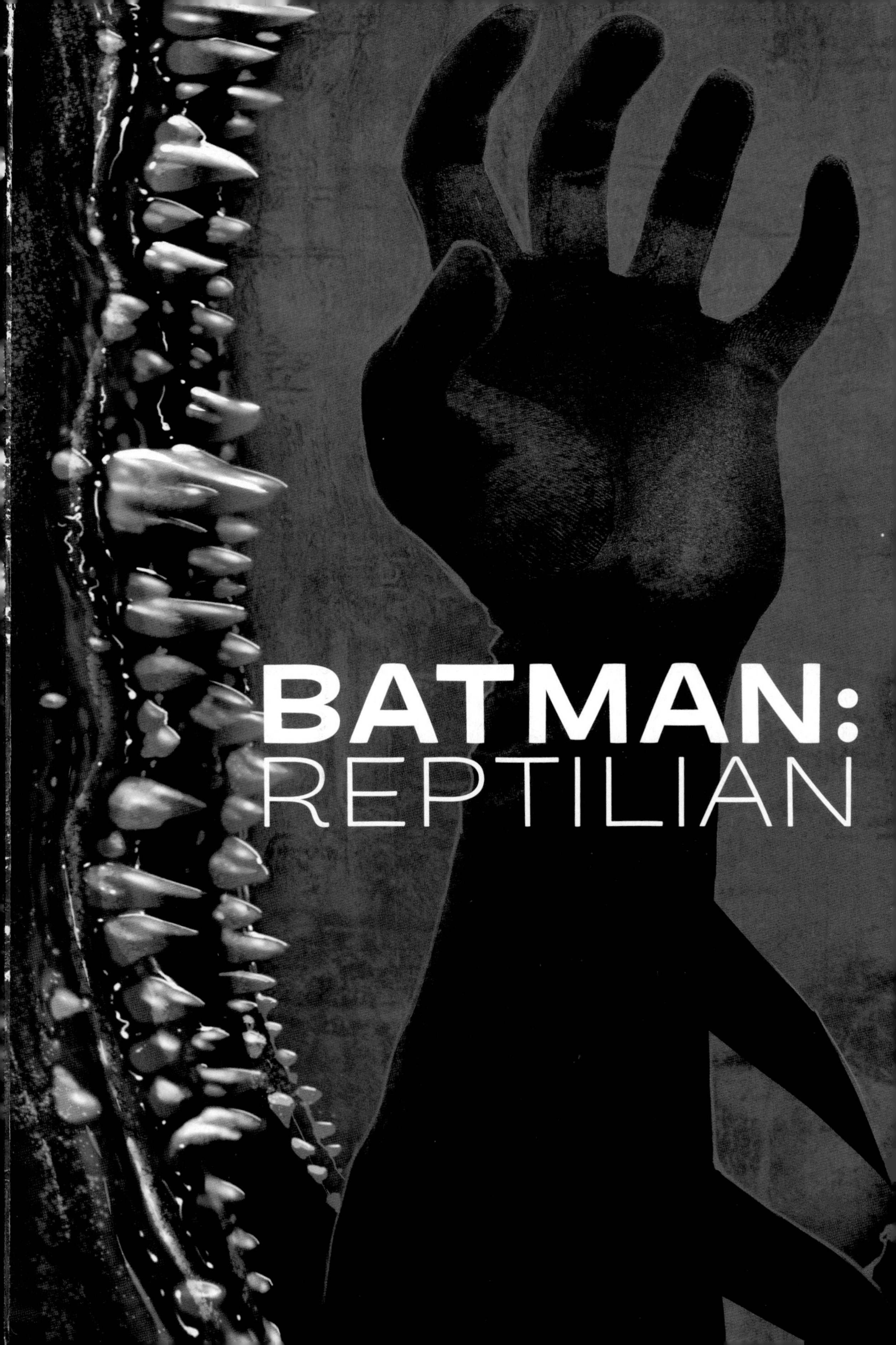
BATMAN:
REPTILIAN

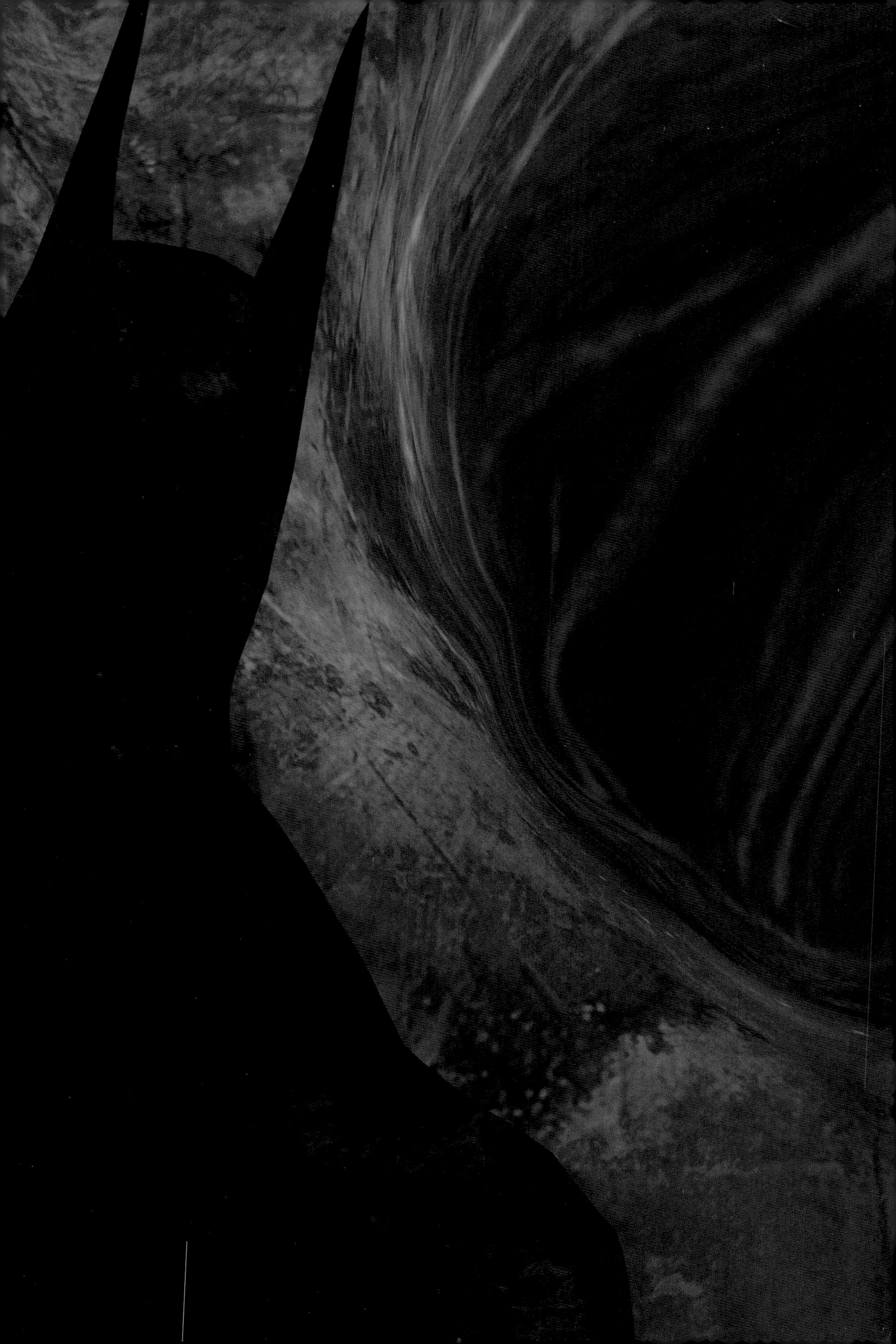

BATMAN: REPTILIAN

GARTH ENNIS writer
LIAM SHARP artist, colorist, cover artist
ROB STEEN letterer
BATMAN created by BOB KANE with BILL FINGER

For Steve Dillon—a big brother to many of us. The script to this book was meant for him, and I would rather have him here by far than be drawing it myself. I'm doing my best to make him proud, but that said, I can feel him over my shoulder, chuckling a little, saying "No mate! You do you! Shame to waste it!"

LS

Jessica Chen .... Editor – Original Series & Collected Edition
Ben Meares .... Associate Editor – Original Series
Steve Cook .... Design Director – Books
Louis Prandi .... Publication Design
Danielle Ramondelli .... Publication Production

Marie Javins .... Editor-in-Chief, DC Comics

Anne DePies .... Senior VP – General Manager
Jim Lee .... Publisher & Chief Creative Officer
Don Falletti .... VP – Manufacturing Operations & Workflow Management
Lawrence Ganem .... VP – Talent Services
Alison Gill .... Senior VP – Manufacturing & Operations
Jeffrey Kaufman .... VP – Editorial Strategy & Programming
Nick J. Napolitano .... VP – Manufacturing Administration & Design
Nancy Spears .... VP – Revenue

BATMAN: REPTILIAN

Published by DC Comics. Compilation and all new material Copyright © 2022 DC Comics. All Rights Reserved. Originally published in single magazine form in *Batman: Reptilian* 1-6. Copyright © 2021 DC Comics. All Rights Reserved. All characters, their distinctive likenesses, and related elements featured in this publication are trademarks of DC Comics. The stories, characters, and incidents featured in this publication are entirely fictional. DC Comics does not read or accept unsolicited submissions of ideas, stories, or artwork. DC – a WarnerMedia Company. DC Comics, 2900 West Alameda Ave., Burbank, CA 91505. Printed by Transcontinental Interglobe, Beauceville, QC, Canada. 4/4/22. First Printing. ISBN: 978-1-77951-533-9.

Library of Congress Cataloging-in-Publication Data is available.

PEFC Certified

This product is from sustainably managed forests and controlled sources

PEFC/01-31-106   www.pefc.org

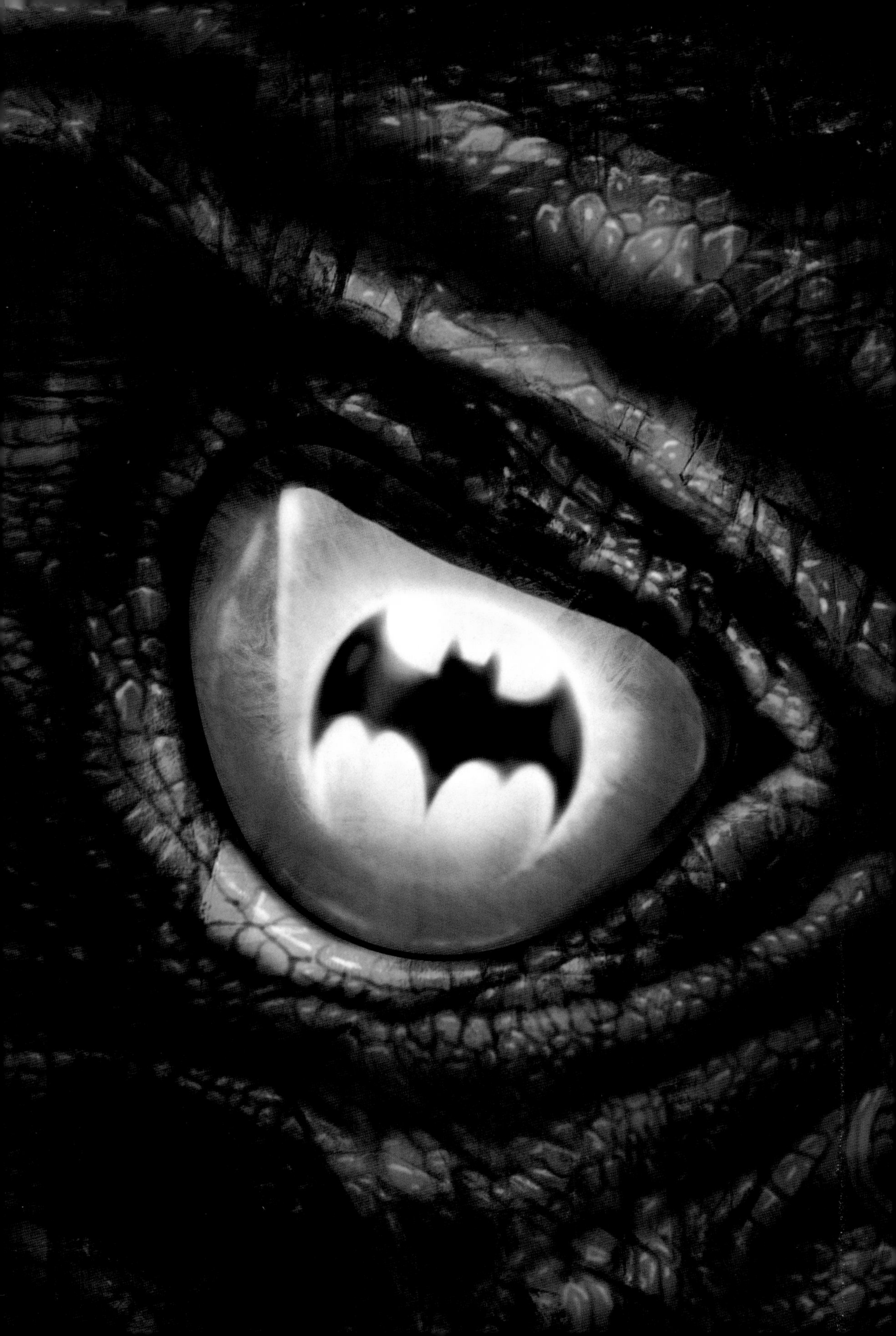

Batman: Reptilian #1 1:25 variant cover by BILL SIENKIEWICZ

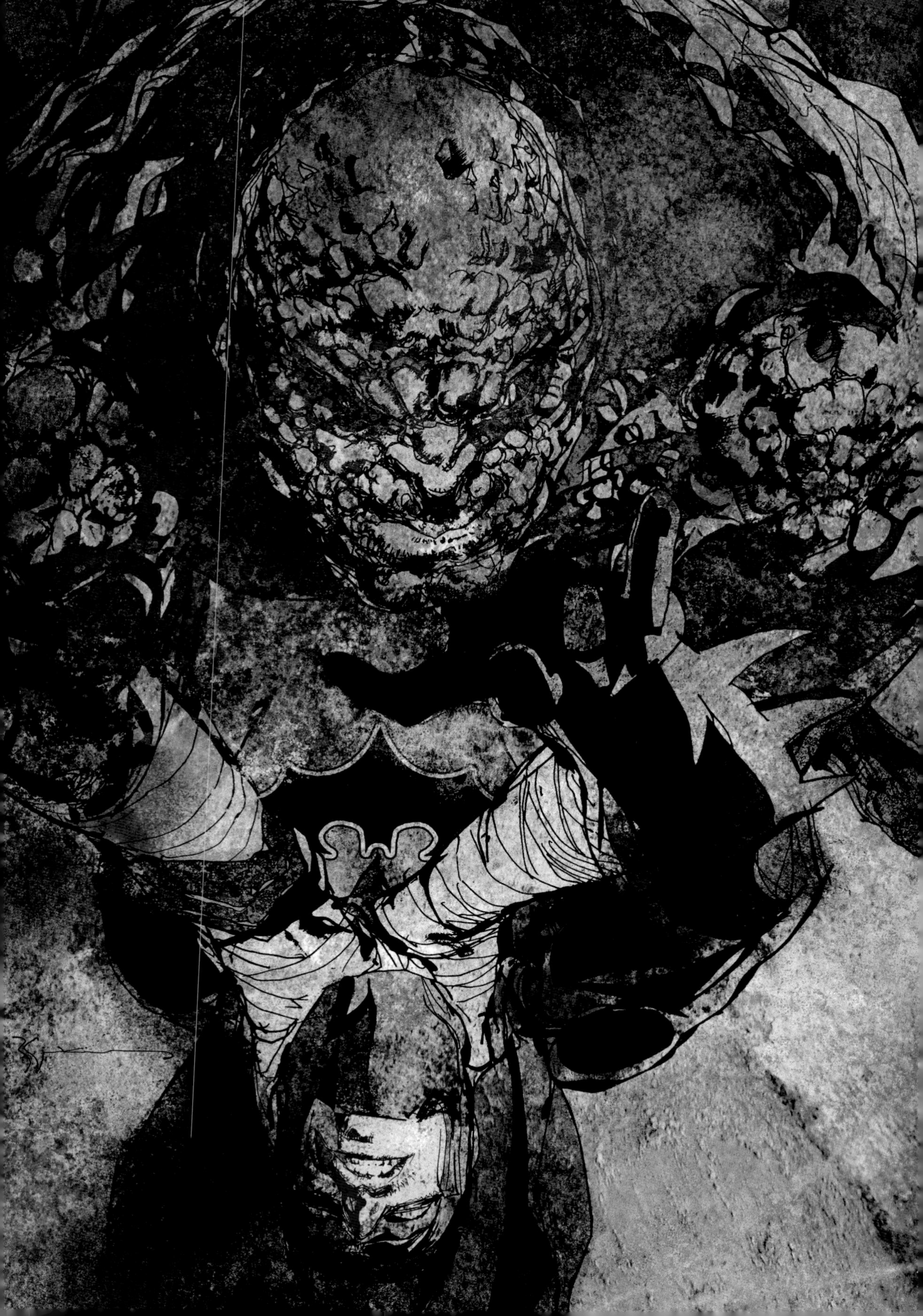

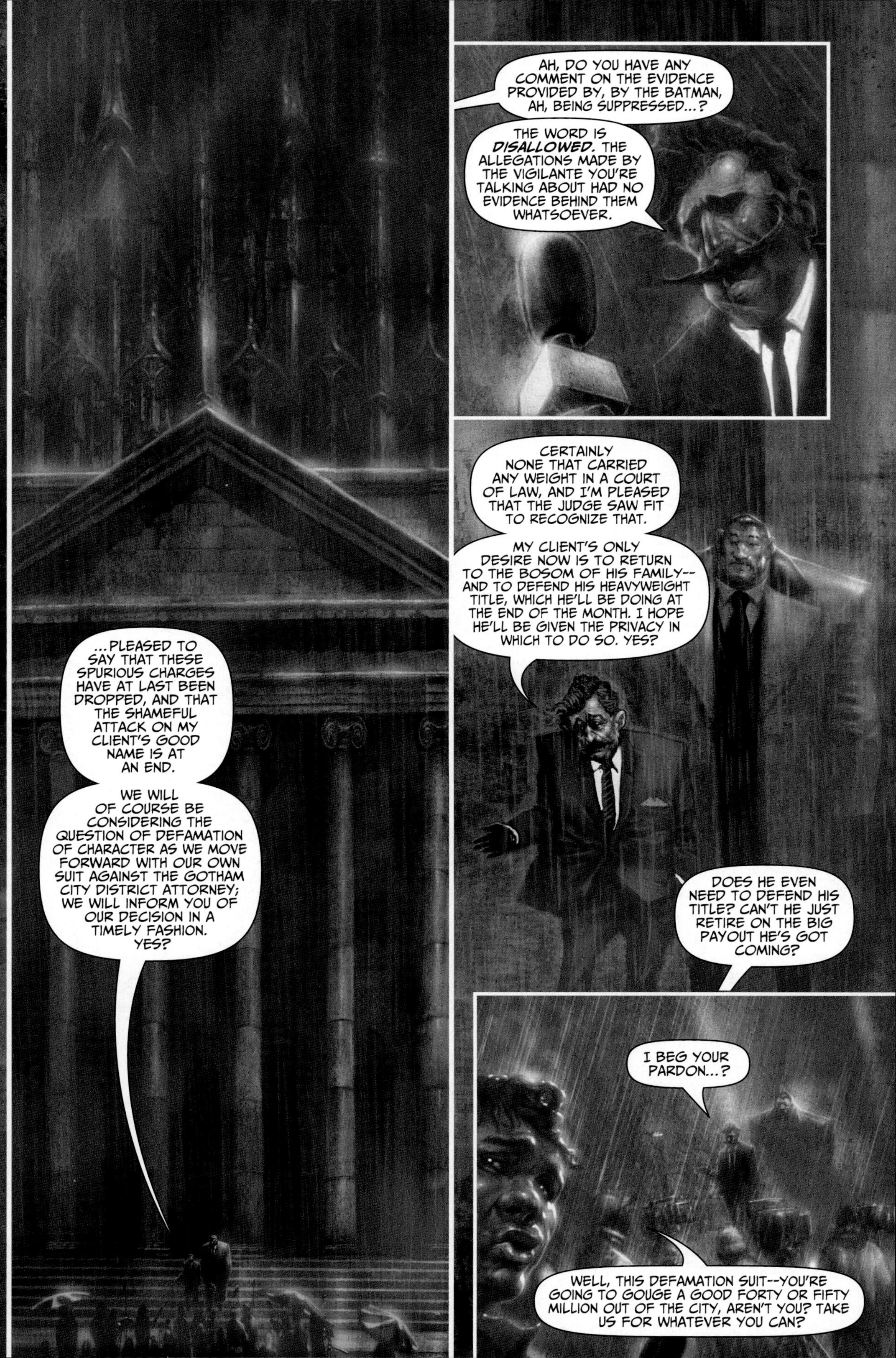
...PLEASED TO SAY THAT THESE SPURIOUS CHARGES HAVE AT LAST BEEN DROPPED, AND THAT THE SHAMEFUL ATTACK ON MY CLIENT'S GOOD NAME IS AT AN END.
WE WILL OF COURSE BE CONSIDERING THE QUESTION OF DEFAMATION OF CHARACTER AS WE MOVE FORWARD WITH OUR OWN SUIT AGAINST THE GOTHAM CITY DISTRICT ATTORNEY; WE WILL INFORM YOU OF OUR DECISION IN A TIMELY FASHION. YES?
AH, DO YOU HAVE ANY COMMENT ON THE EVIDENCE PROVIDED BY, BY THE BATMAN, AH, BEING SUPPRESSED...?
THE WORD IS *DISALLOWED.* THE ALLEGATIONS MADE BY THE VIGILANTE YOU'RE TALKING ABOUT HAD NO EVIDENCE BEHIND THEM WHATSOEVER.
CERTAINLY NONE THAT CARRIED ANY WEIGHT IN A COURT OF LAW, AND I'M PLEASED THAT THE JUDGE SAW FIT TO RECOGNIZE THAT.
MY CLIENT'S ONLY DESIRE NOW IS TO RETURN TO THE BOSOM OF HIS FAMILY--AND TO DEFEND HIS HEAVYWEIGHT TITLE, WHICH HE'LL BE DOING AT THE END OF THE MONTH. I HOPE HE'LL BE GIVEN THE PRIVACY IN WHICH TO DO SO. YES?
DOES HE EVEN NEED TO DEFEND HIS TITLE? CAN'T HE JUST RETIRE ON THE BIG PAYOUT HE'S GOT COMING?
I BEG YOUR PARDON...?
WELL, THIS DEFAMATION SUIT--YOU'RE GOING TO GOUGE A GOOD FORTY OR FIFTY MILLION OUT OF THE CITY, AREN'T YOU? TAKE US FOR WHATEVER YOU CAN?

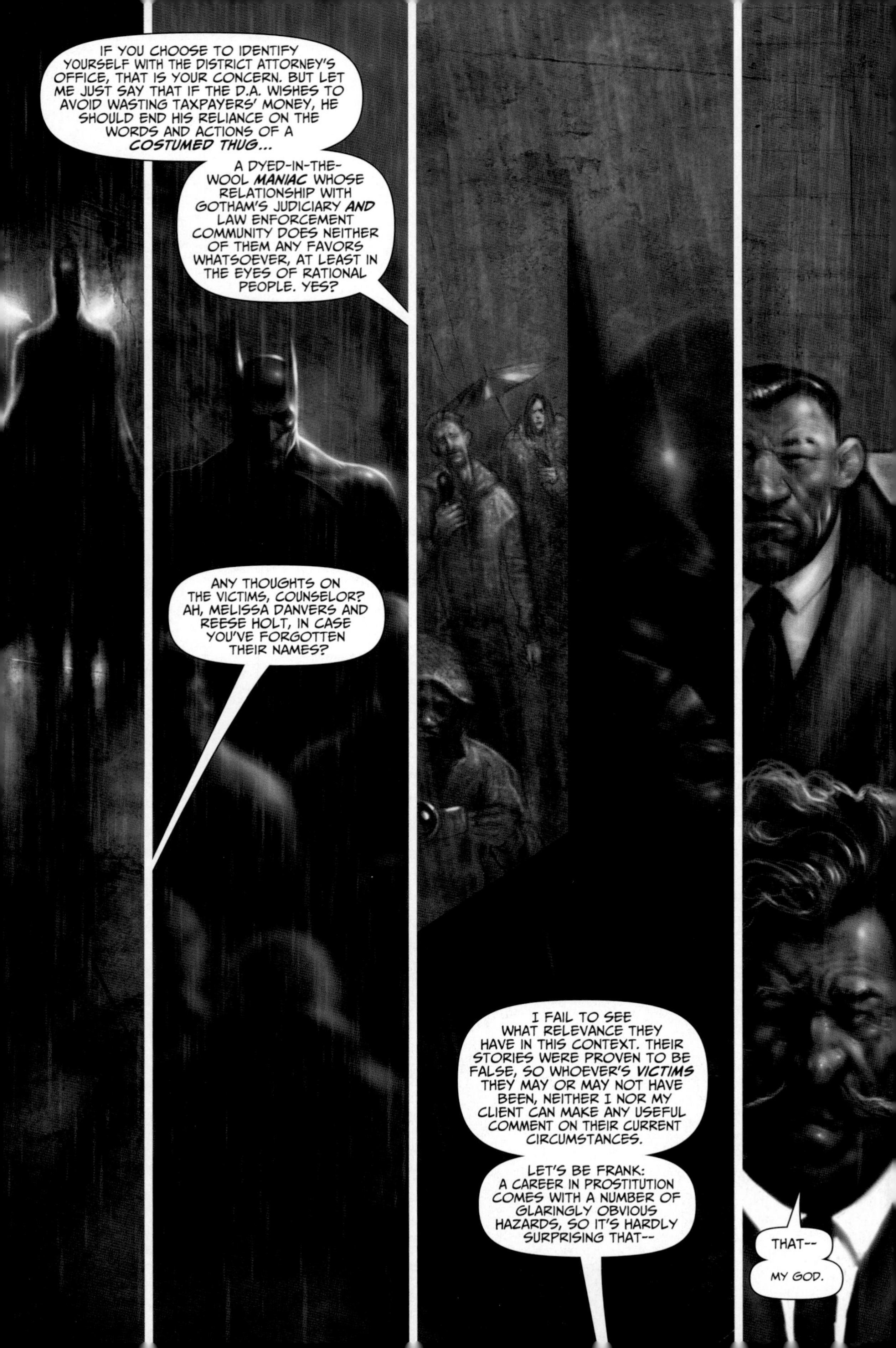
IF YOU CHOOSE TO IDENTIFY YOURSELF WITH THE DISTRICT ATTORNEY'S OFFICE, THAT IS YOUR CONCERN. BUT LET ME JUST SAY THAT IF THE D.A. WISHES TO AVOID WASTING TAXPAYERS' MONEY, HE SHOULD END HIS RELIANCE ON THE WORDS AND ACTIONS OF A ***COSTUMED THUG...***
A DYED-IN-THE-WOOL ***MANIAC*** WHOSE RELATIONSHIP WITH GOTHAM'S JUDICIARY ***AND*** LAW ENFORCEMENT COMMUNITY DOES NEITHER OF THEM ANY FAVORS WHATSOEVER, AT LEAST IN THE EYES OF RATIONAL PEOPLE. YES?
ANY THOUGHTS ON THE VICTIMS, COUNSELOR? AH, MELISSA DANVERS AND REESE HOLT, IN CASE YOU'VE FORGOTTEN THEIR NAMES?
I FAIL TO SEE WHAT RELEVANCE THEY HAVE IN THIS CONTEXT. THEIR STORIES WERE PROVEN TO BE FALSE, SO WHOEVER'S ***VICTIMS*** THEY MAY OR MAY NOT HAVE BEEN, NEITHER I NOR MY CLIENT CAN MAKE ANY USEFUL COMMENT ON THEIR CURRENT CIRCUMSTANCES.
LET'S BE FRANK: A CAREER IN PROSTITUTION COMES WITH A NUMBER OF GLARINGLY OBVIOUS HAZARDS, SO IT'S HARDLY SURPRISING THAT--
THAT--
MY GOD.

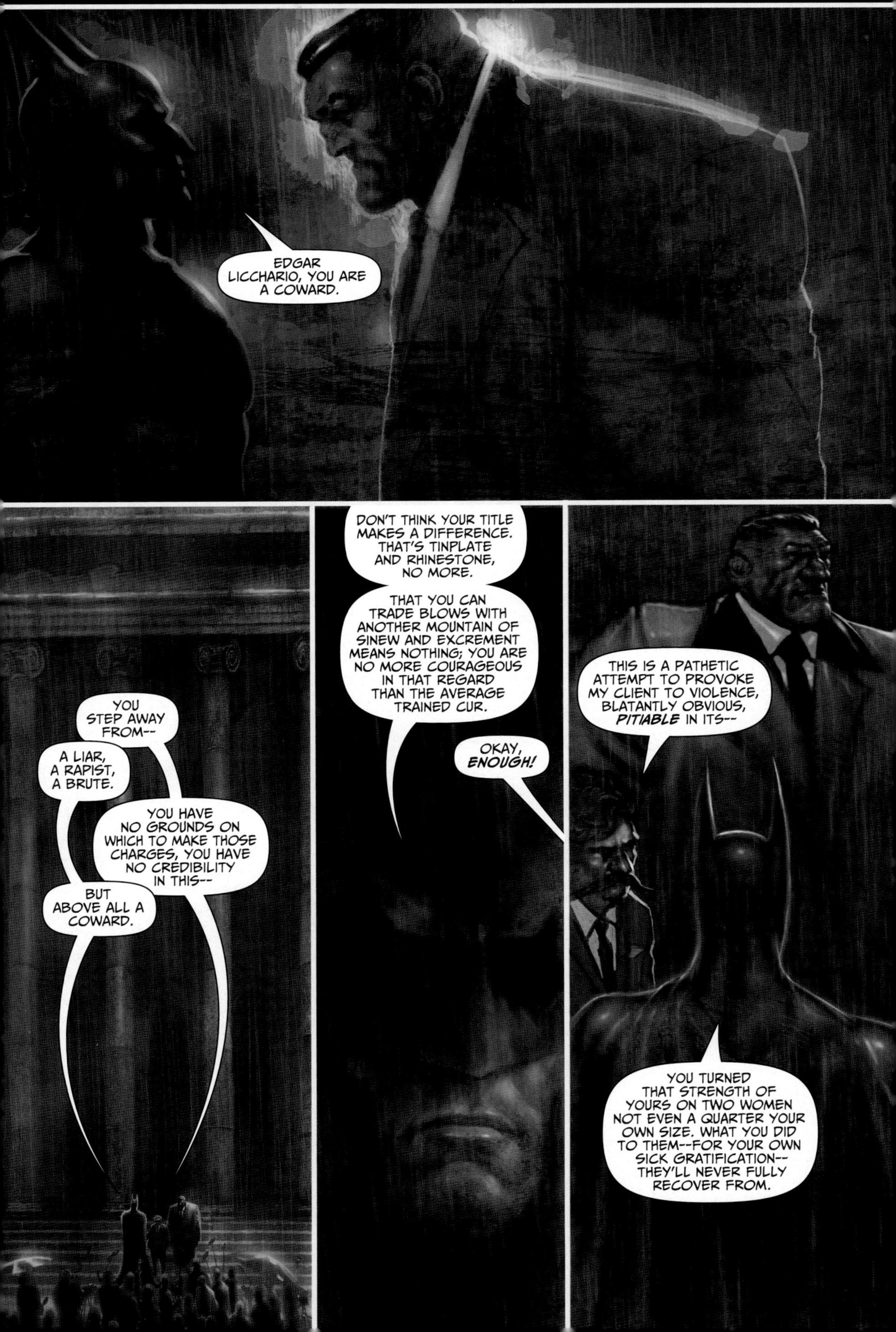
EDGAR LICCHARIO, YOU ARE A COWARD.
YOU STEP AWAY FROM--
A LIAR, A RAPIST, A BRUTE.
YOU HAVE NO GROUNDS ON WHICH TO MAKE THOSE CHARGES, YOU HAVE NO CREDIBILITY IN THIS--
BUT ABOVE ALL A COWARD.
DON'T THINK YOUR TITLE MAKES A DIFFERENCE. THAT'S TINPLATE AND RHINESTONE, NO MORE.
THAT YOU CAN TRADE BLOWS WITH ANOTHER MOUNTAIN OF SINEW AND EXCREMENT MEANS NOTHING; YOU ARE NO MORE COURAGEOUS IN THAT REGARD THAN THE AVERAGE TRAINED CUR.
OKAY, ***ENOUGH!***
THIS IS A PATHETIC ATTEMPT TO PROVOKE MY CLIENT TO VIOLENCE, BLATANTLY OBVIOUS, ***PITIABLE*** IN ITS--
YOU TURNED THAT STRENGTH OF YOURS ON TWO WOMEN NOT EVEN A QUARTER YOUR OWN SIZE. WHAT YOU DID TO THEM--FOR YOUR OWN SICK GRATIFICATION--THEY'LL NEVER FULLY RECOVER FROM.

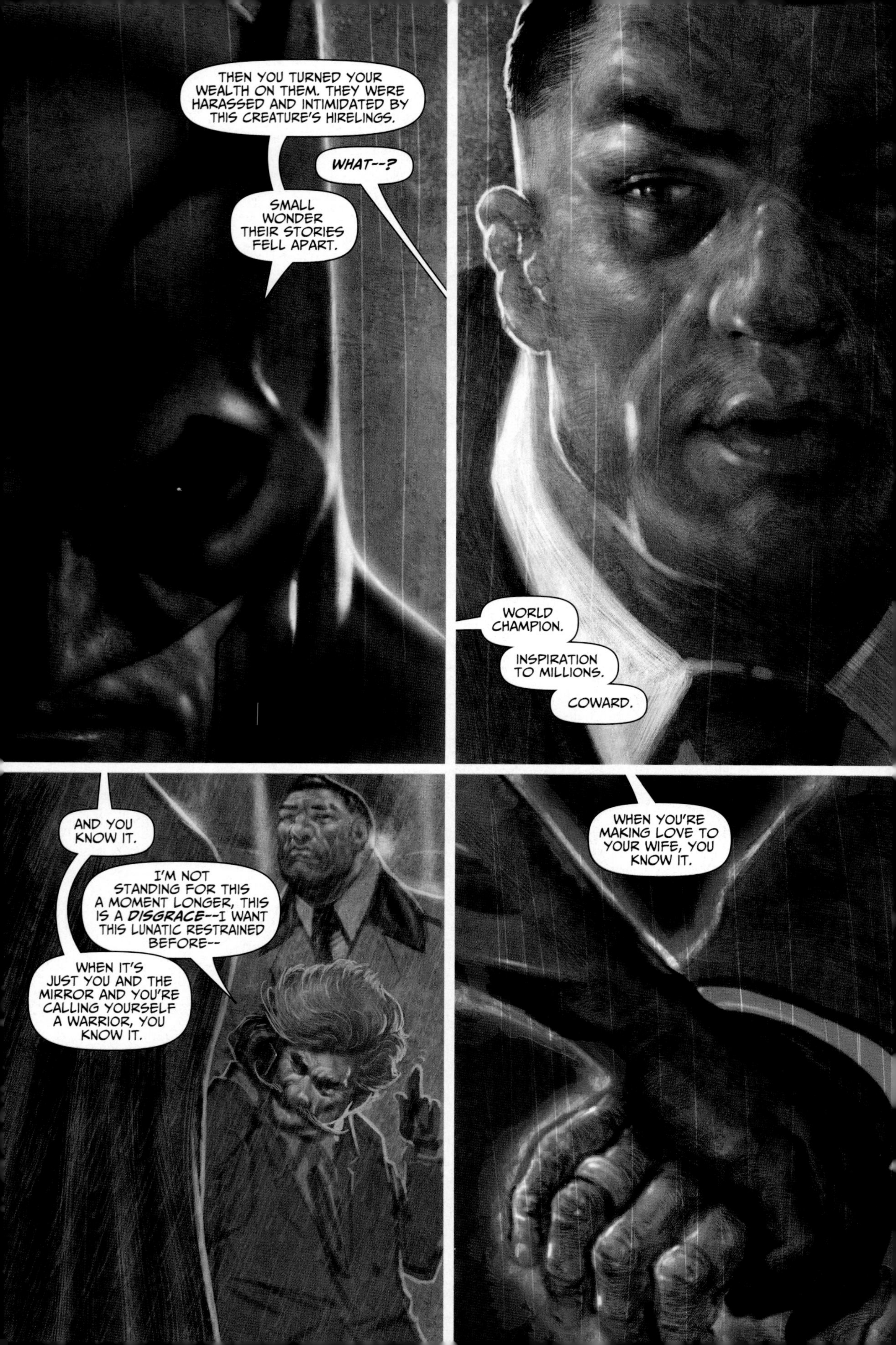
THEN YOU TURNED YOUR WEALTH ON THEM. THEY WERE HARASSED AND INTIMIDATED BY THIS CREATURE'S HIRELINGS.
SMALL WONDER THEIR STORIES FELL APART.
WHAT--?
WORLD CHAMPION.
INSPIRATION TO MILLIONS.
COWARD.
AND YOU KNOW IT.
I'M NOT STANDING FOR THIS A MOMENT LONGER, THIS IS A DISGRACE--I WANT THIS LUNATIC RESTRAINED BEFORE--
WHEN IT'S JUST YOU AND THE MIRROR AND YOU'RE CALLING YOURSELF A WARRIOR, YOU KNOW IT.
WHEN YOU'RE MAKING LOVE TO YOUR WIFE, YOU KNOW IT.

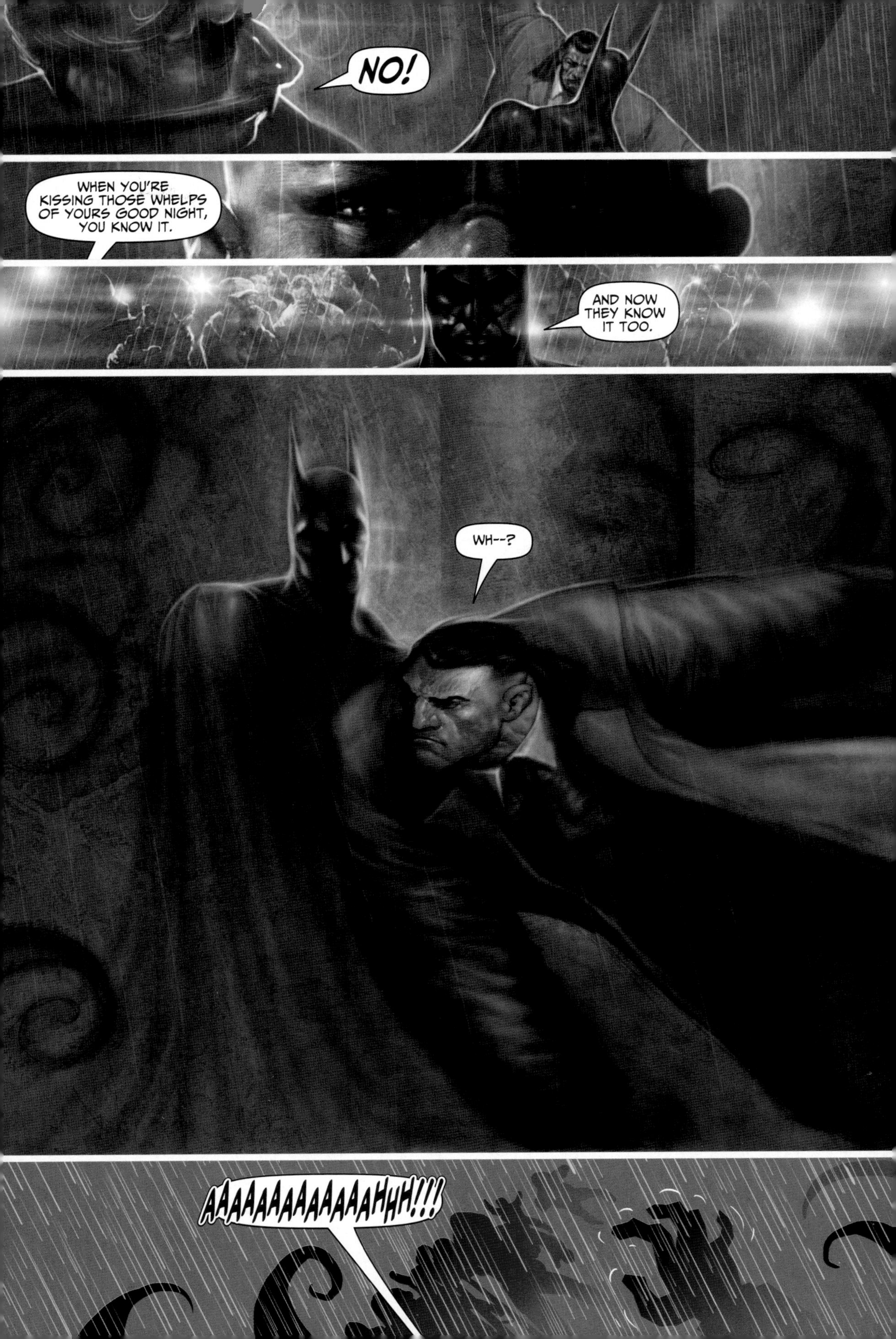
NO!
WHEN YOU'RE KISSING THOSE WHELPS OF YOURS GOOD NIGHT, YOU KNOW IT.
AND NOW THEY KNOW IT TOO.
WH--?
AAAAAAAAAAAAAHHH!!!!

1: QUICK & DIRTY

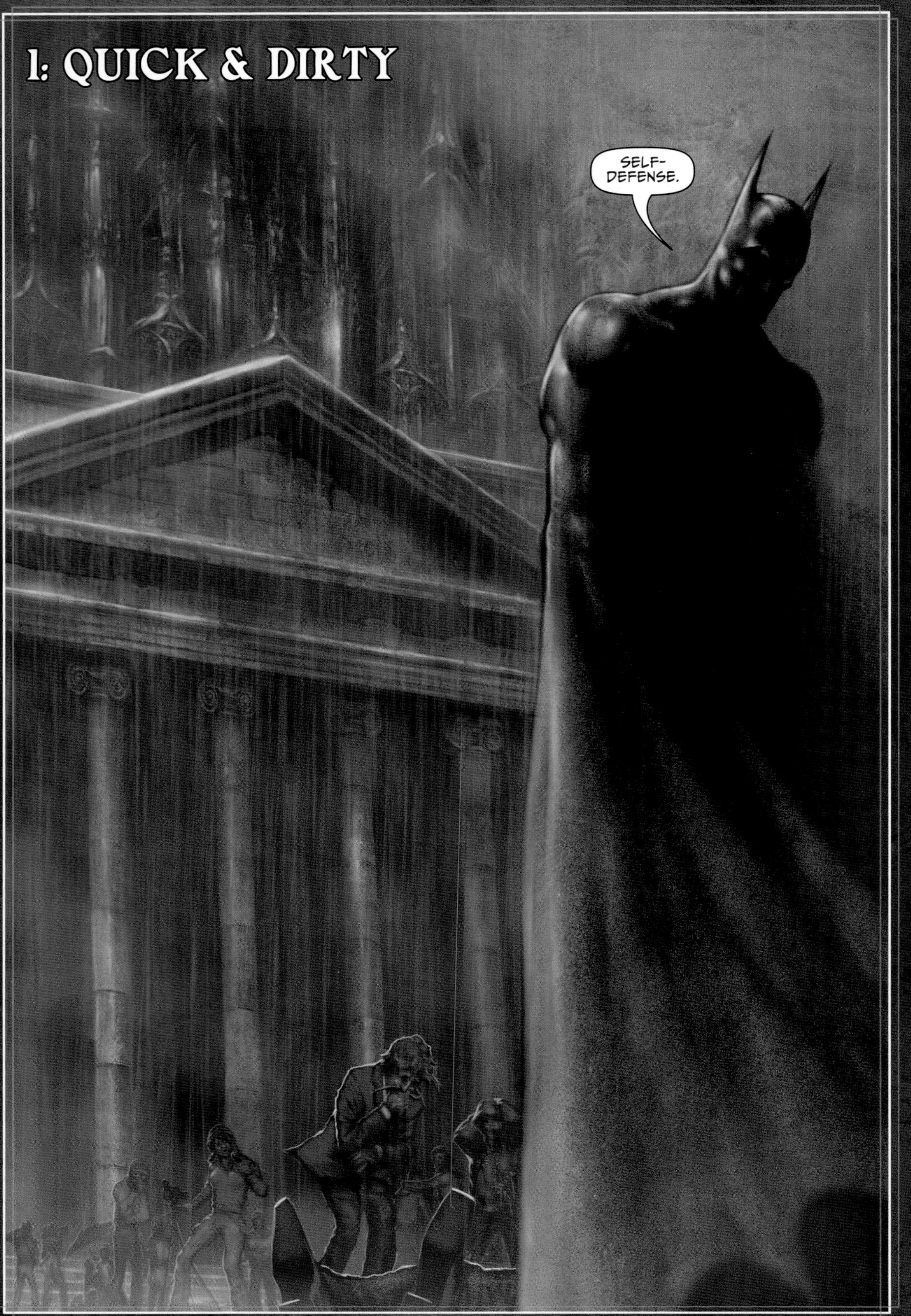
SELF-DEFENSE.

WERE I A BETTING MAN, I WOULD WAGER A TIDY SUM THAT HIS WIFE'LL BE STUPID ENOUGH TO STICK BY HIM...

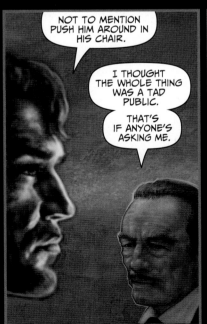

NOT TO MENTION PUSH HIM AROUND IN HIS CHAIR.

I THOUGHT THE WHOLE THING WAS A TAD PUBLIC.

THAT'S IF ANYONE'S ASKING ME.

WHAT SHOULD I HAVE DONE? LURKED ON A ROOFTOP AND HISSED FROM THE SHADOWS?

KEEP THE SCUM GUESSING, THAT'S THE BEST...HELLO.

MM?

9-1-1 CALL HALF AN HOUR AGO, WITH PARAMEDICS AND PD RESPONSE...GOOD LORD, CONFIRMING THE SCARECROW AND THE MAD HATTER FOUND TOGETHER.

ASSAULTED.

GUTTED, IN FACT.

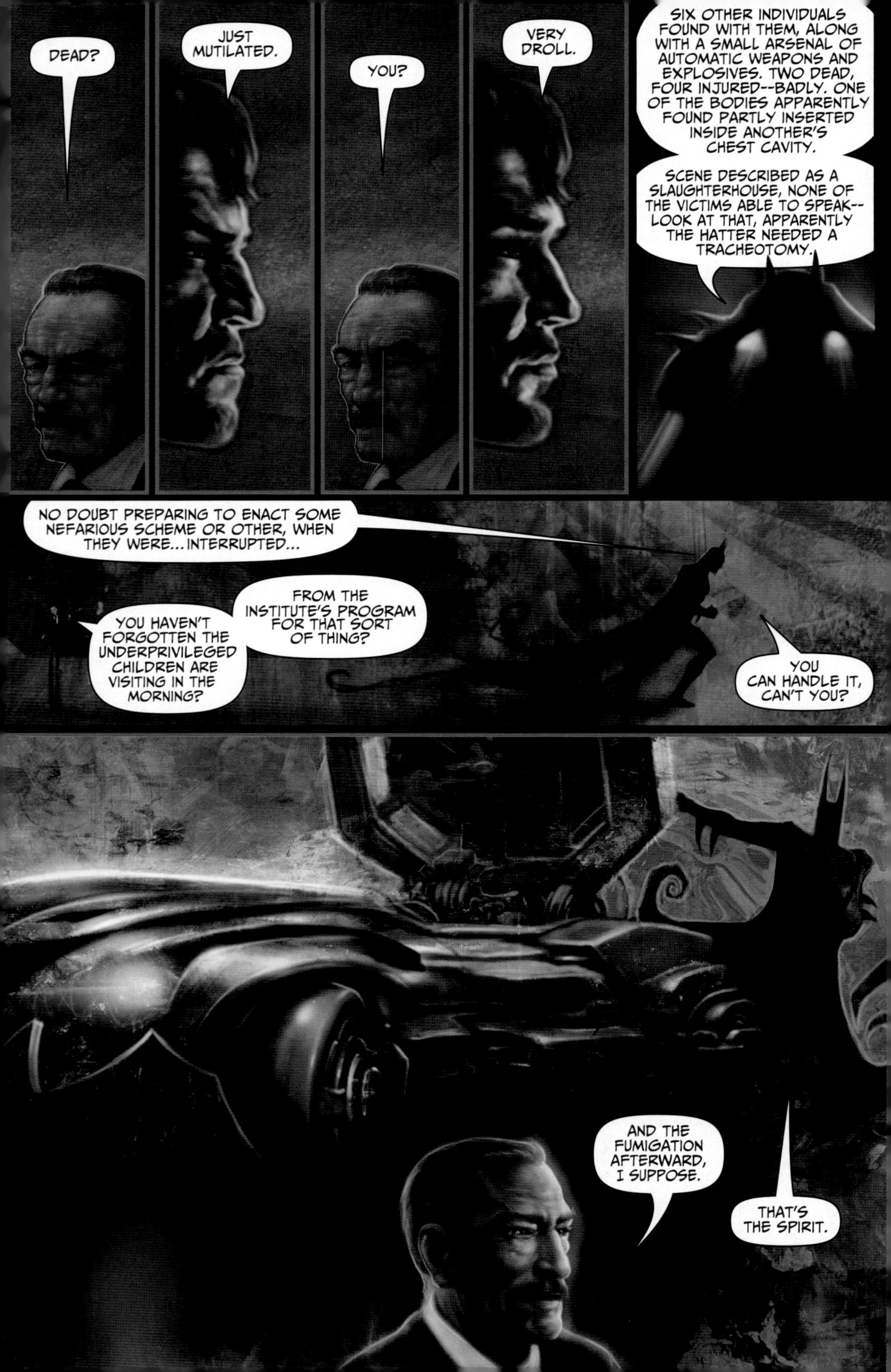
DEAD?
JUST MUTILATED.
YOU?
VERY DROLL.
SIX OTHER INDIVIDUALS FOUND WITH THEM, ALONG WITH A SMALL ARSENAL OF AUTOMATIC WEAPONS AND EXPLOSIVES. TWO DEAD, FOUR INJURED--BADLY. ONE OF THE BODIES APPARENTLY FOUND PARTLY INSERTED INSIDE ANOTHER'S CHEST CAVITY.
SCENE DESCRIBED AS A SLAUGHTERHOUSE, NONE OF THE VICTIMS ABLE TO SPEAK-- LOOK AT THAT, APPARENTLY THE HATTER NEEDED A TRACHEOTOMY.
NO DOUBT PREPARING TO ENACT SOME NEFARIOUS SCHEME OR OTHER, WHEN THEY WERE...INTERRUPTED...
YOU HAVEN'T FORGOTTEN THE UNDERPRIVILEGED CHILDREN ARE VISITING IN THE MORNING?
FROM THE INSTITUTE'S PROGRAM FOR THAT SORT OF THING?
YOU CAN HANDLE IT, CAN'T YOU?
AND THE FUMIGATION AFTERWARD, I SUPPOSE.
THAT'S THE SPIRIT.

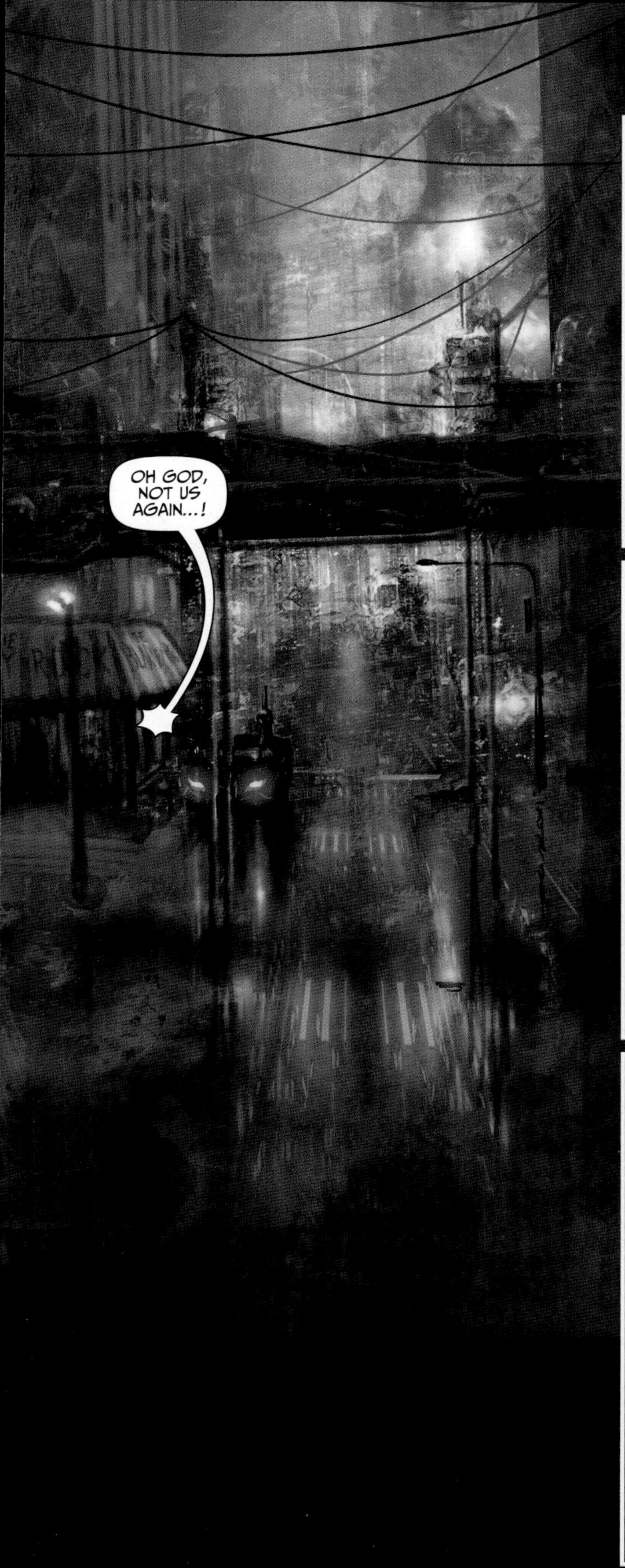
OH GOD, NOT US AGAIN...!

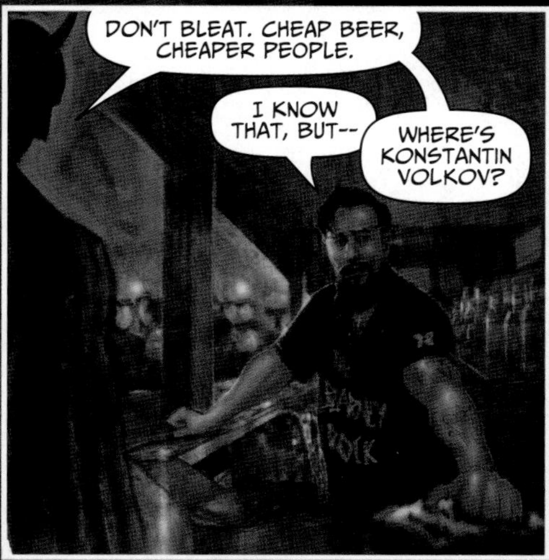
DON'T BLEAT. CHEAP BEER, CHEAPER PEOPLE.
I KNOW THAT, BUT--
WHERE'S KONSTANTIN VOLKOV?

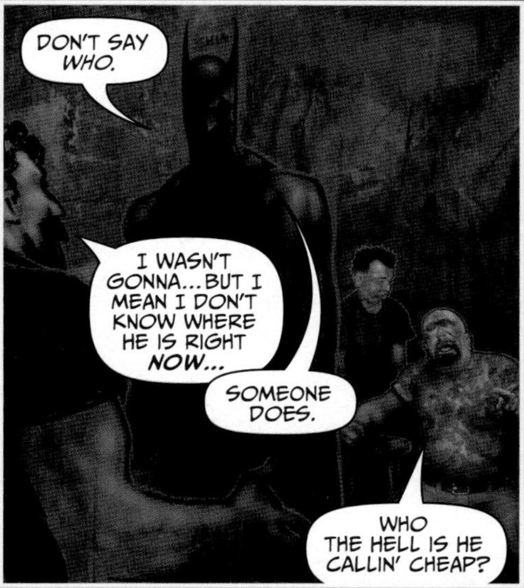
DON'T SAY *WHO.*
I WASN'T GONNA...BUT I MEAN I DON'T KNOW WHERE HE IS RIGHT ***NOW...***
SOMEONE DOES.
WHO THE HELL IS HE CALLIN' CHEAP?

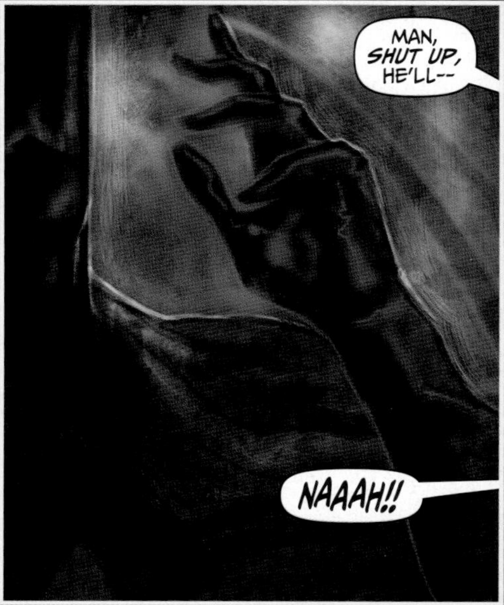
MAN, ***SHUT UP,*** HE'LL--
NAAAH!!

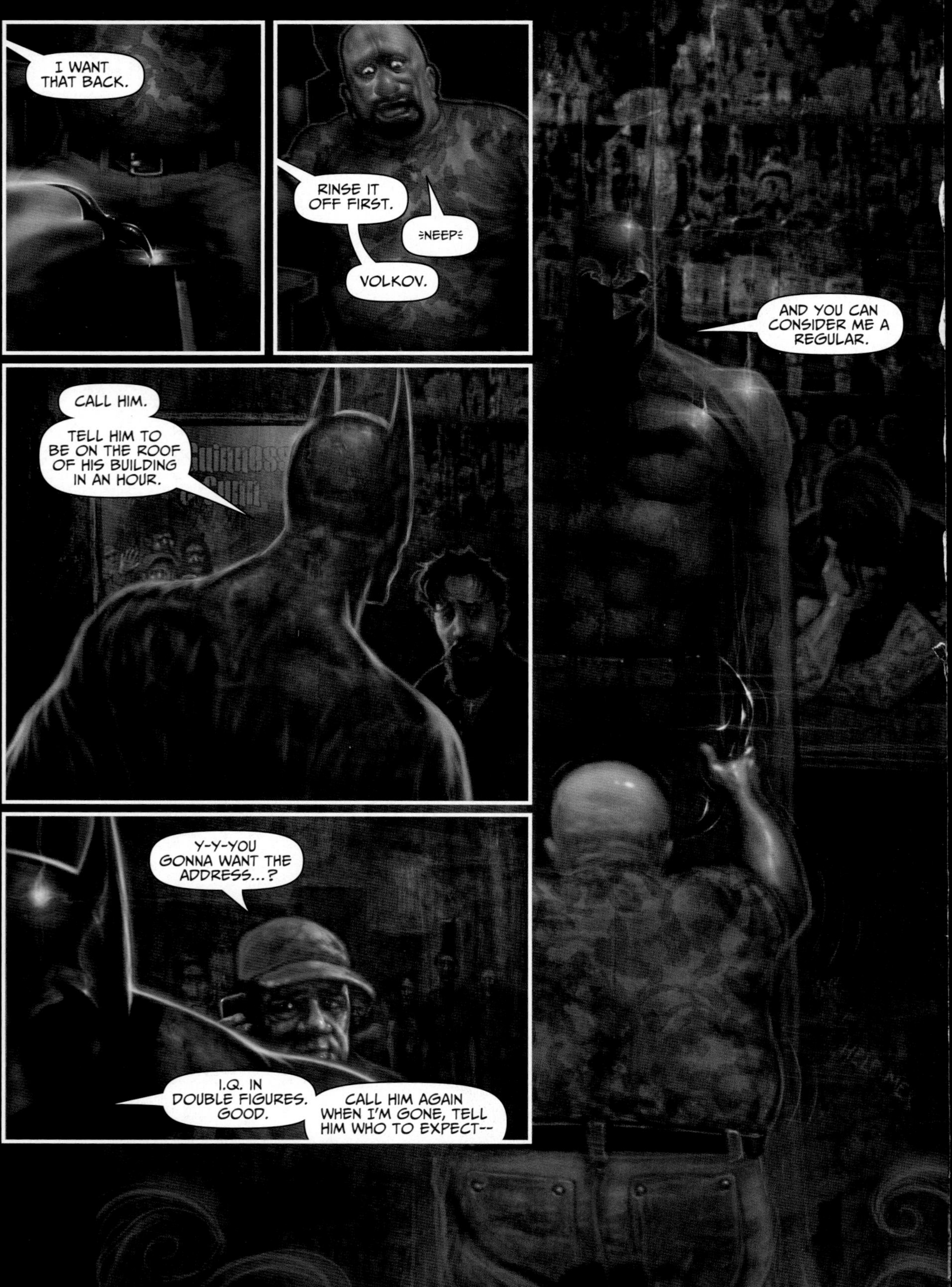

I WANT THAT BACK.
RINSE IT OFF FIRST.
VOLKOV.
≠NEEP≠
AND YOU CAN CONSIDER ME A REGULAR.
CALL HIM.
TELL HIM TO BE ON THE ROOF OF HIS BUILDING IN AN HOUR.
Y-Y-YOU GONNA WANT THE ADDRESS...?
I.Q. IN DOUBLE FIGURES. GOOD.
CALL HIM AGAIN WHEN I'M GONE, TELL HIM WHO TO EXPECT--

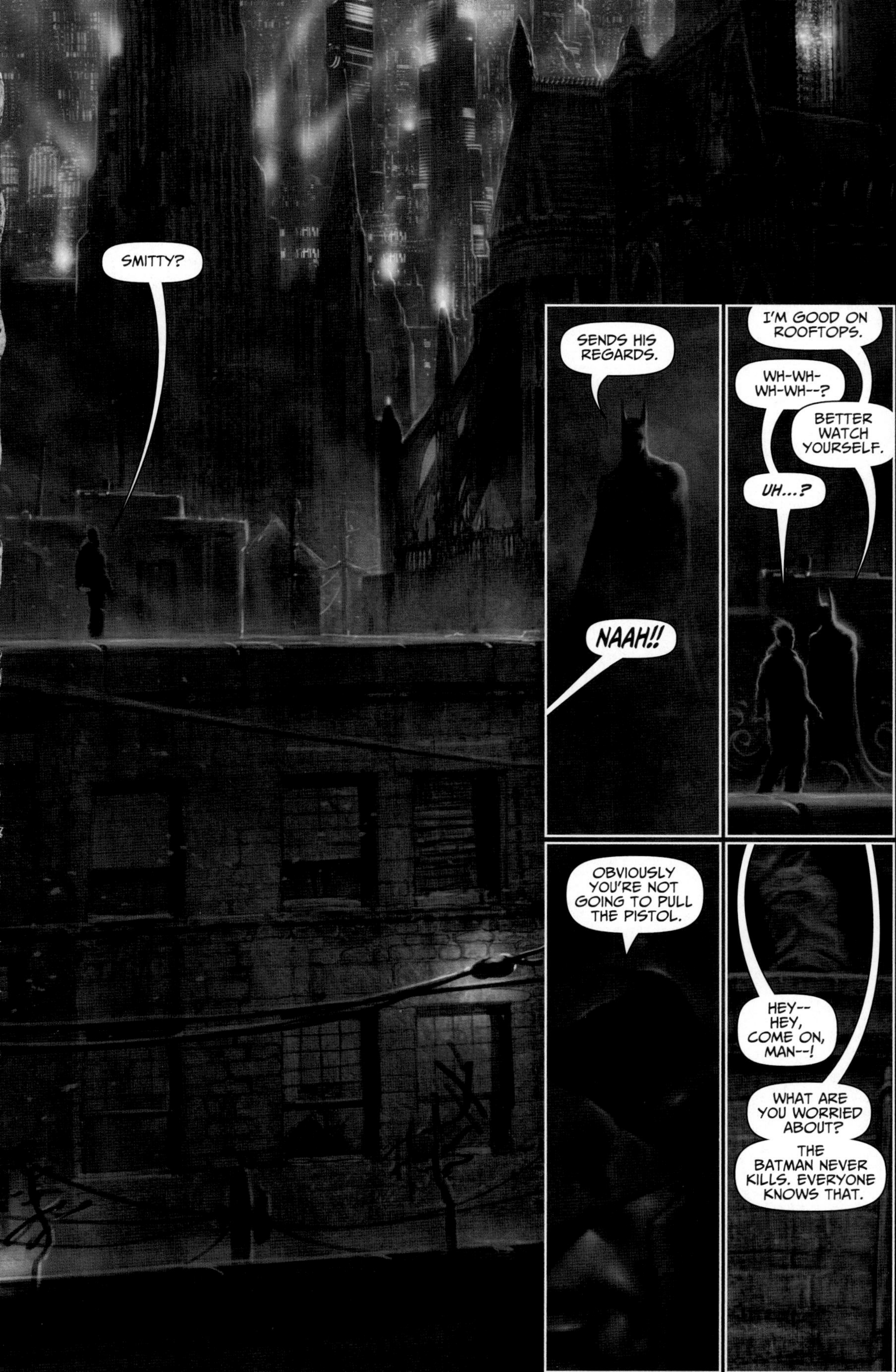
SMITTY?
SENDS HIS REGARDS.
NAAH!!
I'M GOOD ON ROOFTOPS.
WH-WH-WH-WH--?
BETTER WATCH YOURSELF.
UH...?
OBVIOUSLY YOU'RE NOT GOING TO PULL THE PISTOL.
HEY--HEY, COME ON, MAN--!
WHAT ARE YOU WORRIED ABOUT?
THE BATMAN NEVER KILLS. EVERYONE KNOWS THAT.

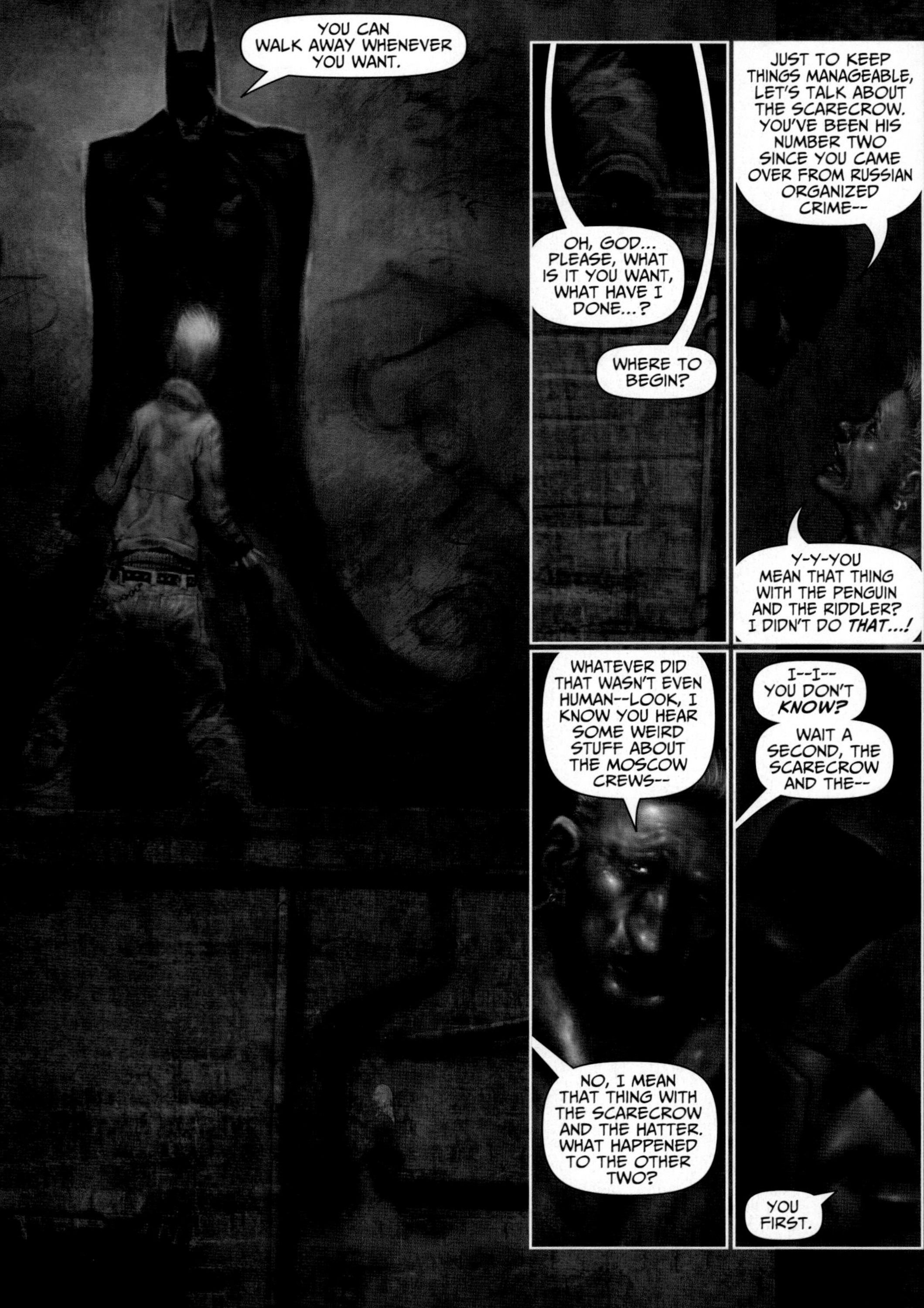
YOU CAN WALK AWAY WHENEVER YOU WANT.
OH, GOD... PLEASE, WHAT IS IT YOU WANT, WHAT HAVE I DONE...?
WHERE TO BEGIN?
JUST TO KEEP THINGS MANAGEABLE, LET'S TALK ABOUT THE SCARECROW. YOU'VE BEEN HIS NUMBER TWO SINCE YOU CAME OVER FROM RUSSIAN ORGANIZED CRIME--
Y-Y-YOU MEAN THAT THING WITH THE PENGUIN AND THE RIDDLER? I DIDN'T DO *THAT...!*
WHATEVER DID THAT WASN'T EVEN HUMAN--LOOK, I KNOW YOU HEAR SOME WEIRD STUFF ABOUT THE MOSCOW CREWS--
NO, I MEAN THAT THING WITH THE SCARECROW AND THE HATTER. WHAT HAPPENED TO THE OTHER TWO?
I--I-- YOU DON'T ***KNOW?***
WAIT A SECOND, THE SCARECROW AND THE--
YOU FIRST.

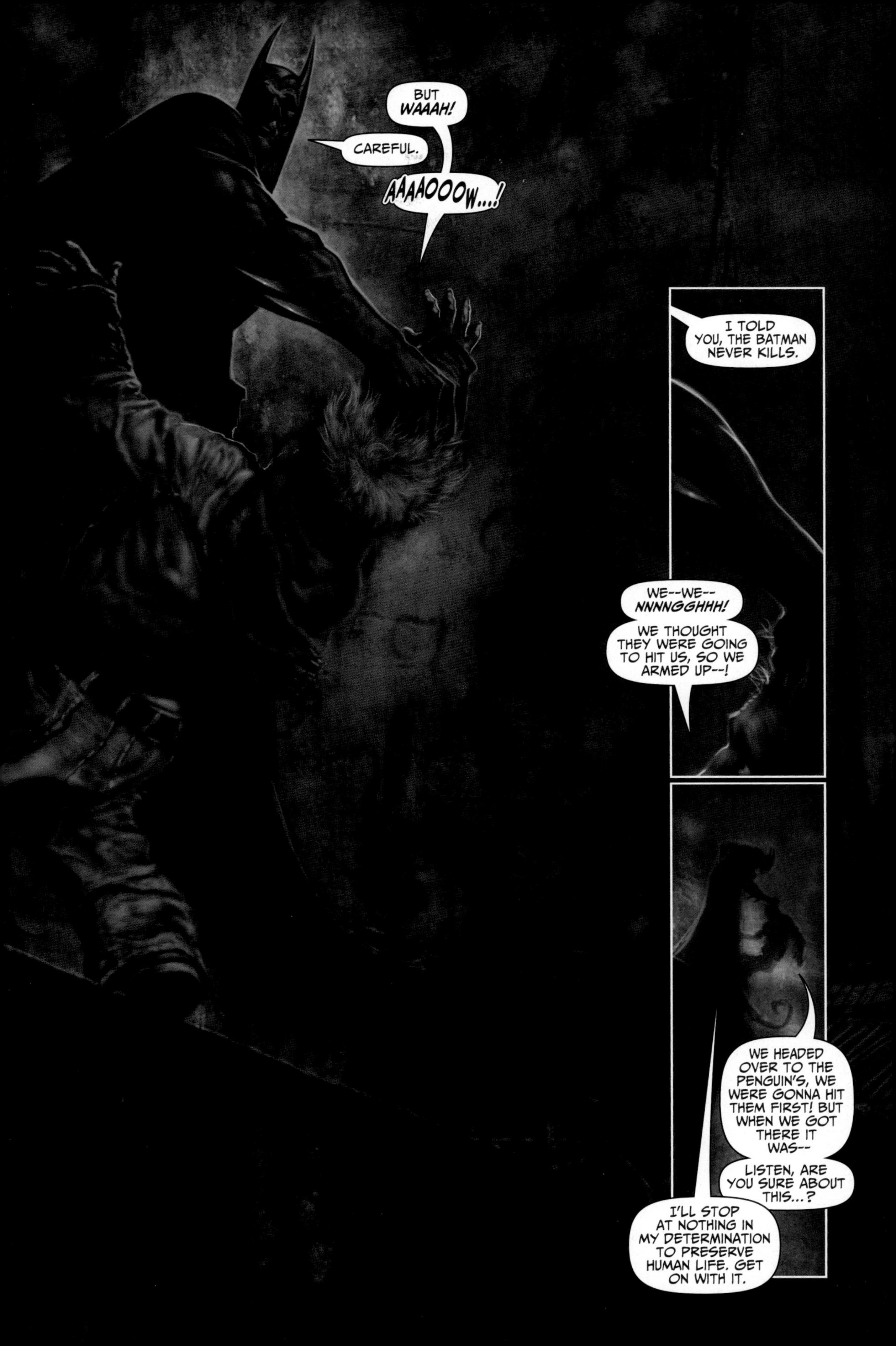
CAREFUL.
BUT WAAAH!
AAAAOOOW...!
I TOLD YOU, THE BATMAN NEVER KILLS.
WE--WE-- NNNNGGHHH!
WE THOUGHT THEY WERE GOING TO HIT US, SO WE ARMED UP--!
WE HEADED OVER TO THE PENGUIN'S, WE WERE GONNA HIT THEM FIRST! BUT WHEN WE GOT THERE IT WAS--
LISTEN, ARE YOU SURE ABOUT THIS...?
I'LL STOP AT NOTHING IN MY DETERMINATION TO PRESERVE HUMAN LIFE. GET ON WITH IT.

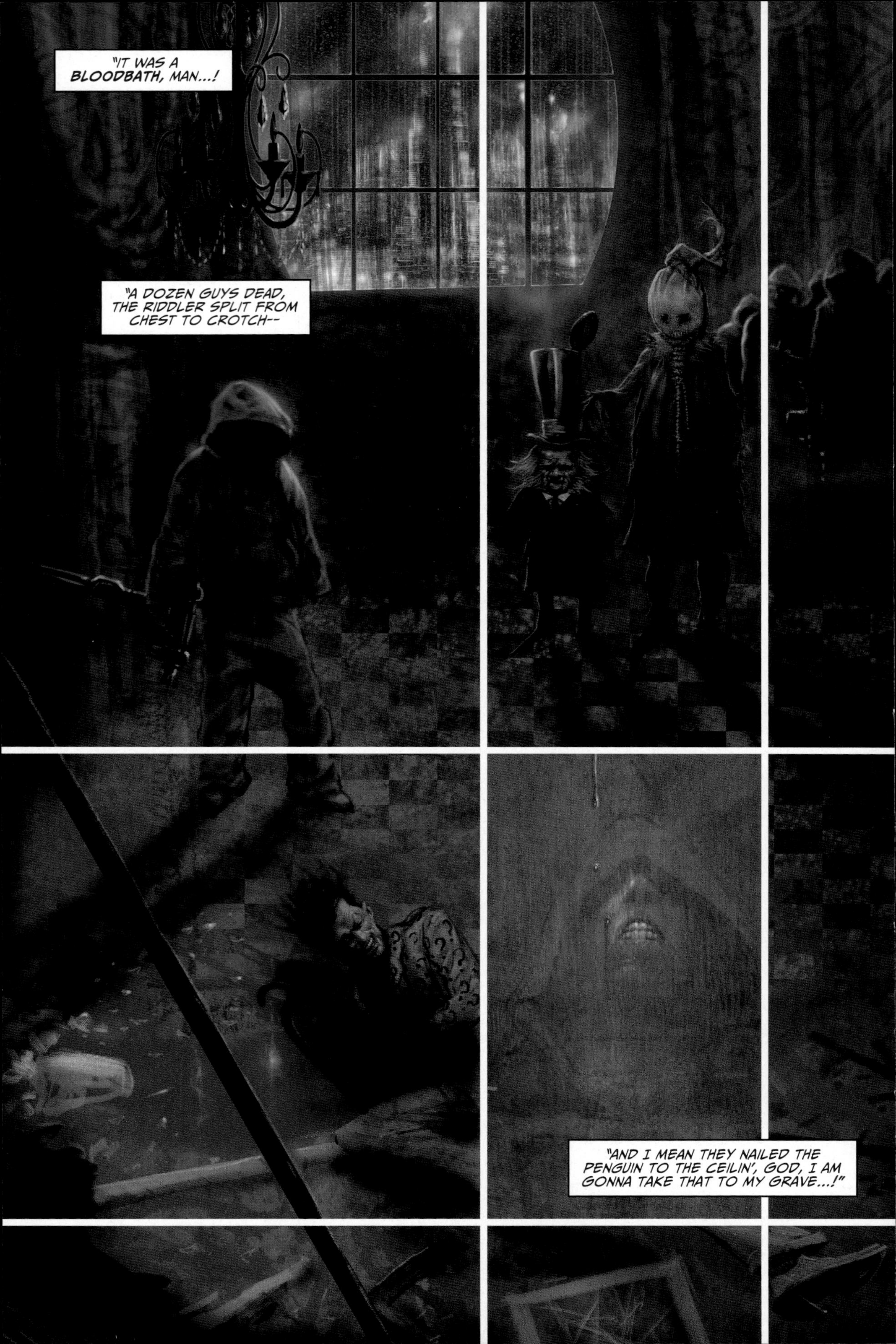
"IT WAS A BLOODBATH, MAN...!
"A DOZEN GUYS DEAD, THE RIDDLER SPLIT FROM CHEST TO CROTCH--
"AND I MEAN THEY NAILED THE PENGUIN TO THE CEILIN', GOD, I AM GONNA TAKE THAT TO MY GRAVE...!"

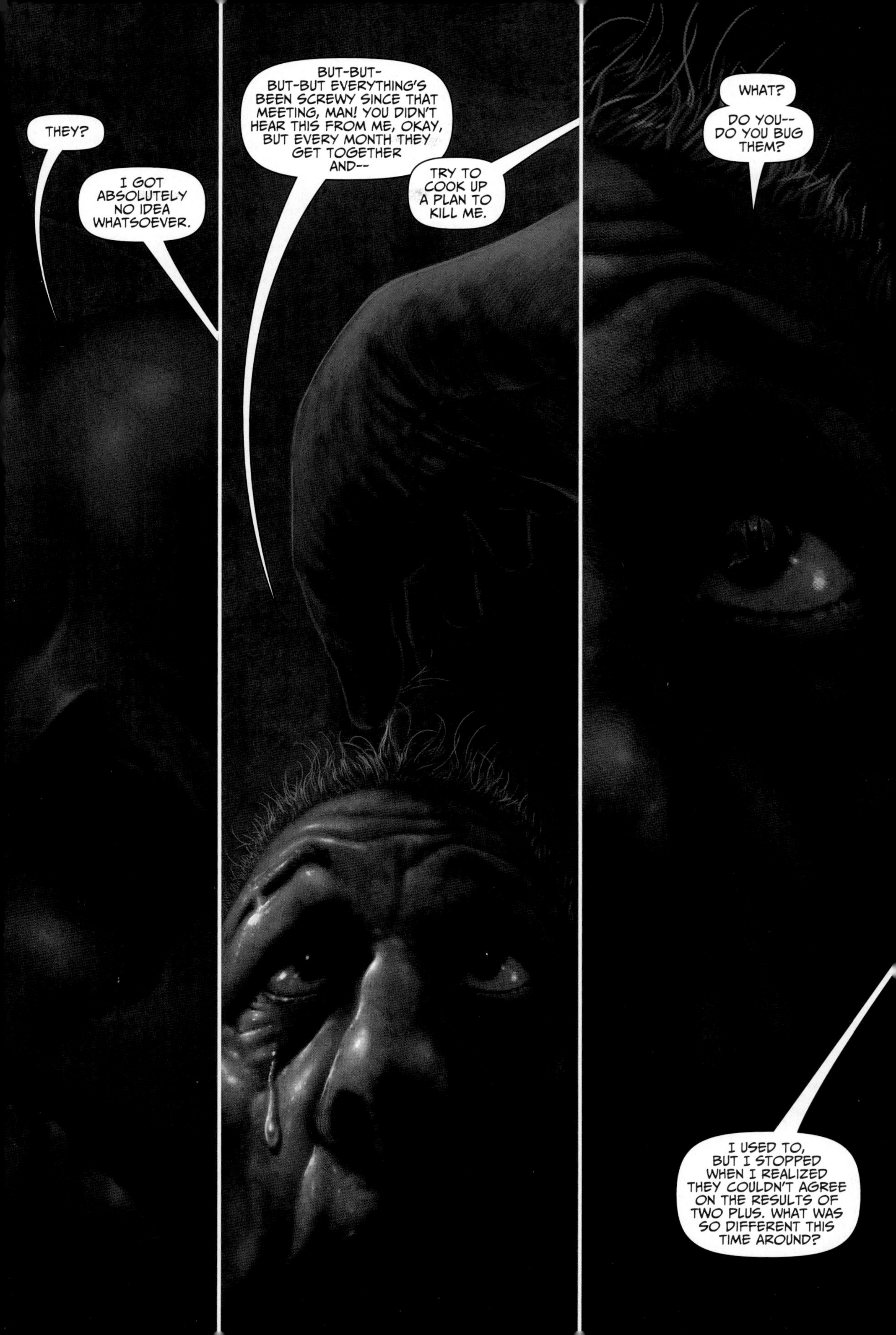
THEY?
I GOT ABSOLUTELY NO IDEA WHATSOEVER.
BUT-BUT- BUT-BUT EVERYTHING'S BEEN SCREWY SINCE THAT MEETING, MAN! YOU DIDN'T HEAR THIS FROM ME, OKAY, BUT EVERY MONTH THEY GET TOGETHER AND--
TRY TO COOK UP A PLAN TO KILL ME.
WHAT?
DO YOU-- DO YOU BUG THEM?
I USED TO, BUT I STOPPED WHEN I REALIZED THEY COULDN'T AGREE ON THE RESULTS OF TWO PLUS. WHAT WAS SO DIFFERENT THIS TIME AROUND?

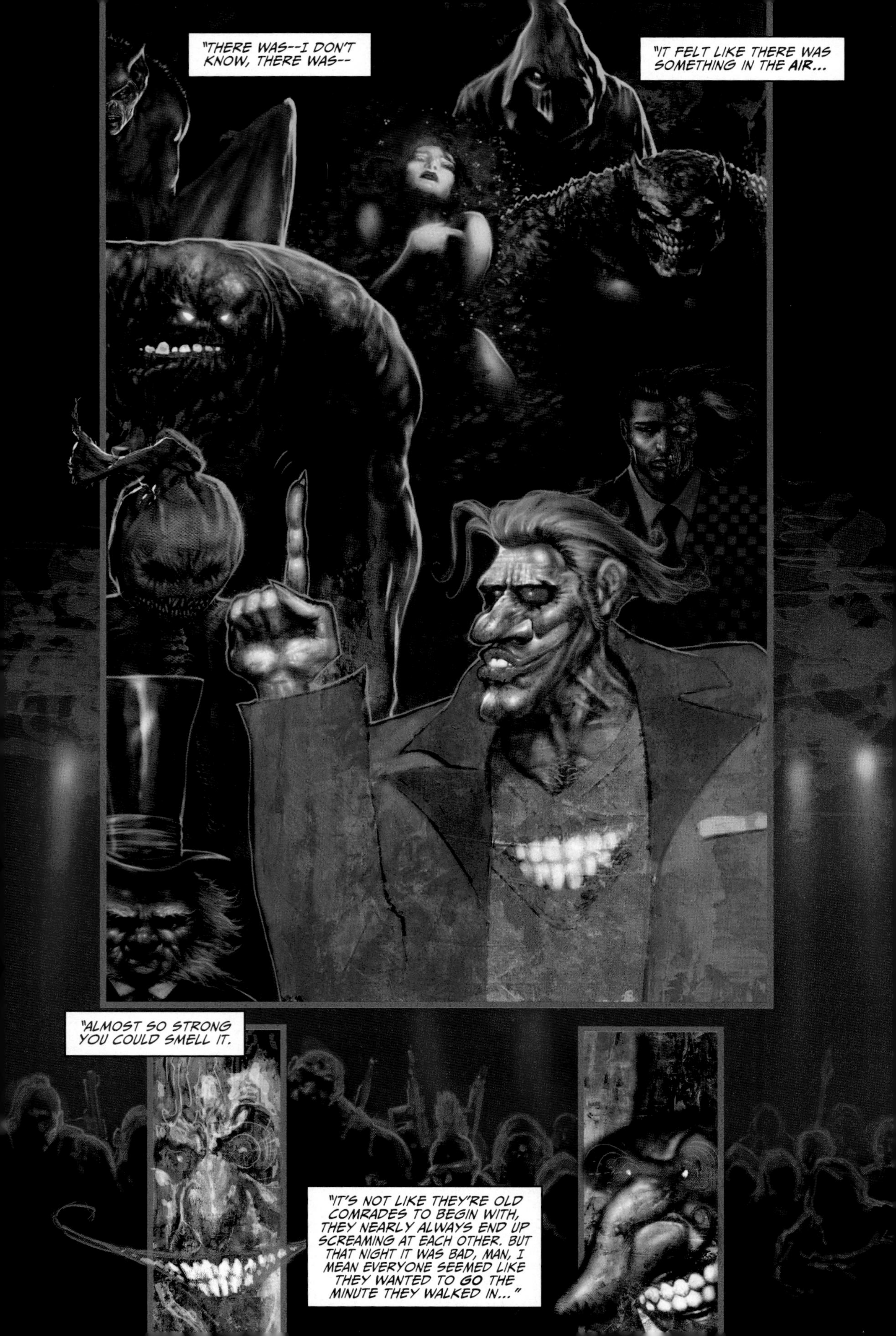
"THERE WAS--I DON'T KNOW, THERE WAS--
"IT FELT LIKE THERE WAS SOMETHING IN THE AIR...
"ALMOST SO STRONG YOU COULD SMELL IT.
"IT'S NOT LIKE THEY'RE OLD COMRADES TO BEGIN WITH, THEY NEARLY ALWAYS END UP SCREAMING AT EACH OTHER. BUT THAT NIGHT IT WAS BAD, MAN, I MEAN EVERYONE SEEMED LIKE THEY WANTED TO GO THE MINUTE THEY WALKED IN..."

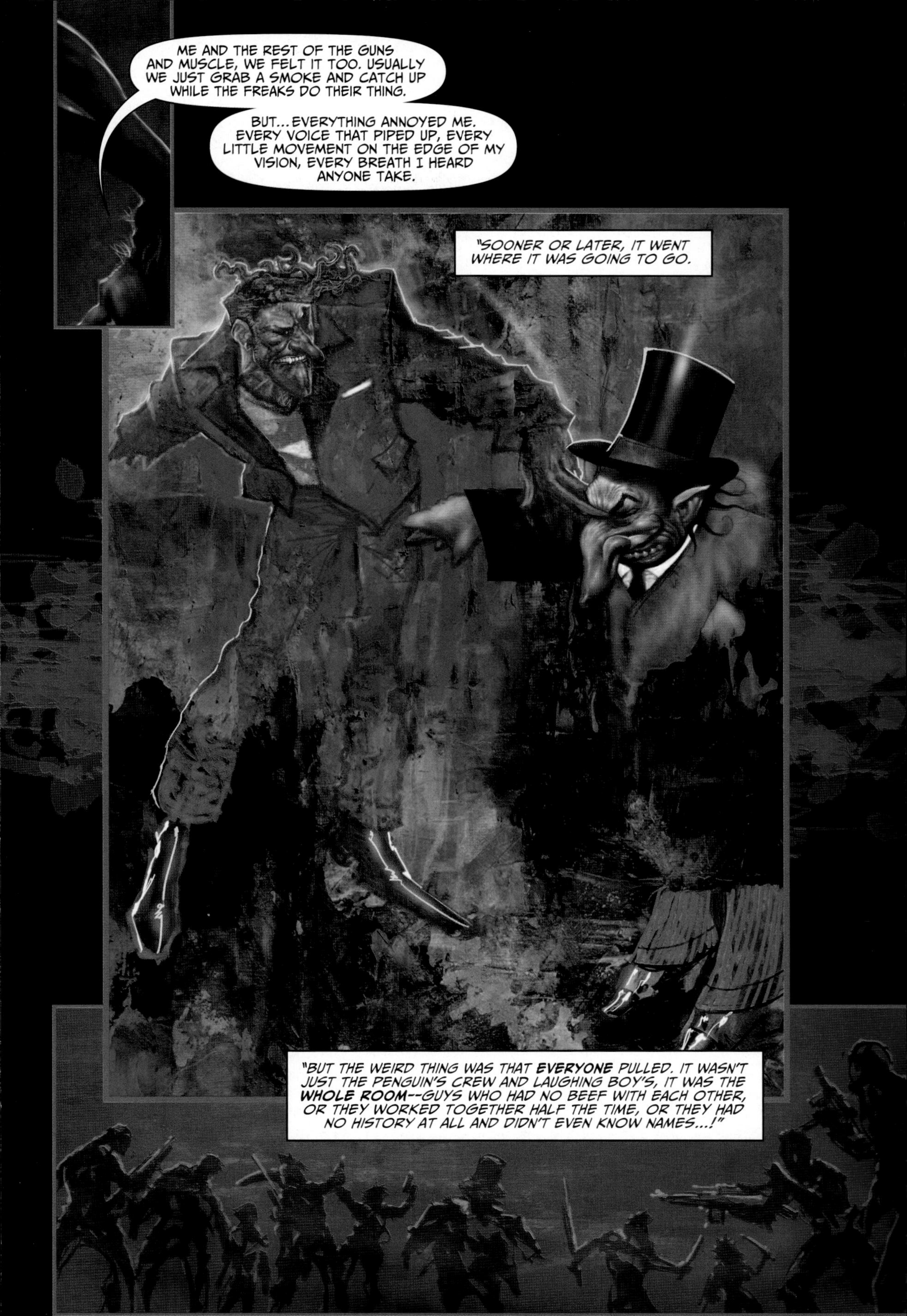

ME AND THE REST OF THE GUNS AND MUSCLE, WE FELT IT TOO. USUALLY WE JUST GRAB A SMOKE AND CATCH UP WHILE THE FREAKS DO THEIR THING.
BUT... EVERYTHING ANNOYED ME. EVERY VOICE THAT PIPED UP, EVERY LITTLE MOVEMENT ON THE EDGE OF MY VISION, EVERY BREATH I HEARD ANYONE TAKE.
"SOONER OR LATER, IT WENT WHERE IT WAS GOING TO GO.
"BUT THE WEIRD THING WAS THAT **EVERYONE** PULLED. IT WASN'T JUST THE PENGUIN'S CREW AND LAUGHING BOY'S, IT WAS THE **WHOLE ROOM**--GUYS WHO HAD NO BEEF WITH EACH OTHER, OR THEY WORKED TOGETHER HALF THE TIME, OR THEY HAD NO HISTORY AT ALL AND DIDN'T EVEN KNOW NAMES...!"

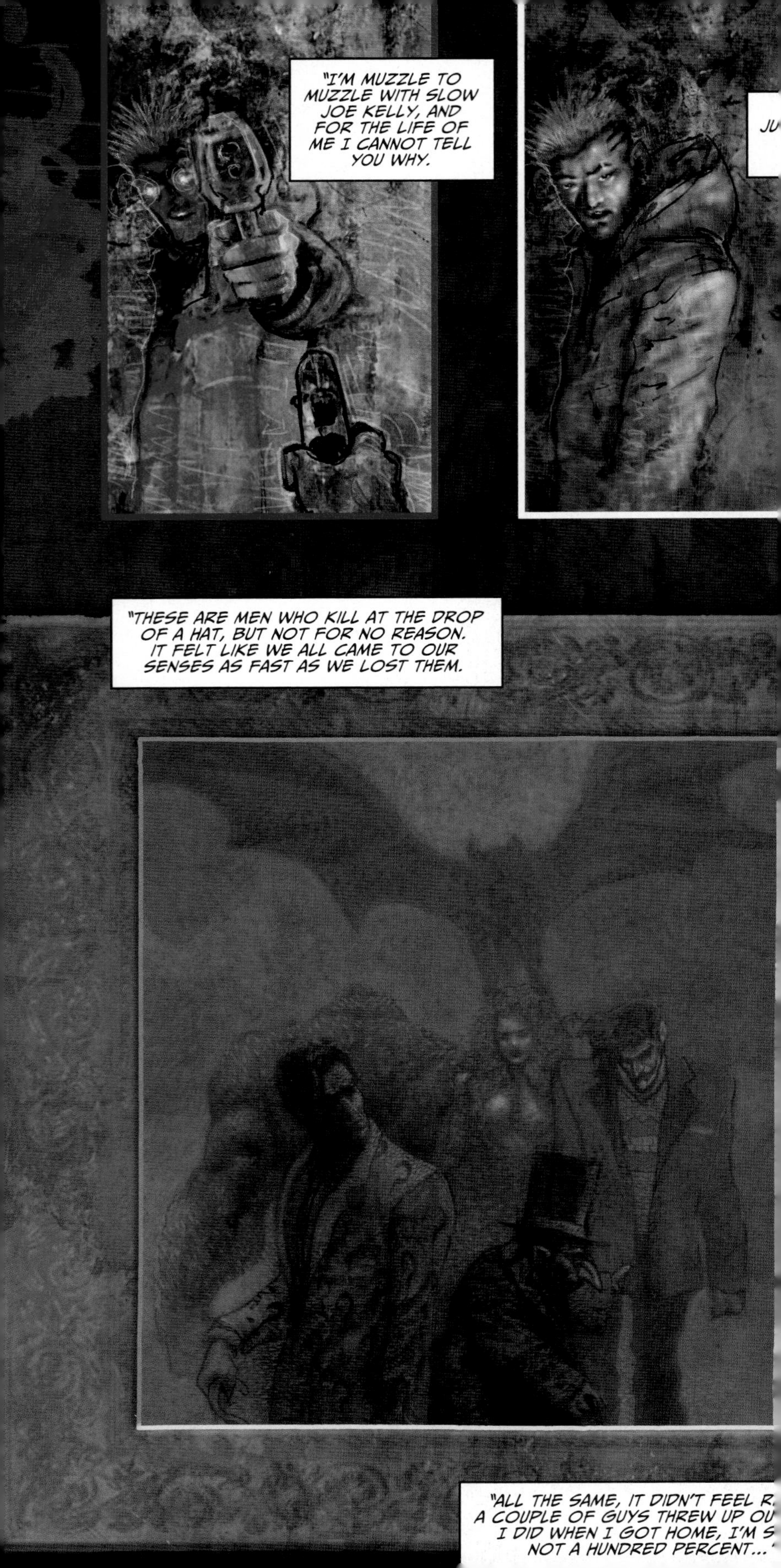
"I'M MUZZLE TO MUZZLE WITH SLOW JOE KELLY, AND FOR THE LIFE OF ME I CANNOT TELL YOU WHY.
"THESE ARE MEN WHO KILL AT THE DROP OF A HAT, BUT NOT FOR NO REASON. IT FELT LIKE WE ALL CAME TO OUR SENSES AS FAST AS WE LOST THEM.
"ALL THE SAME, IT DIDN'T FEEL
A COUPLE OF GUYS THREW UP
I DID WHEN I GOT HOME, I'M
NOT A HUNDRED PERCENT...

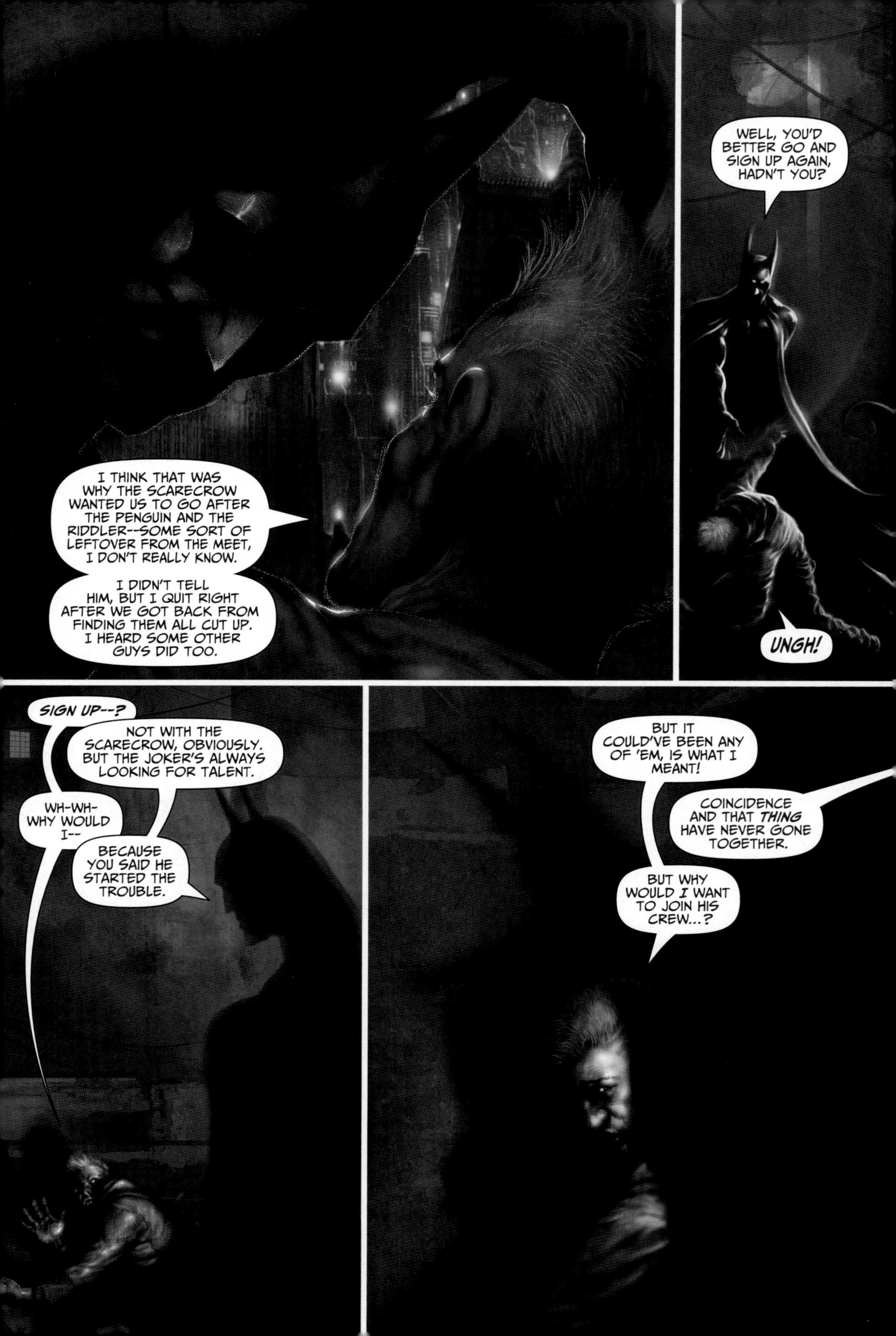
I THINK THAT WAS WHY THE SCARECROW WANTED US TO GO AFTER THE PENGUIN AND THE RIDDLER--SOME SORT OF LEFTOVER FROM THE MEET, I DON'T REALLY KNOW.
I DIDN'T TELL HIM, BUT I QUIT RIGHT AFTER WE GOT BACK FROM FINDING THEM ALL CUT UP. I HEARD SOME OTHER GUYS DID TOO.
WELL, YOU'D BETTER GO AND SIGN UP AGAIN, HADN'T YOU?
UNGH!
SIGN UP--?
NOT WITH THE SCARECROW, OBVIOUSLY. BUT THE JOKER'S ALWAYS LOOKING FOR TALENT.
WH-WH-WHY WOULD I--
BECAUSE YOU SAID HE STARTED THE TROUBLE.
BUT IT COULD'VE BEEN ANY OF 'EM, IS WHAT I MEANT!
COINCIDENCE AND THAT THING HAVE NEVER GONE TOGETHER.
BUT WHY WOULD I WANT TO JOIN HIS CREW...?

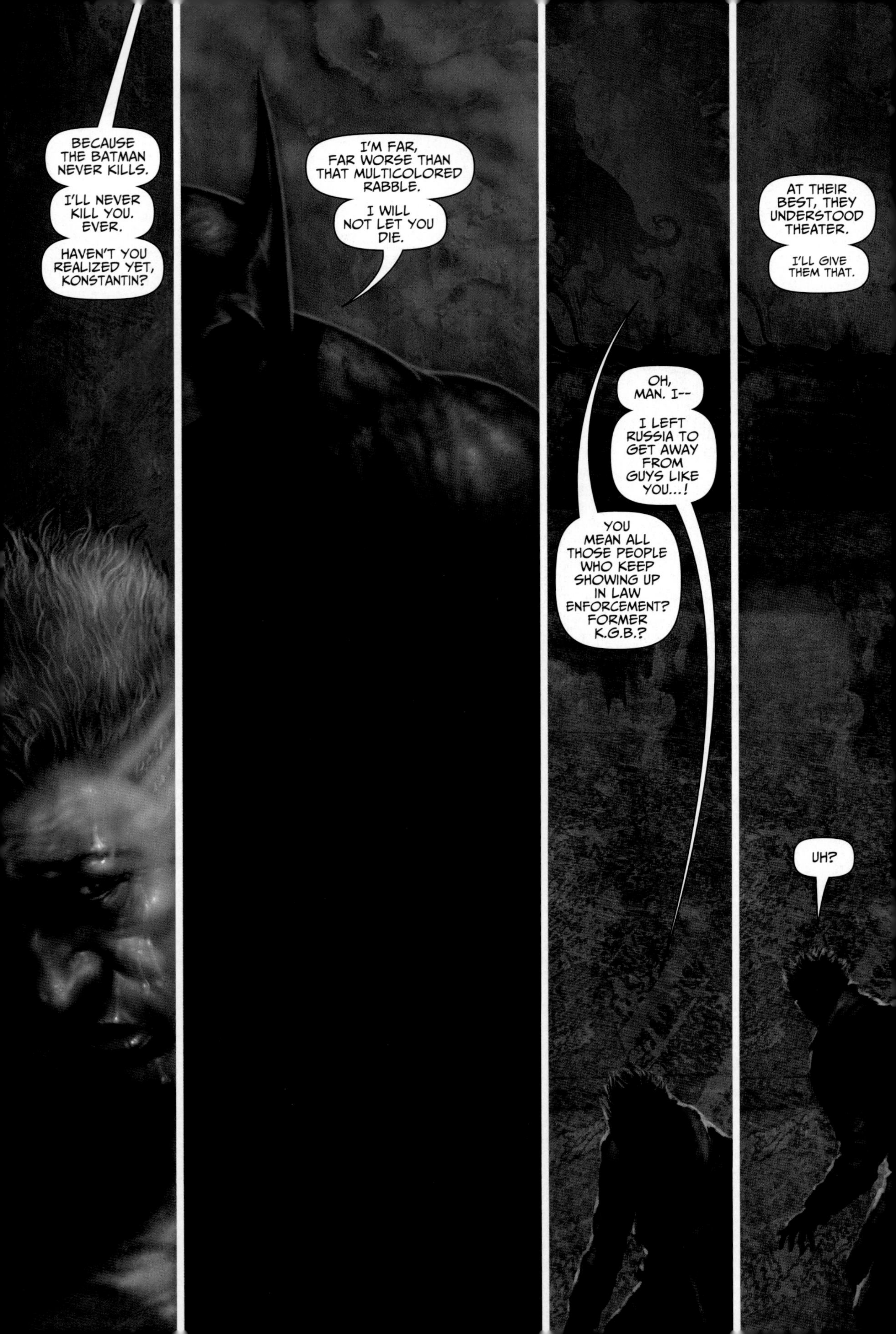
BECAUSE THE BATMAN NEVER KILLS.
I'LL NEVER KILL YOU. EVER.
HAVEN'T YOU REALIZED YET, KONSTANTIN?
I'M FAR, FAR WORSE THAN THAT MULTICOLORED RABBLE.
I WILL NOT LET YOU DIE.
OH, MAN. I--
I LEFT RUSSIA TO GET AWAY FROM GUYS LIKE YOU...!
YOU MEAN ALL THOSE PEOPLE WHO KEEP SHOWING UP IN LAW ENFORCEMENT? FORMER K.G.B.?
AT THEIR BEST, THEY UNDERSTOOD THEATER.
I'LL GIVE THEM THAT.
UH?

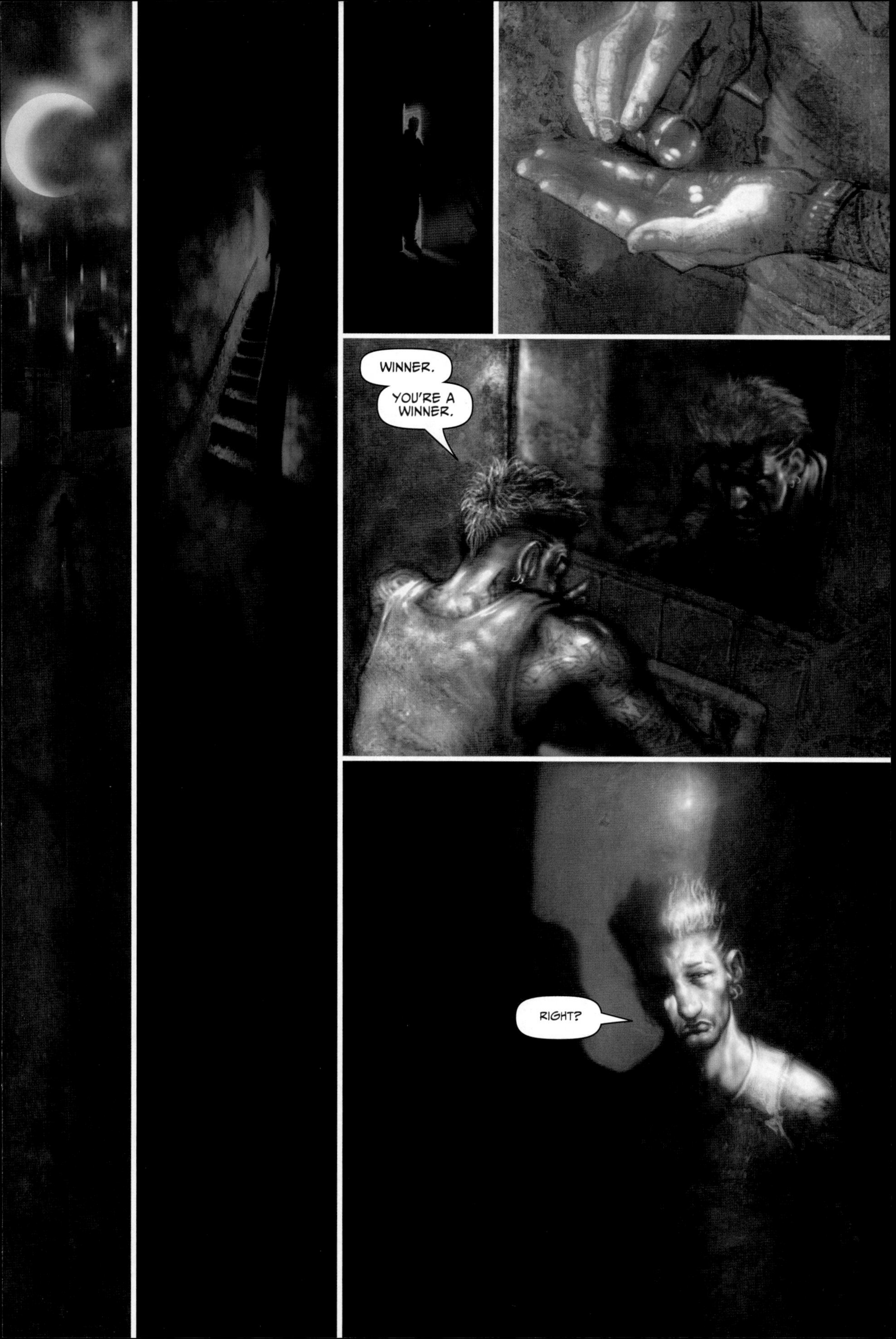
WINNER.
YOU'RE A WINNER.
RIGHT?

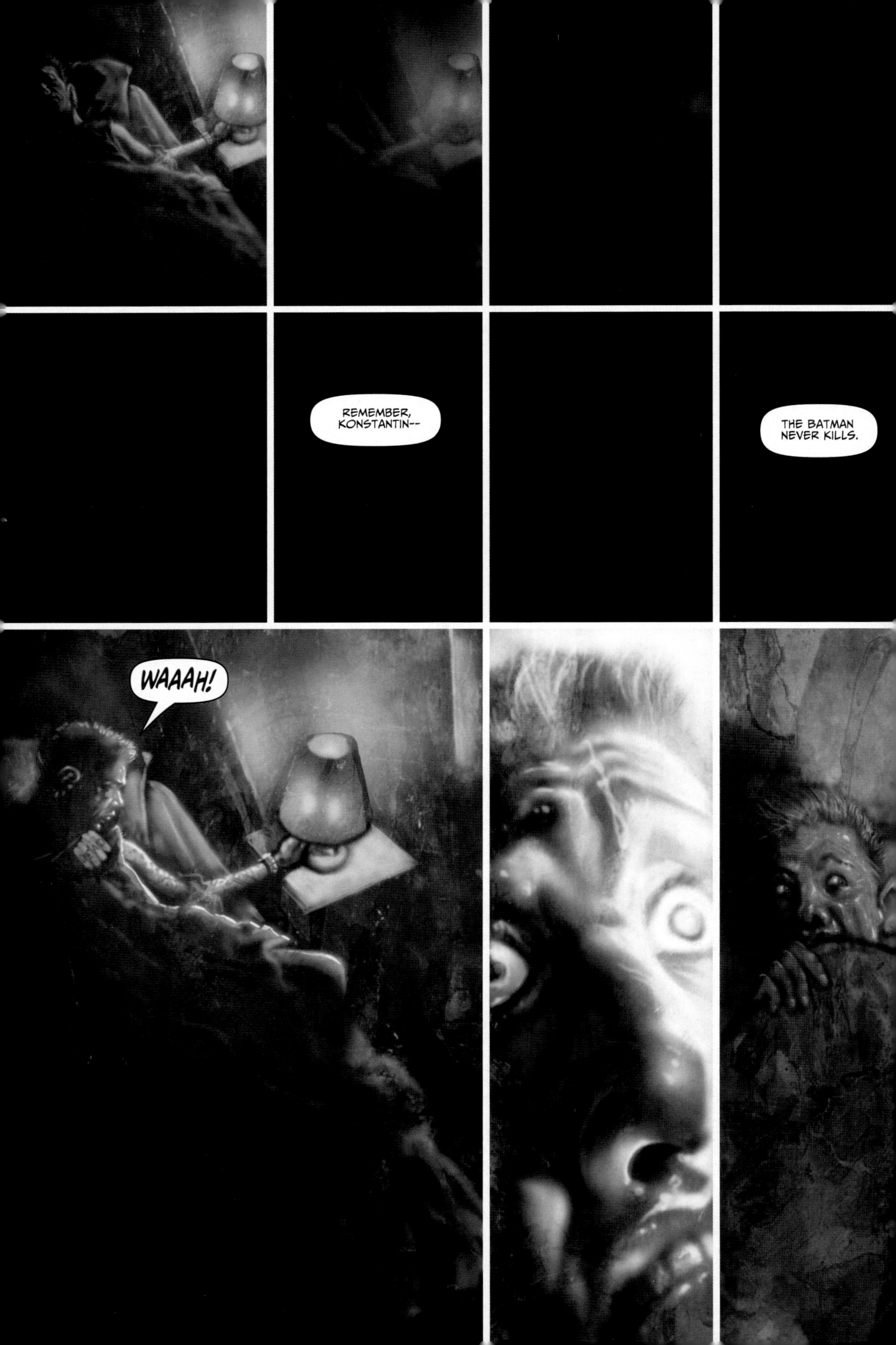
REMEMBER, KONSTANTIN--
THE BATMAN NEVER KILLS.
WAAAH!

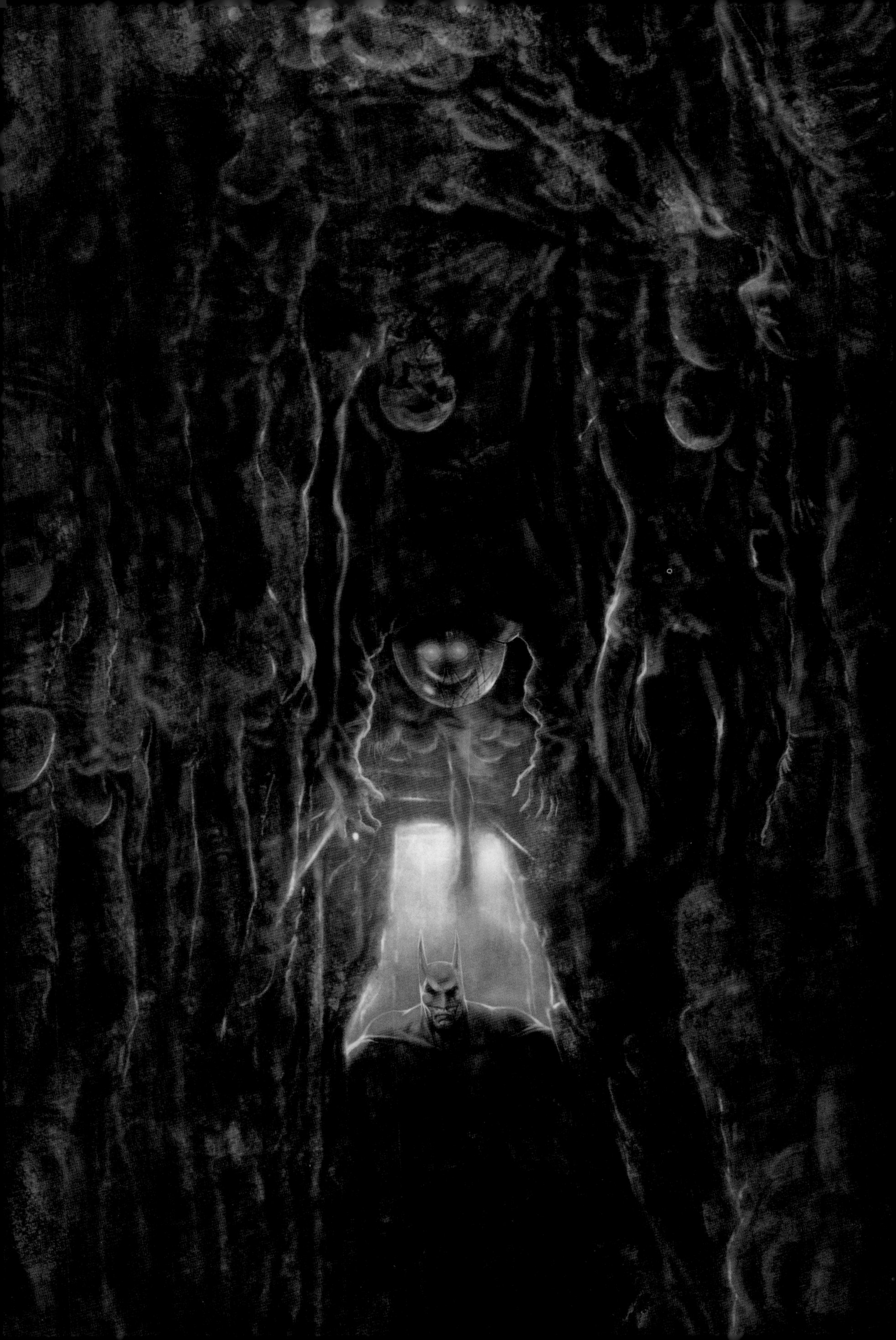

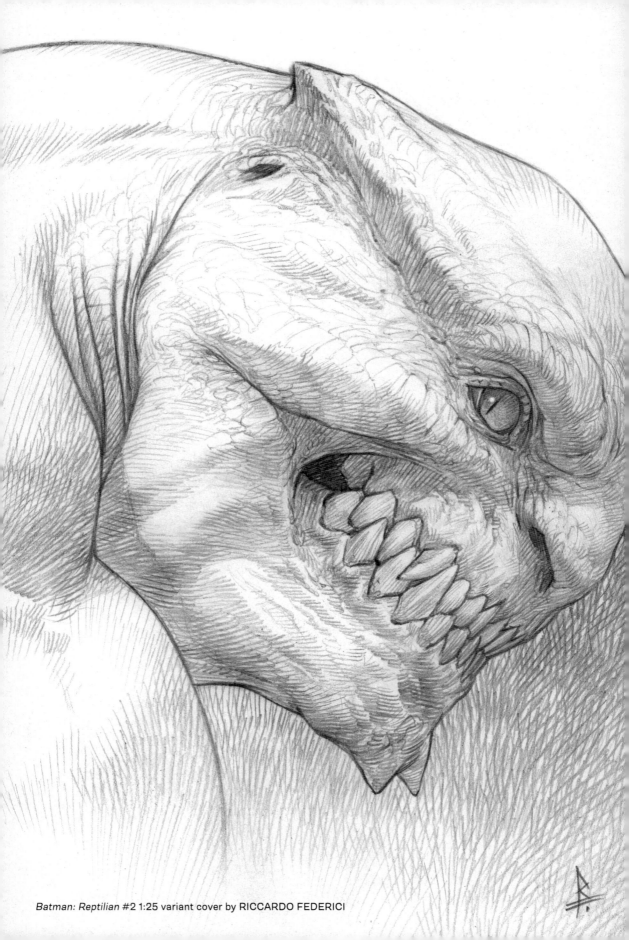

Batman: Reptilian #2 1:25 variant cover by RICCARDO FEDERICI

PENGUIN?

PENGUIN...?

ORK

NOT YOU.

PENGUIN, ARE YOU HERE?

UHHHH...

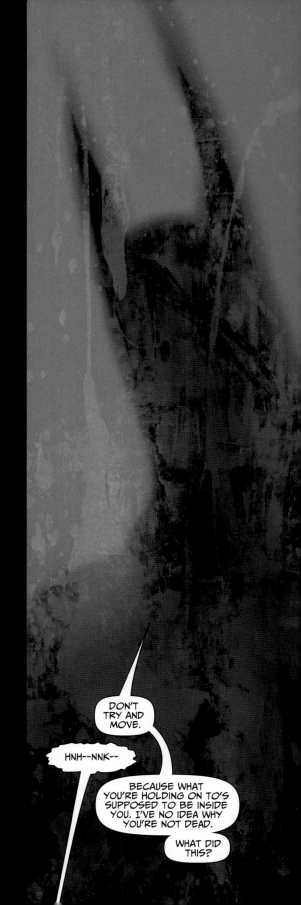

DON'T TRY AND MOVE.

HNH--NNK--

BECAUSE WHAT YOU'RE HOLDING ON TO'S SUPPOSED TO BE INSIDE YOU. I'VE NO IDEA WHY YOU'RE NOT DEAD.

WHAT DID THIS?

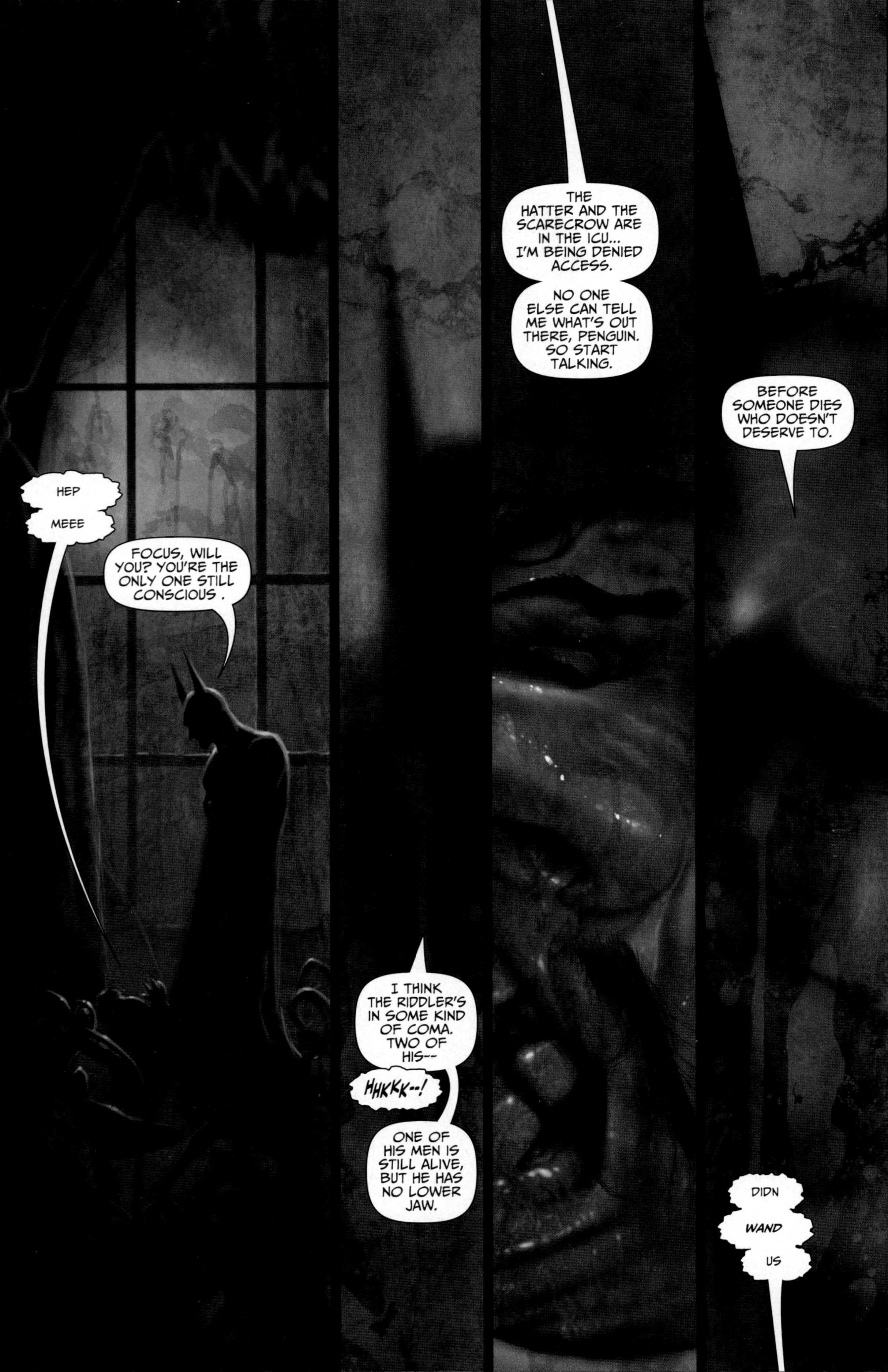
HEP
MEEE
FOCUS, WILL YOU? YOU'RE THE ONLY ONE STILL CONSCIOUS .
I THINK THE RIDDLER'S IN SOME KIND OF COMA. TWO OF HIS--
HHKKK--!
ONE OF HIS MEN IS STILL ALIVE, BUT HE HAS NO LOWER JAW.
THE HATTER AND THE SCARECROW ARE IN THE ICU... I'M BEING DENIED ACCESS.
NO ONE ELSE CAN TELL ME WHAT'S OUT THERE, PENGUIN. SO START TALKING.
BEFORE SOMEONE DIES WHO DOESN'T DESERVE TO.
DIDN
WAND
US

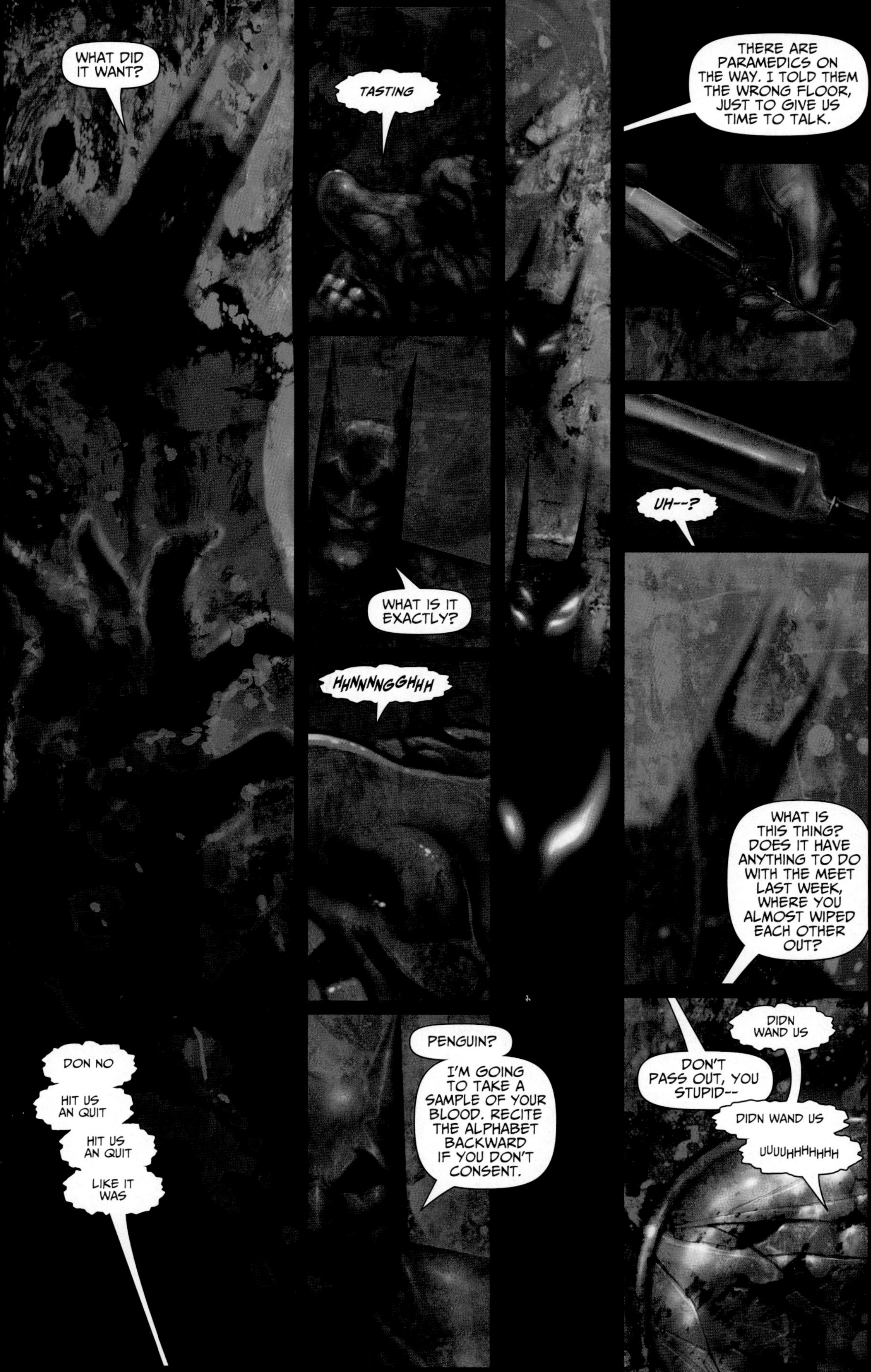
WHAT DID IT WANT?
TASTING
THERE ARE PARAMEDICS ON THE WAY. I TOLD THEM THE WRONG FLOOR, JUST TO GIVE US TIME TO TALK.
UH--?
WHAT IS IT EXACTLY?
HHNNNNGGHHH
WHAT IS THIS THING? DOES IT HAVE ANYTHING TO DO WITH THE MEET LAST WEEK, WHERE YOU ALMOST WIPED EACH OTHER OUT?
DON NO
HIT US AN QUIT
HIT US AN QUIT
LIKE IT WAS
PENGUIN?
I'M GOING TO TAKE A SAMPLE OF YOUR BLOOD. RECITE THE ALPHABET BACKWARD IF YOU DON'T CONSENT.
DIDN WAND US
DON'T PASS OUT, YOU STUPID--
DIDN WAND US
UUUUHHHHHHH

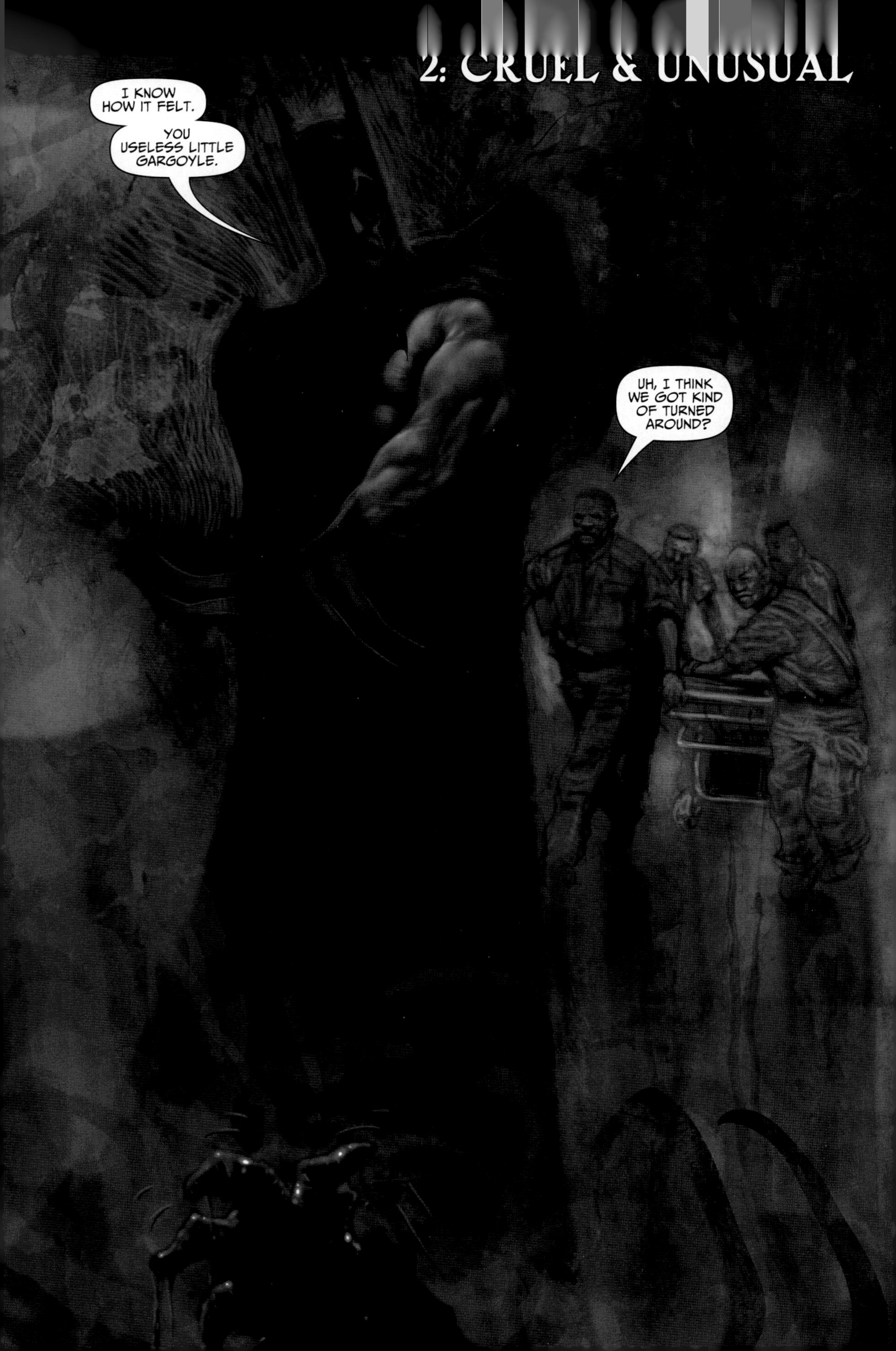
2: CRUEL & UNUSUAL
I KNOW HOW IT FELT.
YOU USELESS LITTLE GARGOYLE.
UH, I THINK WE GOT KIND OF TURNED AROUND?

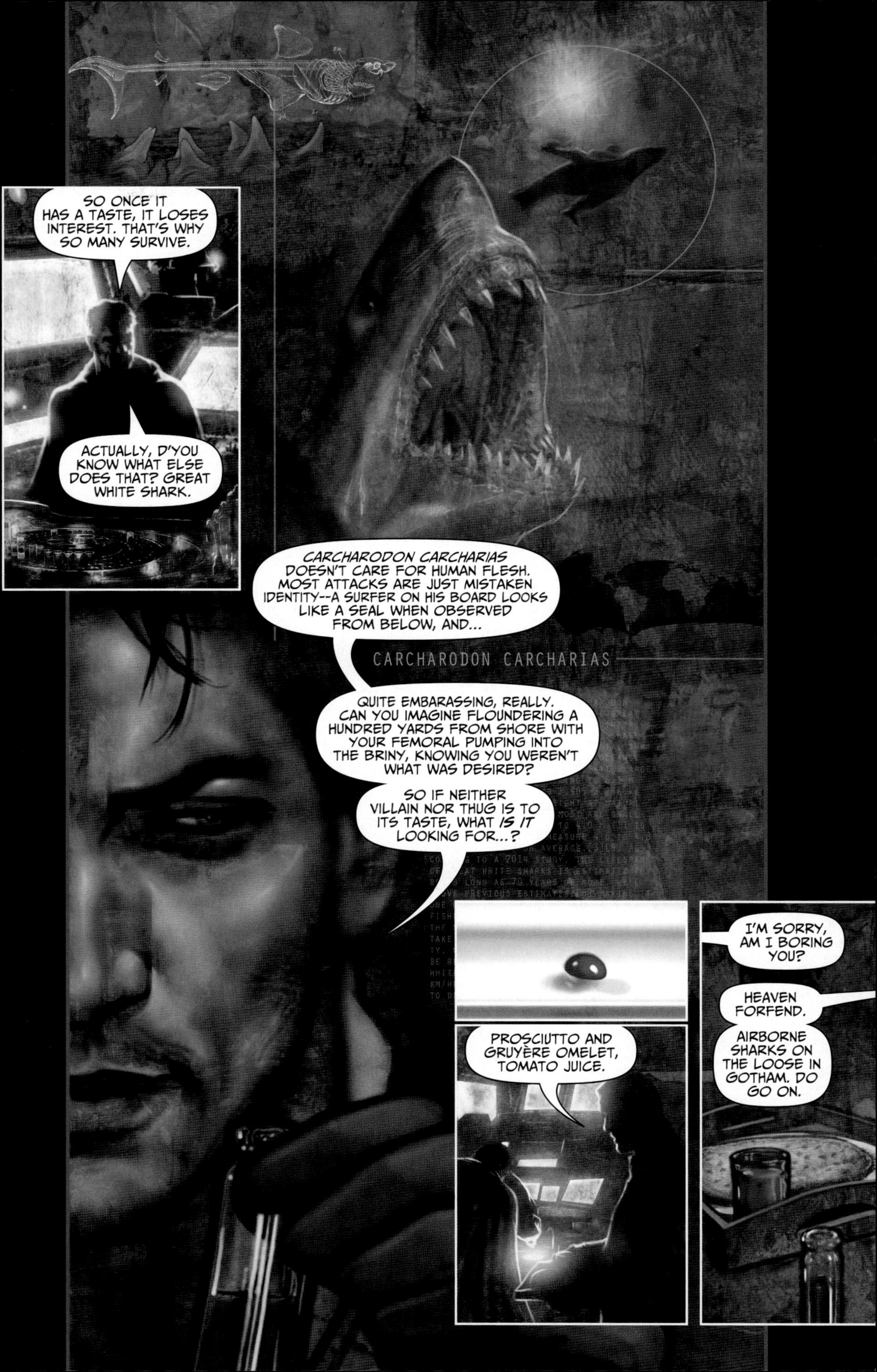
SO ONCE IT HAS A TASTE, IT LOSES INTEREST. THAT'S WHY SO MANY SURVIVE.
ACTUALLY, D'YOU KNOW WHAT ELSE DOES THAT? GREAT WHITE SHARK.
CARCHARODON CARCHARIAS DOESN'T CARE FOR HUMAN FLESH. MOST ATTACKS ARE JUST MISTAKEN IDENTITY--A SURFER ON HIS BOARD LOOKS LIKE A SEAL WHEN OBSERVED FROM BELOW, AND...
CARCHARODON CARCHARIAS
QUITE EMBARASSING, REALLY. CAN YOU IMAGINE FLOUNDERING A HUNDRED YARDS FROM SHORE WITH YOUR FEMORAL PUMPING INTO THE BRINY, KNOWING YOU WEREN'T WHAT WAS DESIRED?
SO IF NEITHER VILLAIN NOR THUG IS TO ITS TASTE, WHAT *IS IT* LOOKING FOR...?
PROSCIUTTO AND GRUYÈRE OMELET, TOMATO JUICE.
I'M SORRY, AM I BORING YOU?
HEAVEN FORFEND.
AIRBORNE SHARKS ON THE LOOSE IN GOTHAM. DO GO ON.

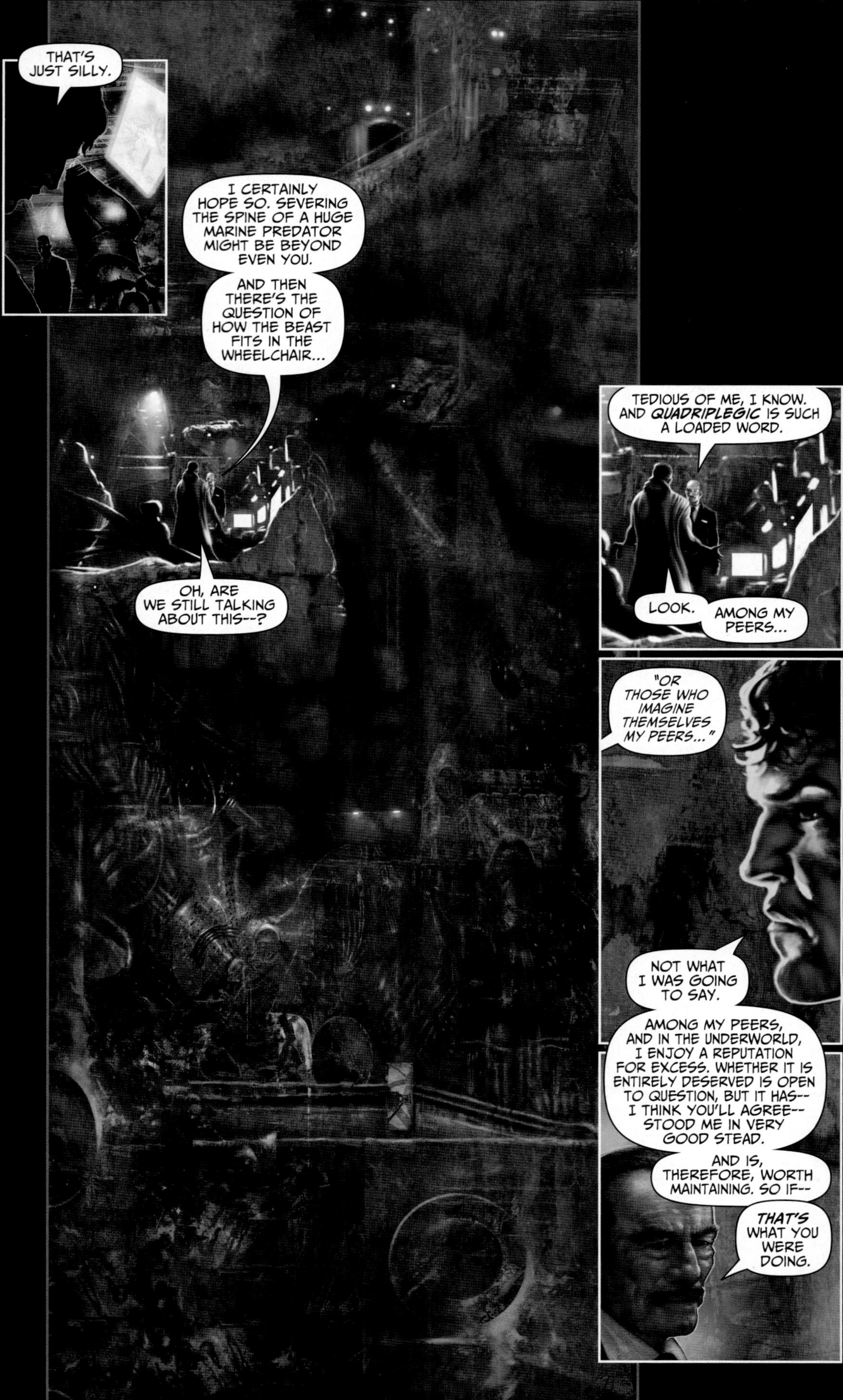
THAT'S JUST SILLY.
I CERTAINLY HOPE SO. SEVERING THE SPINE OF A HUGE MARINE PREDATOR MIGHT BE BEYOND EVEN YOU.
AND THEN THERE'S THE QUESTION OF HOW THE BEAST FITS IN THE WHEELCHAIR...
OH, ARE WE STILL TALKING ABOUT THIS--?
TEDIOUS OF ME, I KNOW. AND *QUADRIPLEGIC* IS SUCH A LOADED WORD.
LOOK.
AMONG MY PEERS...
"OR THOSE WHO IMAGINE THEMSELVES MY PEERS..."
NOT WHAT I WAS GOING TO SAY.
AMONG MY PEERS, AND IN THE UNDERWORLD, I ENJOY A REPUTATION FOR EXCESS. WHETHER IT IS ENTIRELY DESERVED IS OPEN TO QUESTION, BUT IT HAS-- I THINK YOU'LL AGREE-- STOOD ME IN VERY GOOD STEAD.
AND IS, THEREFORE, WORTH MAINTAINING. SO IF--
THAT'S WHAT YOU WERE DOING.

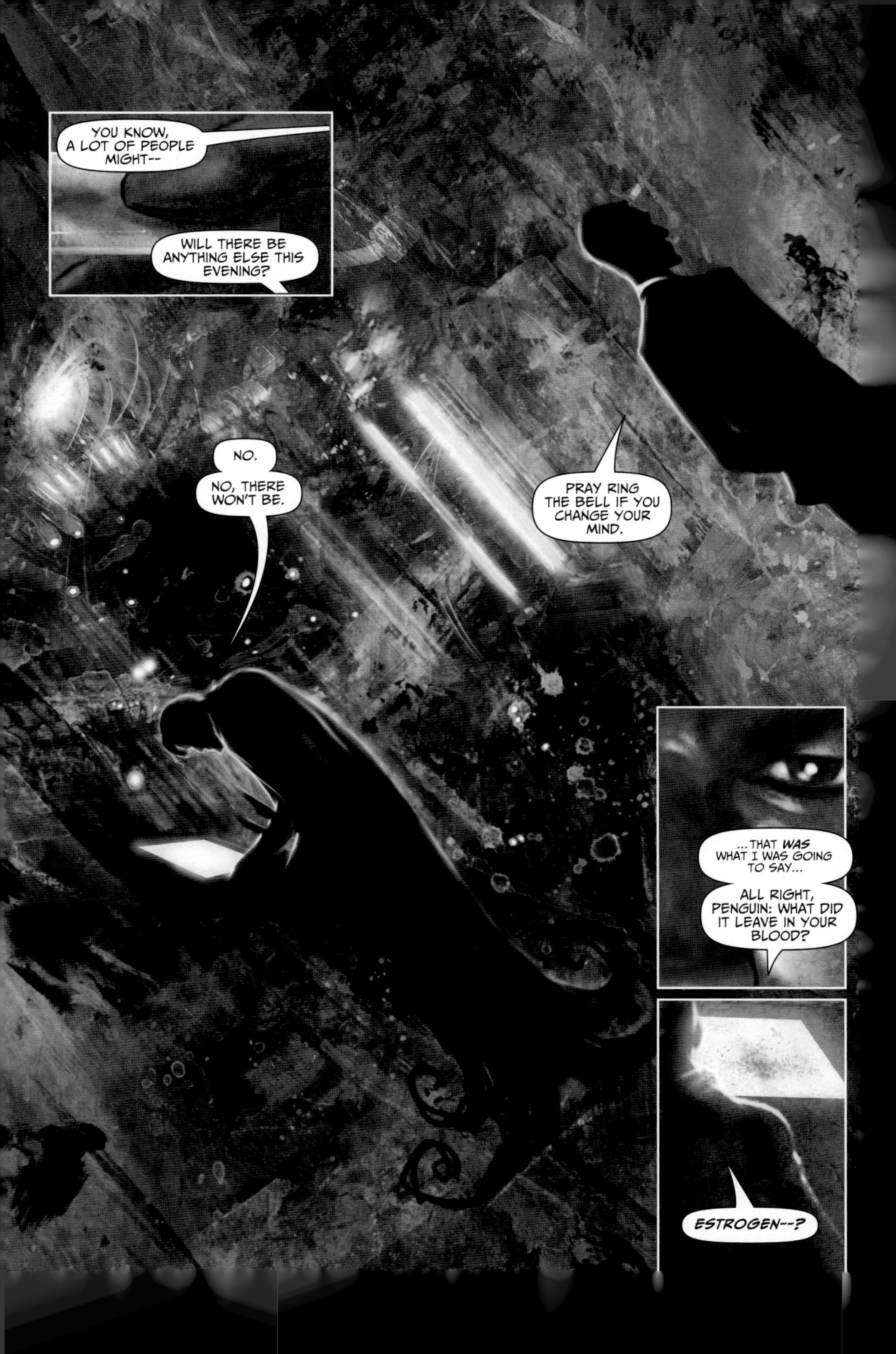
YOU KNOW, A LOT OF PEOPLE MIGHT--
WILL THERE BE ANYTHING ELSE THIS EVENING?
NO.
NO, THERE WON'T BE.
PRAY RING THE BELL IF YOU CHANGE YOUR MIND.
...THAT WAS WHAT I WAS GOING TO SAY...
ALL RIGHT, PENGUIN: WHAT DID IT LEAVE IN YOUR BLOOD?
ESTROGEN--?

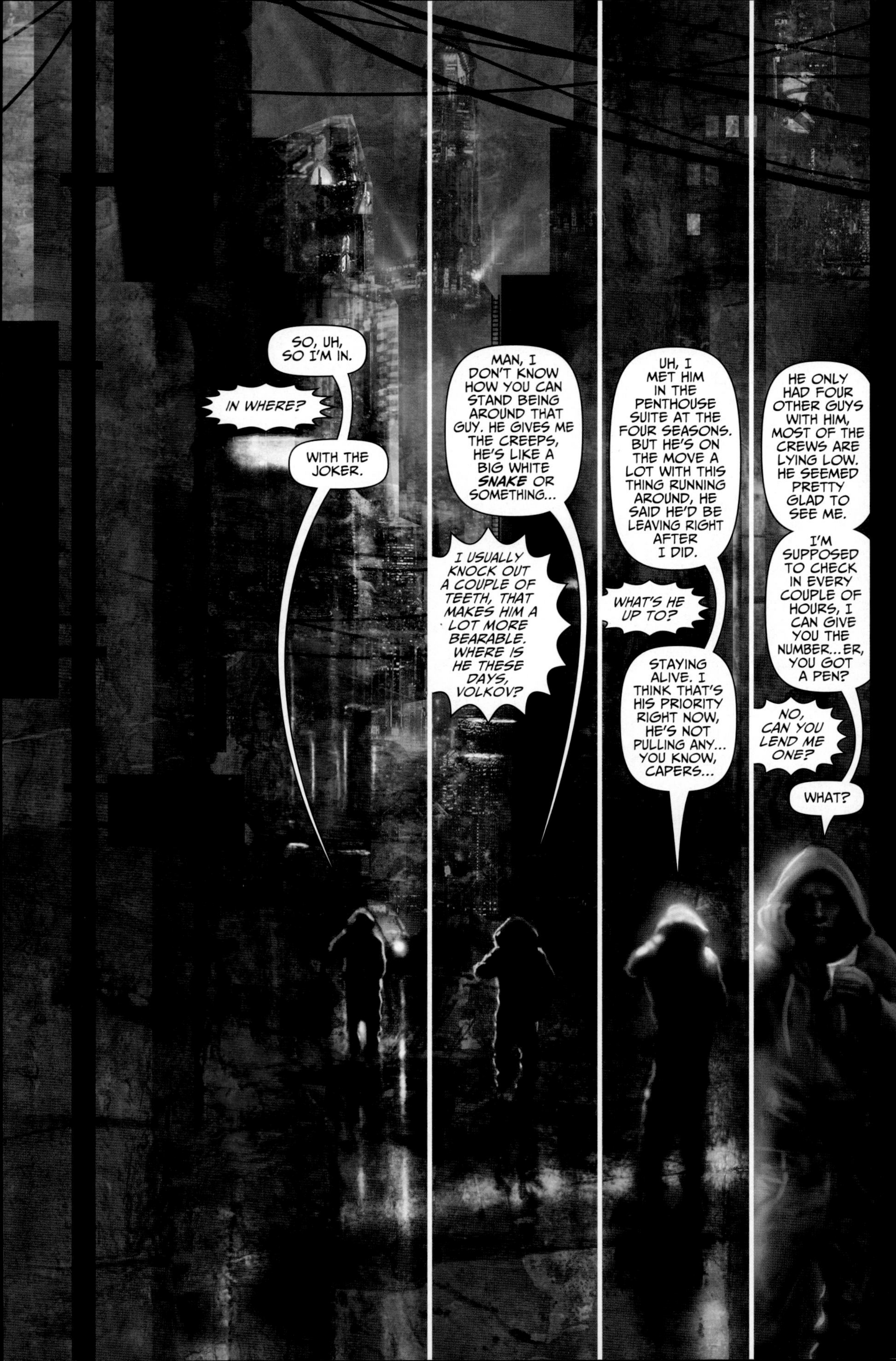
SO, UH, SO I'M IN.
IN WHERE?
WITH THE JOKER.
MAN, I DON'T KNOW HOW YOU CAN STAND BEING AROUND THAT GUY. HE GIVES ME THE CREEPS, HE'S LIKE A BIG WHITE SNAKE OR SOMETHING...
I USUALLY KNOCK OUT A COUPLE OF TEETH, THAT MAKES HIM A LOT MORE BEARABLE. WHERE IS HE THESE DAYS, VOLKOV?
UH, I MET HIM IN THE PENTHOUSE SUITE AT THE FOUR SEASONS. BUT HE'S ON THE MOVE A LOT WITH THIS THING RUNNING AROUND, HE SAID HE'D BE LEAVING RIGHT AFTER I DID.
WHAT'S HE UP TO?
STAYING ALIVE. I THINK THAT'S HIS PRIORITY RIGHT NOW, HE'S NOT PULLING ANY... YOU KNOW, CAPERS...
HE ONLY HAD FOUR OTHER GUYS WITH HIM, MOST OF THE CREWS ARE LYING LOW. HE SEEMED PRETTY GLAD TO SEE ME.
I'M SUPPOSED TO CHECK IN EVERY COUPLE OF HOURS, I CAN GIVE YOU THE NUMBER...ER, YOU GOT A PEN?
NO, CAN YOU LEND ME ONE?
WHAT?

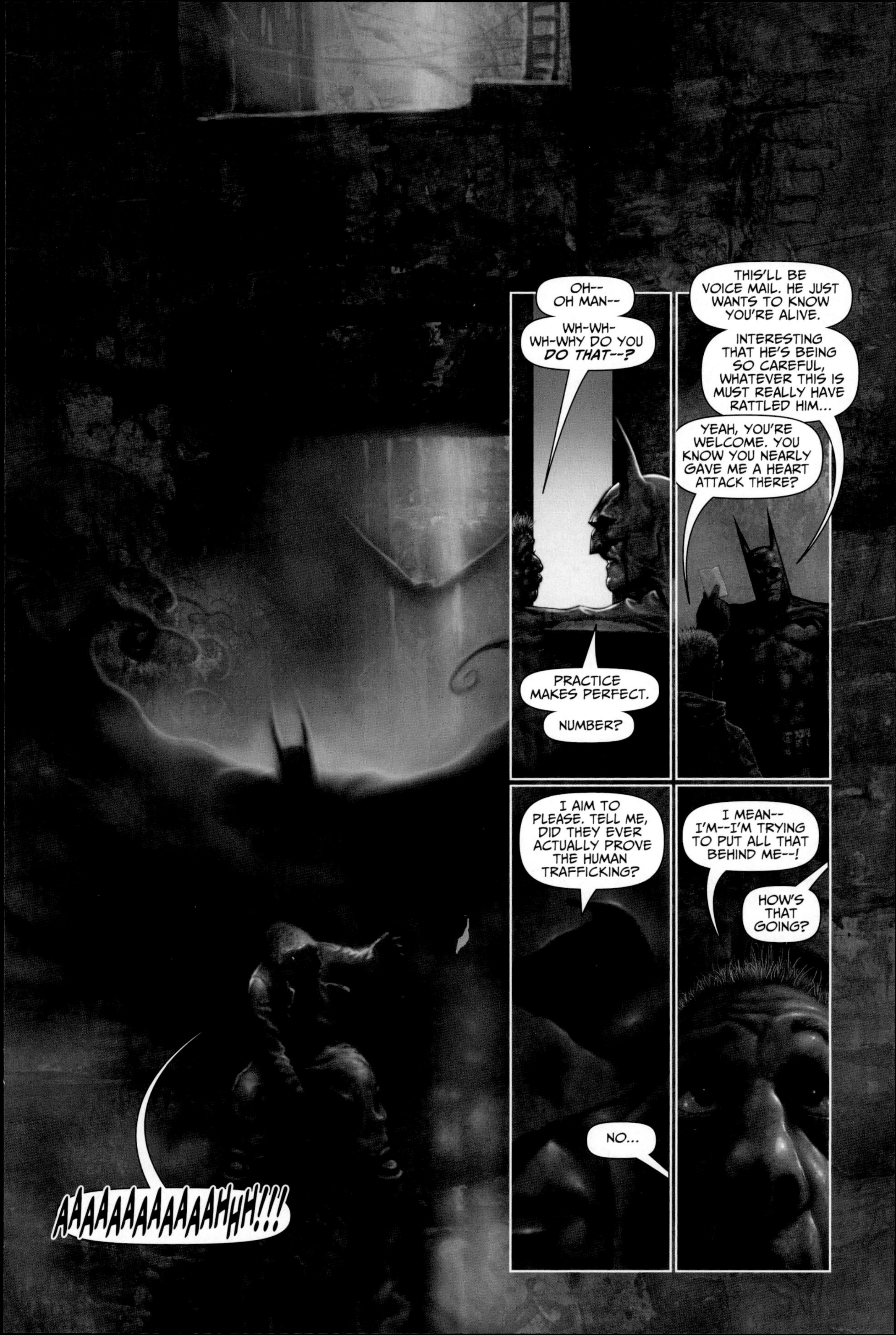
AAAAAAAAAAAHHH!!!
OH--
OH MAN--
WH-WH-
WH-WHY DO YOU
DO THAT--?
PRACTICE
MAKES PERFECT.
NUMBER?
THIS'LL BE
VOICE MAIL. HE JUST
WANTS TO KNOW
YOU'RE ALIVE.
INTERESTING
THAT HE'S BEING
SO CAREFUL,
WHATEVER THIS IS
MUST REALLY HAVE
RATTLED HIM...
YEAH, YOU'RE
WELCOME. YOU
KNOW YOU NEARLY
GAVE ME A HEART
ATTACK THERE?
I AIM TO
PLEASE. TELL ME,
DID THEY EVER
ACTUALLY PROVE
THE HUMAN
TRAFFICKING?
NO...
I MEAN--
I'M--I'M TRYING
TO PUT ALL THAT
BEHIND ME--!
HOW'S
THAT
GOING?

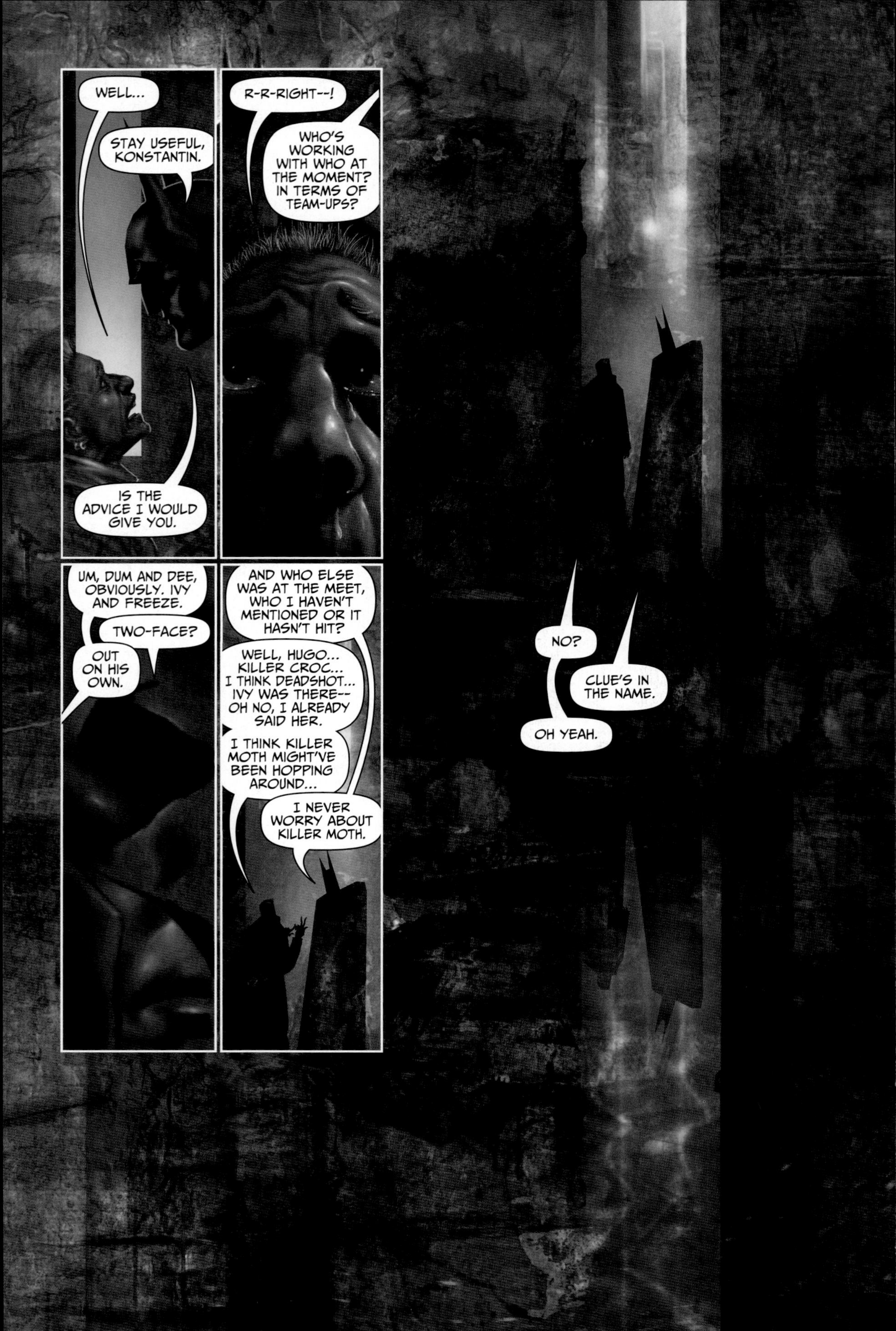
WELL...
STAY USEFUL, KONSTANTIN.
IS THE ADVICE I WOULD GIVE YOU.
R-R-RIGHT--!
WHO'S WORKING WITH WHO AT THE MOMENT? IN TERMS OF TEAM-UPS?
UM, DUM AND DEE, OBVIOUSLY. IVY AND FREEZE.
TWO-FACE?
OUT ON HIS OWN.
AND WHO ELSE WAS AT THE MEET, WHO I HAVEN'T MENTIONED OR IT HASN'T HIT?
WELL, HUGO... KILLER CROC... I THINK DEADSHOT... IVY WAS THERE-- OH NO, I ALREADY SAID HER.
I THINK KILLER MOTH MIGHT'VE BEEN HOPPING AROUND...
I NEVER WORRY ABOUT KILLER MOTH.
NO?
CLUE'S IN THE NAME.
OH YEAH.

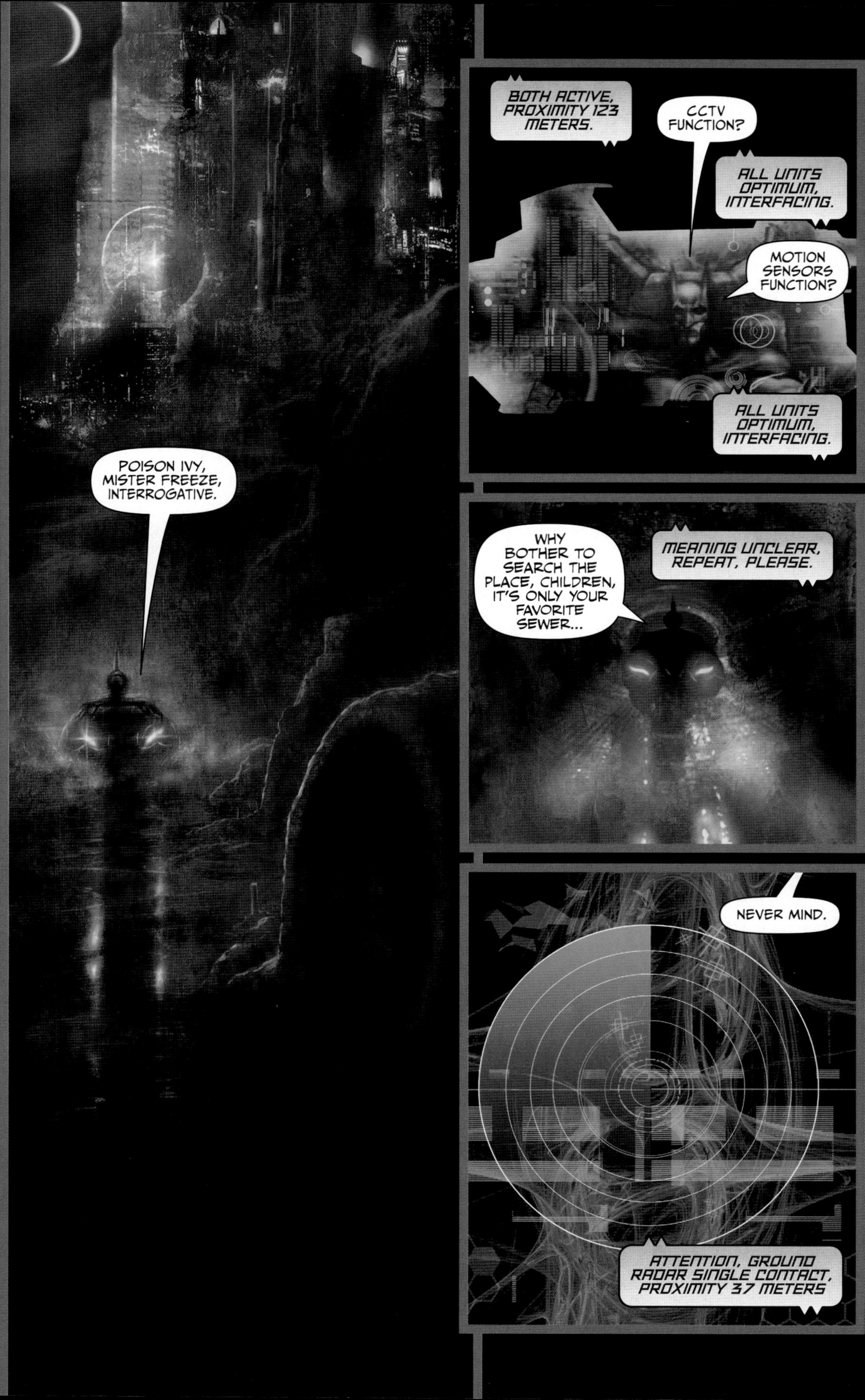
POISON IVY, MISTER FREEZE, INTERROGATIVE.
BOTH ACTIVE, PROXIMITY 123 METERS.
CCTV FUNCTION?
ALL UNITS OPTIMUM, INTERFACING.
MOTION SENSORS FUNCTION?
ALL UNITS OPTIMUM, INTERFACING.
WHY BOTHER TO SEARCH THE PLACE, CHILDREN, IT'S ONLY YOUR FAVORITE SEWER...
MEANING UNCLEAR, REPEAT, PLEASE.
NEVER MIND.
ATTENTION, GROUND RADAR SINGLE CONTACT, PROXIMITY 37 METERS

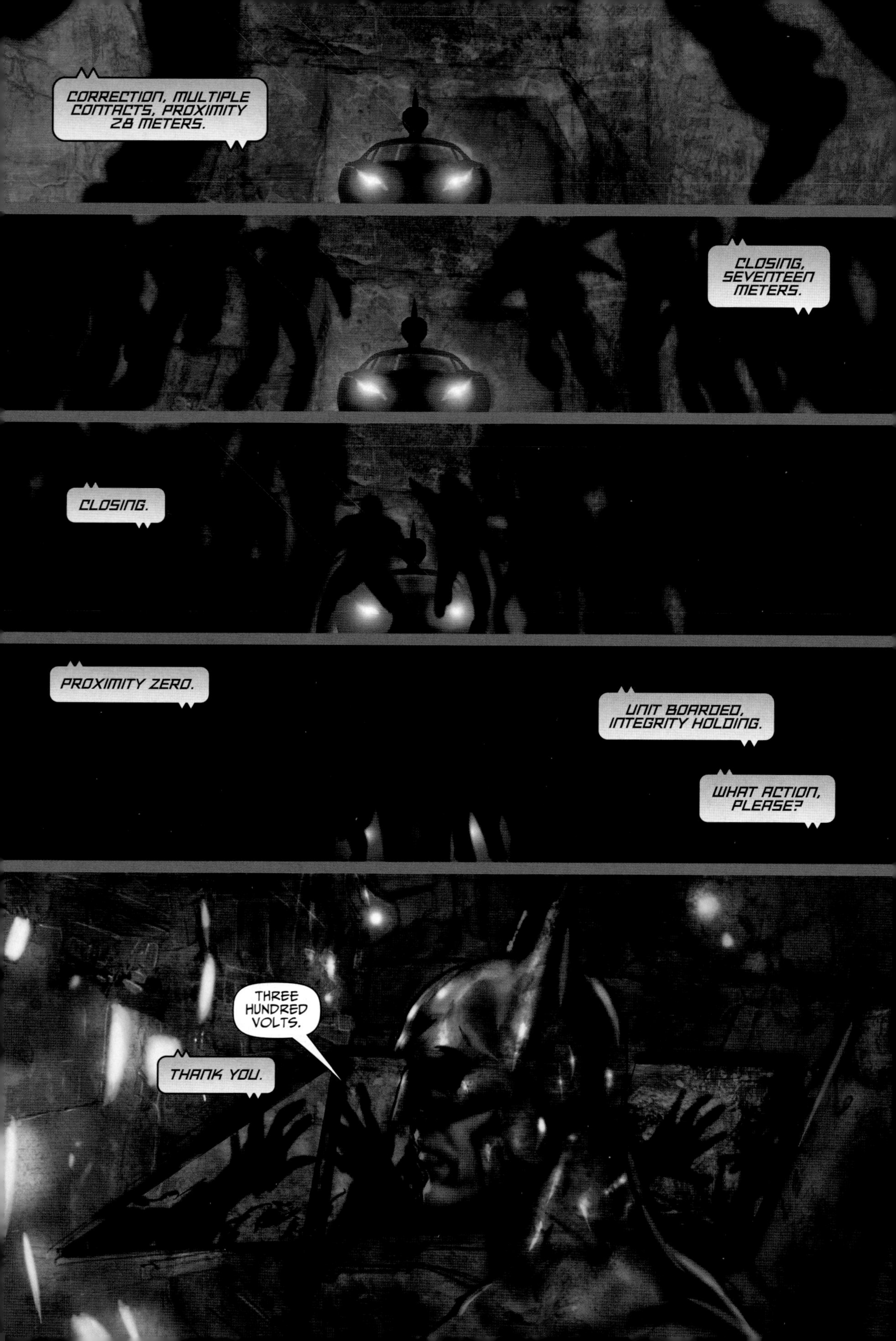
CORRECTION, MULTIPLE CONTACTS, PROXIMITY 28 METERS.
CLOSING, SEVENTEEN METERS.
CLOSING.
PROXIMITY ZERO.
UNIT BOARDED, INTEGRITY HOLDING.
WHAT ACTION, PLEASE?
THREE HUNDRED VOLTS.
THANK YOU.

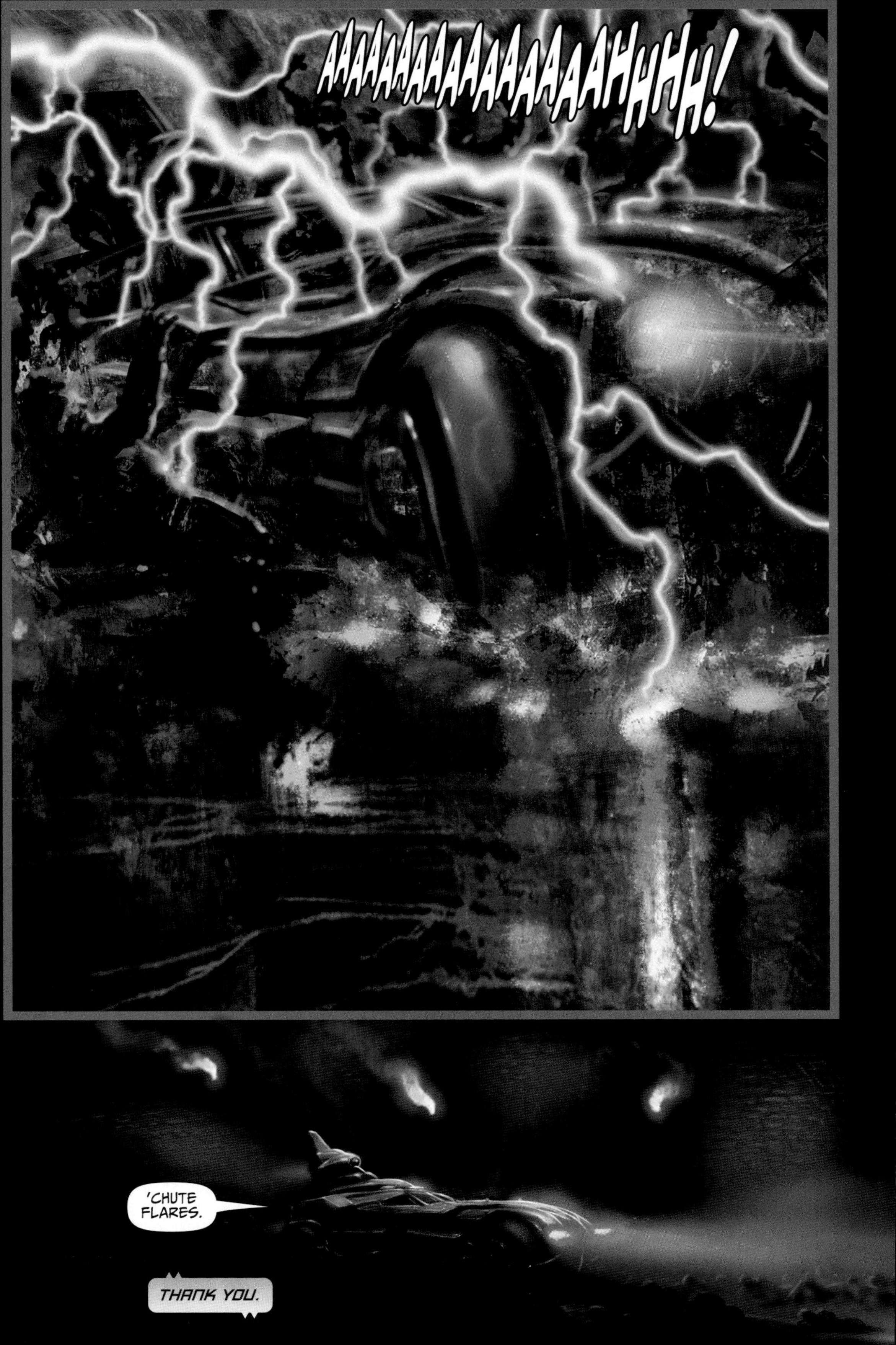
AAAAAAAAAAAAAAAAAAHHHH!
'CHUTE FLARES.
THANK YOU.

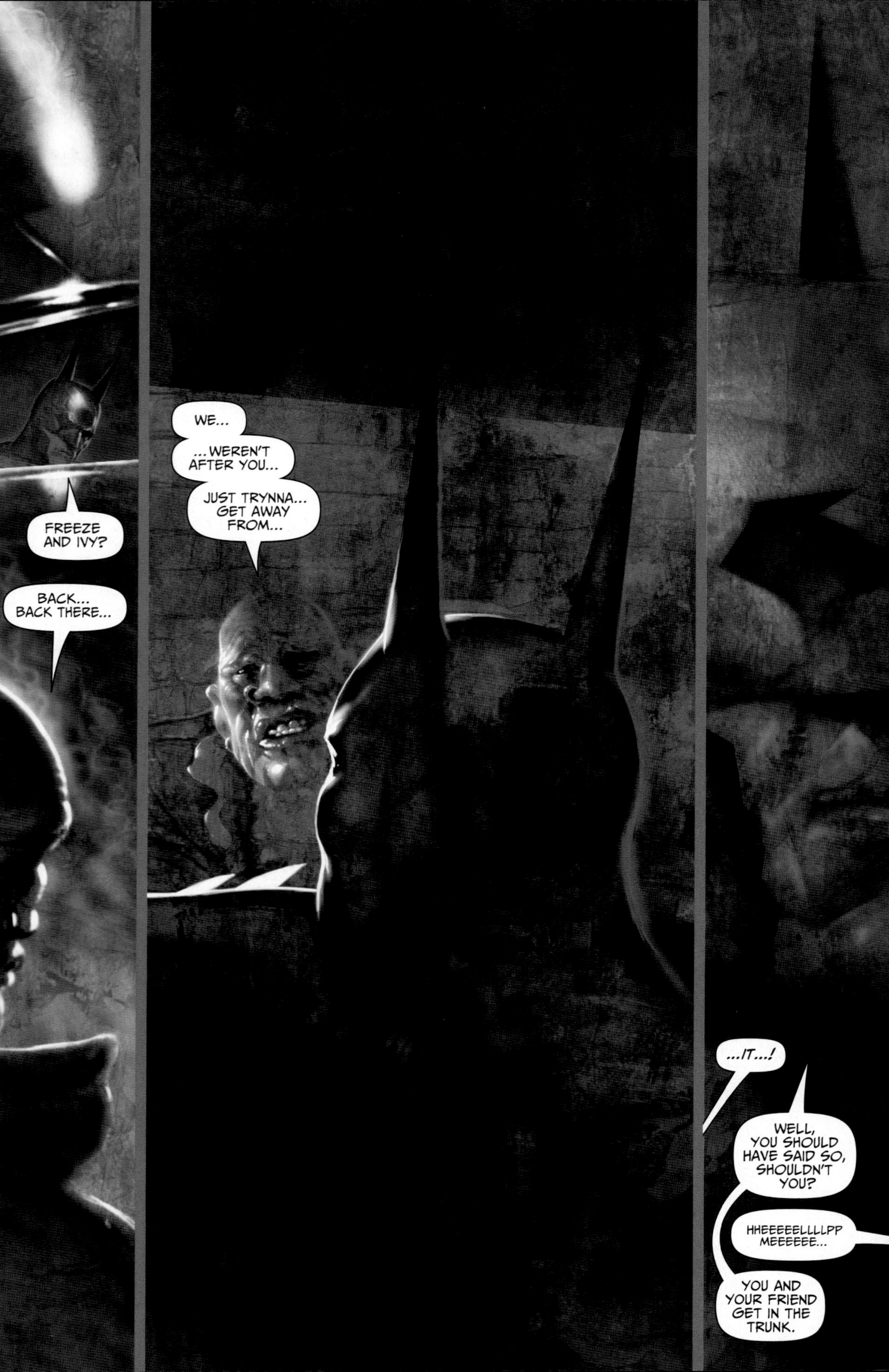
FREEZE AND IVY?
BACK... BACK THERE...
WE...
...WEREN'T AFTER YOU...
JUST TRYNNA... GET AWAY FROM...
...IT...!
WELL, YOU SHOULD HAVE SAID SO, SHOULDN'T YOU?
HHEEEEELLLLPP MEEEEEE...
YOU AND YOUR FRIEND GET IN THE TRUNK.

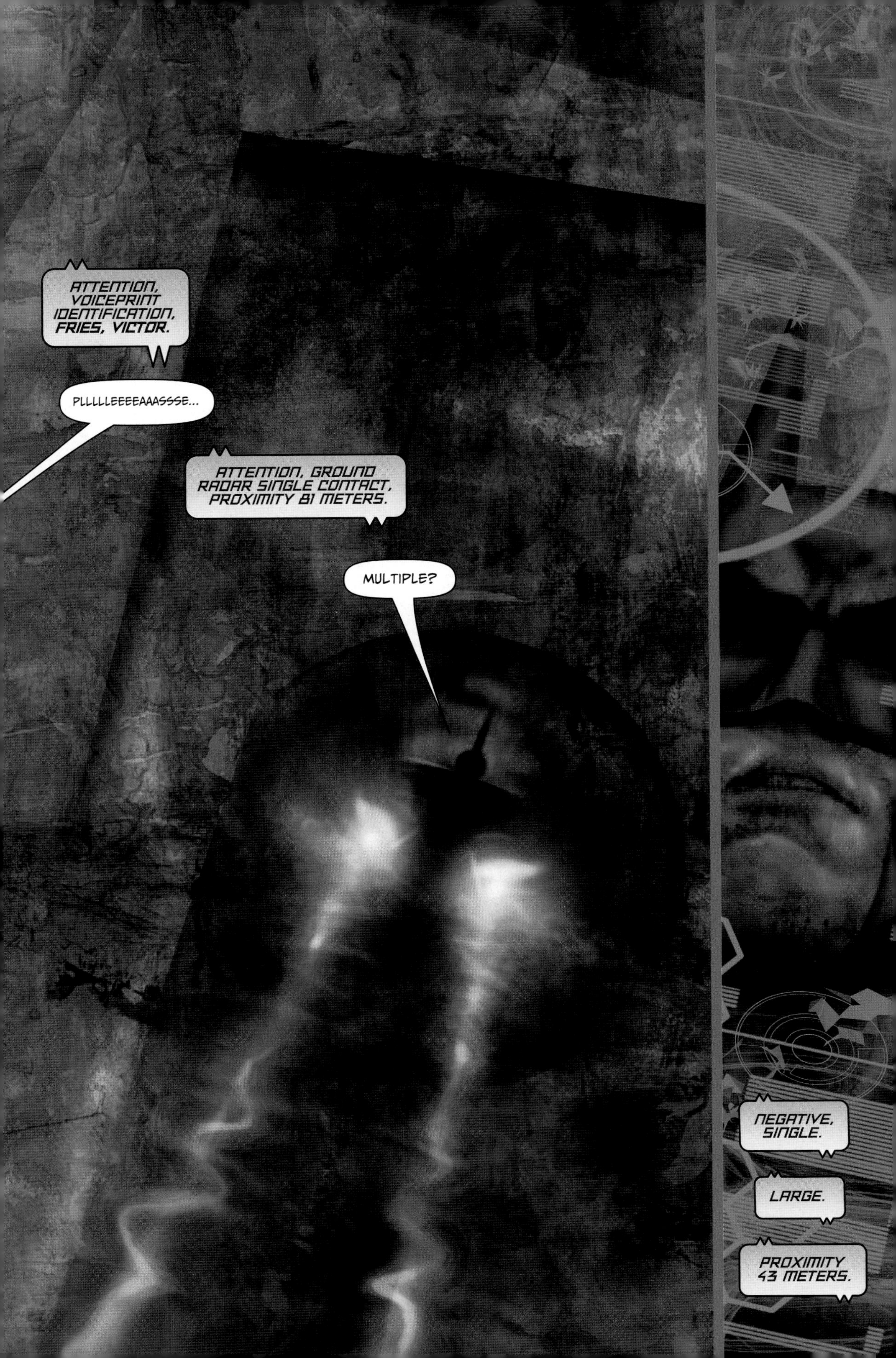
ATTENTION, VOICEPRINT IDENTIFICATION, FRIES, VICTOR.
PLLLLLEEEEAAASSSE...
ATTENTION, GROUND RADAR SINGLE CONTACT, PROXIMITY 81 METERS.
MULTIPLE?
NEGATIVE, SINGLE.
LARGE.
PROXIMITY 43 METERS.

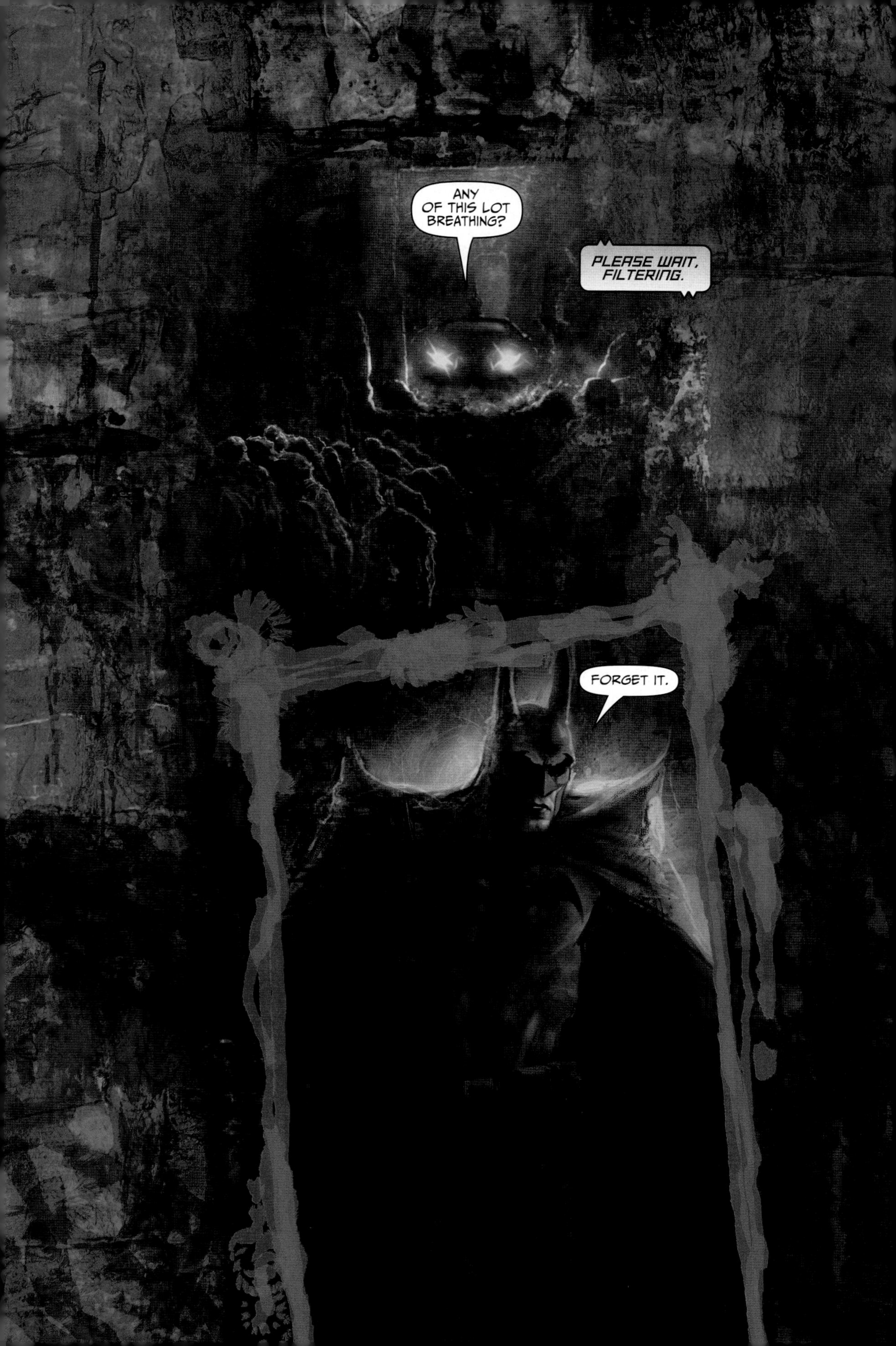
ANY OF THIS LOT BREATHING?
PLEASE WAIT, FILTERING.
FORGET IT.

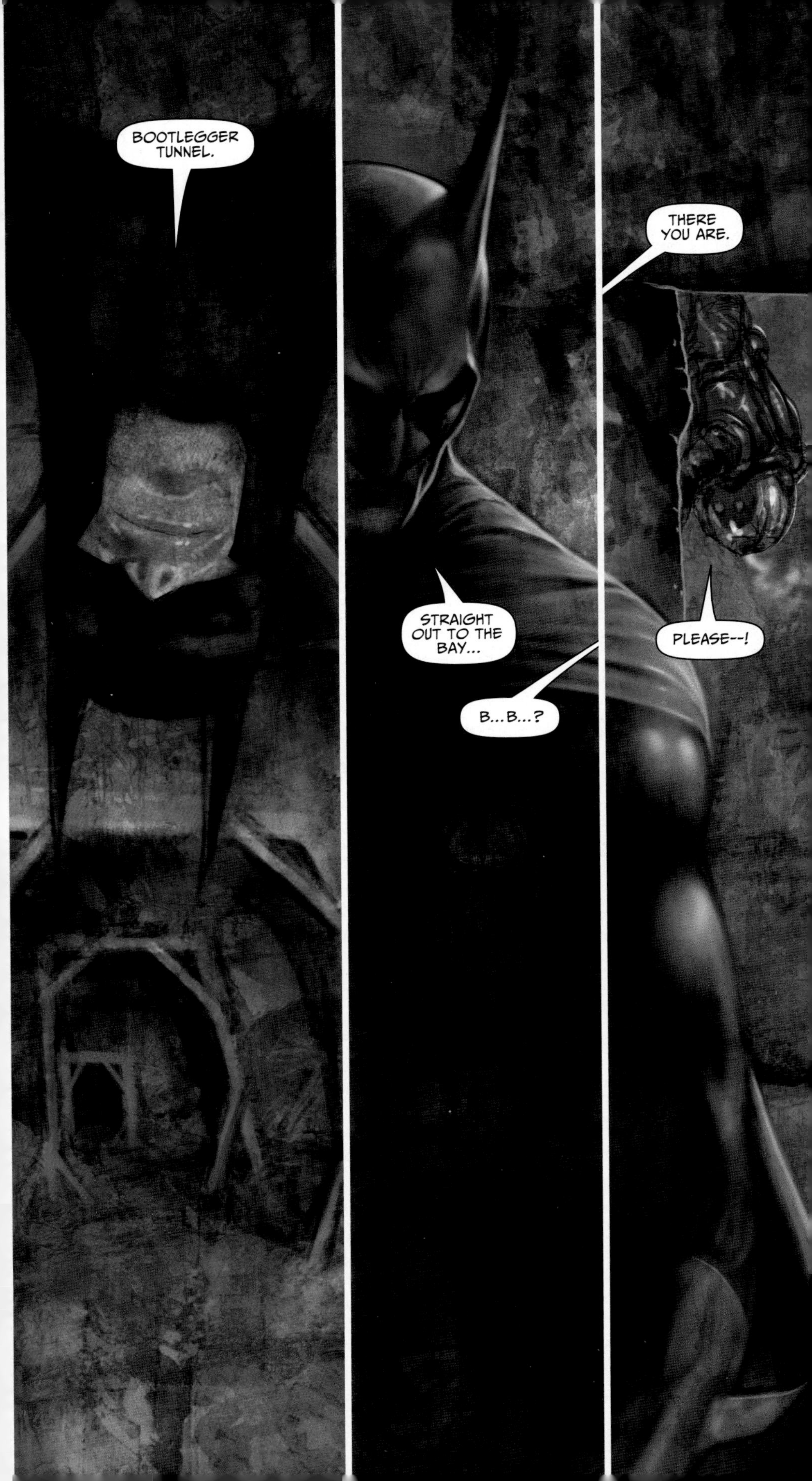
BOOTLEGGER TUNNEL.
STRAIGHT OUT TO THE BAY...
B...B...?
THERE YOU ARE.
PLEASE--!

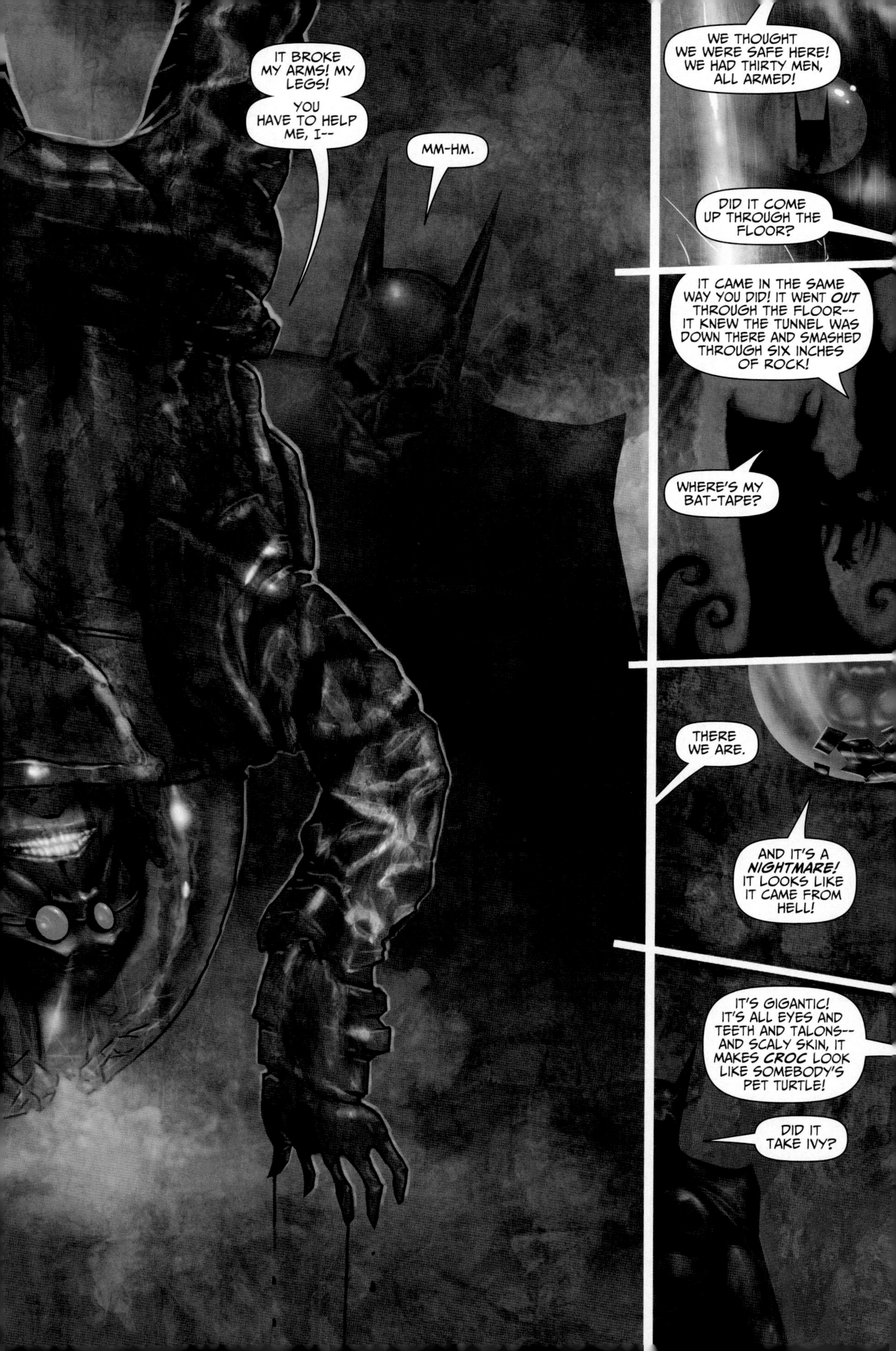
IT BROKE MY ARMS! MY LEGS!
YOU HAVE TO HELP ME, I--
MM-HM.
WE THOUGHT WE WERE SAFE HERE! WE HAD THIRTY MEN, ALL ARMED!
DID IT COME UP THROUGH THE FLOOR?
IT CAME IN THE SAME WAY YOU DID! IT WENT OUT THROUGH THE FLOOR-- IT KNEW THE TUNNEL WAS DOWN THERE AND SMASHED THROUGH SIX INCHES OF ROCK!
WHERE'S MY BAT-TAPE?
THERE WE ARE.
AND IT'S A NIGHTMARE! IT LOOKS LIKE IT CAME FROM HELL!
IT'S GIGANTIC! IT'S ALL EYES AND TEETH AND TALONS-- AND SCALY SKIN, IT MAKES CROC LOOK LIKE SOMEBODY'S PET TURTLE!
DID IT TAKE IVY?

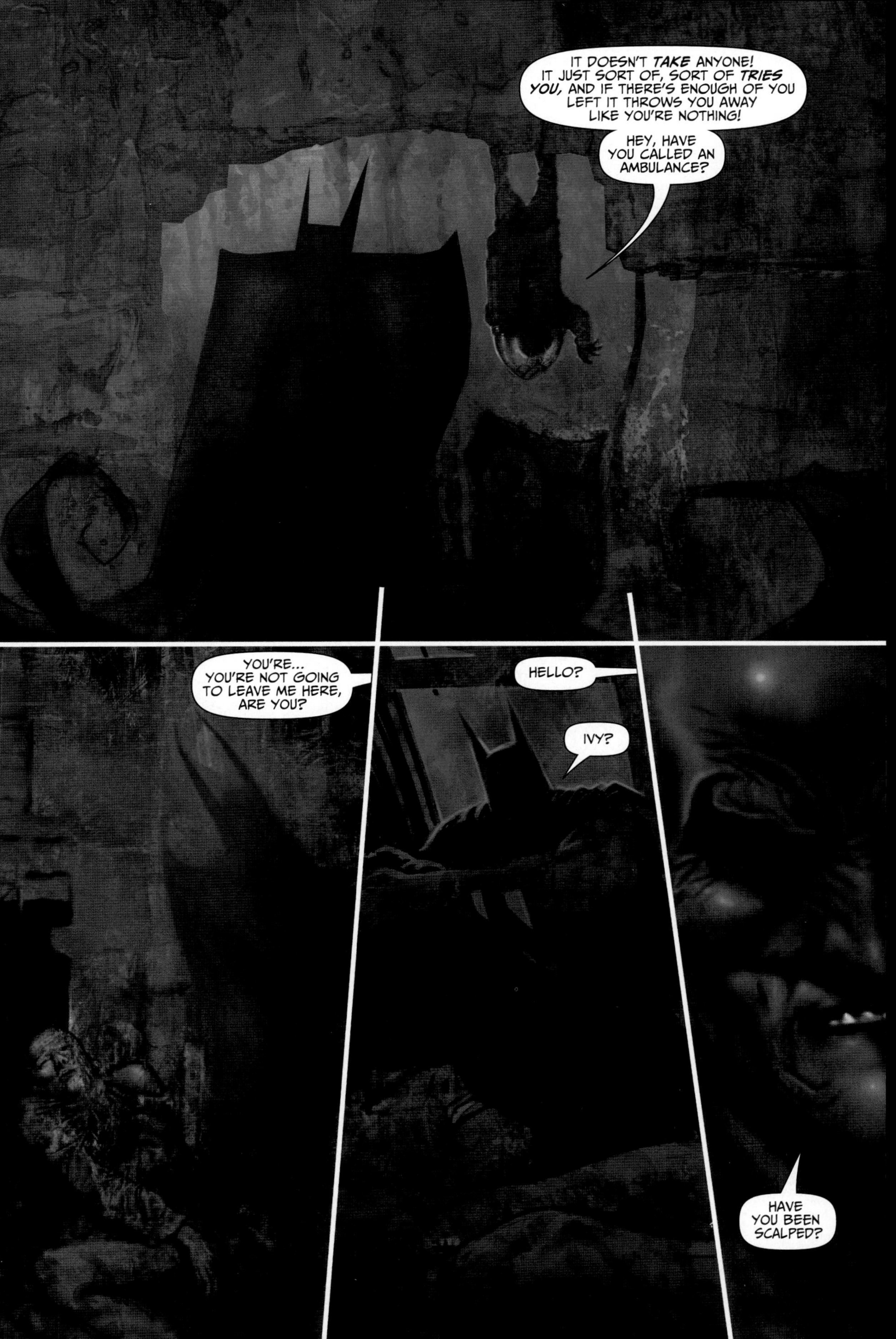
IT DOESN'T TAKE ANYONE! IT JUST SORT OF, SORT OF TRIES YOU, AND IF THERE'S ENOUGH OF YOU LEFT IT THROWS YOU AWAY LIKE YOU'RE NOTHING!
HEY, HAVE YOU CALLED AN AMBULANCE?
YOU'RE... YOU'RE NOT GOING TO LEAVE ME HERE, ARE YOU?
HELLO?
IVY?
HAVE YOU BEEN SCALPED?

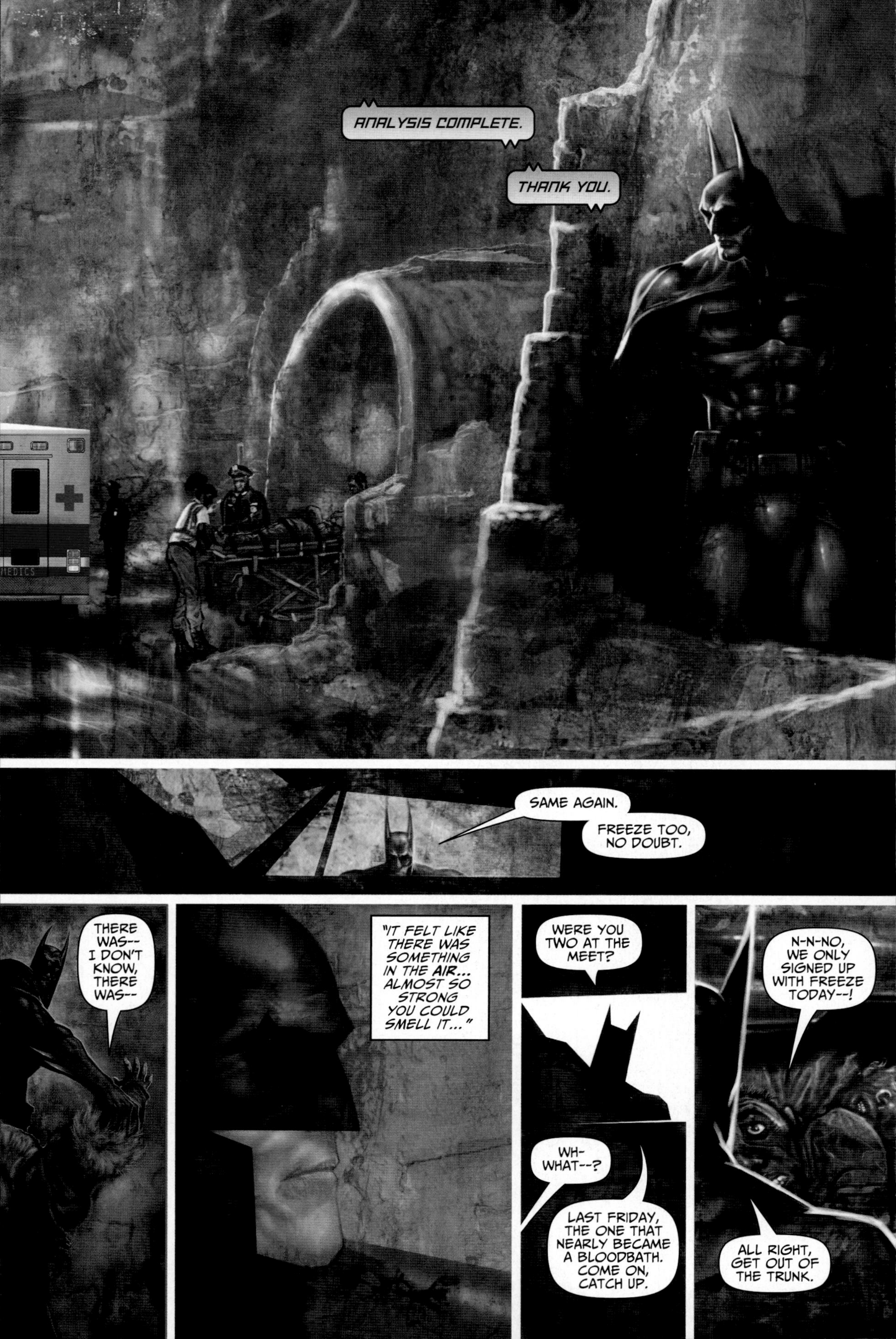
ANALYSIS COMPLETE.
THANK YOU.
MEDICS
SAME AGAIN.
FREEZE TOO, NO DOUBT.
THERE WAS-- I DON'T KNOW, THERE WAS--
"IT FELT LIKE THERE WAS SOMETHING IN THE AIR... ALMOST SO STRONG YOU COULD SMELL IT..."
WERE YOU TWO AT THE MEET?
WH- WHAT--?
LAST FRIDAY, THE ONE THAT NEARLY BECAME A BLOODBATH. COME ON, CATCH UP.
N-N-NO, WE ONLY SIGNED UP WITH FREEZE TODAY--!
ALL RIGHT, GET OUT OF THE TRUNK.

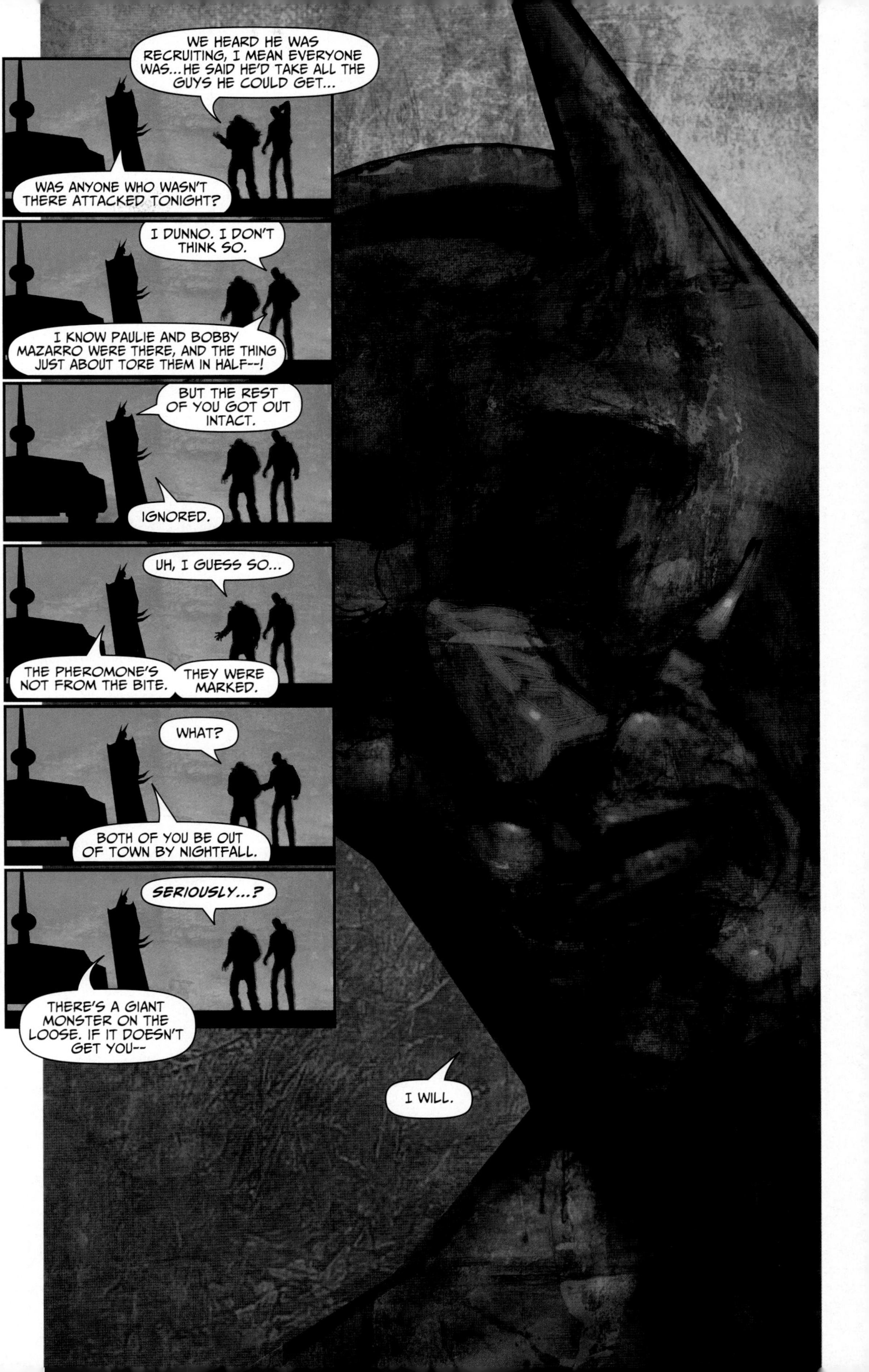

WE HEARD HE WAS RECRUITING, I MEAN EVERYONE WAS... HE SAID HE'D TAKE ALL THE GUYS HE COULD GET...
WAS ANYONE WHO WASN'T THERE ATTACKED TONIGHT?
I DUNNO. I DON'T THINK SO.
I KNOW PAULIE AND BOBBY MAZARRO WERE THERE, AND THE THING JUST ABOUT TORE THEM IN HALF--!
BUT THE REST OF YOU GOT OUT INTACT.
IGNORED.
UH, I GUESS SO...
THE PHEROMONE'S NOT FROM THE BITE.
THEY WERE MARKED.
WHAT?
BOTH OF YOU BE OUT OF TOWN BY NIGHTFALL.
SERIOUSLY...?
THERE'S A GIANT MONSTER ON THE LOOSE. IF IT DOESN'T GET YOU--
I WILL.

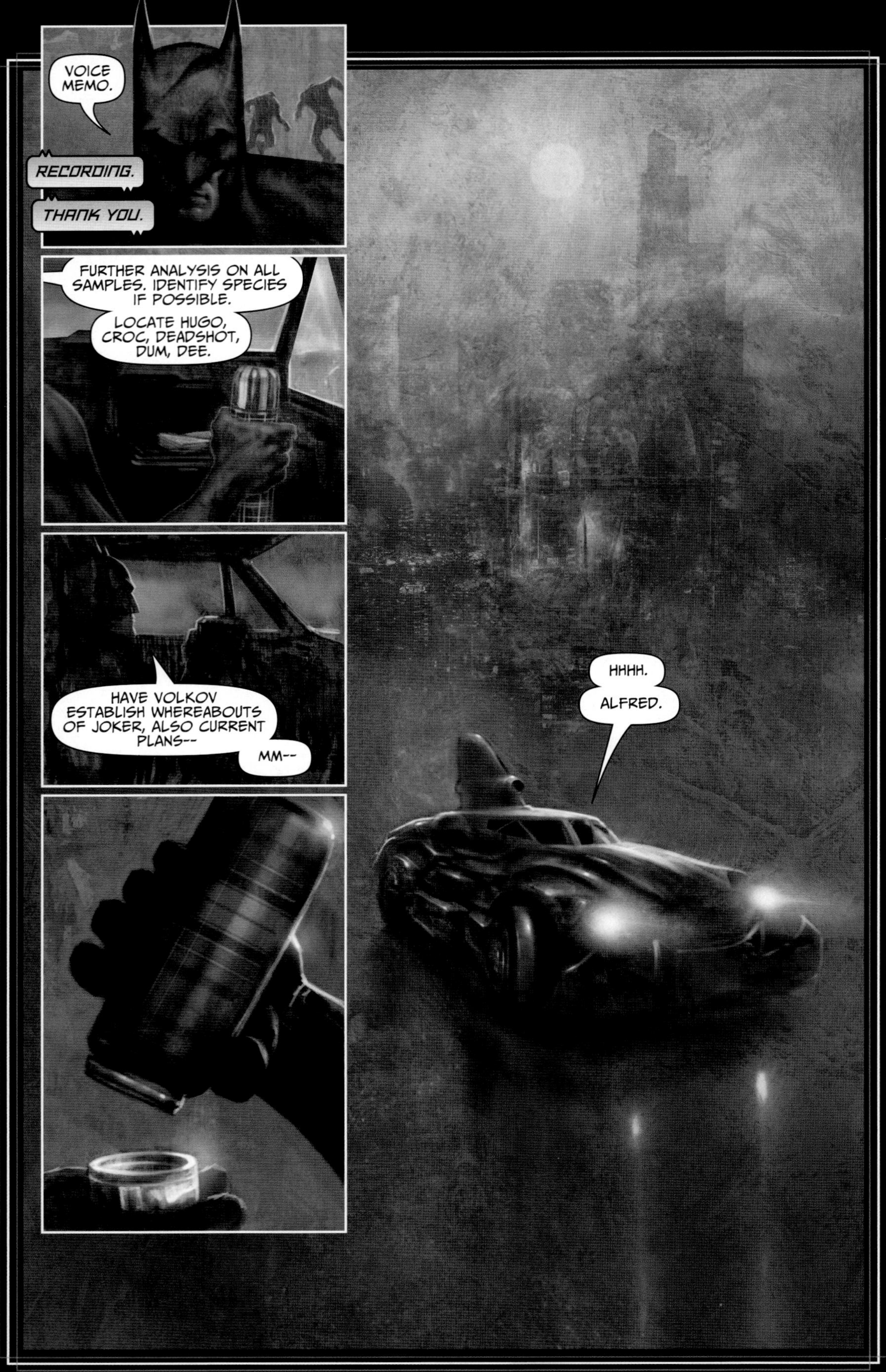
VOICE MEMO.
RECORDING.
THANK YOU.
FURTHER ANALYSIS ON ALL SAMPLES. IDENTIFY SPECIES IF POSSIBLE.
LOCATE HUGO, CROC, DEADSHOT, DUM, DEE.
HAVE VOLKOV ESTABLISH WHEREABOUTS OF JOKER, ALSO CURRENT PLANS--
MM--
HHHH.
ALFRED.

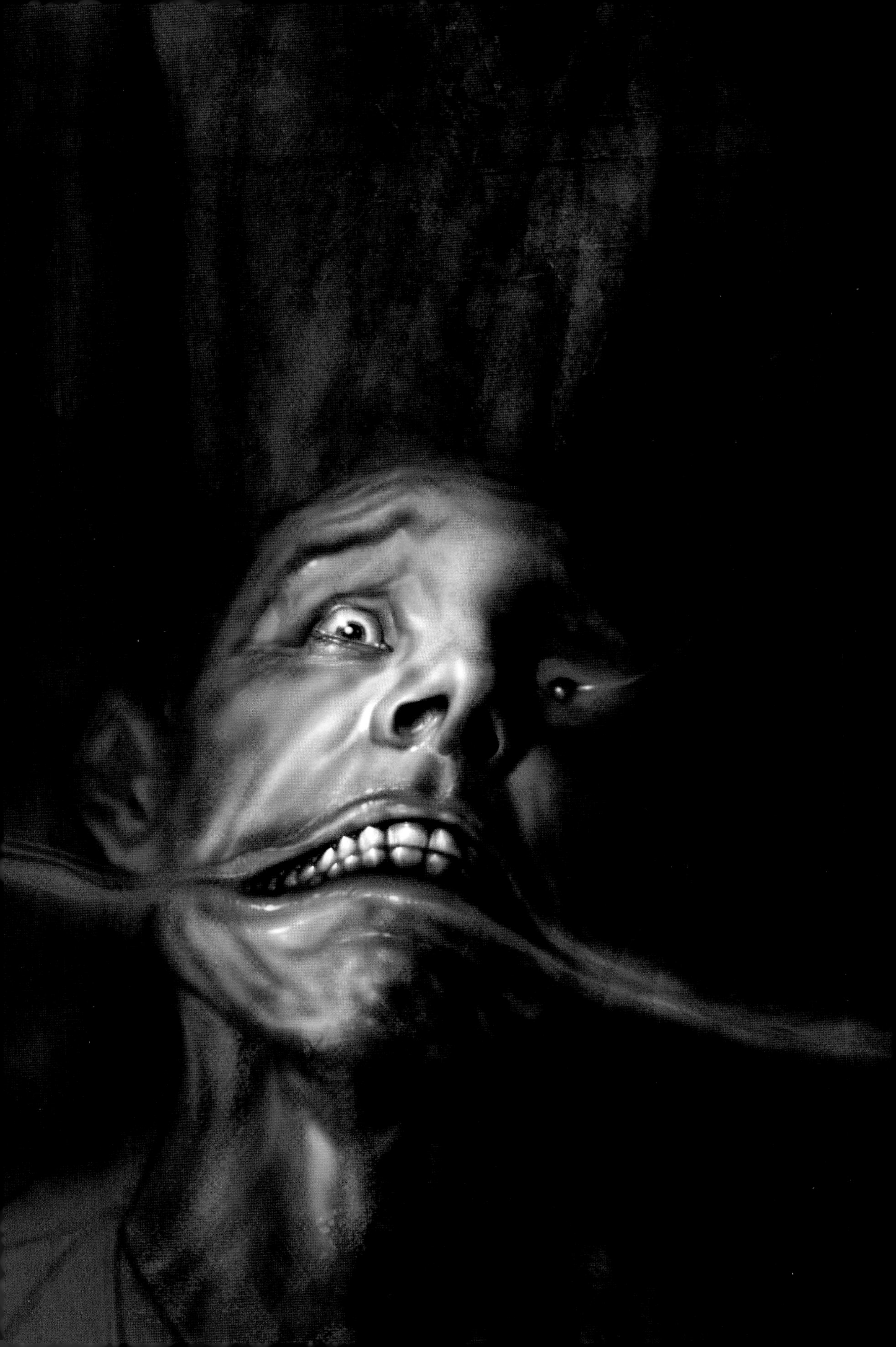

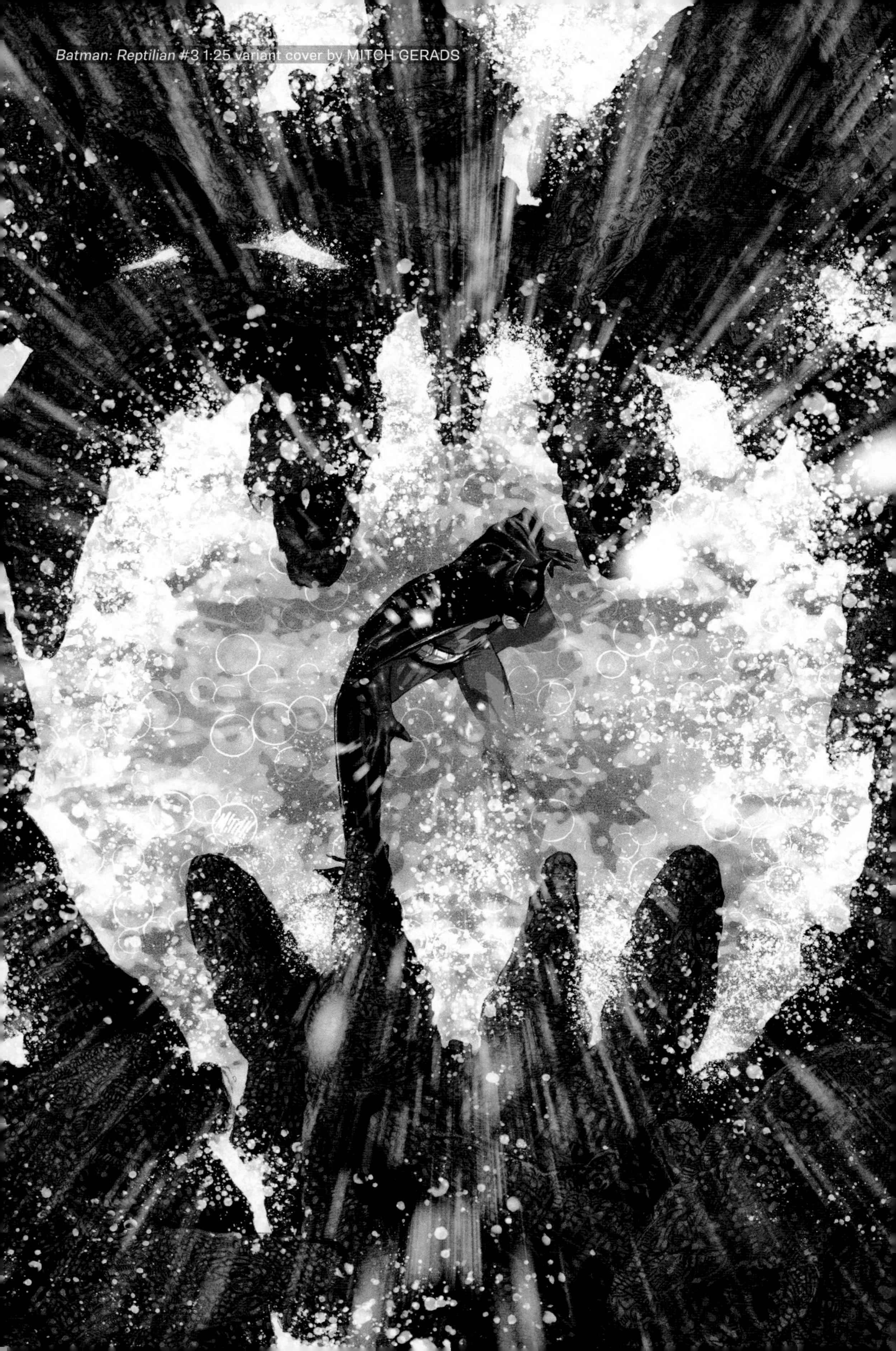

Batman: Reptilian #3 1:25 variant cover by MITCH GERADS

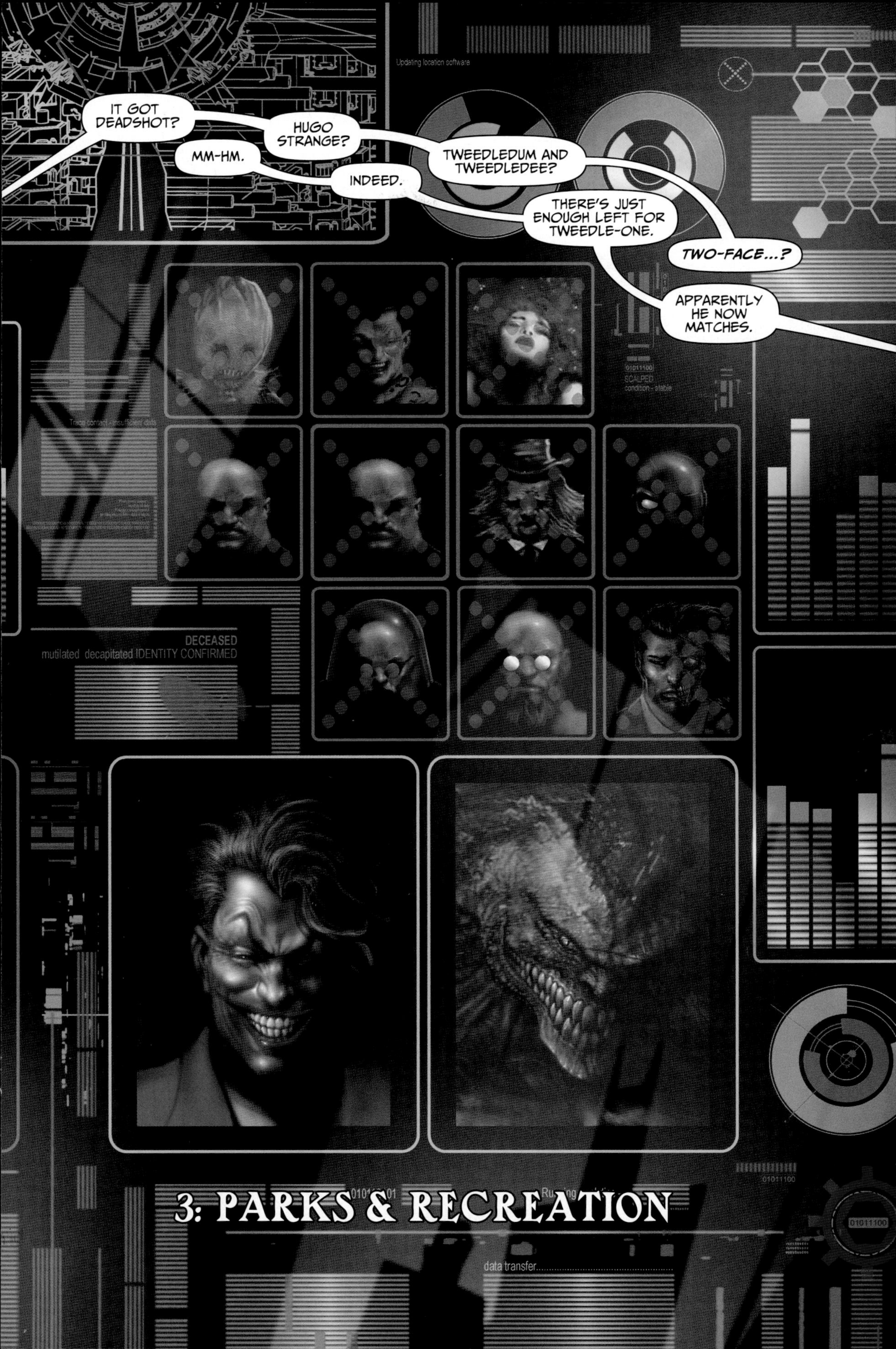
Updating location software
IT GOT DEADSHOT?
MM-HM.
HUGO STRANGE?
INDEED.
TWEEDLEDUM AND TWEEDLEDEE?
THERE'S JUST ENOUGH LEFT FOR TWEEDLE-ONE.
TWO-FACE...?
APPARENTLY HE NOW MATCHES.
01011100
SCALPED
condition - stable
DECEASED
mutilated decapitated IDENTITY CONFIRMED
01011100
3: PARKS & RECREATION
01011100
data transfer.......................

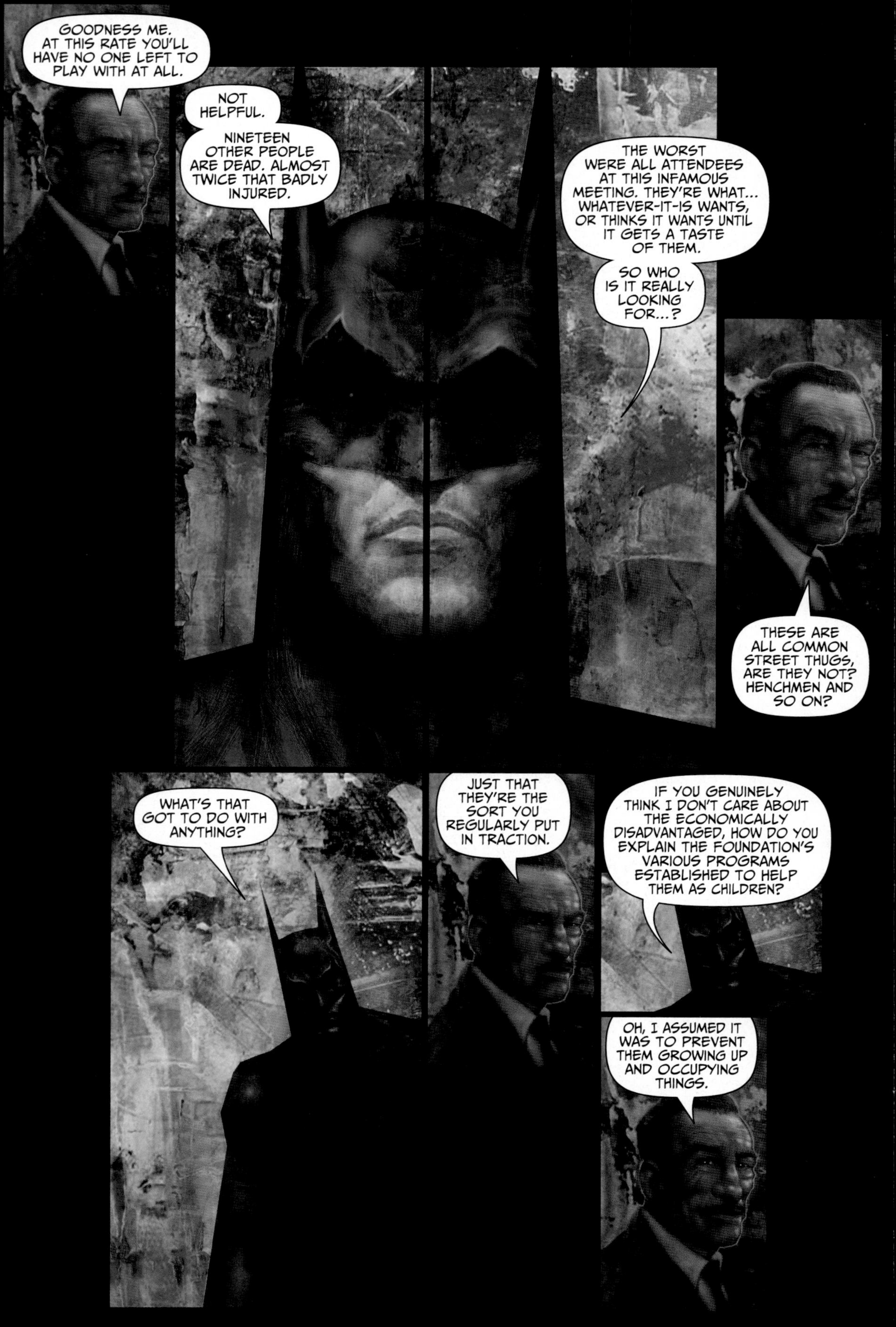
GOODNESS ME. AT THIS RATE YOU'LL HAVE NO ONE LEFT TO PLAY WITH AT ALL.
NOT HELPFUL.
NINETEEN OTHER PEOPLE ARE DEAD. ALMOST TWICE THAT BADLY INJURED.
THE WORST WERE ALL ATTENDEES AT THIS INFAMOUS MEETING. THEY'RE WHAT... WHATEVER-IT-IS WANTS, OR THINKS IT WANTS UNTIL IT GETS A TASTE OF THEM.
SO WHO IS IT REALLY LOOKING FOR...?
THESE ARE ALL COMMON STREET THUGS, ARE THEY NOT? HENCHMEN AND SO ON?
WHAT'S THAT GOT TO DO WITH ANYTHING?
JUST THAT THEY'RE THE SORT YOU REGULARLY PUT IN TRACTION.
IF YOU GENUINELY THINK I DON'T CARE ABOUT THE ECONOMICALLY DISADVANTAGED, HOW DO YOU EXPLAIN THE FOUNDATION'S VARIOUS PROGRAMS ESTABLISHED TO HELP THEM AS CHILDREN?
OH, I ASSUMED IT WAS TO PREVENT THEM GROWING UP AND OCCUPYING THINGS.

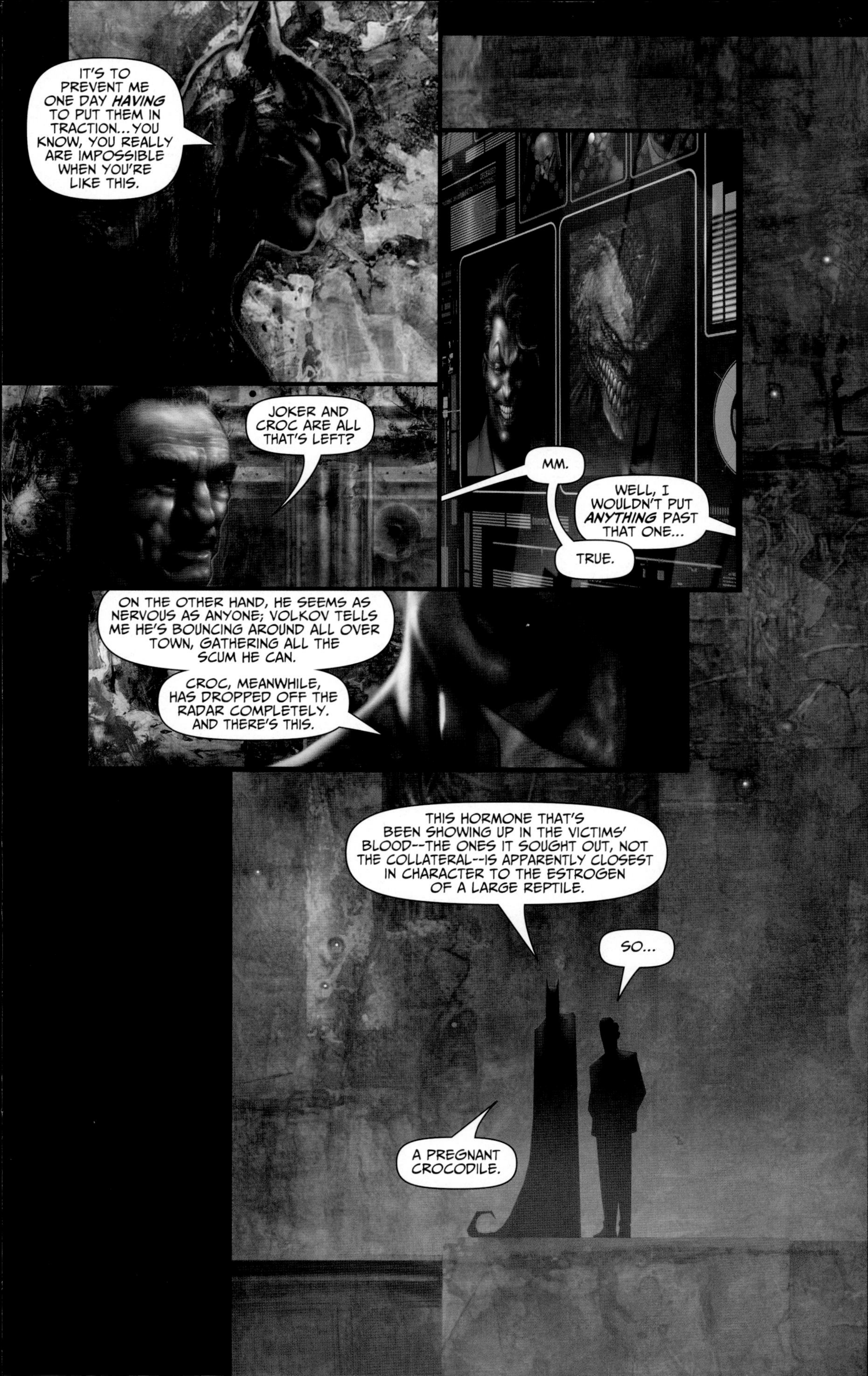
IT'S TO PREVENT ME ONE DAY *HAVING* TO PUT THEM IN TRACTION...YOU KNOW, YOU REALLY ARE IMPOSSIBLE WHEN YOU'RE LIKE THIS.
JOKER AND CROC ARE ALL THAT'S LEFT?
MM.
WELL, I WOULDN'T PUT *ANYTHING* PAST THAT ONE...
TRUE.
ON THE OTHER HAND, HE SEEMS AS NERVOUS AS ANYONE; VOLKOV TELLS ME HE'S BOUNCING AROUND ALL OVER TOWN, GATHERING ALL THE SCUM HE CAN.
CROC, MEANWHILE, HAS DROPPED OFF THE RADAR COMPLETELY. AND THERE'S THIS.
THIS HORMONE THAT'S BEEN SHOWING UP IN THE VICTIMS' BLOOD--THE ONES IT SOUGHT OUT, NOT THE COLLATERAL--IS APPARENTLY CLOSEST IN CHARACTER TO THE ESTROGEN OF A LARGE REPTILE.
SO...
A PREGNANT CROCODILE.

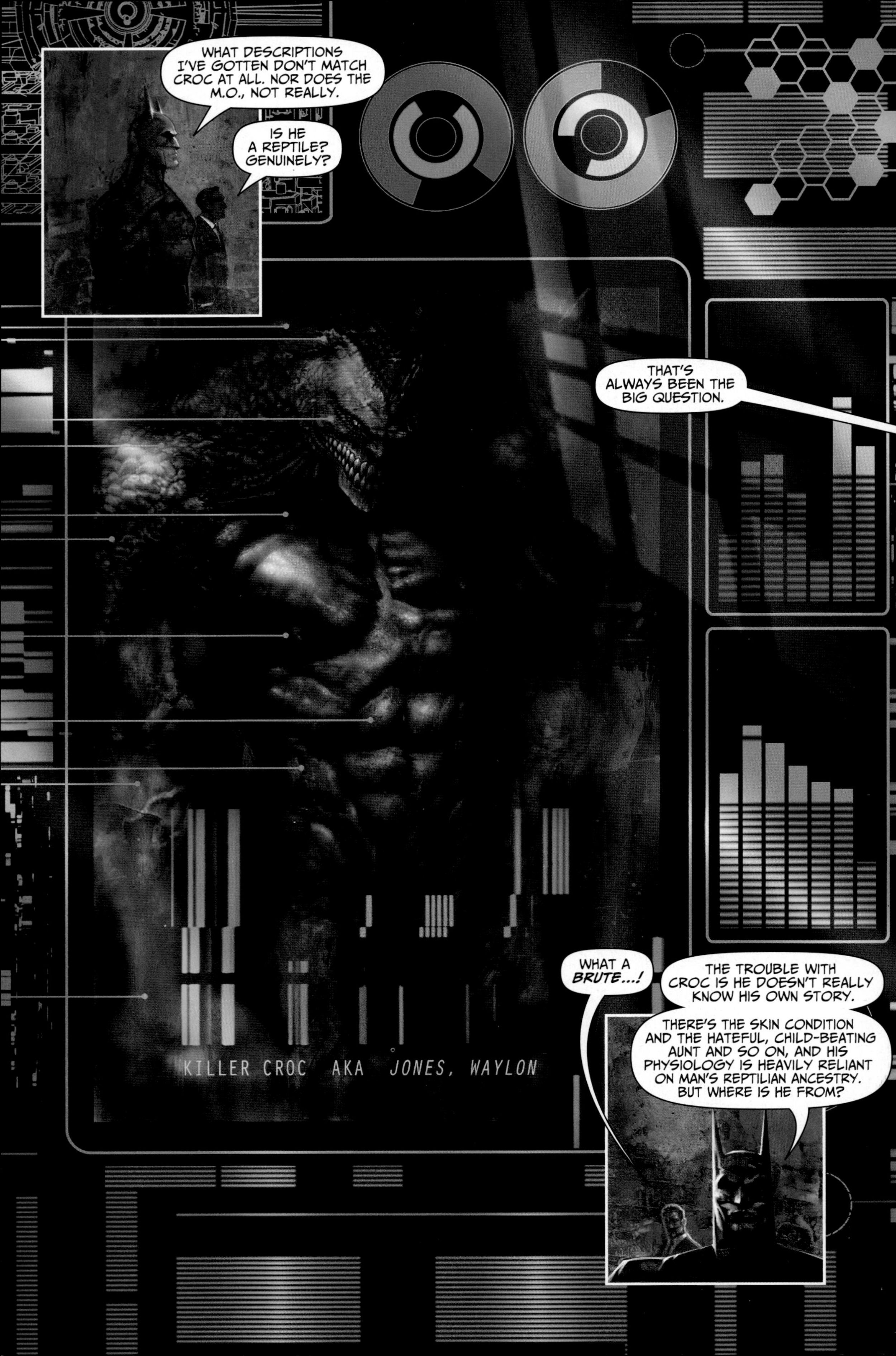
WHAT DESCRIPTIONS I'VE GOTTEN DON'T MATCH CROC AT ALL. NOR DOES THE M.O., NOT REALLY.
IS HE A REPTILE? GENUINELY?
THAT'S ALWAYS BEEN THE BIG QUESTION.
KILLER CROC AKA JONES, WAYLON
WHAT A BRUTE...!
THE TROUBLE WITH CROC IS HE DOESN'T REALLY KNOW HIS OWN STORY.
THERE'S THE SKIN CONDITION AND THE HATEFUL, CHILD-BEATING AUNT AND SO ON, AND HIS PHYSIOLOGY IS HEAVILY RELIANT ON MAN'S REPTILIAN ANCESTRY. BUT WHERE IS HE FROM?

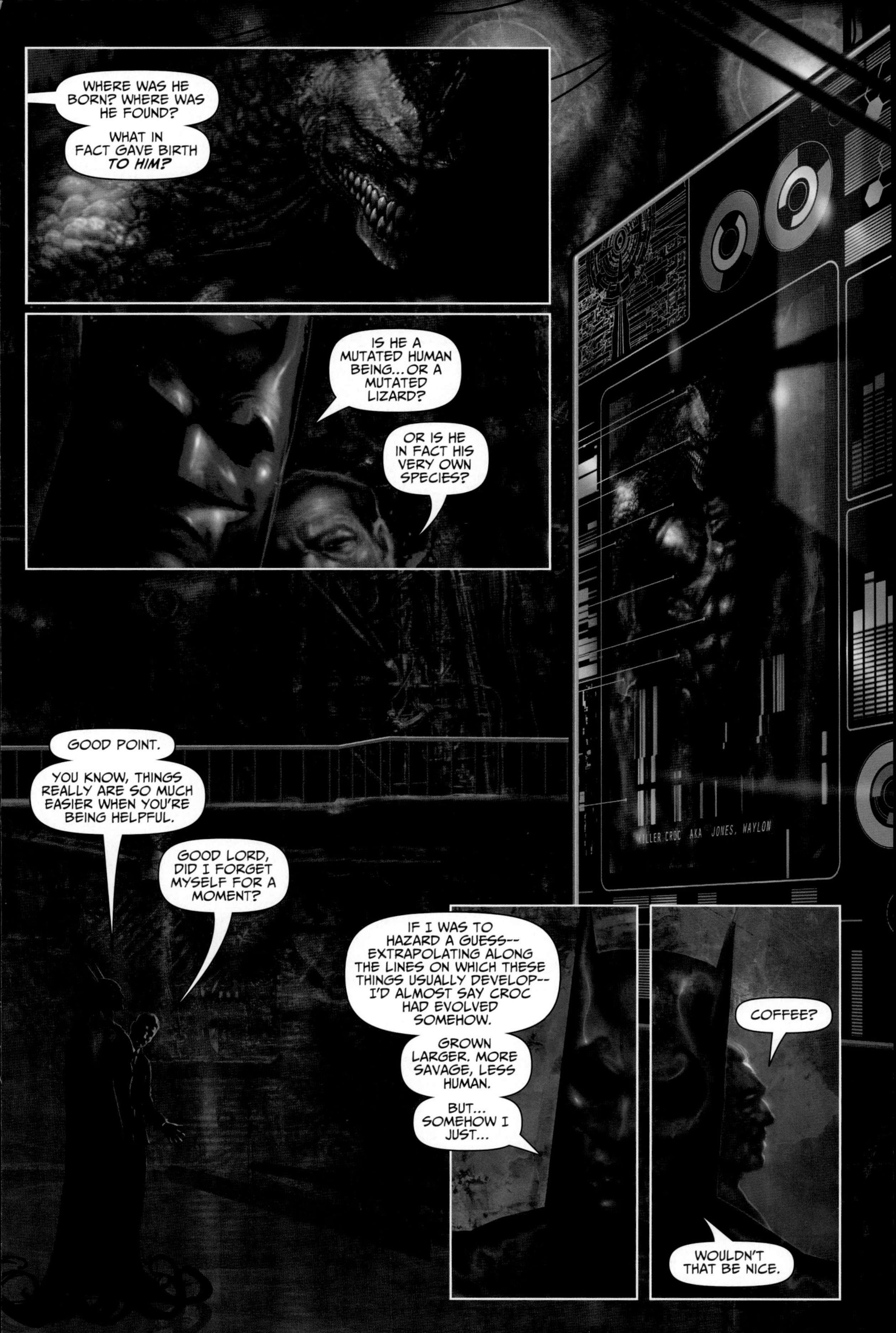

WHERE WAS HE BORN? WHERE WAS HE FOUND?
WHAT IN FACT GAVE BIRTH TO HIM?
IS HE A MUTATED HUMAN BEING...OR A MUTATED LIZARD?
OR IS HE IN FACT HIS VERY OWN SPECIES?
GOOD POINT.
YOU KNOW, THINGS REALLY ARE SO MUCH EASIER WHEN YOU'RE BEING HELPFUL.
GOOD LORD, DID I FORGET MYSELF FOR A MOMENT?
KILLER CROC AKA JONES, WAYLON
IF I WAS TO HAZARD A GUESS--EXTRAPOLATING ALONG THE LINES ON WHICH THESE THINGS USUALLY DEVELOP--I'D ALMOST SAY CROC HAD EVOLVED SOMEHOW.
GROWN LARGER. MORE SAVAGE, LESS HUMAN.
BUT... SOMEHOW I JUST...
COFFEE?
WOULDN'T THAT BE NICE.

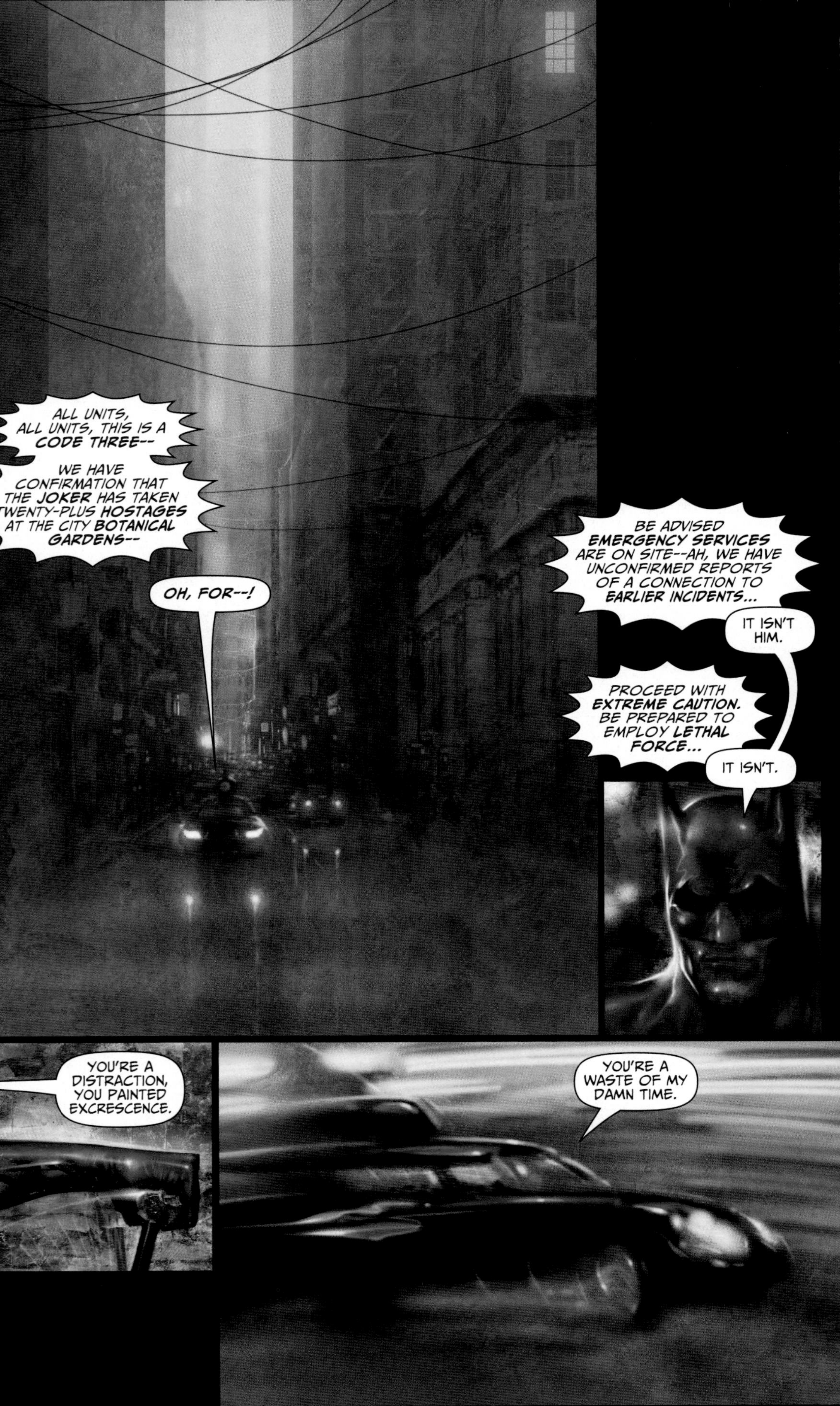
ALL UNITS, ALL UNITS, THIS IS A CODE THREE--
WE HAVE CONFIRMATION THAT THE JOKER HAS TAKEN TWENTY-PLUS HOSTAGES AT THE CITY BOTANICAL GARDENS--
OH, FOR--!
BE ADVISED EMERGENCY SERVICES ARE ON SITE--AH, WE HAVE UNCONFIRMED REPORTS OF A CONNECTION TO EARLIER INCIDENTS...
IT ISN'T HIM.
PROCEED WITH EXTREME CAUTION. BE PREPARED TO EMPLOY LETHAL FORCE...
IT ISN'T.
YOU'RE A DISTRACTION, YOU PAINTED EXCRESCENCE.
YOU'RE A WASTE OF MY DAMN TIME.

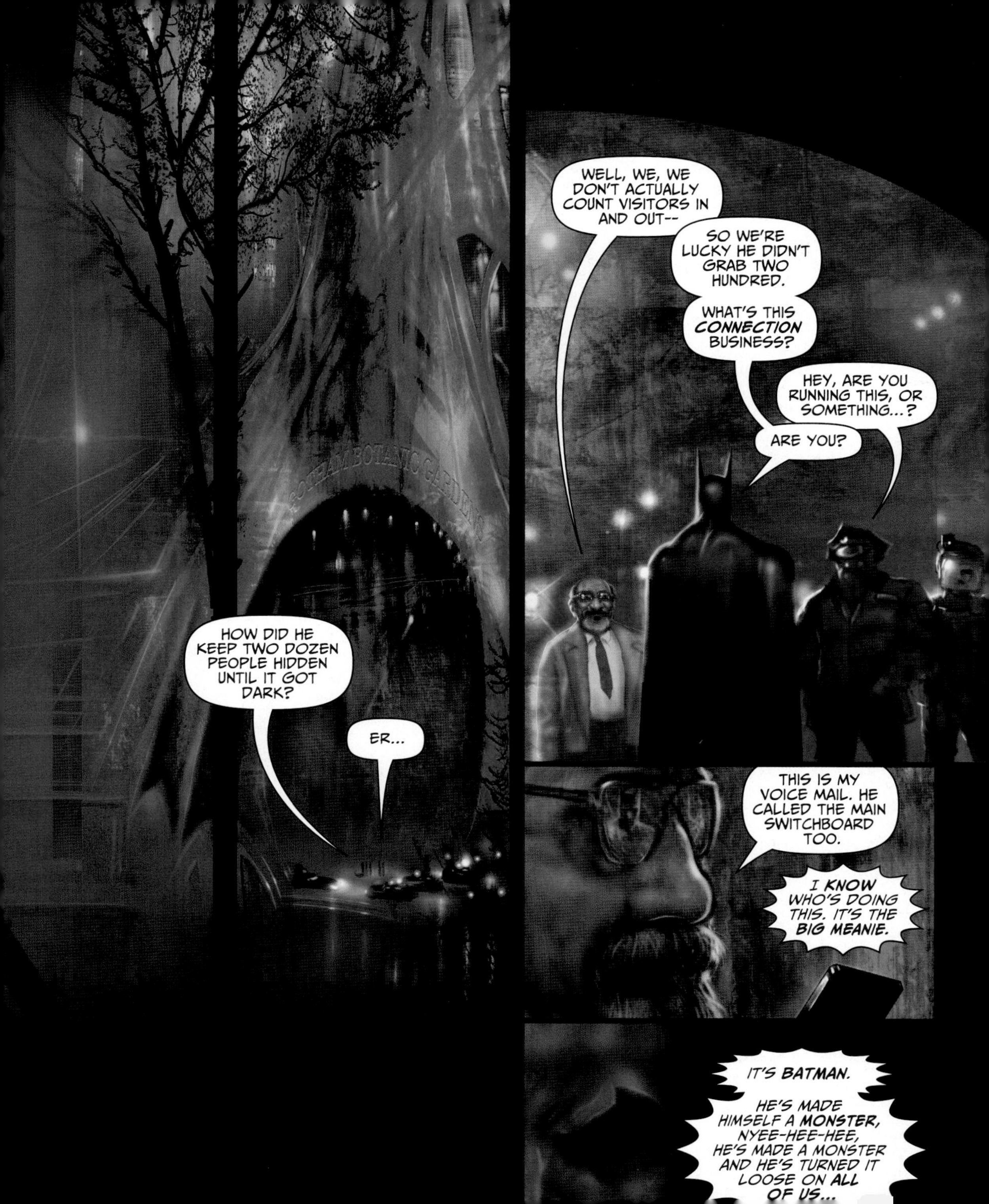

GOTHAM BOTANIC GARDENS
HOW DID HE KEEP TWO DOZEN PEOPLE HIDDEN UNTIL IT GOT DARK?
ER...
WELL, WE, WE DON'T ACTUALLY COUNT VISITORS IN AND OUT--
SO WE'RE LUCKY HE DIDN'T GRAB TWO HUNDRED.
WHAT'S THIS *CONNECTION* BUSINESS?
HEY, ARE YOU RUNNING THIS, OR SOMETHING...?
ARE YOU?
THIS IS MY VOICE MAIL. HE CALLED THE MAIN SWITCHBOARD TOO.
*I **KNOW** WHO'S DOING THIS. IT'S THE **BIG MEANIE.***
*IT'S **BATMAN.***
*HE'S MADE HIMSELF A **MONSTER,** NYEE-HEE-HEE, HE'S MADE A MONSTER AND HE'S TURNED IT LOOSE ON **ALL OF US...***

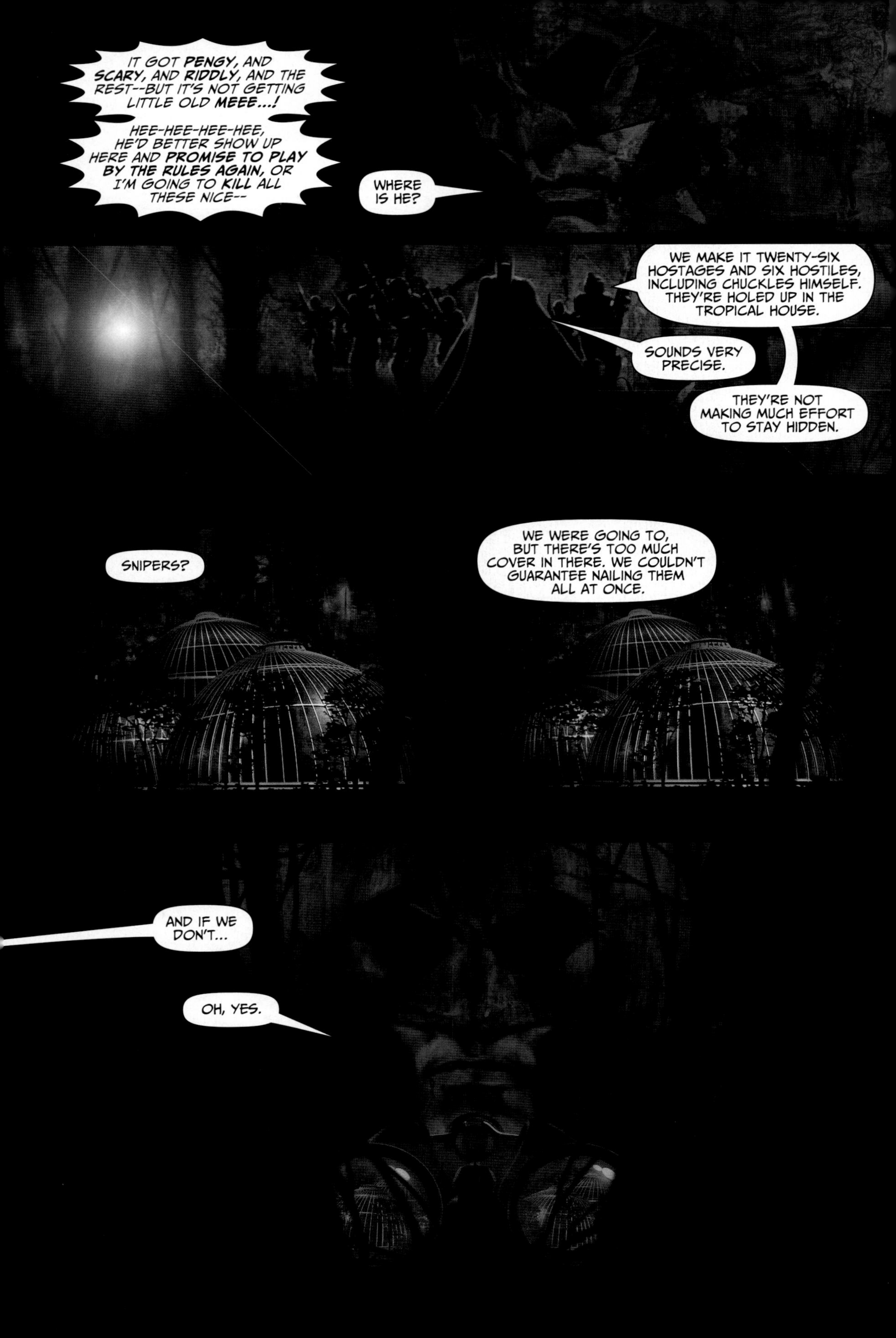
IT GOT **PENGY**, AND **SCARY**, AND **RIDDLY**, AND THE REST--BUT IT'S NOT GETTING LITTLE OLD **MEEE...!**
HEE-HEE-HEE-HEE, HE'D BETTER SHOW UP HERE AND **PROMISE TO PLAY BY THE RULES AGAIN,** OR I'M GOING TO **KILL** ALL THESE NICE--
WHERE IS HE?
WE MAKE IT TWENTY-SIX HOSTAGES AND SIX HOSTILES, INCLUDING CHUCKLES HIMSELF. THEY'RE HOLED UP IN THE TROPICAL HOUSE.
SOUNDS VERY PRECISE.
THEY'RE NOT MAKING MUCH EFFORT TO STAY HIDDEN.
SNIPERS?
WE WERE GOING TO, BUT THERE'S TOO MUCH COVER IN THERE. WE COULDN'T GUARANTEE NAILING THEM ALL AT ONCE.
AND IF WE DON'T...
OH, YES.

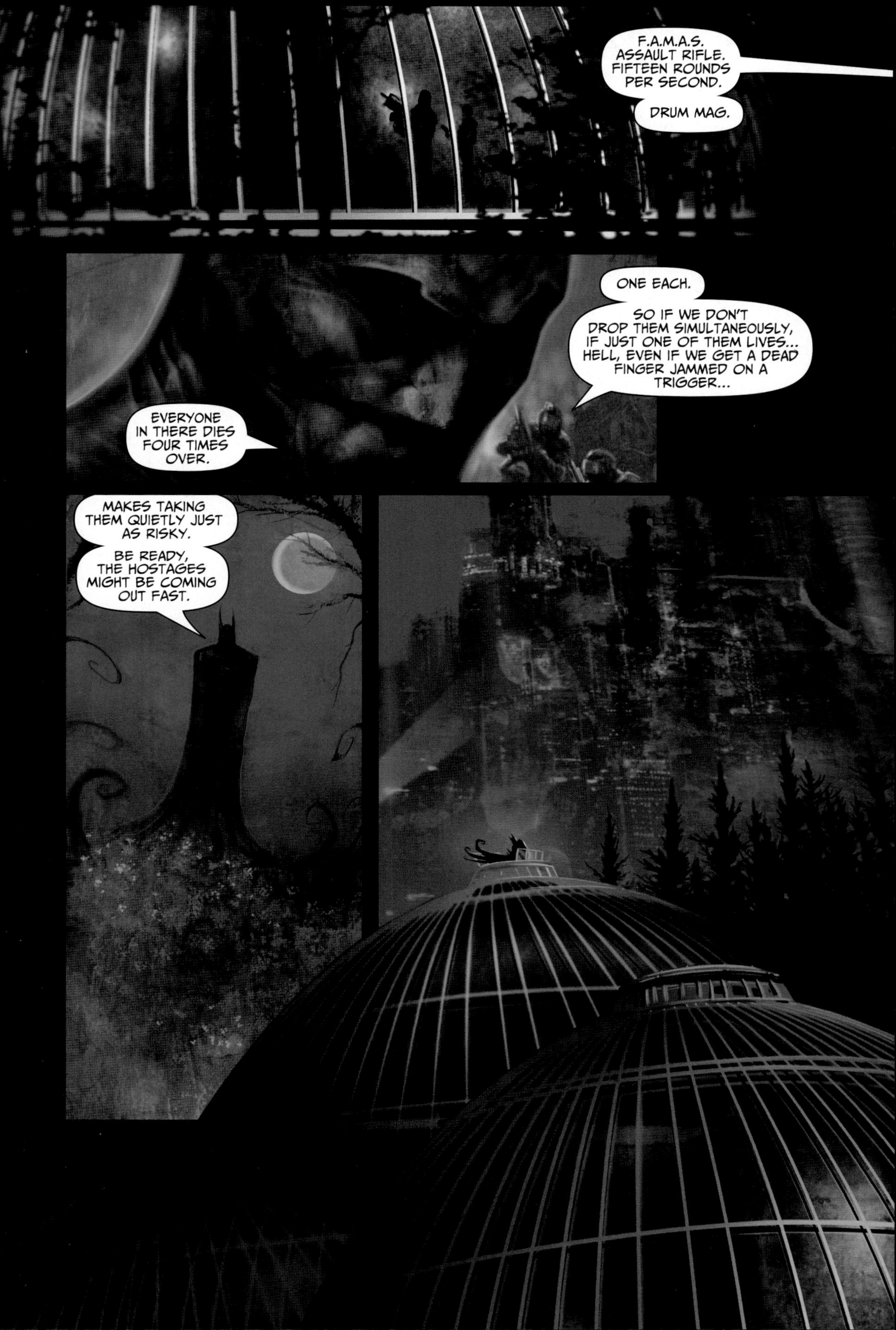
F.A.M.A.S. ASSAULT RIFLE. FIFTEEN ROUNDS PER SECOND.
DRUM MAG.
ONE EACH.
SO IF WE DON'T DROP THEM SIMULTANEOUSLY, IF JUST ONE OF THEM LIVES... HELL, EVEN IF WE GET A DEAD FINGER JAMMED ON A TRIGGER...
EVERYONE IN THERE DIES FOUR TIMES OVER.
MAKES TAKING THEM QUIETLY JUST AS RISKY.
BE READY, THE HOSTAGES MIGHT BE COMING OUT FAST.

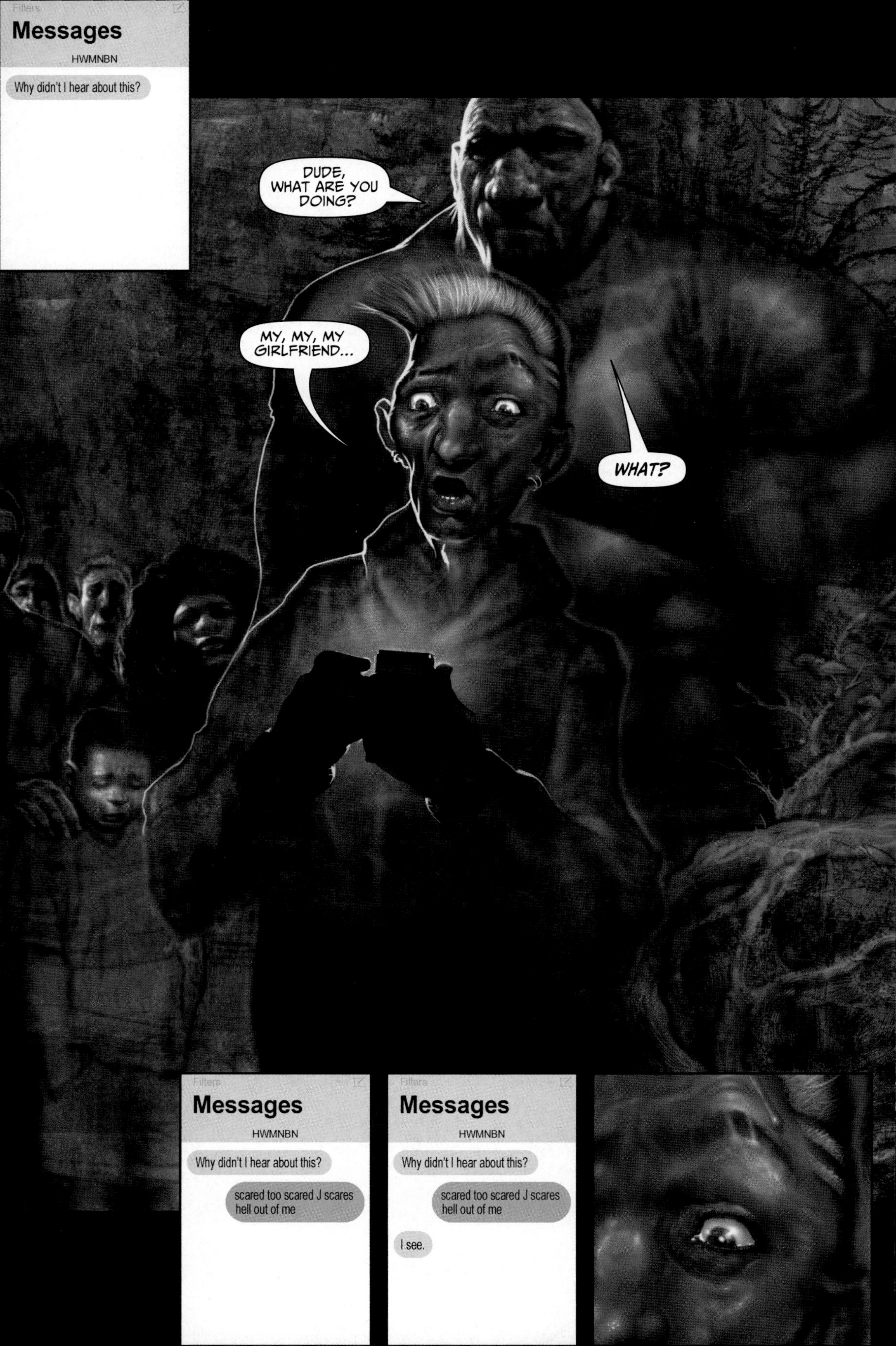

Filters
Messages
HWMNBN
Why didn't I hear about this?
DUDE, WHAT ARE YOU DOING?
MY, MY, MY GIRLFRIEND...
WHAT?
Filters
Messages
HWMNBN
Why didn't I hear about this?
scared too scared J scares hell out of me
Filters
Messages
HWMNBN
Why didn't I hear about this?
scared too scared J scares hell out of me
I see.

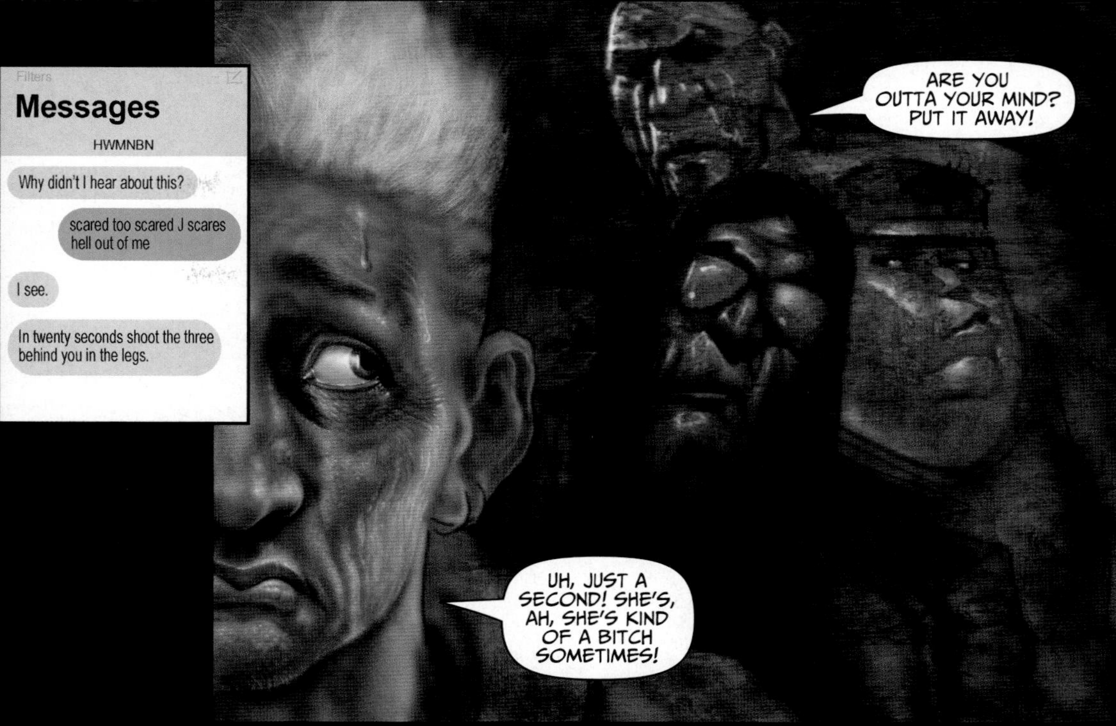
Filters
Messages
HWMNBN
Why didn't I hear about this?
scared too scared J scares hell out of me
I see.
In twenty seconds shoot the three behind you in the legs.
ARE YOU OUTTA YOUR MIND? PUT IT AWAY!
UH, JUST A SECOND! SHE'S, AH, SHE'S KIND OF A BITCH SOMETIMES!

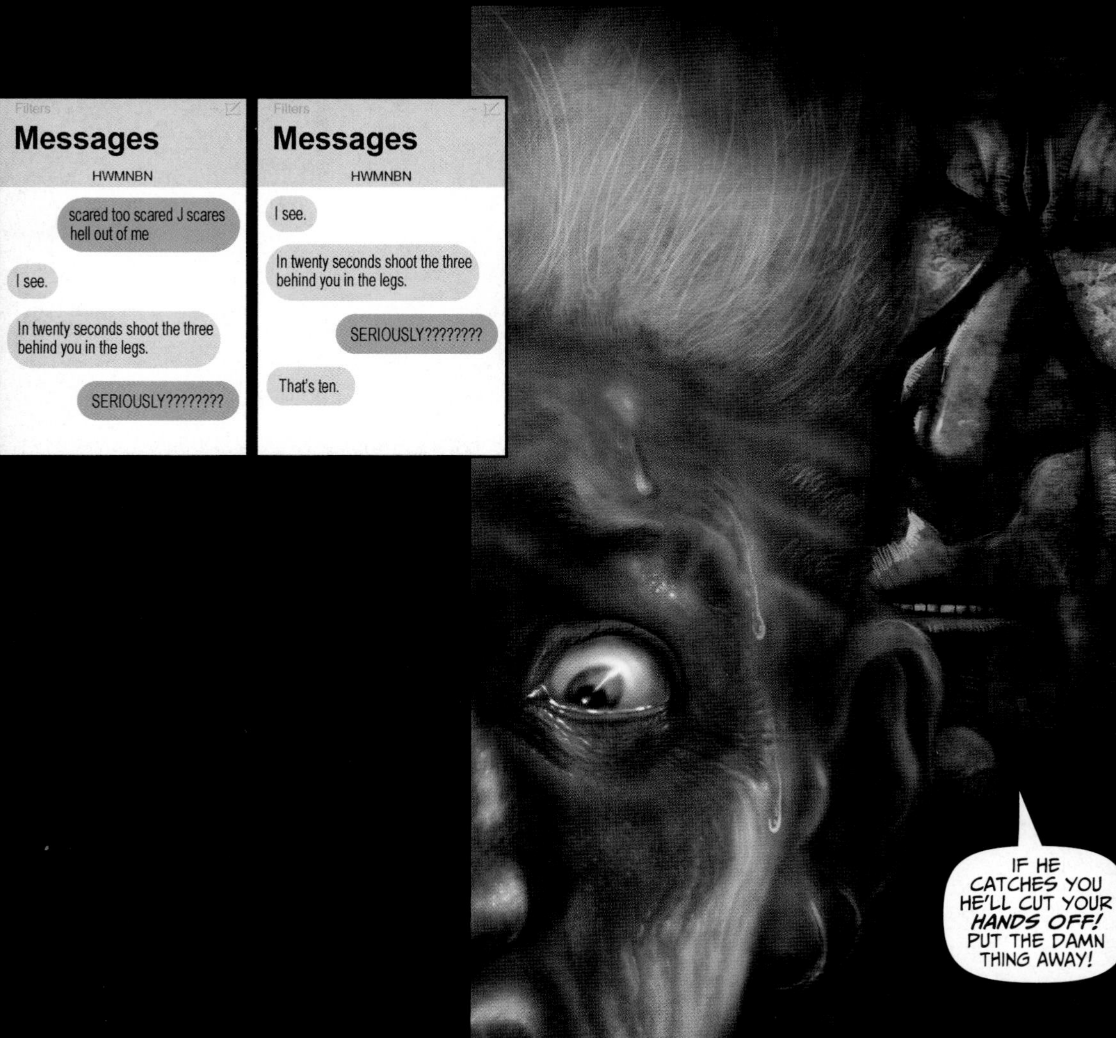
Filters
Messages
HWMNBN
scared too scared J scares hell out of me
I see.
In twenty seconds shoot the three behind you in the legs.
SERIOUSLY????????
Filters
Messages
HWMNBN
I see.
In twenty seconds shoot the three behind you in the legs.
SERIOUSLY????????
That's ten.
IF HE CATCHES YOU HE'LL CUT YOUR ***HANDS OFF!*** PUT THE DAMN THING AWAY!

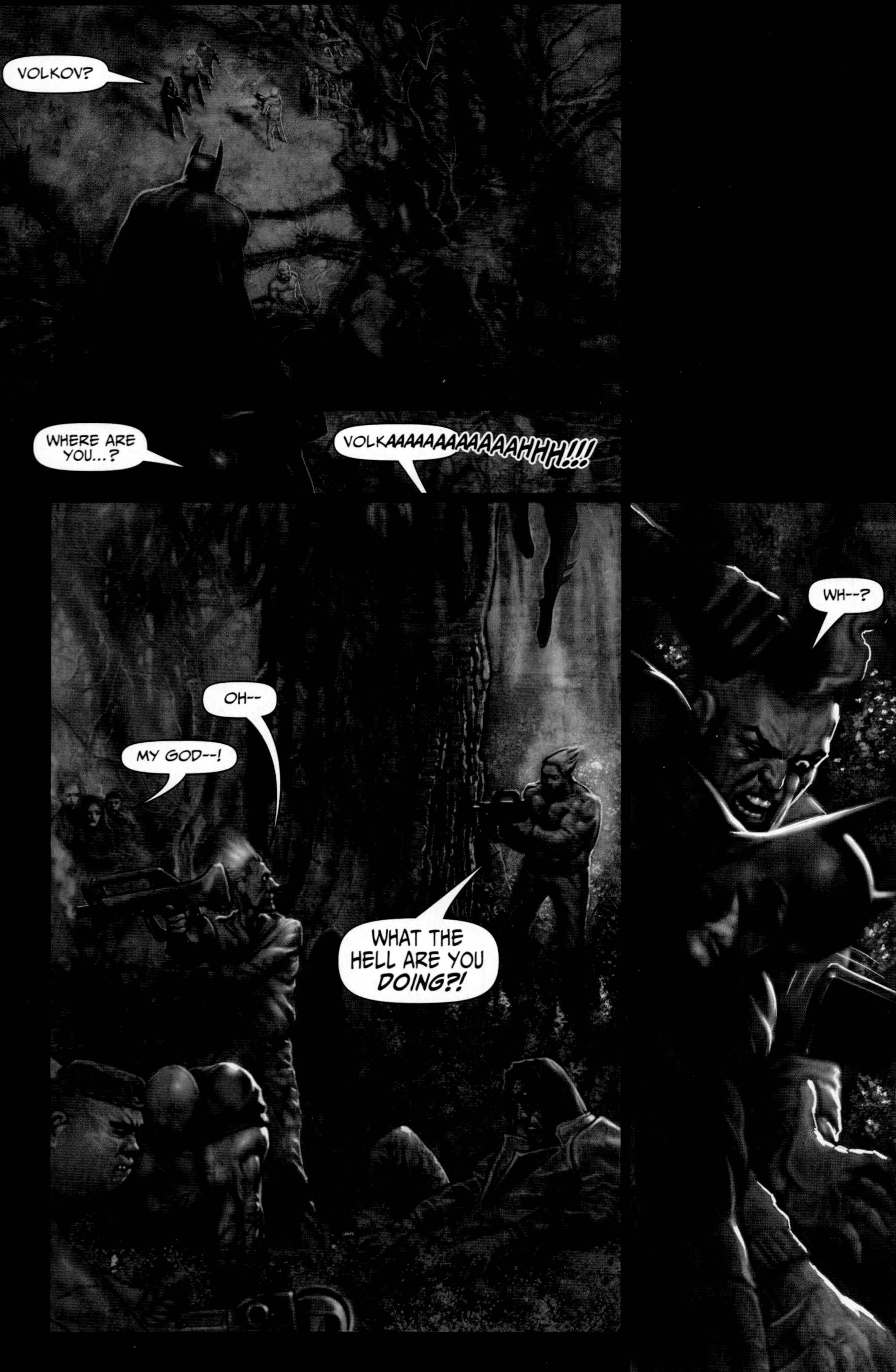
VOLKOV?
WHERE ARE YOU...?
VOLKAAAAAAAAAAAAAHHH!!!
OH--
MY GOD--!
WHAT THE HELL ARE YOU DOING?!
WH--?

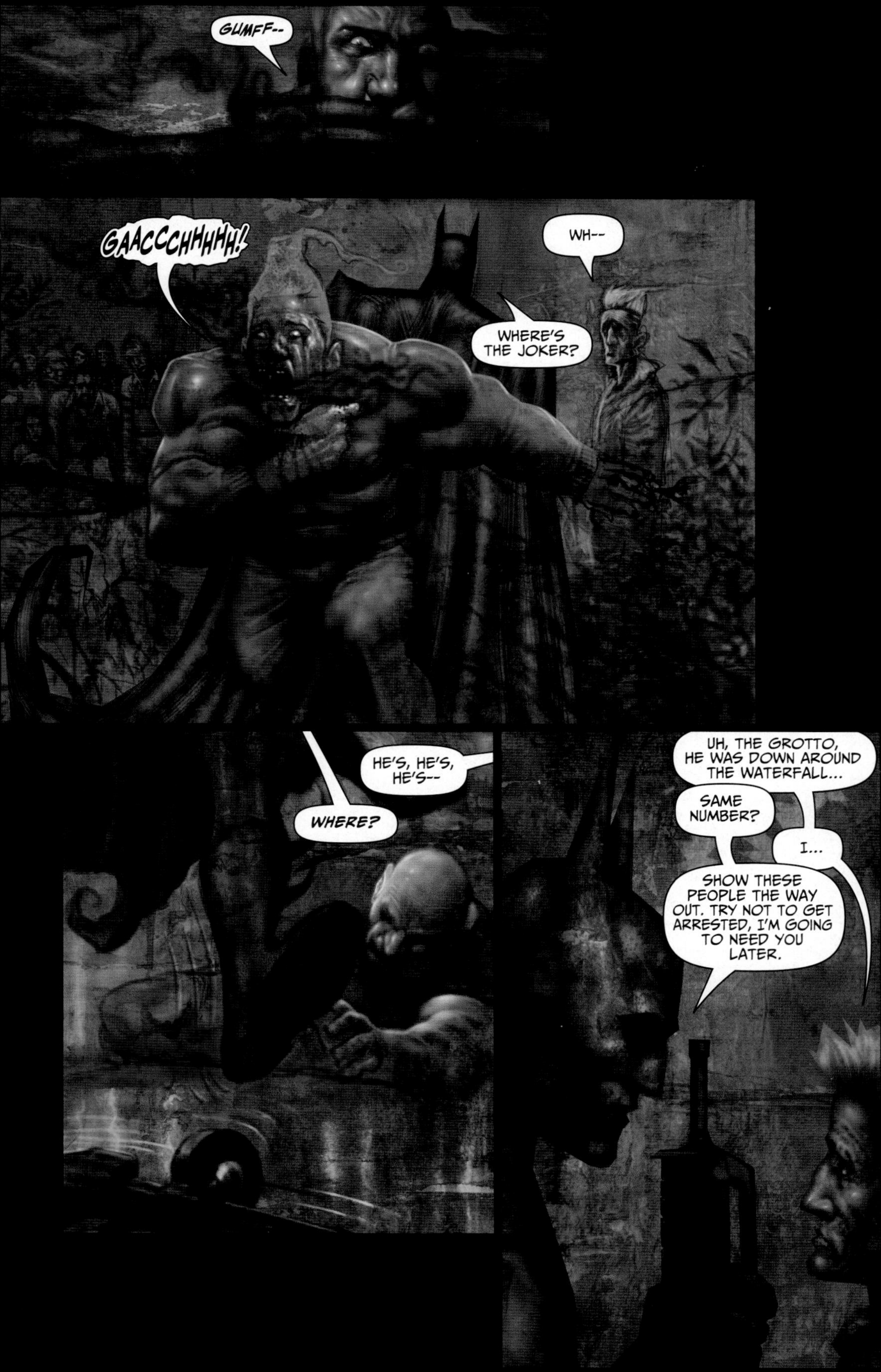
GUMFF--
GAACCCHHHHH!
WH--
WHERE'S THE JOKER?
HE'S, HE'S, HE'S--
WHERE?
UH, THE GROTTO, HE WAS DOWN AROUND THE WATERFALL...
SAME NUMBER?
I...
SHOW THESE PEOPLE THE WAY OUT. TRY NOT TO GET ARRESTED, I'M GOING TO NEED YOU LATER.

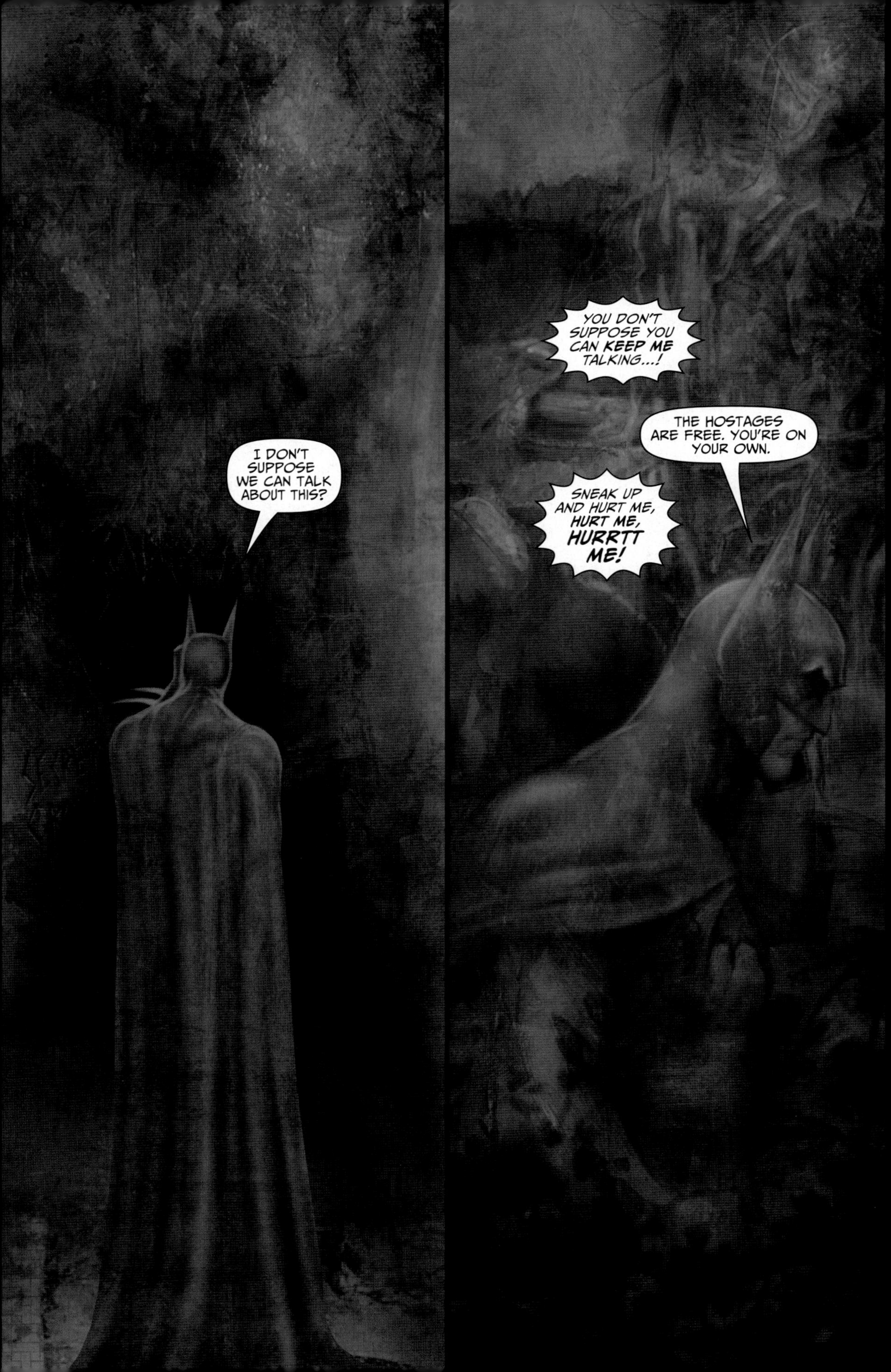
I DON'T SUPPOSE WE CAN TALK ABOUT THIS?
YOU DON'T SUPPOSE YOU CAN KEEP ME TALKING...!
THE HOSTAGES ARE FREE. YOU'RE ON YOUR OWN.
SNEAK UP AND HURT ME, HURT ME, HURRTT ME!

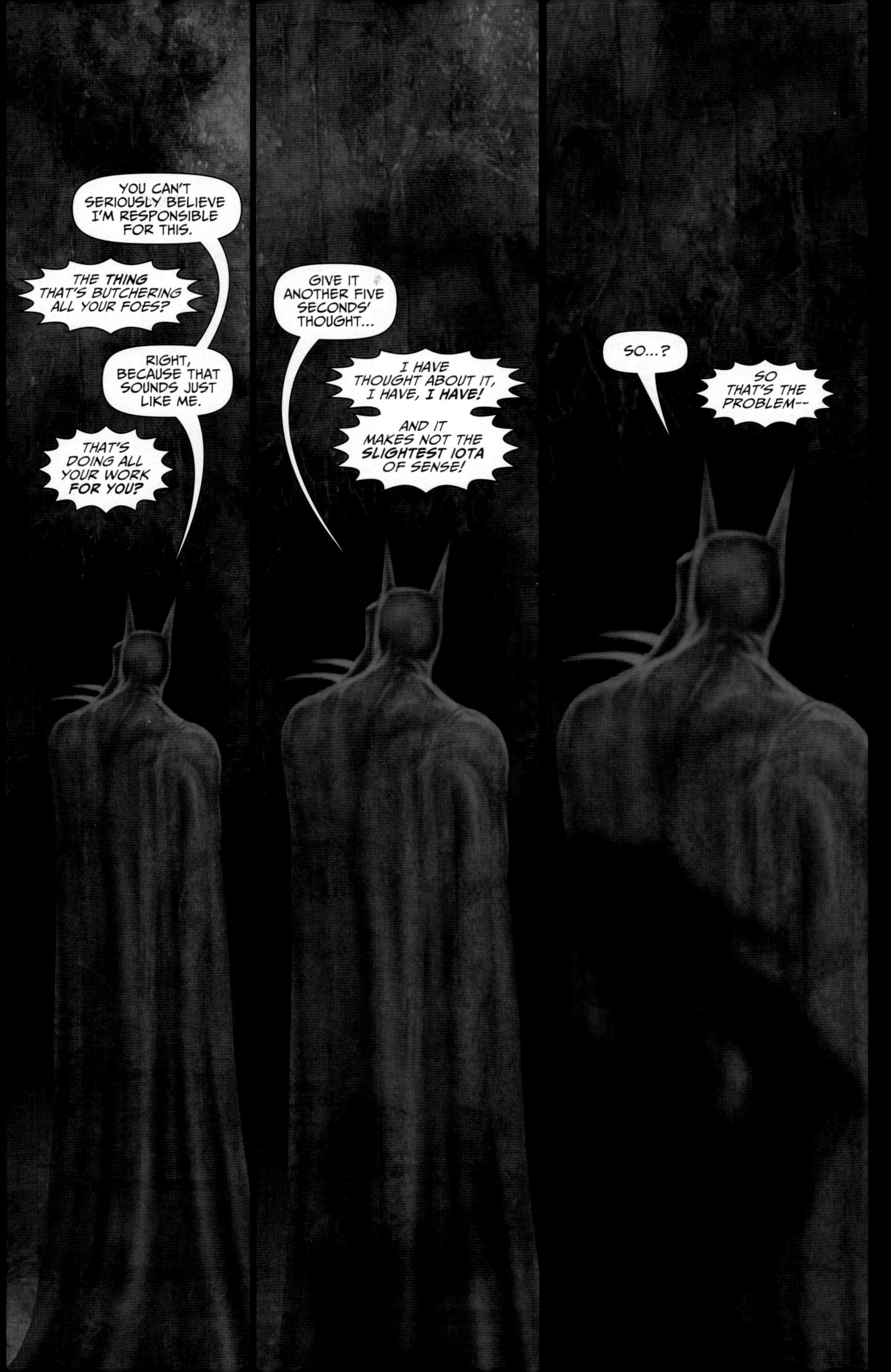
YOU CAN'T SERIOUSLY BELIEVE I'M RESPONSIBLE FOR THIS.
THE THING THAT'S BUTCHERING ALL YOUR FOES?
RIGHT, BECAUSE THAT SOUNDS JUST LIKE ME.
THAT'S DOING ALL YOUR WORK FOR YOU?
GIVE IT ANOTHER FIVE SECONDS' THOUGHT...
I HAVE THOUGHT ABOUT IT, I HAVE, I HAVE!
AND IT MAKES NOT THE SLIGHTEST IOTA OF SENSE!
SO...?
SO THAT'S THE PROBLEM--

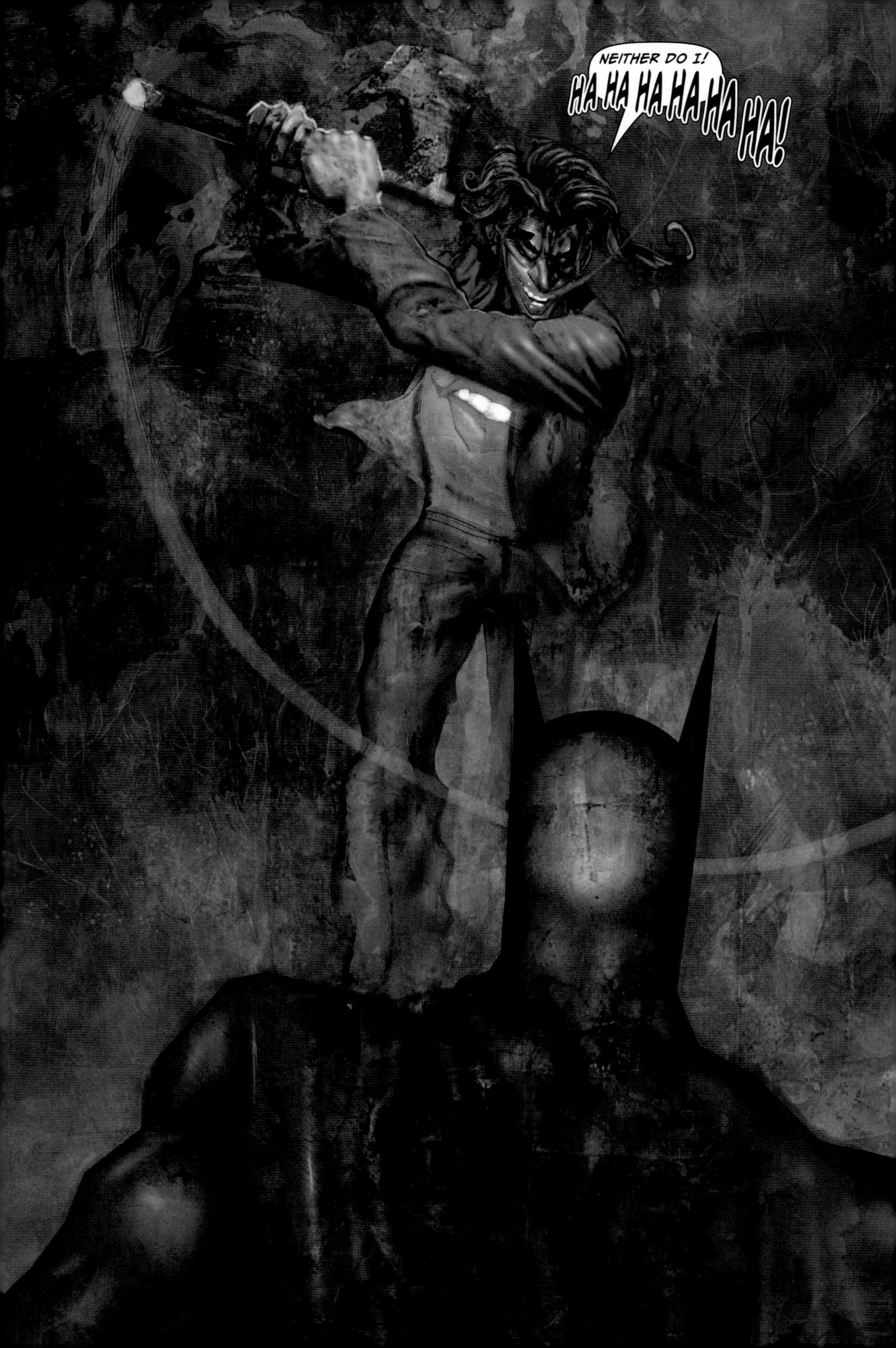
NEITHER DO I!
HA HA HA HA HA HA HA!

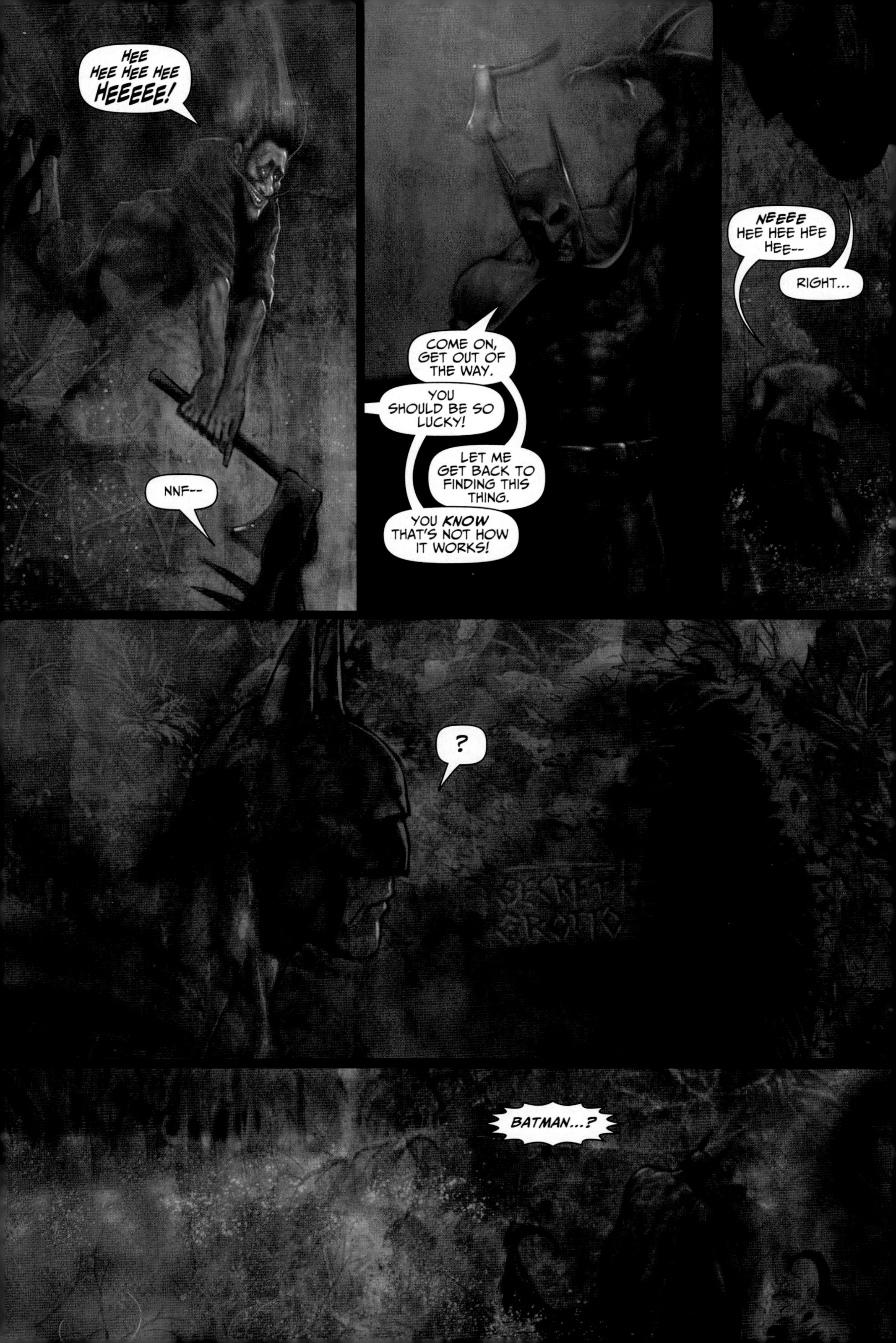
HEE HEE HEE HEE HEEEEE!
NNF--
COME ON, GET OUT OF THE WAY.
YOU SHOULD BE SO LUCKY!
LET ME GET BACK TO FINDING THIS THING.
YOU KNOW THAT'S NOT HOW IT WORKS!
NEEEE HEE HEE HEE HEE--
RIGHT...
?
BATMAN...?

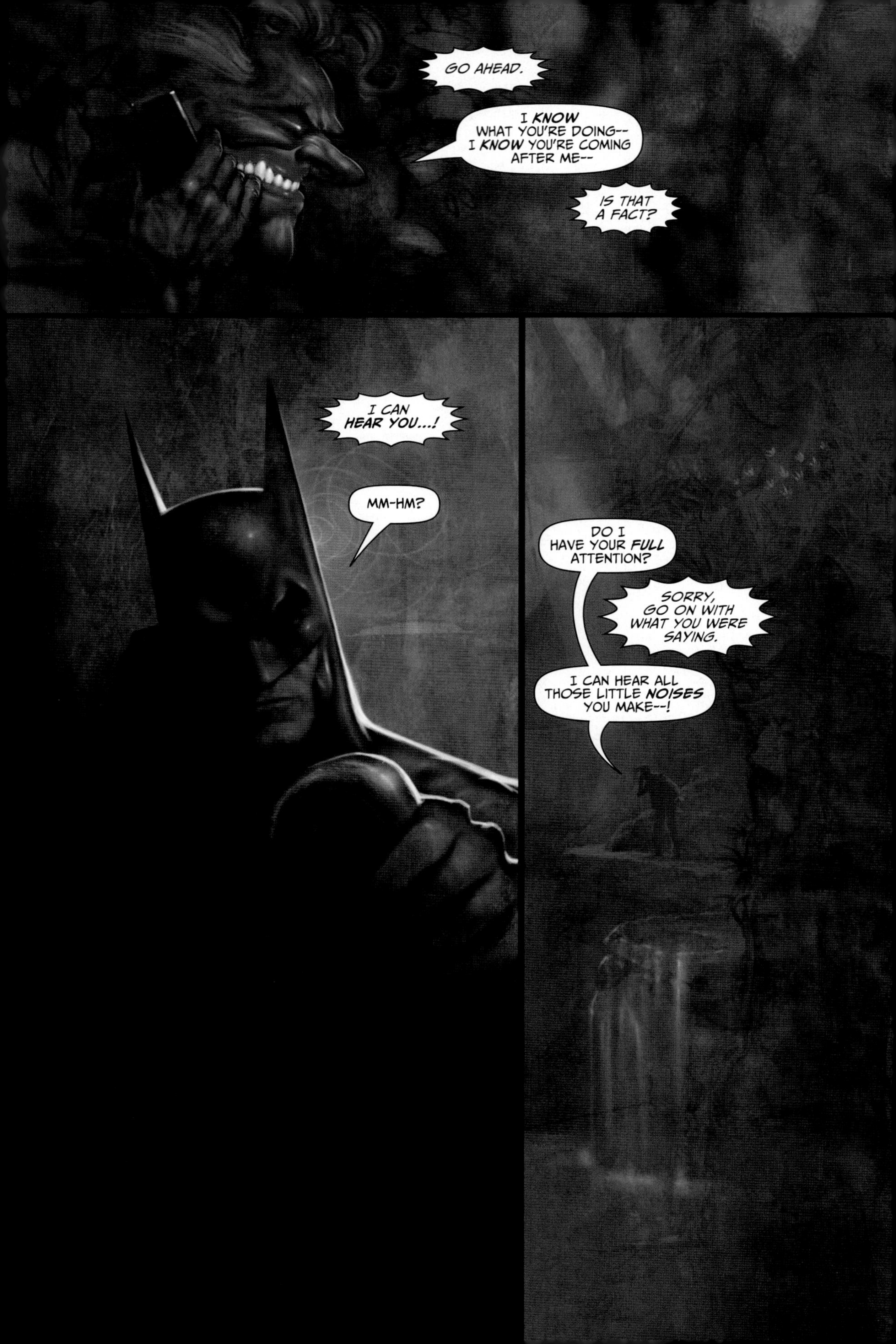
GO AHEAD.
I KNOW WHAT YOU'RE DOING-- I KNOW YOU'RE COMING AFTER ME--
IS THAT A FACT?
I CAN HEAR YOU...!
MM-HM?
DO I HAVE YOUR FULL ATTENTION?
SORRY, GO ON WITH WHAT YOU WERE SAYING.
I CAN HEAR ALL THOSE LITTLE NOISES YOU MAKE--!

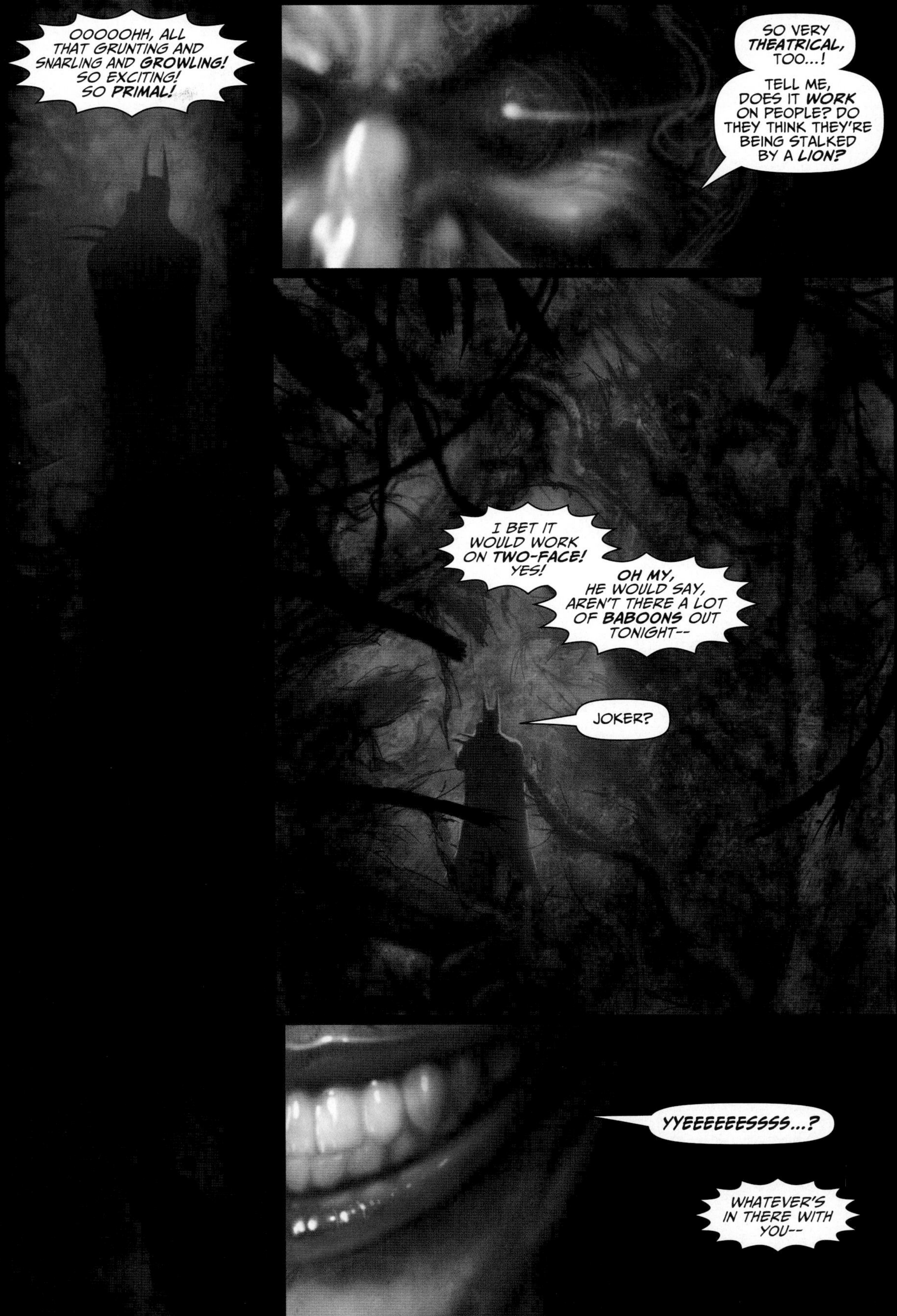
OOOOOHH, ALL THAT GRUNTING AND SNARLING AND GROWLING! SO EXCITING! SO PRIMAL!
SO VERY THEATRICAL, TOO...!
TELL ME, DOES IT WORK ON PEOPLE? DO THEY THINK THEY'RE BEING STALKED BY A LION?
I BET IT WOULD WORK ON TWO-FACE! YES!
OH MY, HE WOULD SAY, AREN'T THERE A LOT OF BABOONS OUT TONIGHT--
JOKER?
YYEEEEEEESSSS...?
WHATEVER'S IN THERE WITH YOU--

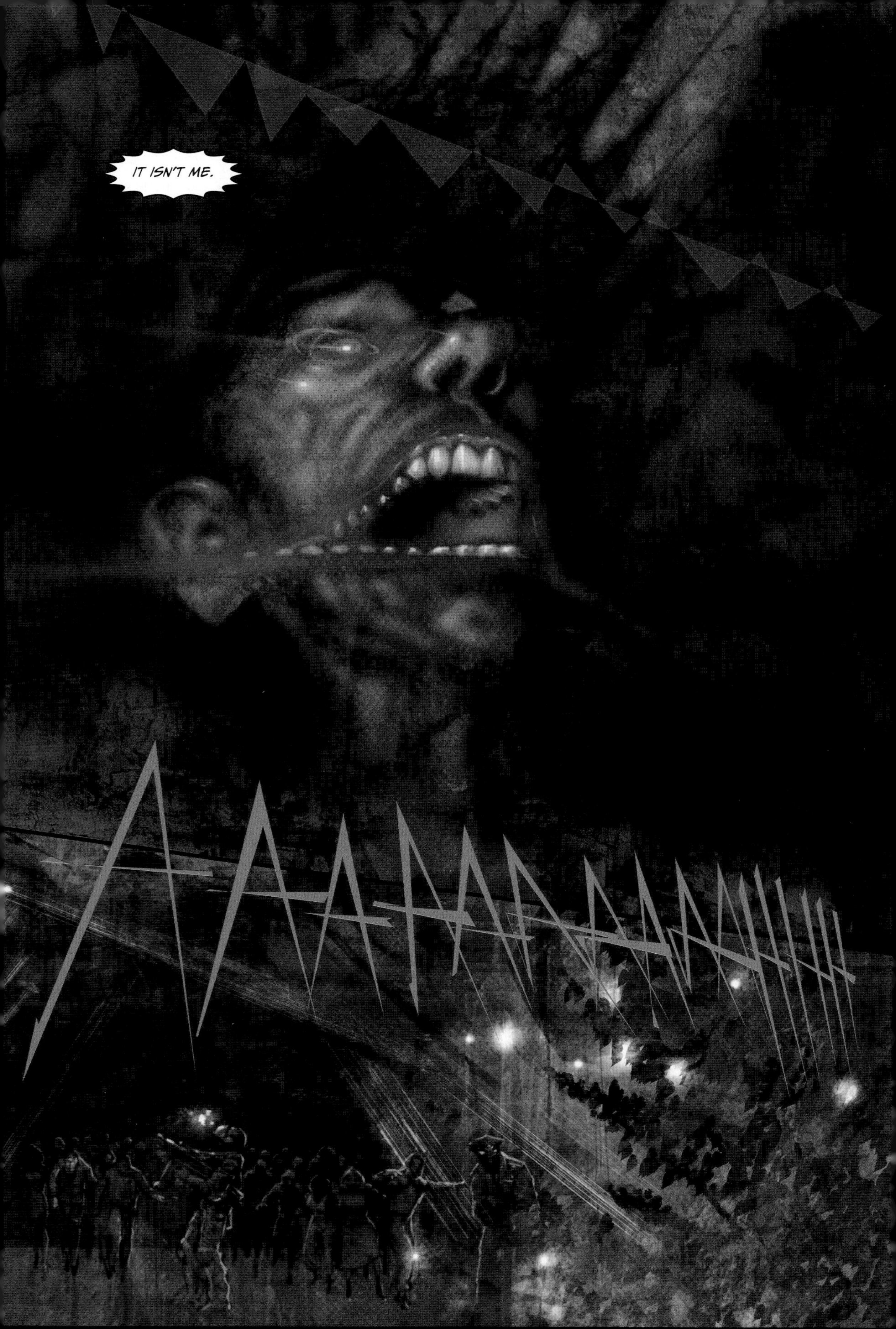
IT ISN'T ME.
AAAAAAAAAHHHH

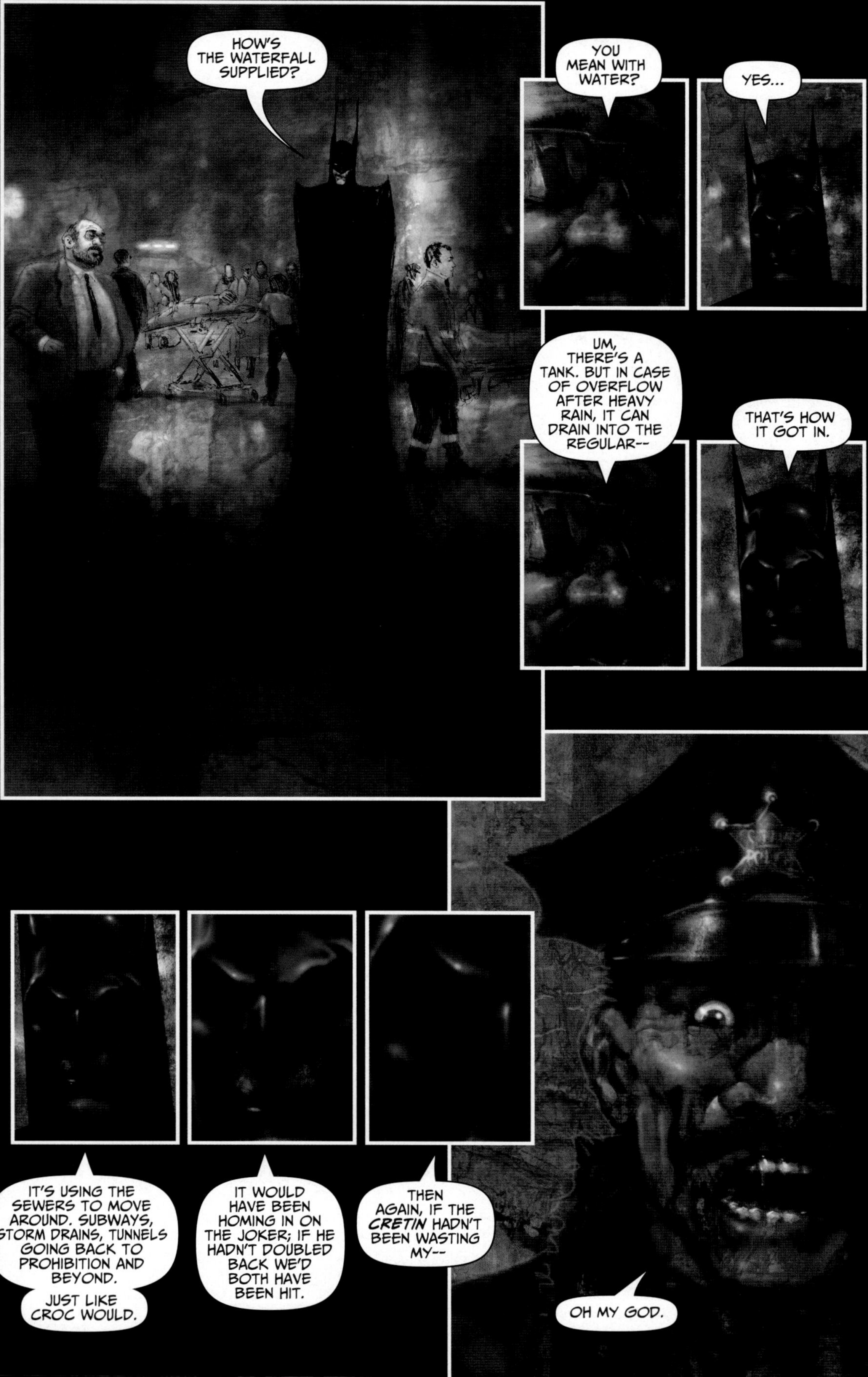
HOW'S THE WATERFALL SUPPLIED?
YOU MEAN WITH WATER?
YES...
UM, THERE'S A TANK. BUT IN CASE OF OVERFLOW AFTER HEAVY RAIN, IT CAN DRAIN INTO THE REGULAR--
THAT'S HOW IT GOT IN.
IT'S USING THE SEWERS TO MOVE AROUND. SUBWAYS, STORM DRAINS, TUNNELS GOING BACK TO PROHIBITION AND BEYOND.
JUST LIKE CROC WOULD.
IT WOULD HAVE BEEN HOMING IN ON THE JOKER; IF HE HADN'T DOUBLED BACK WE'D BOTH HAVE BEEN HIT.
THEN AGAIN, IF THE *CRETIN* HADN'T BEEN WASTING MY--
OH MY GOD.

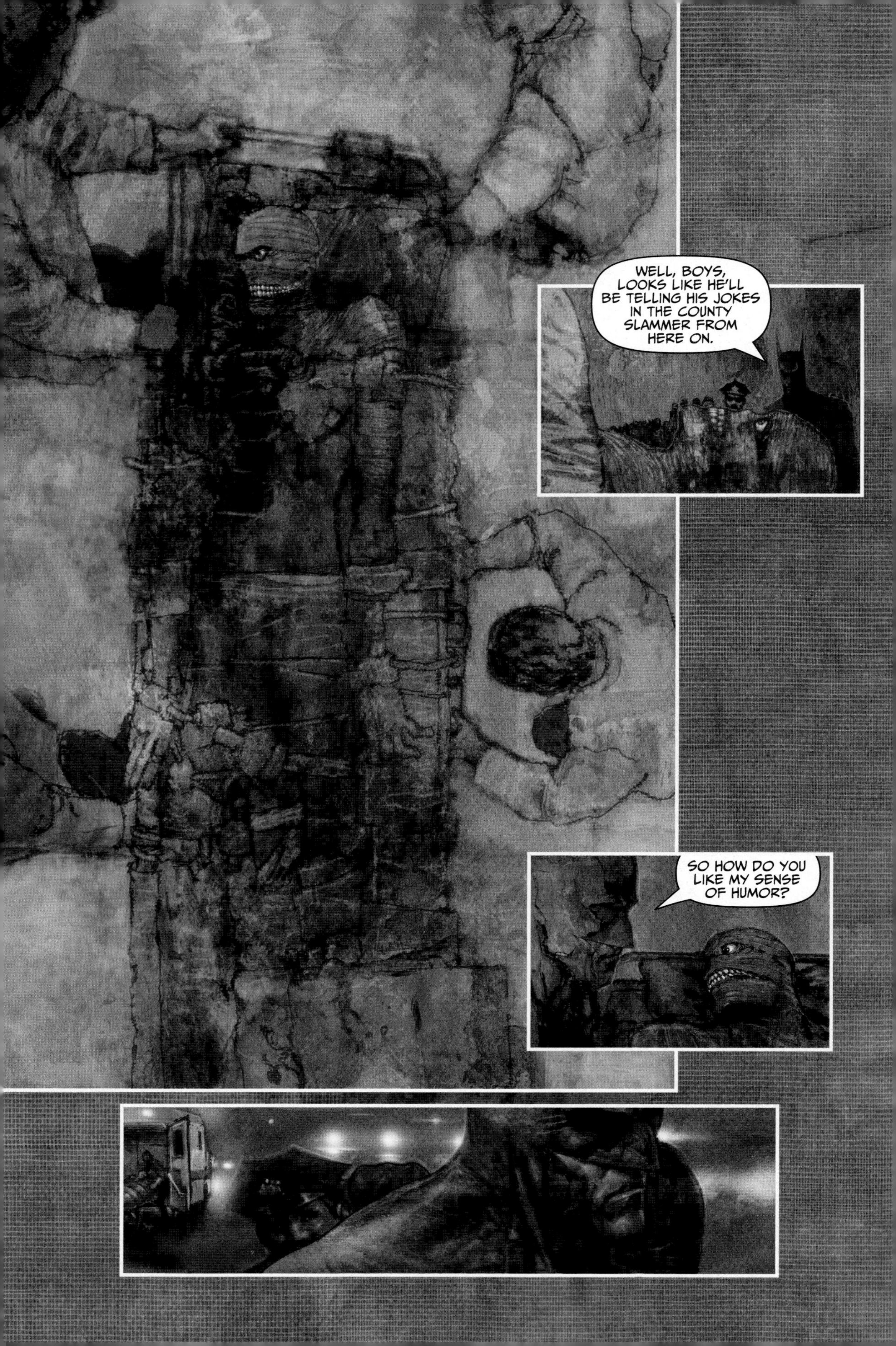
WELL, BOYS, LOOKS LIKE HE'LL BE TELLING HIS JOKES IN THE COUNTY SLAMMER FROM HERE ON.
SO HOW DO YOU LIKE MY SENSE OF HUMOR?

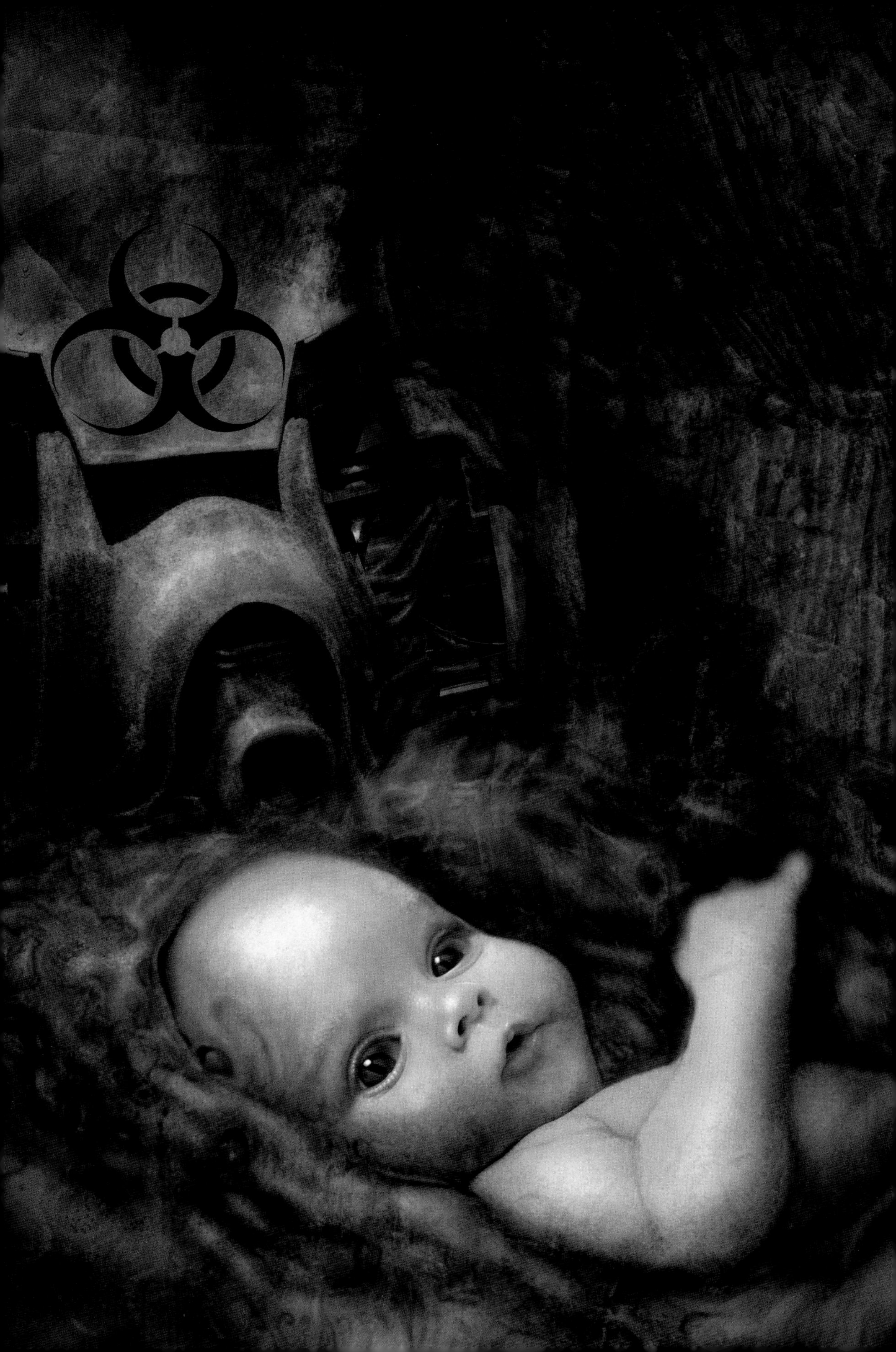

Batman: Reptilian #4 1:25 variant cover by DECLAN SHALVEY

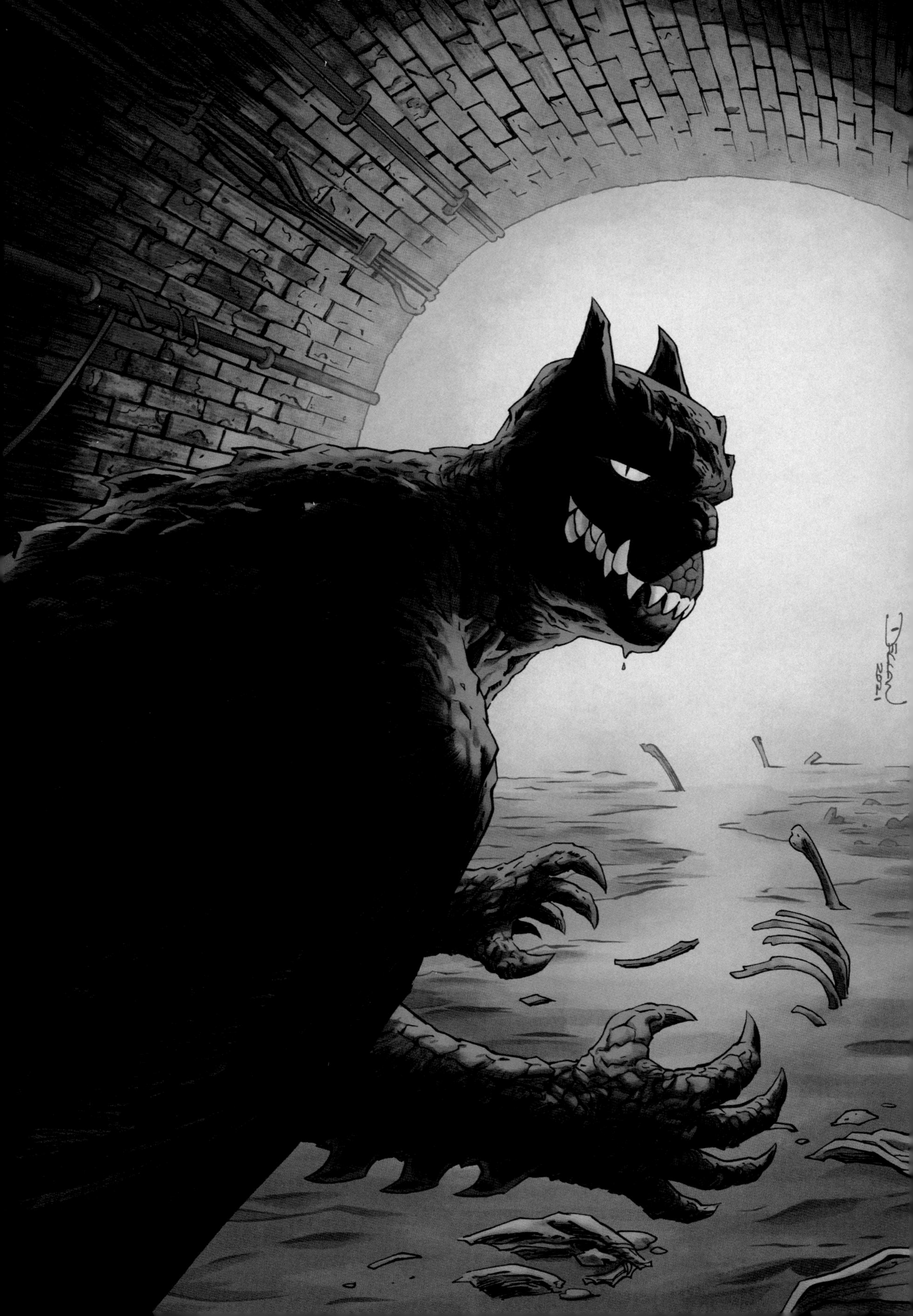

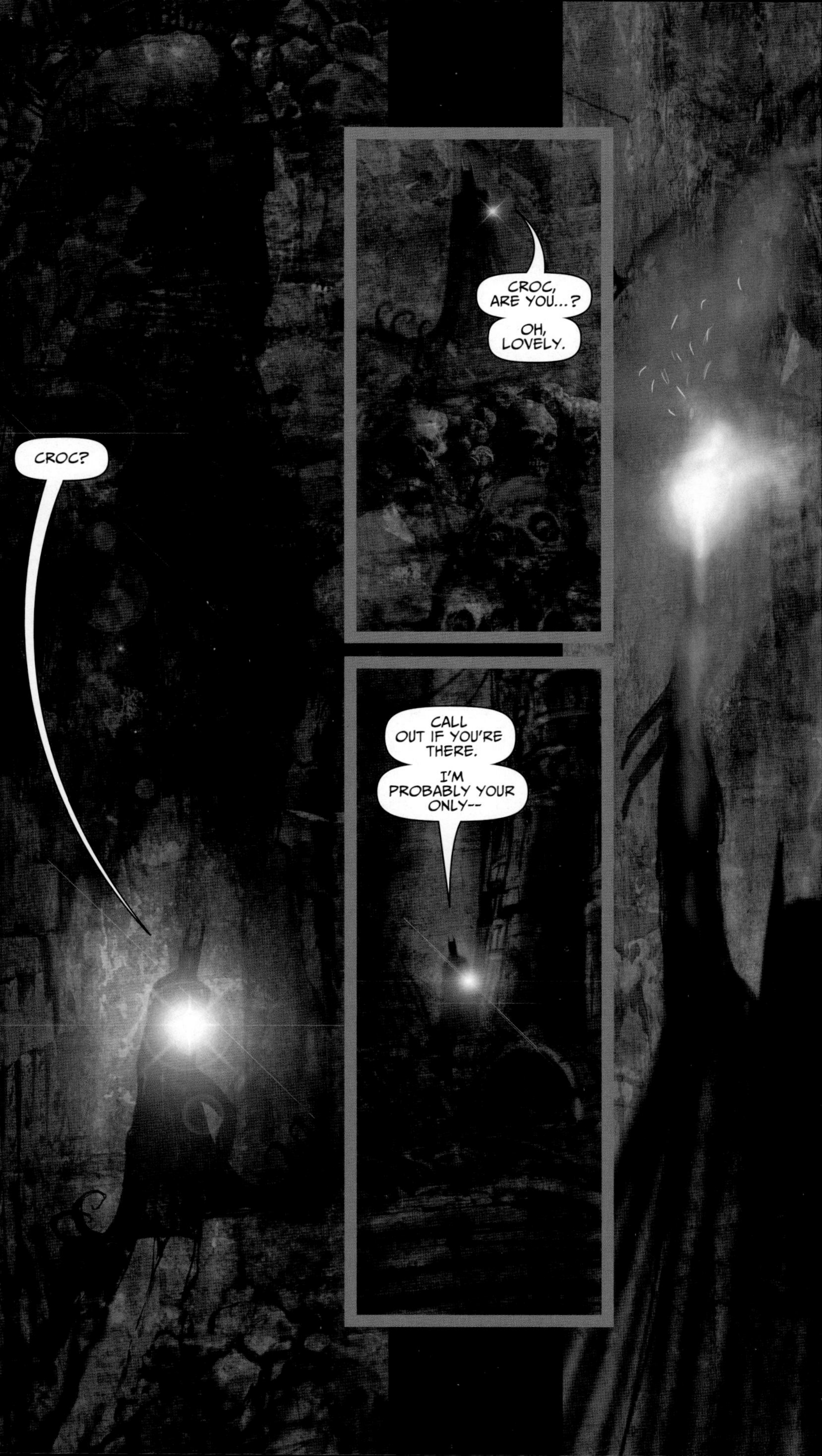
CROC?
CROC, ARE YOU...?
OH, LOVELY.
CALL OUT IF YOU'RE THERE.
I'M PROBABLY YOUR ONLY--

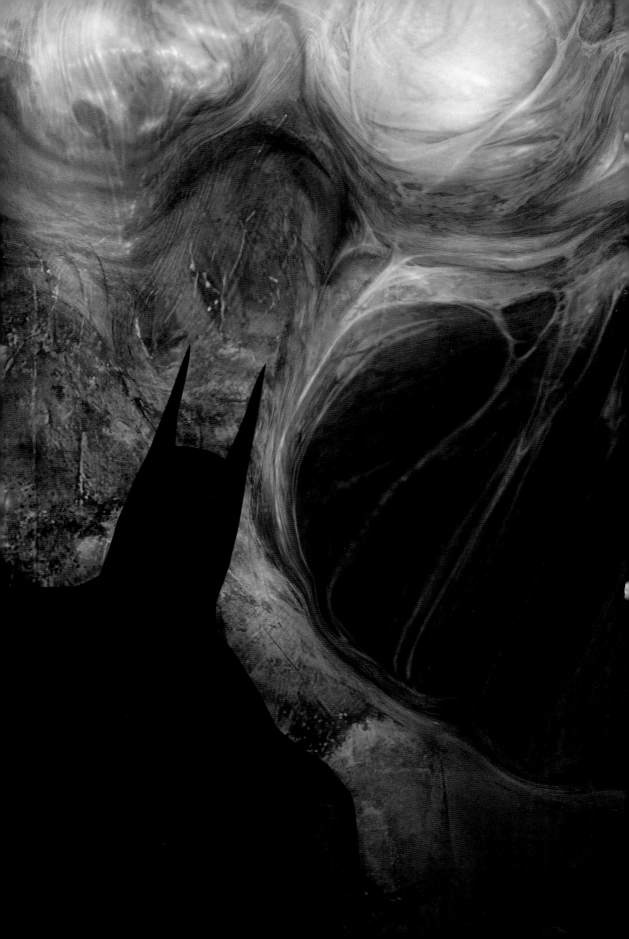

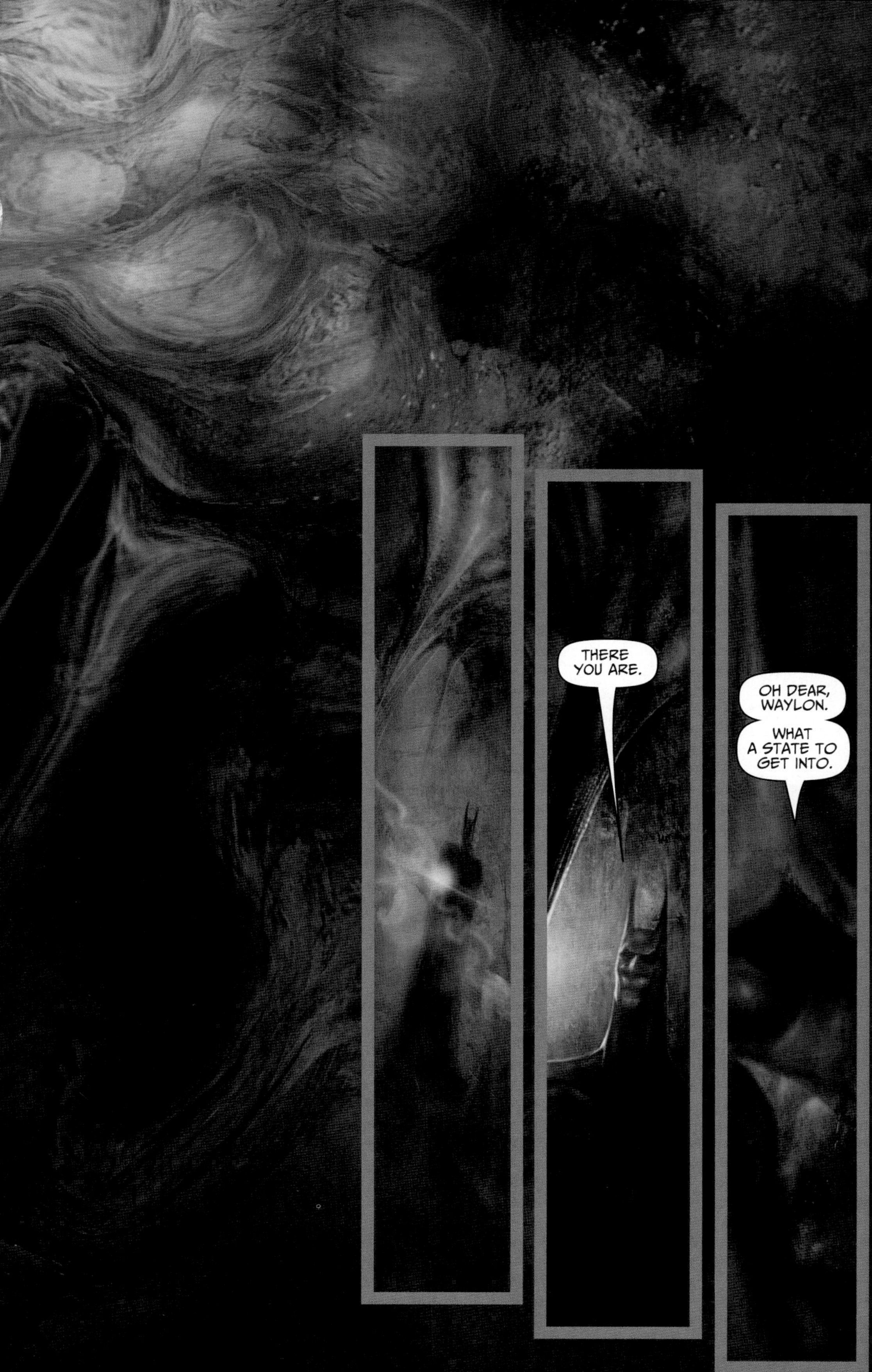
THERE YOU ARE.
OH DEAR, WAYLON.
WHAT A STATE TO GET INTO.

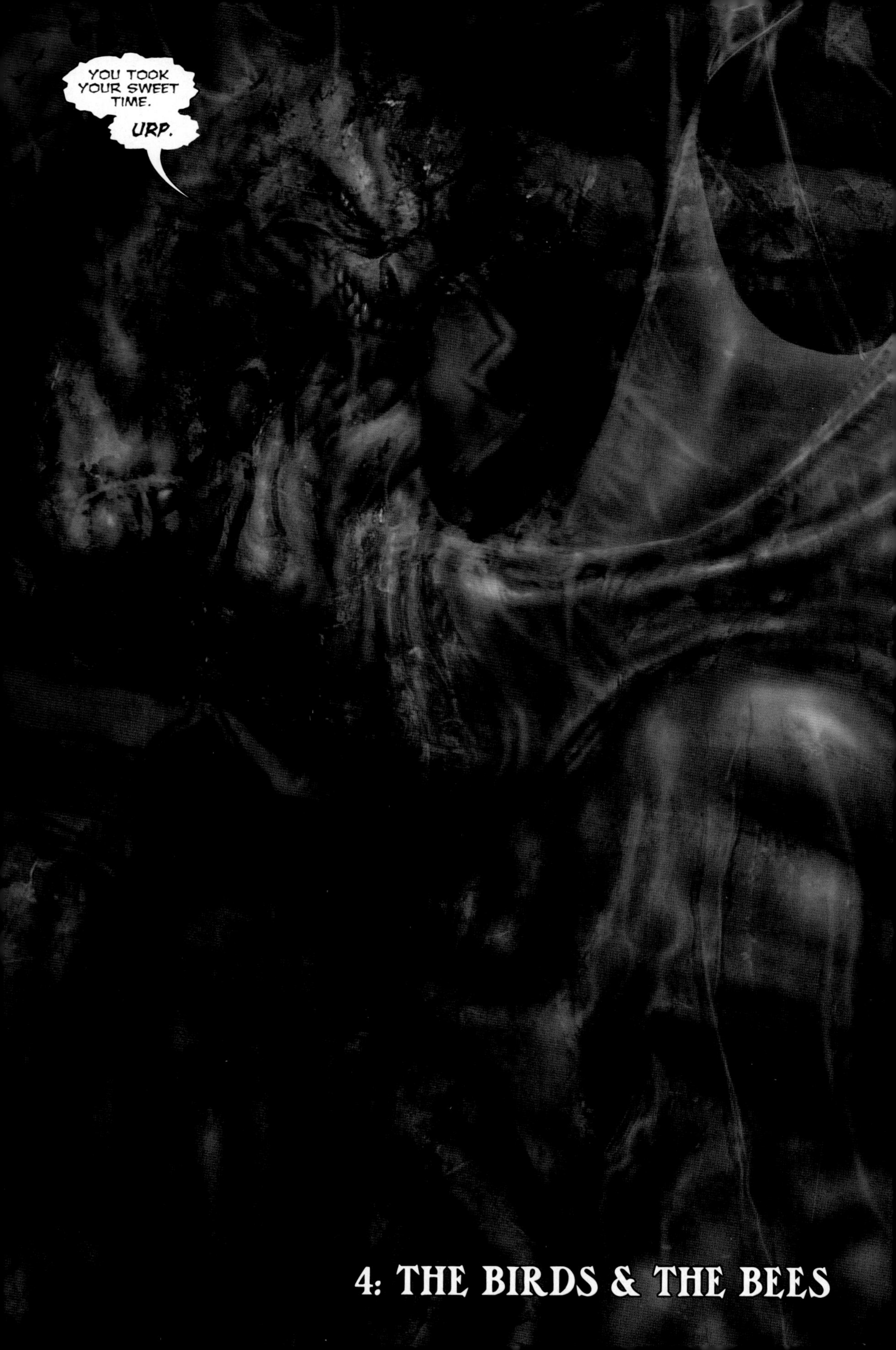
YOU TOOK YOUR SWEET TIME.
URP.
4: THE BIRDS & THE BEES

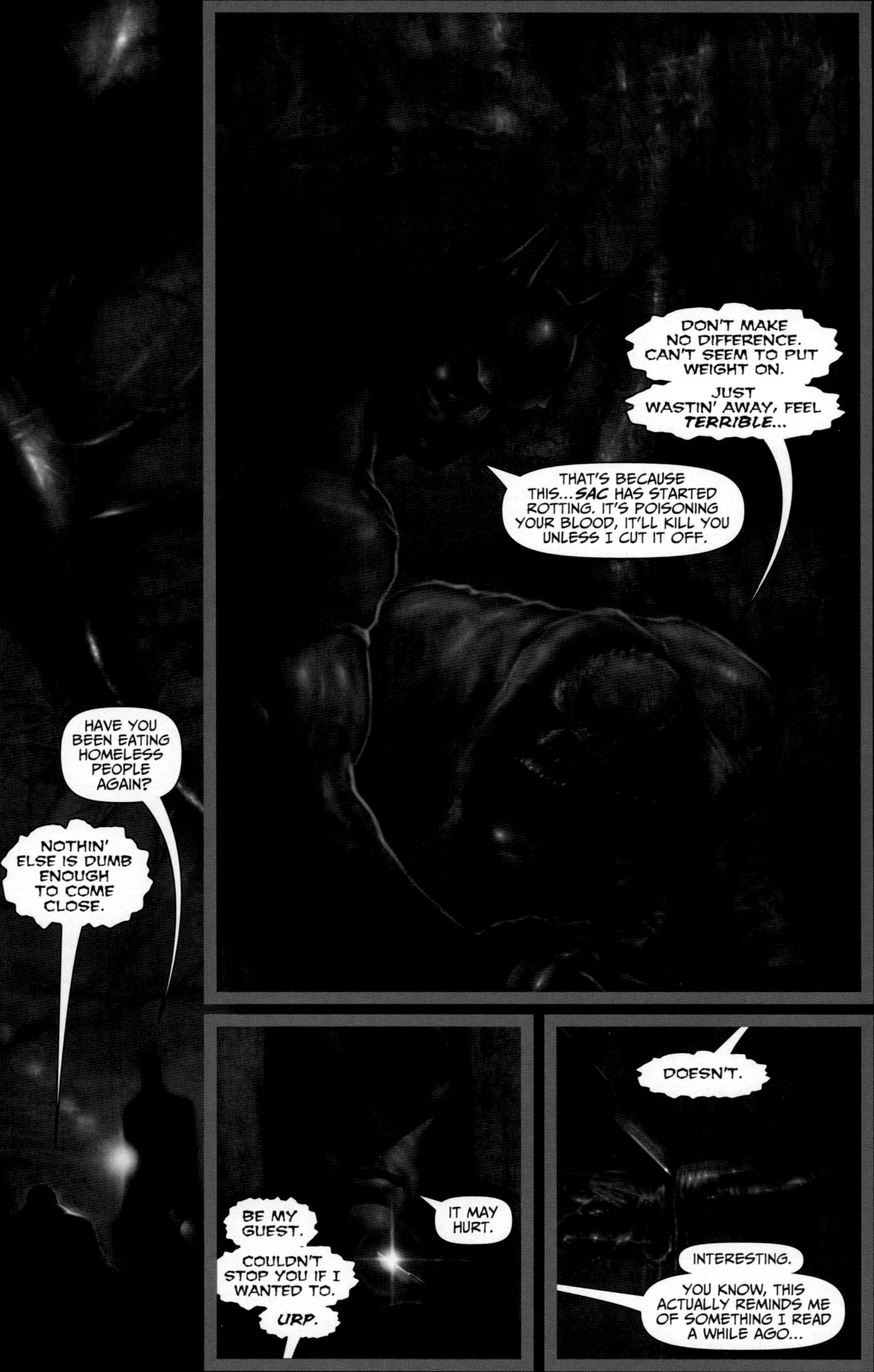
DON'T MAKE NO DIFFERENCE. CAN'T SEEM TO PUT WEIGHT ON.
JUST WASTIN' AWAY, FEEL *TERRIBLE*...
THAT'S BECAUSE THIS...*SAC* HAS STARTED ROTTING. IT'S POISONING YOUR BLOOD, IT'LL KILL YOU UNLESS I CUT IT OFF.
HAVE YOU BEEN EATING HOMELESS PEOPLE AGAIN?
NOTHIN' ELSE IS DUMB ENOUGH TO COME CLOSE.
IT MAY HURT.
BE MY GUEST.
COULDN'T STOP YOU IF I WANTED TO.
URP.
DOESN'T.
INTERESTING.
YOU KNOW, THIS ACTUALLY REMINDS ME OF SOMETHING I READ A WHILE AGO...

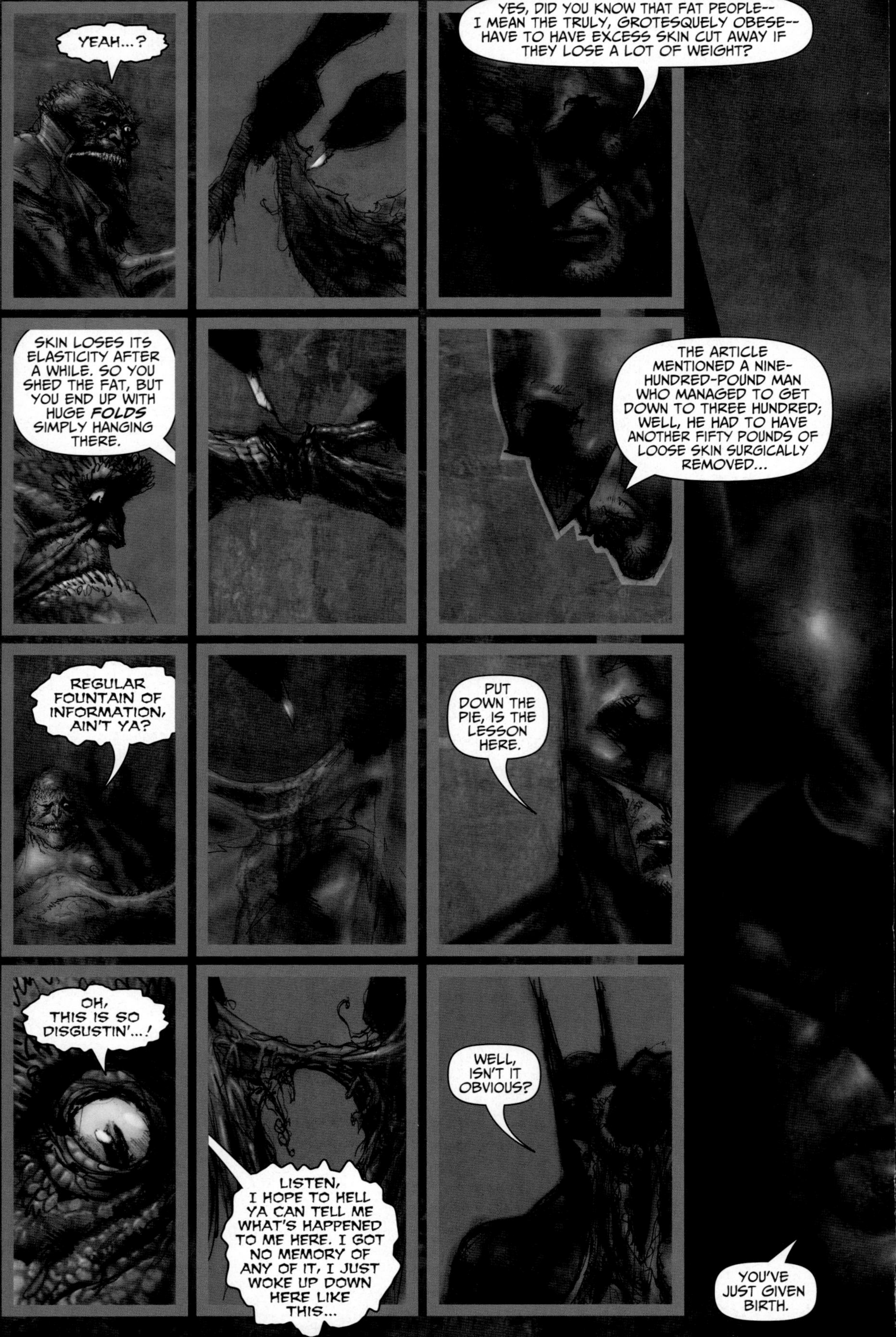
YEAH...?
YES, DID YOU KNOW THAT FAT PEOPLE-- I MEAN THE TRULY, GROTESQUELY OBESE-- HAVE TO HAVE EXCESS SKIN CUT AWAY IF THEY LOSE A LOT OF WEIGHT?
SKIN LOSES ITS ELASTICITY AFTER A WHILE. SO YOU SHED THE FAT, BUT YOU END UP WITH HUGE FOLDS SIMPLY HANGING THERE.
THE ARTICLE MENTIONED A NINE-HUNDRED-POUND MAN WHO MANAGED TO GET DOWN TO THREE HUNDRED; WELL, HE HAD TO HAVE ANOTHER FIFTY POUNDS OF LOOSE SKIN SURGICALLY REMOVED...
REGULAR FOUNTAIN OF INFORMATION, AIN'T YA?
PUT DOWN THE PIE, IS THE LESSON HERE.
OH, THIS IS SO DISGUSTIN'...!
LISTEN, I HOPE TO HELL YA CAN TELL ME WHAT'S HAPPENED TO ME HERE. I GOT NO MEMORY OF ANY OF IT, I JUST WOKE UP DOWN HERE LIKE THIS...
WELL, ISN'T IT OBVIOUS?
YOU'VE JUST GIVEN BIRTH.

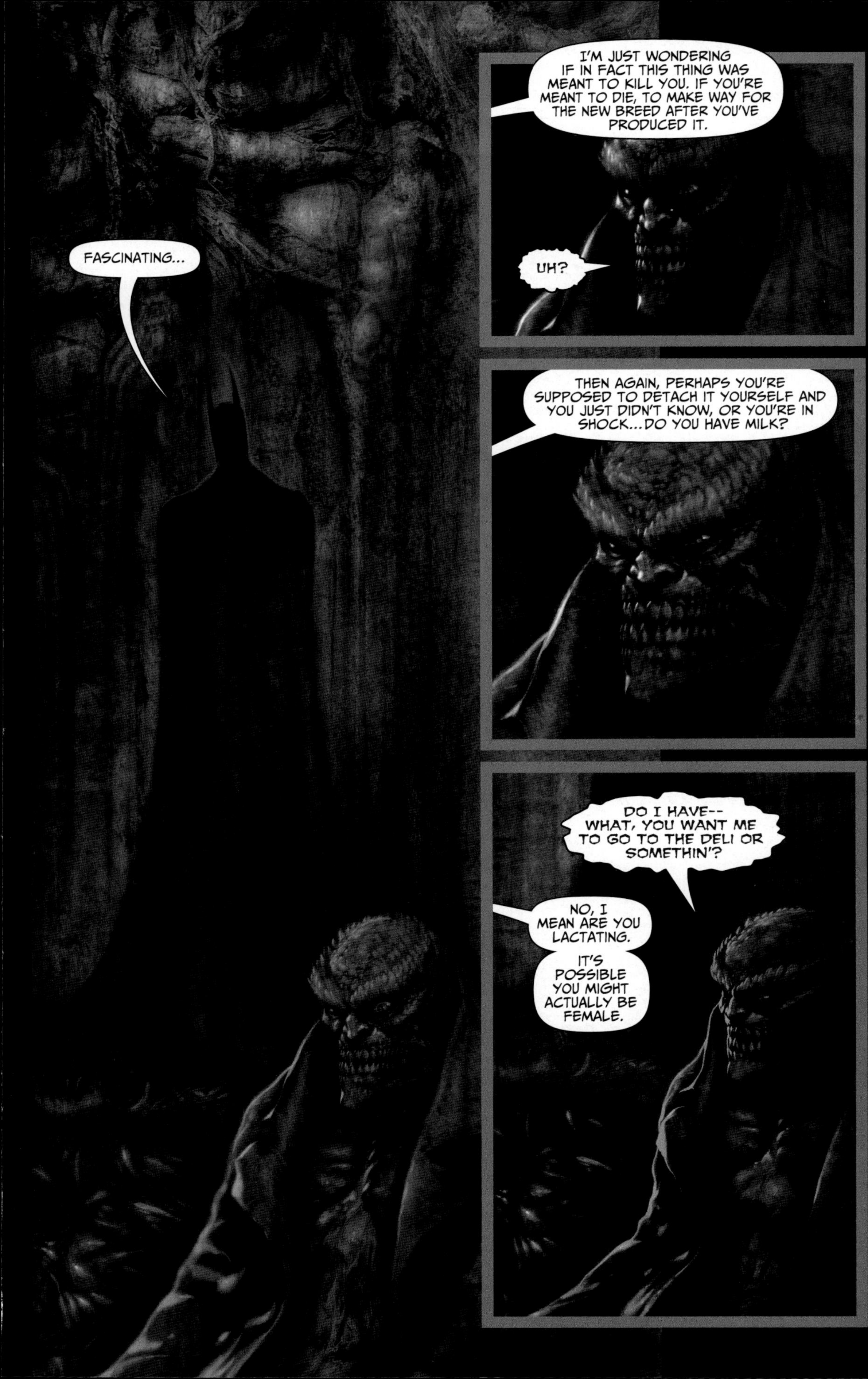
FASCINATING...
I'M JUST WONDERING IF IN FACT THIS THING WAS MEANT TO KILL YOU. IF YOU'RE MEANT TO DIE, TO MAKE WAY FOR THE NEW BREED AFTER YOU'VE PRODUCED IT.
UH?
THEN AGAIN, PERHAPS YOU'RE SUPPOSED TO DETACH IT YOURSELF AND YOU JUST DIDN'T KNOW, OR YOU'RE IN SHOCK...DO YOU HAVE MILK?
DO I HAVE-- WHAT, YOU WANT ME TO GO TO THE DELI OR SOMETHIN'?
NO, I MEAN ARE YOU LACTATING.
IT'S POSSIBLE YOU MIGHT ACTUALLY BE FEMALE.

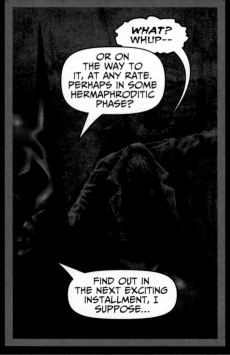

WHAT? WHUP--

OR ON THE WAY TO IT, AT ANY RATE. PERHAPS IN SOME HERMAPHRODITIC PHASE?

FIND OUT IN THE NEXT EXCITING INSTALLMENT, I SUPPOSE...

BUT--BUT I AIN'T GOT-- YA KNOW, STUFF...!

WHAT HAVE YOU GOT?

I--I--

THERE'S SOMETHING LOOSE IN THE CITY, WAYLON. IT'S BEEN KILLING OR MAIMING EVERYONE WHO WAS AT YOUR LAST MEETING.

"THE ONE THAT NEARLY ENDED IN A MASSACRE.

"DO YOU REMEMBER THAT?

"DO YOU REMEMBER FEELING LIKE YOU WANTED TO KILL EVERYBODY, FRIEND AND FOE ALIKE?"

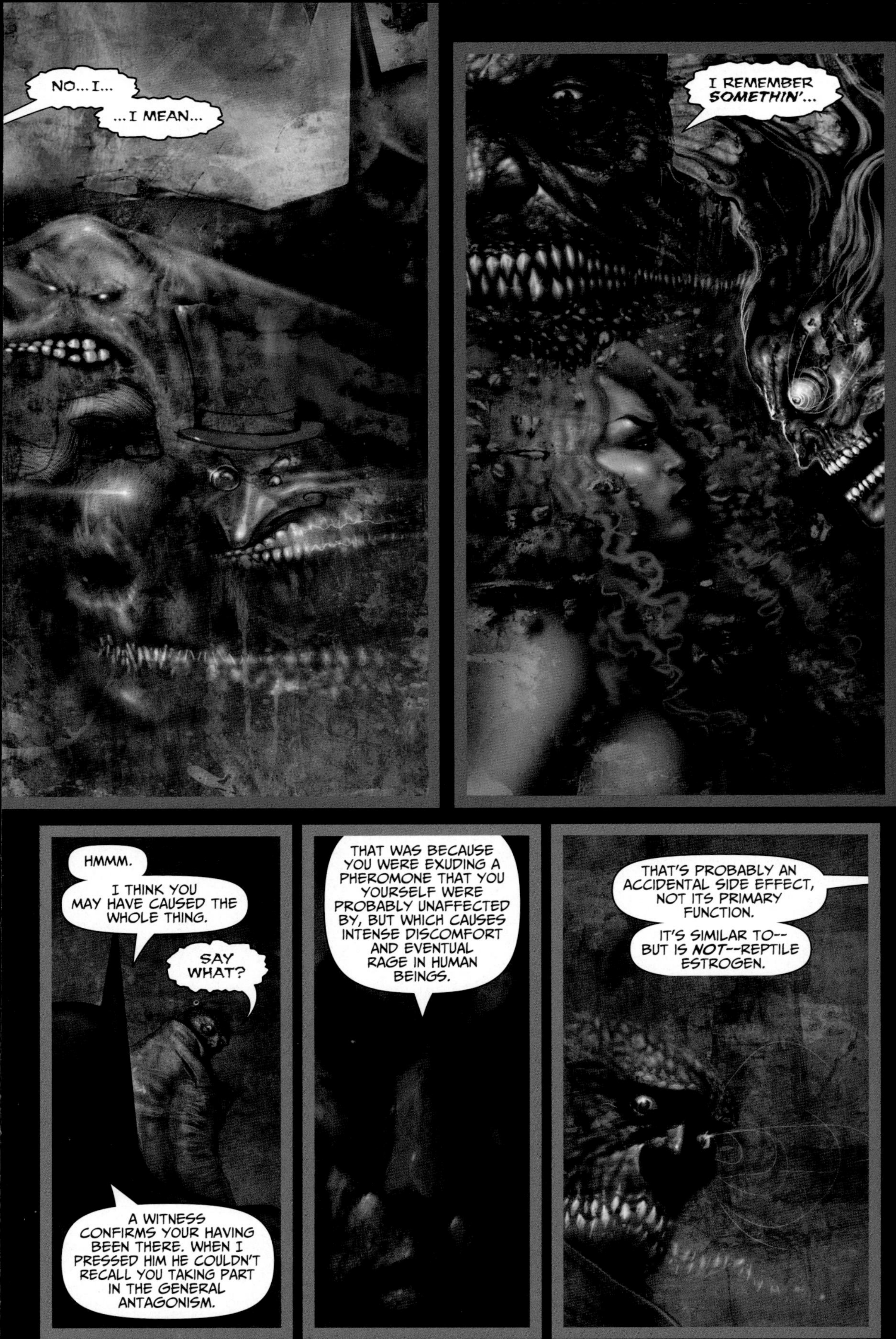

NO... I...
...I MEAN...
I REMEMBER SOMETHIN'...
HMMM.
I THINK YOU MAY HAVE CAUSED THE WHOLE THING.
SAY WHAT?
A WITNESS CONFIRMS YOUR HAVING BEEN THERE. WHEN I PRESSED HIM HE COULDN'T RECALL YOU TAKING PART IN THE GENERAL ANTAGONISM.
THAT WAS BECAUSE YOU WERE EXUDING A PHEROMONE THAT YOU YOURSELF WERE PROBABLY UNAFFECTED BY, BUT WHICH CAUSES INTENSE DISCOMFORT AND EVENTUAL RAGE IN HUMAN BEINGS.
THAT'S PROBABLY AN ACCIDENTAL SIDE EFFECT, NOT ITS PRIMARY FUNCTION.
IT'S SIMILAR TO-- BUT IS NOT--REPTILE ESTROGEN.

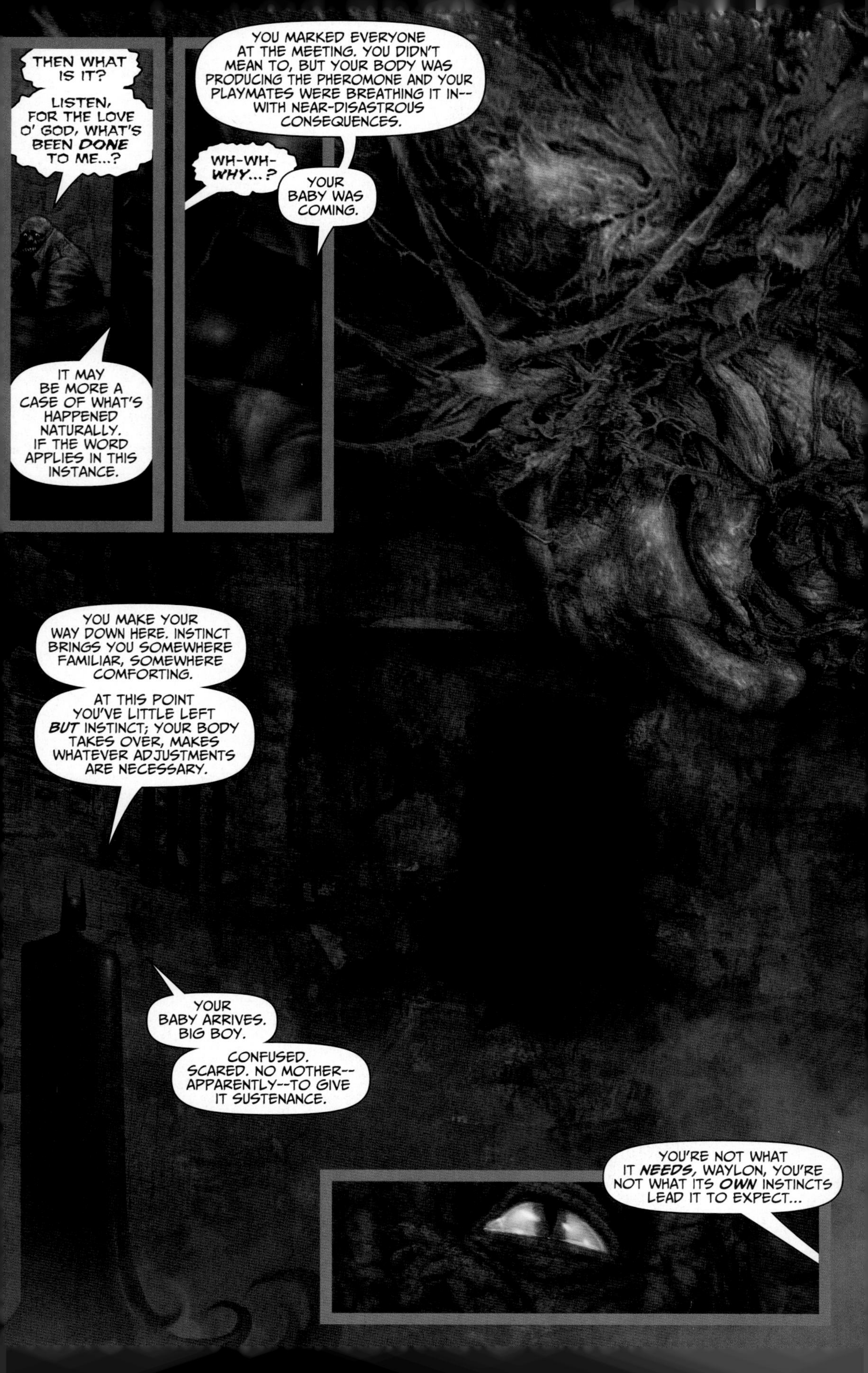
THEN WHAT IS IT?
LISTEN, FOR THE LOVE O' GOD, WHAT'S BEEN *DONE* TO ME...?
IT MAY BE MORE A CASE OF WHAT'S HAPPENED NATURALLY. IF THE WORD APPLIES IN THIS INSTANCE.
YOU MARKED EVERYONE AT THE MEETING. YOU DIDN'T MEAN TO, BUT YOUR BODY WAS PRODUCING THE PHEROMONE AND YOUR PLAYMATES WERE BREATHING IT IN--WITH NEAR-DISASTROUS CONSEQUENCES.
WH-WH-*WHY*...?
YOUR BABY WAS COMING.
YOU MAKE YOUR WAY DOWN HERE. INSTINCT BRINGS YOU SOMEWHERE FAMILIAR, SOMEWHERE COMFORTING.
AT THIS POINT YOU'VE LITTLE LEFT *BUT* INSTINCT; YOUR BODY TAKES OVER, MAKES WHATEVER ADJUSTMENTS ARE NECESSARY.
YOUR BABY ARRIVES. BIG BOY.
CONFUSED. SCARED. NO MOTHER--APPARENTLY--TO GIVE IT SUSTENANCE.
YOU'RE NOT WHAT IT *NEEDS*, WAYLON, YOU'RE NOT WHAT ITS *OWN* INSTINCTS LEAD IT TO EXPECT...

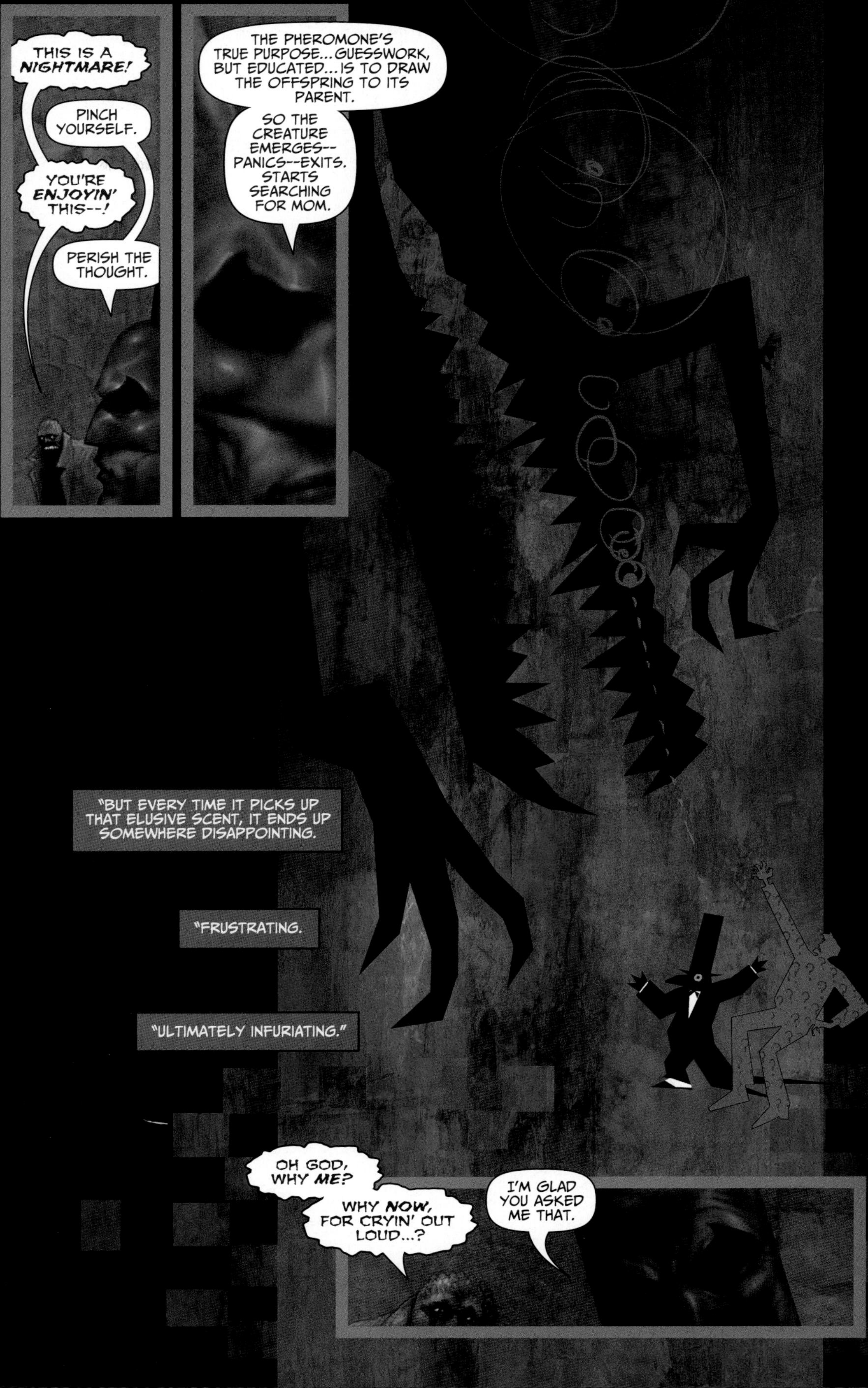
THIS IS A *NIGHTMARE!*
PINCH YOURSELF.
YOU'RE *ENJOYIN'* THIS--!
PERISH THE THOUGHT.
THE PHEROMONE'S TRUE PURPOSE...GUESSWORK, BUT EDUCATED...IS TO DRAW THE OFFSPRING TO ITS PARENT.
SO THE CREATURE EMERGES--PANICS--EXITS. STARTS SEARCHING FOR MOM.
"BUT EVERY TIME IT PICKS UP THAT ELUSIVE SCENT, IT ENDS UP SOMEWHERE DISAPPOINTING.
"FRUSTRATING.
"ULTIMATELY INFURIATING."
OH GOD, WHY *ME?*
WHY *NOW,* FOR CRYIN' OUT LOUD...?
I'M GLAD YOU ASKED ME THAT.

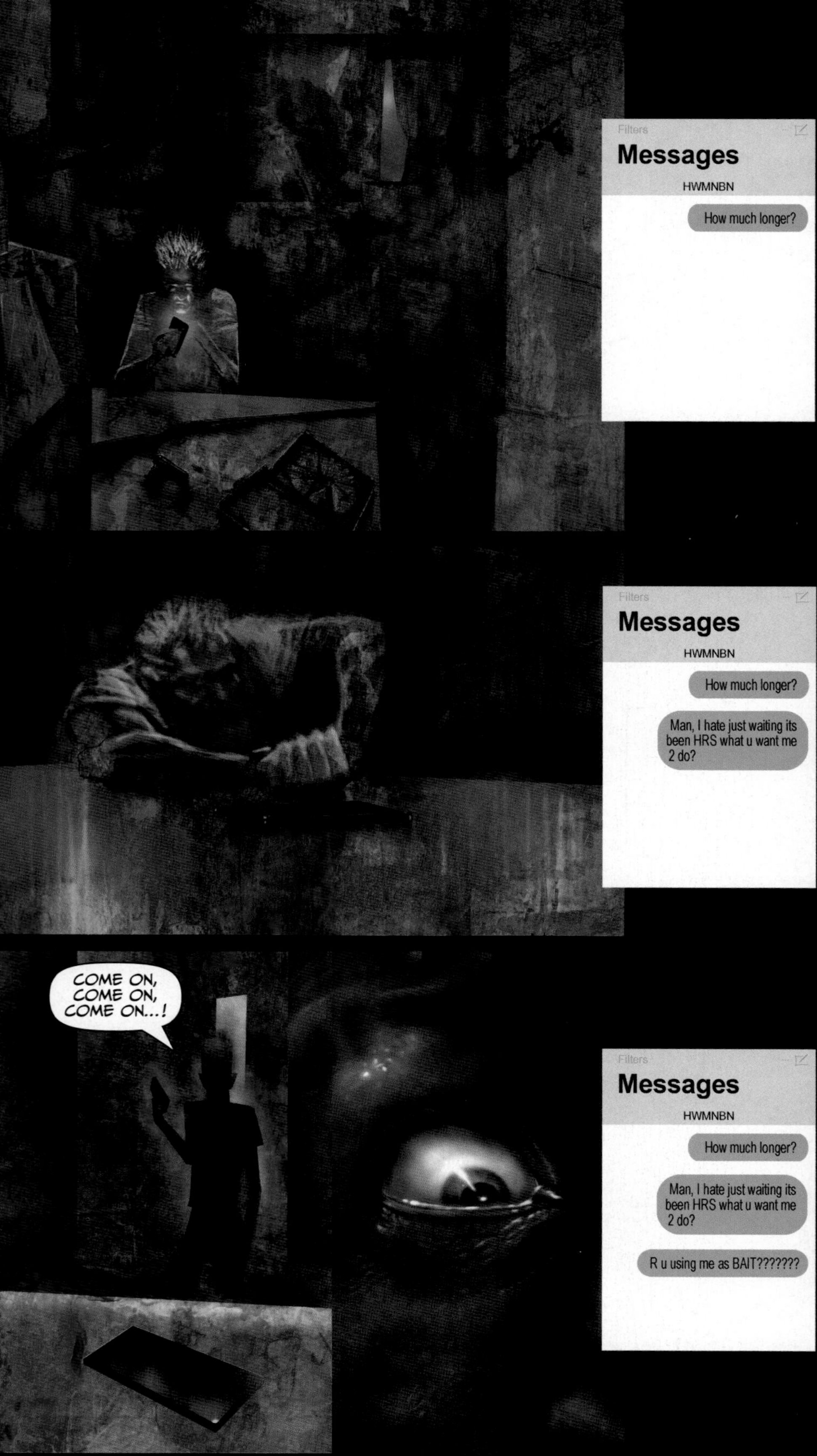
Filters
Messages
HWMNBN
How much longer?
Filters
Messages
HWMNBN
How much longer?
Man, I hate just waiting its been HRS what u want me 2 do?
COME ON, COME ON, COME ON...!
Filters
Messages
HWMNBN
How much longer?
Man, I hate just waiting its been HRS what u want me 2 do?
R u using me as BAIT???????

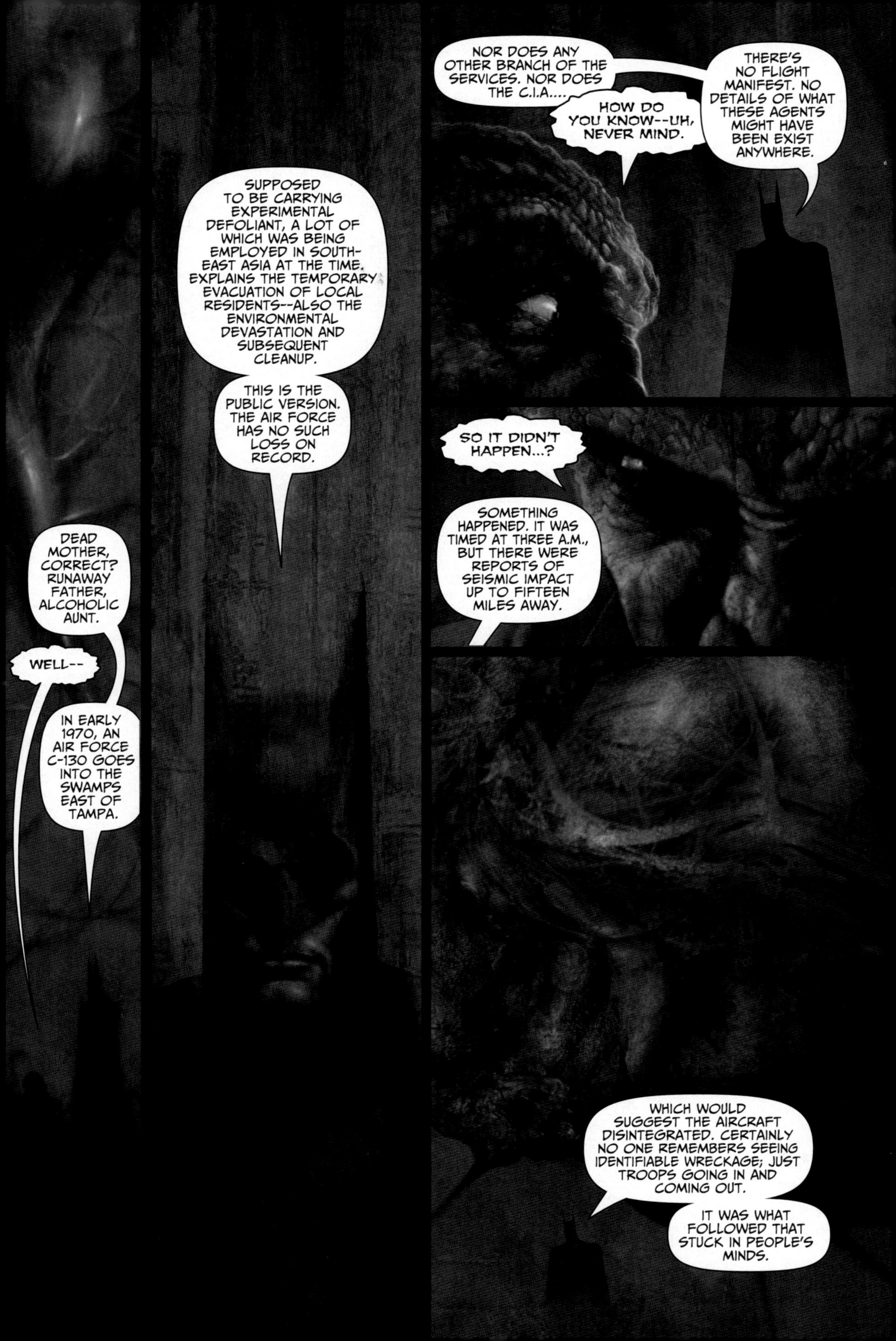
DEAD MOTHER, CORRECT? RUNAWAY FATHER, ALCOHOLIC AUNT.
WELL--
IN EARLY 1970, AN AIR FORCE C-130 GOES INTO THE SWAMPS EAST OF TAMPA.
SUPPOSED TO BE CARRYING EXPERIMENTAL DEFOLIANT, A LOT OF WHICH WAS BEING EMPLOYED IN SOUTH-EAST ASIA AT THE TIME. EXPLAINS THE TEMPORARY EVACUATION OF LOCAL RESIDENTS--ALSO THE ENVIRONMENTAL DEVASTATION AND SUBSEQUENT CLEANUP.
THIS IS THE PUBLIC VERSION. THE AIR FORCE HAS NO SUCH LOSS ON RECORD.
NOR DOES ANY OTHER BRANCH OF THE SERVICES. NOR DOES THE C.I.A....
HOW DO YOU KNOW--UH, NEVER MIND.
THERE'S NO FLIGHT MANIFEST. NO DETAILS OF WHAT THESE AGENTS MIGHT HAVE BEEN EXIST ANYWHERE.
SO IT DIDN'T HAPPEN...?
SOMETHING HAPPENED. IT WAS TIMED AT THREE A.M., BUT THERE WERE REPORTS OF SEISMIC IMPACT UP TO FIFTEEN MILES AWAY.
WHICH WOULD SUGGEST THE AIRCRAFT DISINTEGRATED. CERTAINLY NO ONE REMEMBERS SEEING IDENTIFIABLE WRECKAGE; JUST TROOPS GOING IN AND COMING OUT.
IT WAS WHAT FOLLOWED THAT STUCK IN PEOPLE'S MINDS.

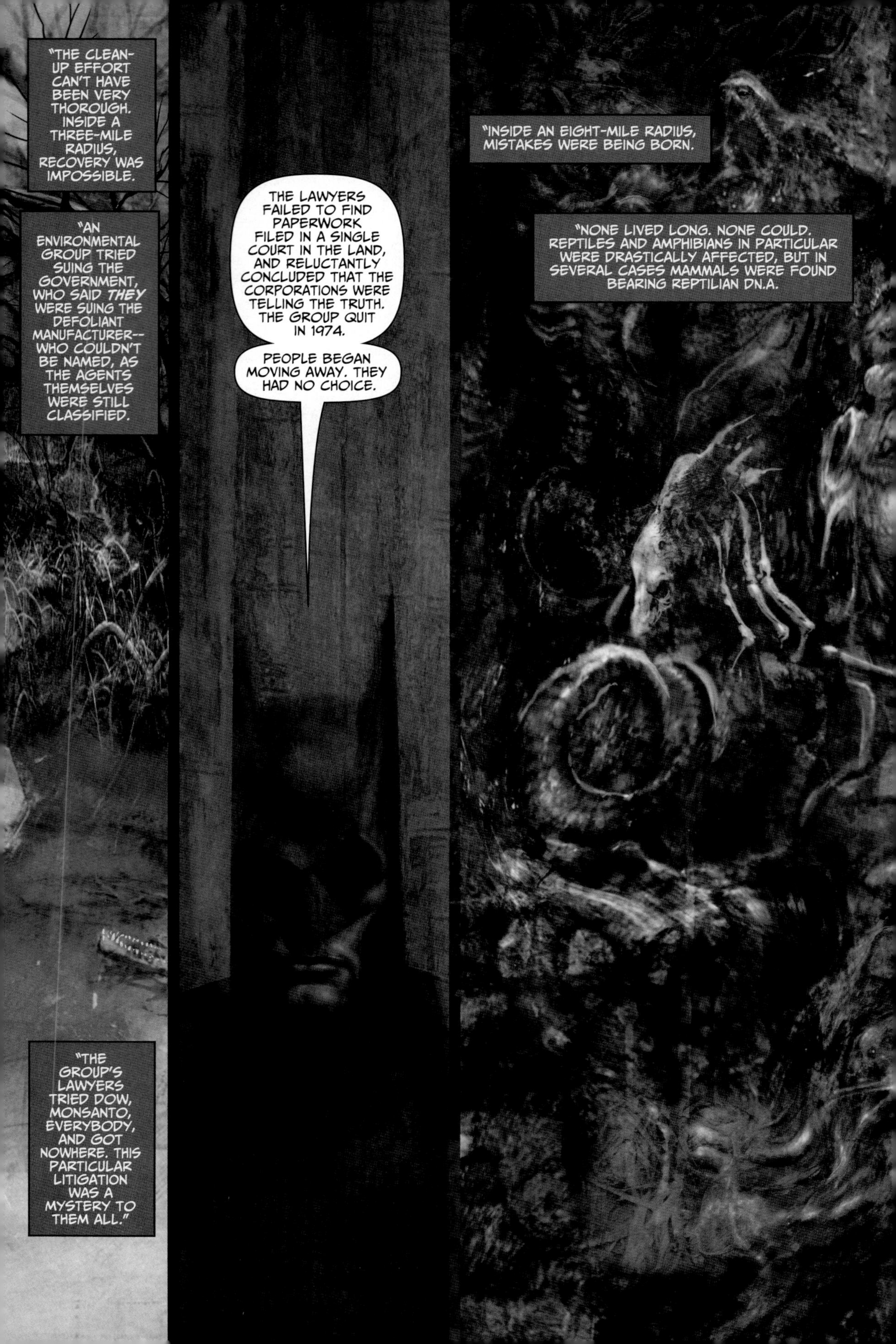
"THE CLEAN-UP EFFORT CAN'T HAVE BEEN VERY THOROUGH. INSIDE A THREE-MILE RADIUS, RECOVERY WAS IMPOSSIBLE.
"AN ENVIRONMENTAL GROUP TRIED SUING THE GOVERNMENT, WHO SAID *THEY* WERE SUING THE DEFOLIANT MANUFACTURER--WHO COULDN'T BE NAMED, AS THE AGENTS THEMSELVES WERE STILL CLASSIFIED.
"THE GROUP'S LAWYERS TRIED DOW, MONSANTO, EVERYBODY, AND GOT NOWHERE. THIS PARTICULAR LITIGATION WAS A MYSTERY TO THEM ALL."
THE LAWYERS FAILED TO FIND PAPERWORK FILED IN A SINGLE COURT IN THE LAND, AND RELUCTANTLY CONCLUDED THAT THE CORPORATIONS WERE TELLING THE TRUTH. THE GROUP QUIT IN 1974.
PEOPLE BEGAN MOVING AWAY. THEY HAD NO CHOICE.
"INSIDE AN EIGHT-MILE RADIUS, MISTAKES WERE BEING BORN.
"NONE LIVED LONG. NONE COULD. REPTILES AND AMPHIBIANS IN PARTICULAR WERE DRASTICALLY AFFECTED, BUT IN SEVERAL CASES MAMMALS WERE FOUND BEARING REPTILIAN DN.A.

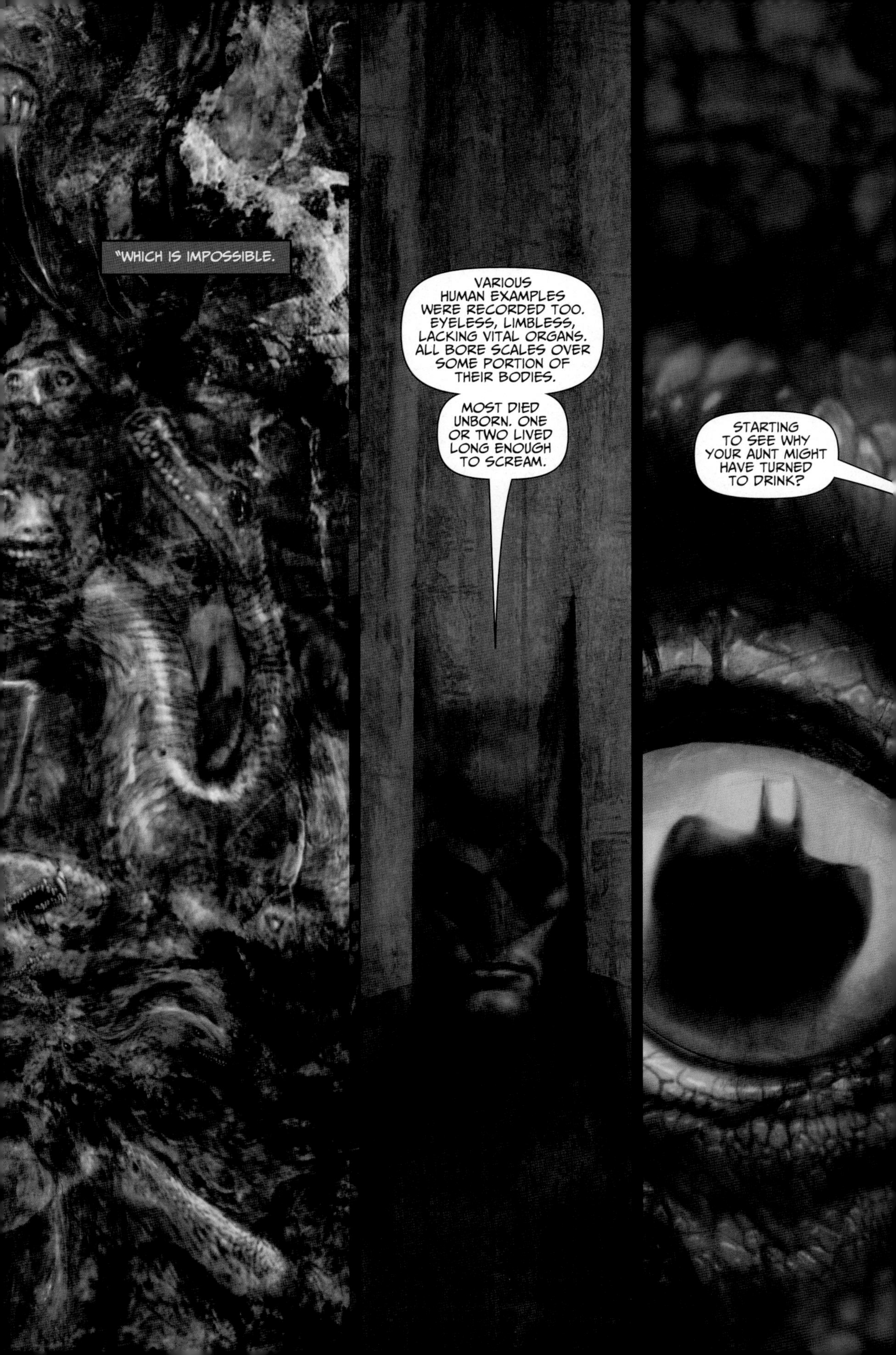
"WHICH IS IMPOSSIBLE.
VARIOUS HUMAN EXAMPLES WERE RECORDED TOO. EYELESS, LIMBLESS, LACKING VITAL ORGANS. ALL BORE SCALES OVER SOME PORTION OF THEIR BODIES.
MOST DIED UNBORN. ONE OR TWO LIVED LONG ENOUGH TO SCREAM.
STARTING TO SEE WHY YOUR AUNT MIGHT HAVE TURNED TO DRINK?

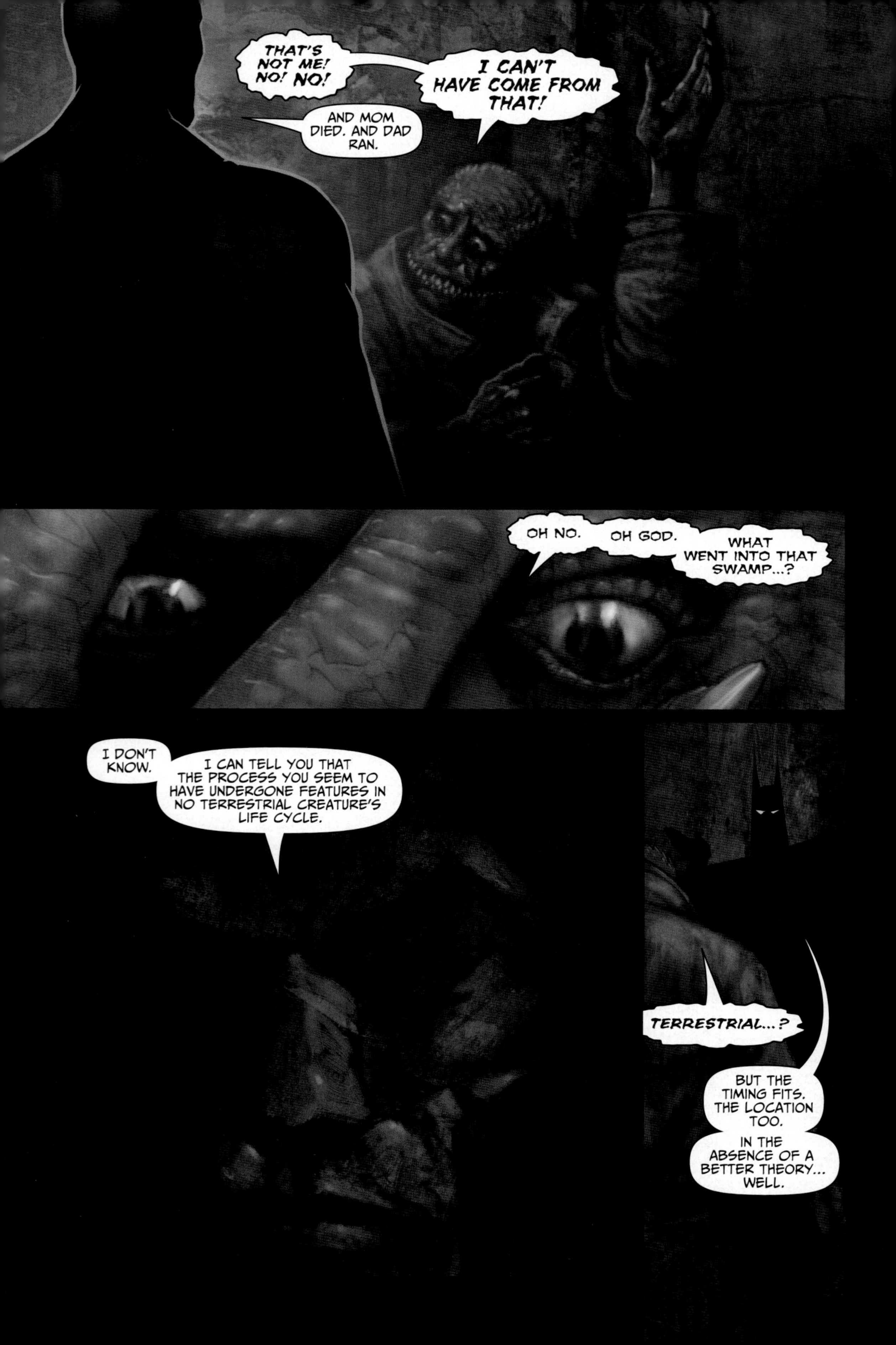
THAT'S NOT ME! NO! NO!
I CAN'T HAVE COME FROM THAT!
AND MOM DIED. AND DAD RAN.
OH NO.
OH GOD.
WHAT WENT INTO THAT SWAMP...?
I DON'T KNOW.
I CAN TELL YOU THAT THE PROCESS YOU SEEM TO HAVE UNDERGONE FEATURES IN NO TERRESTRIAL CREATURE'S LIFE CYCLE.
TERRESTRIAL...?
BUT THE TIMING FITS. THE LOCATION TOO.
IN THE ABSENCE OF A BETTER THEORY... WELL.

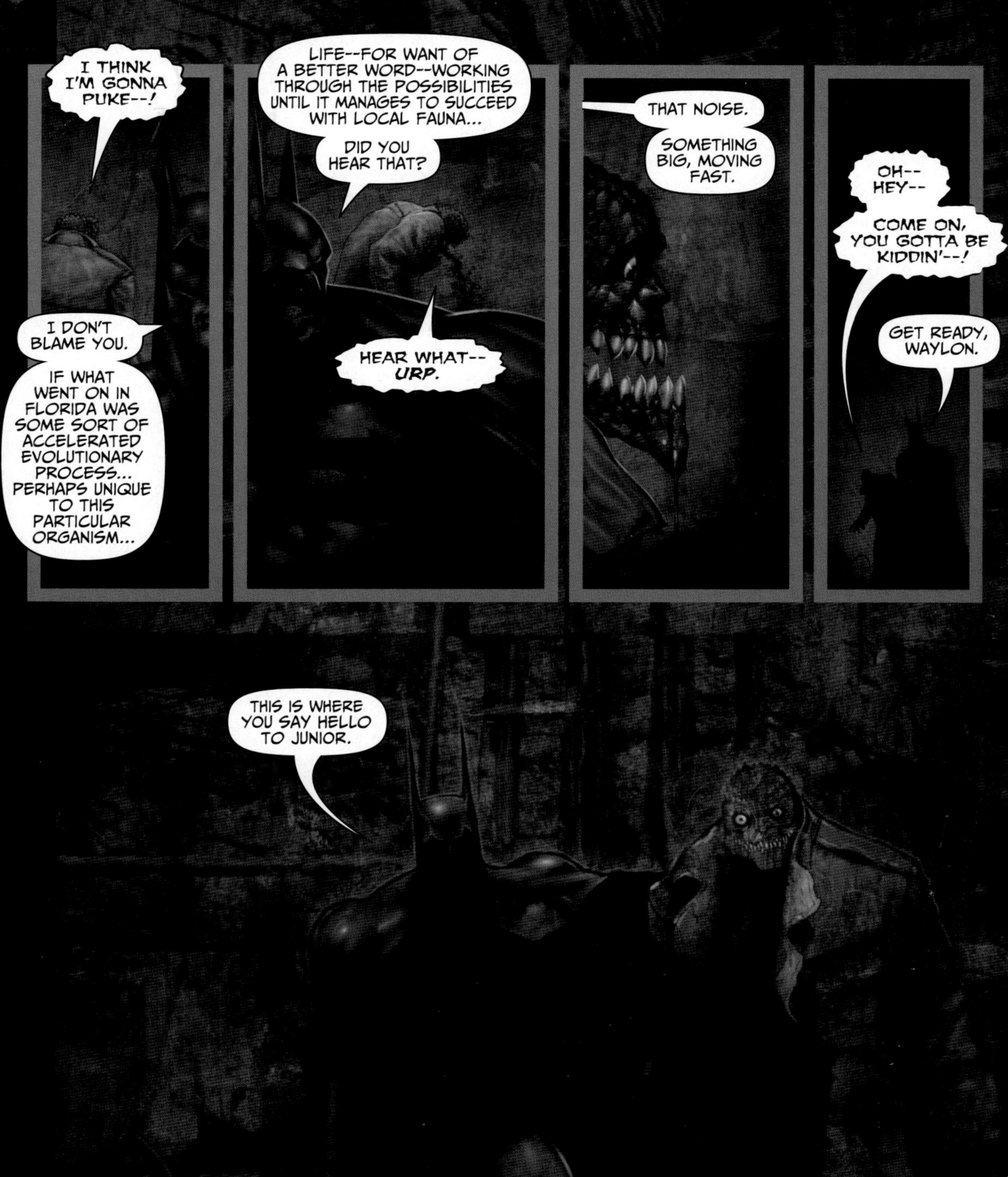
I THINK I'M GONNA PUKE--!
I DON'T BLAME YOU.
IF WHAT WENT ON IN FLORIDA WAS SOME SORT OF ACCELERATED EVOLUTIONARY PROCESS... PERHAPS UNIQUE TO THIS PARTICULAR ORGANISM...
LIFE--FOR WANT OF A BETTER WORD--WORKING THROUGH THE POSSIBILITIES UNTIL IT MANAGES TO SUCCEED WITH LOCAL FAUNA...
DID YOU HEAR THAT?
HEAR WHAT-- *URP.*
THAT NOISE.
SOMETHING BIG, MOVING FAST.
OH-- HEY--
COME ON, YOU GOTTA BE KIDDIN'--!
GET READY, WAYLON.
THIS IS WHERE YOU SAY HELLO TO JUNIOR.

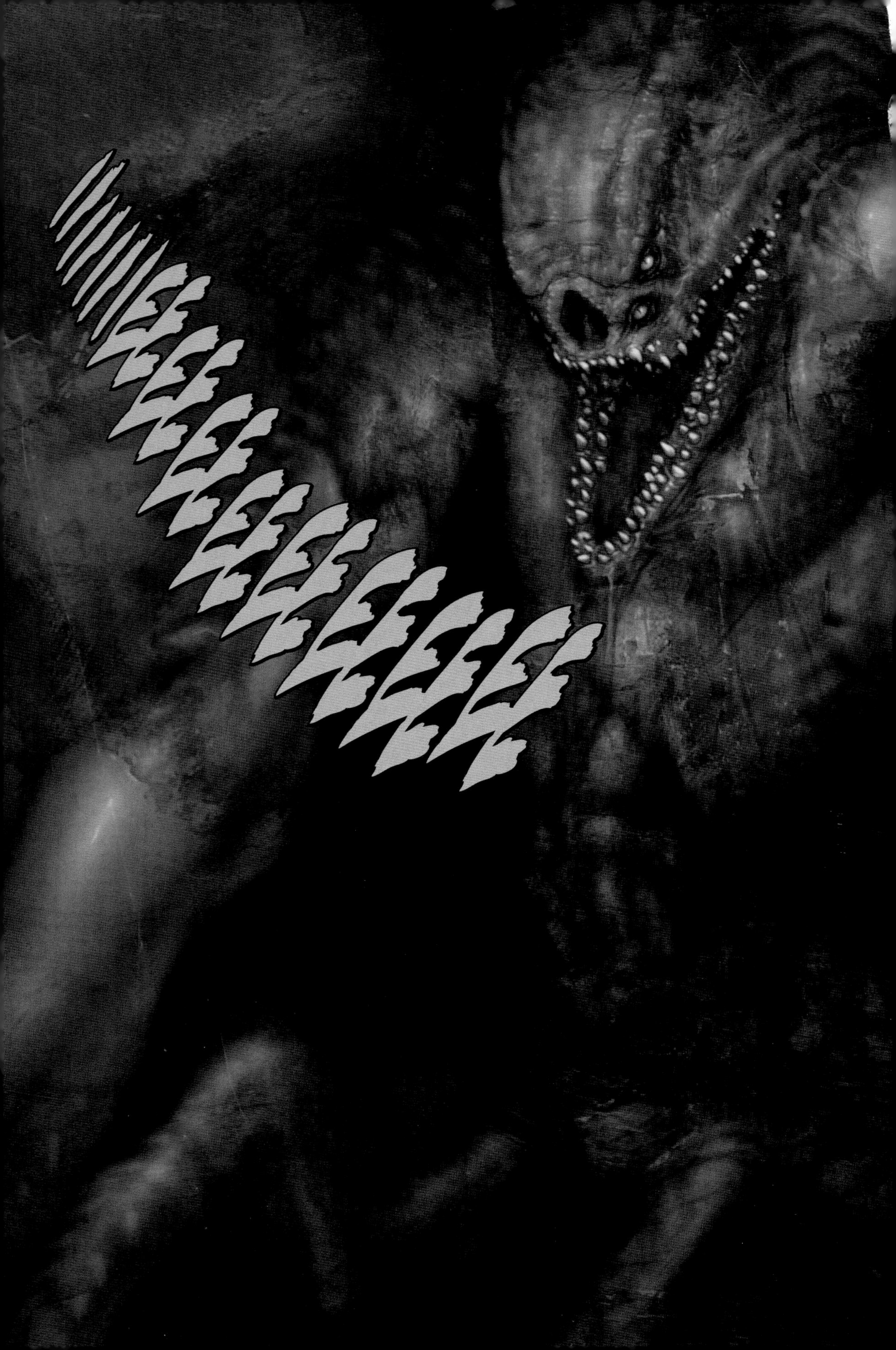
IIIIIIEEEEEEEEEEE

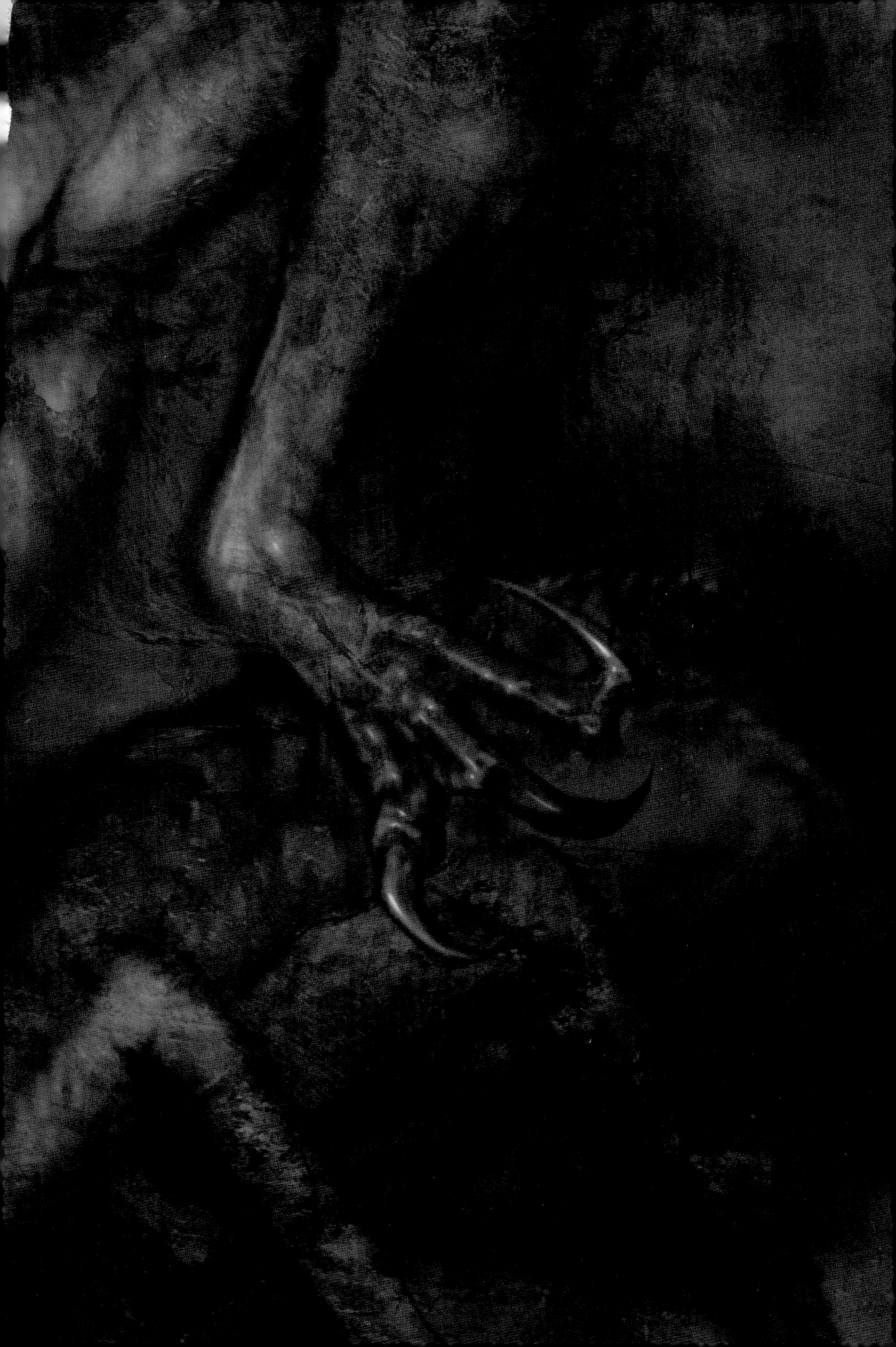

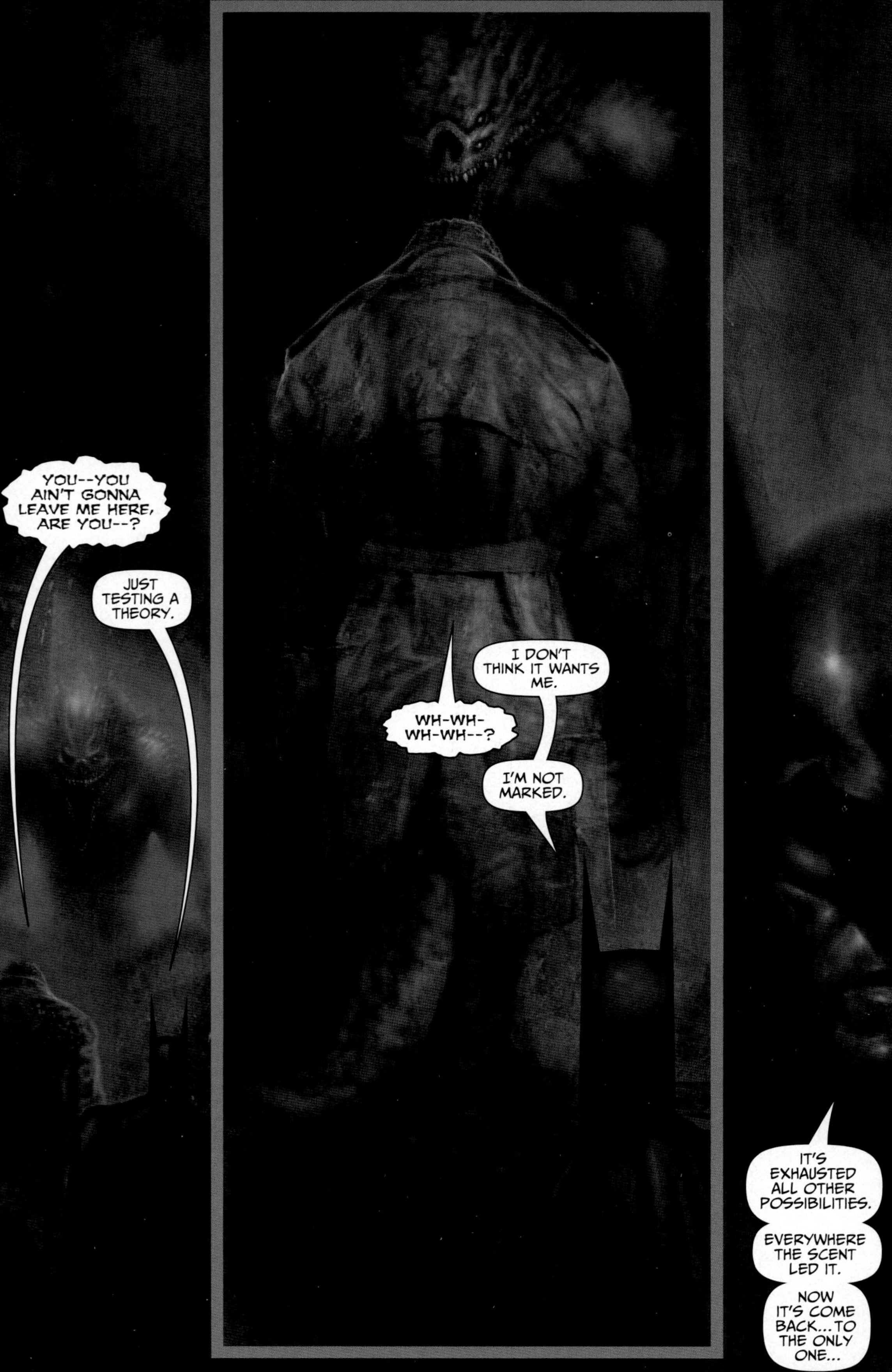
YOU--YOU AIN'T GONNA LEAVE ME HERE, ARE YOU--?
JUST TESTING A THEORY.
WH-WH-WH-WH--?
I DON'T THINK IT WANTS ME.
I'M NOT MARKED.
IT'S EXHAUSTED ALL OTHER POSSIBILITIES.
EVERYWHERE THE SCENT LED IT.
NOW IT'S COME BACK...TO THE ONLY ONE...

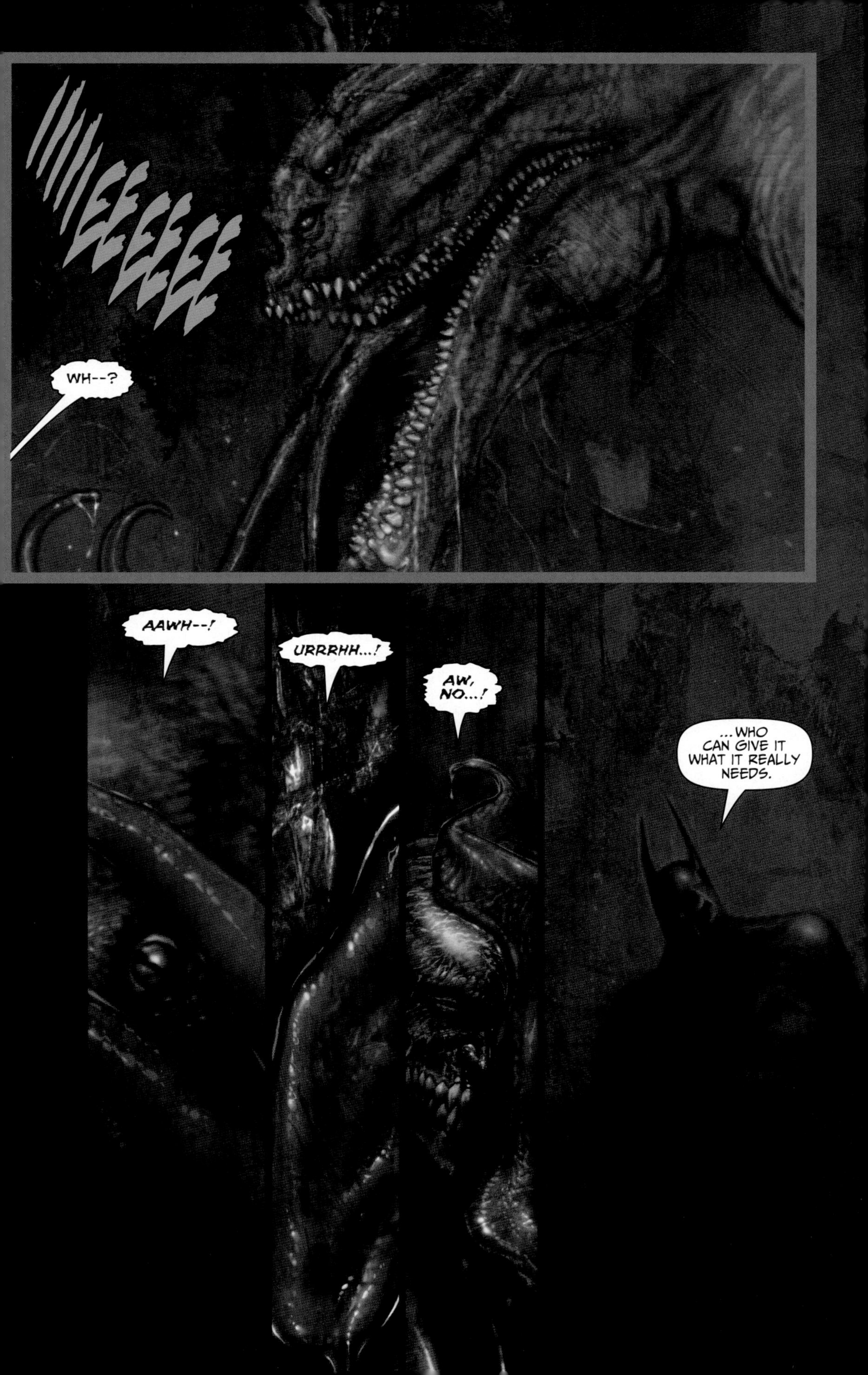
IIIIIEEEEEEE
WH--?
AAWH--!
URRRHH...!
AW, NO...!
...WHO CAN GIVE IT WHAT IT REALLY NEEDS.

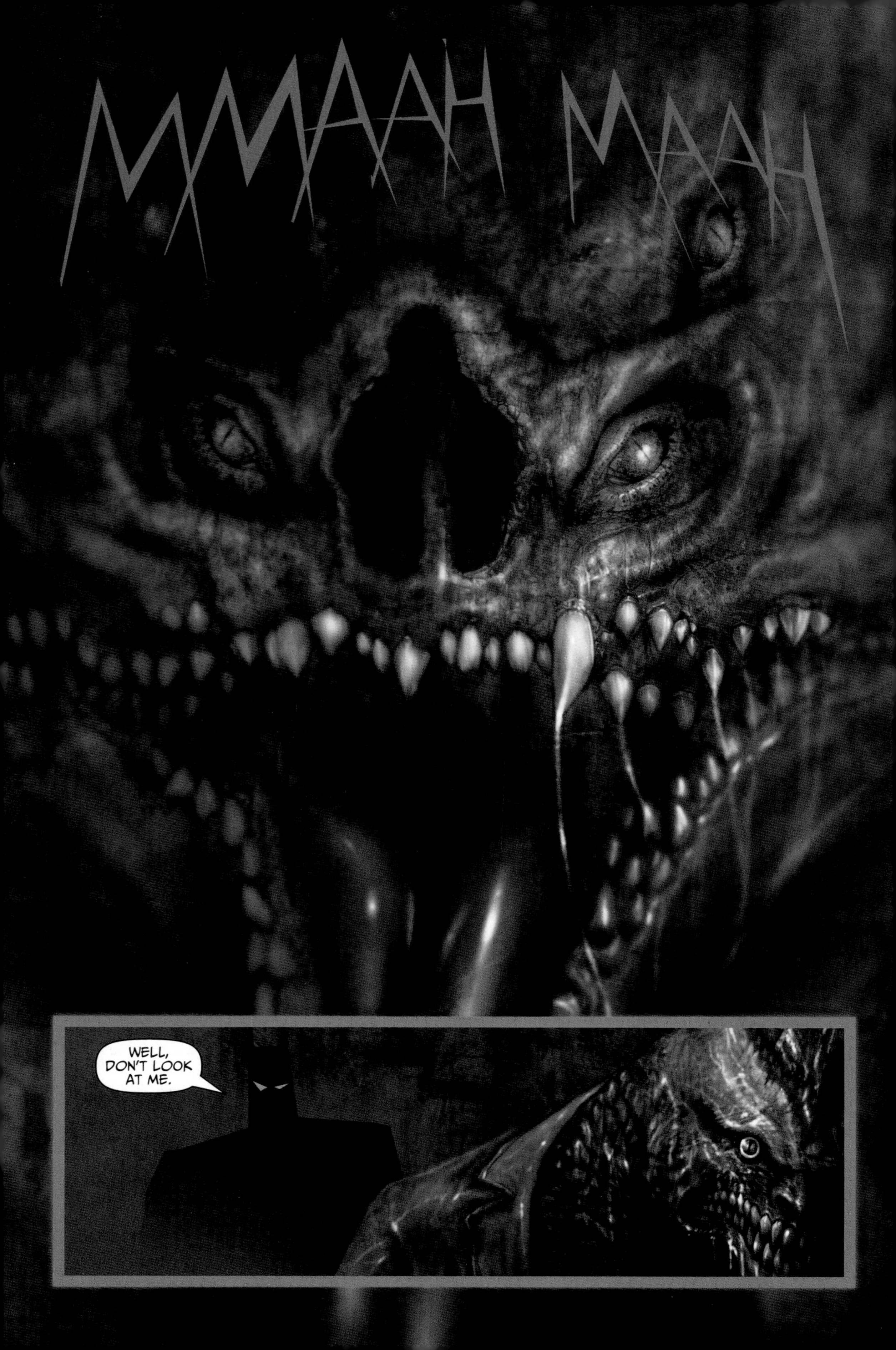
MMAAH MAAH
WELL, DON'T LOOK AT ME.

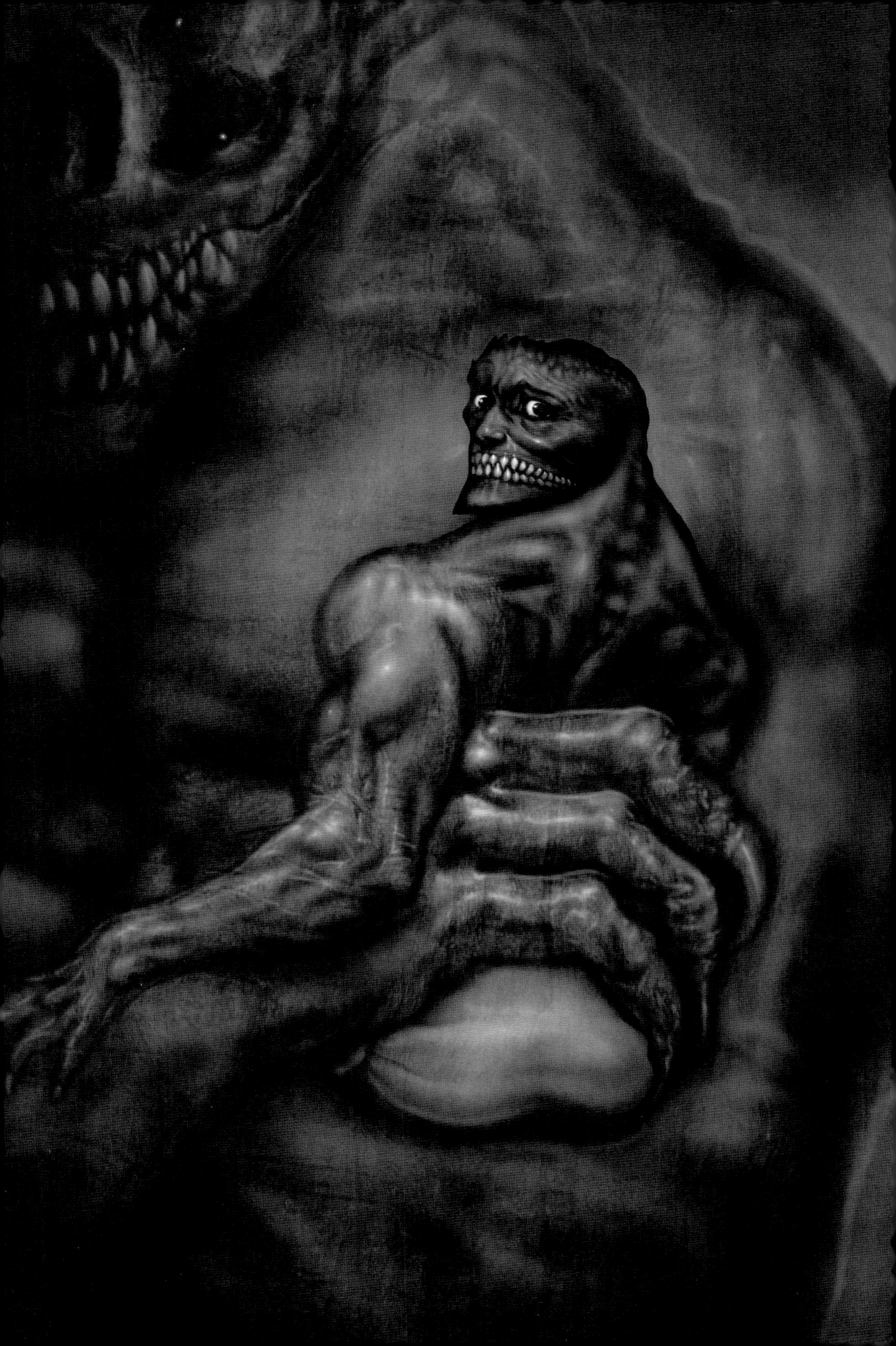

Batman: Reptilian #5 1:25 variant cover by FRANCESCO FRANCAVILLA

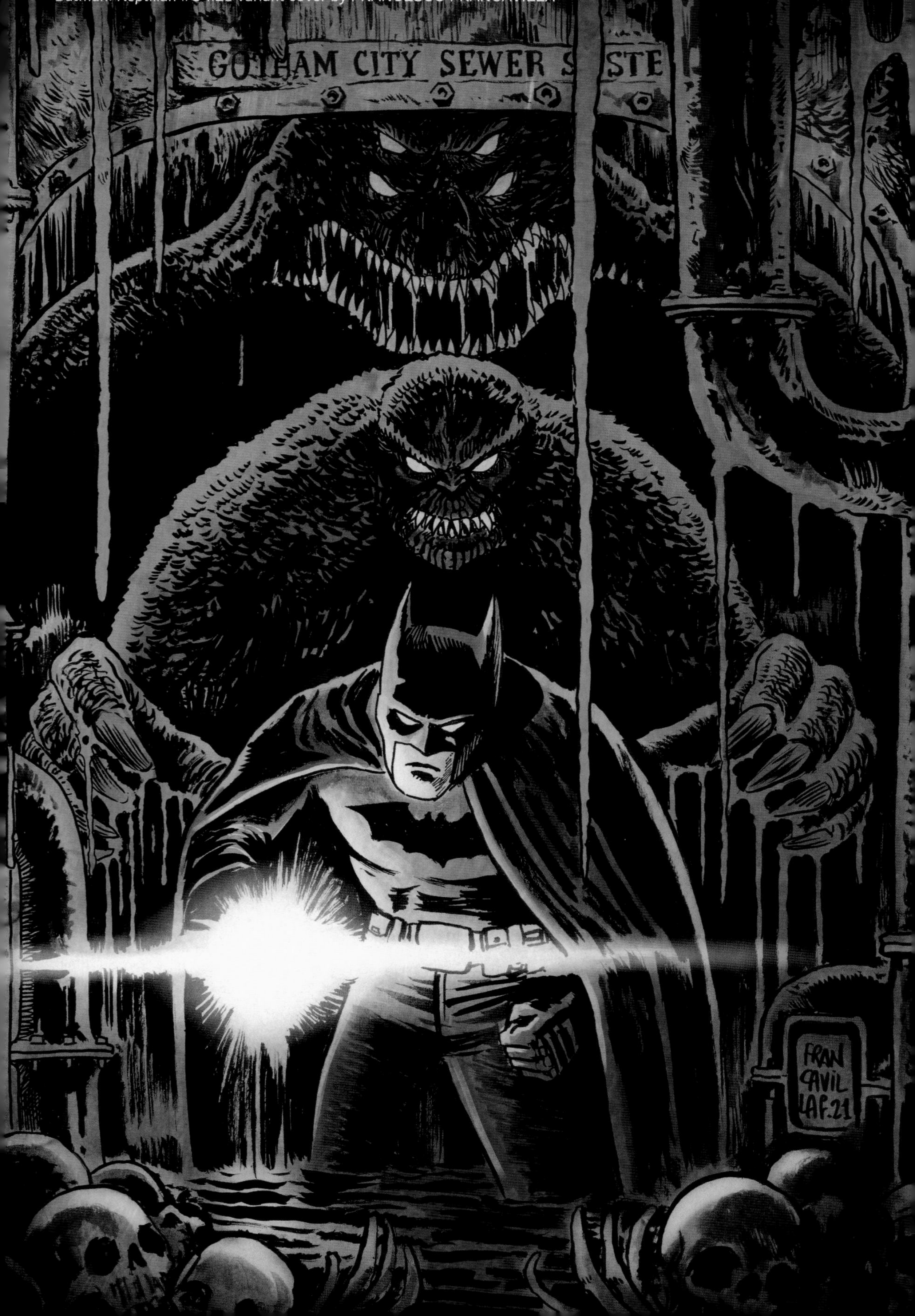
GOTHAM CITY SEWER S STE
FRAN CAVIL LAF.21

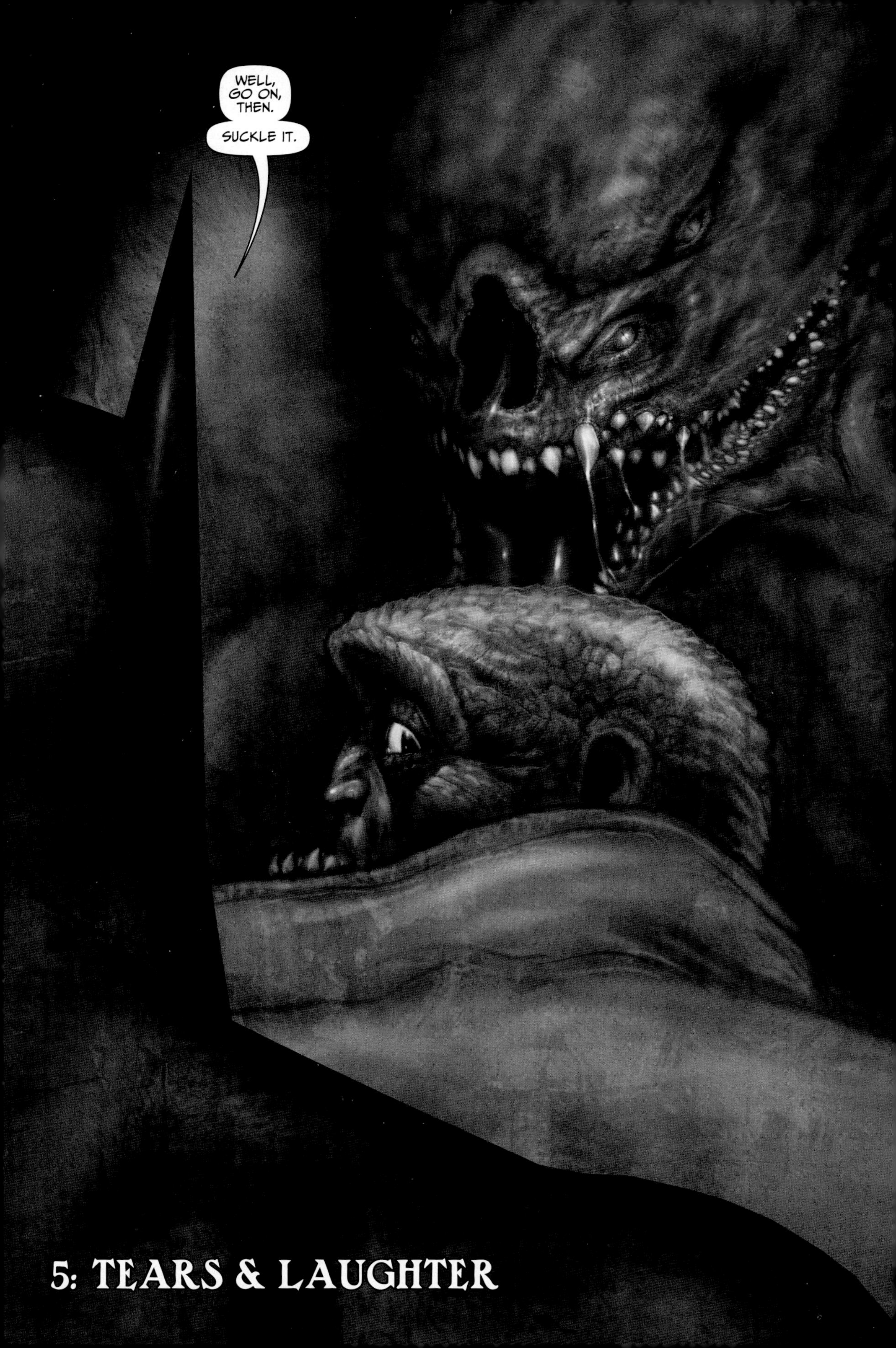
WELL, GO ON, THEN.
SUCKLE IT.
5: TEARS & LAUGHTER

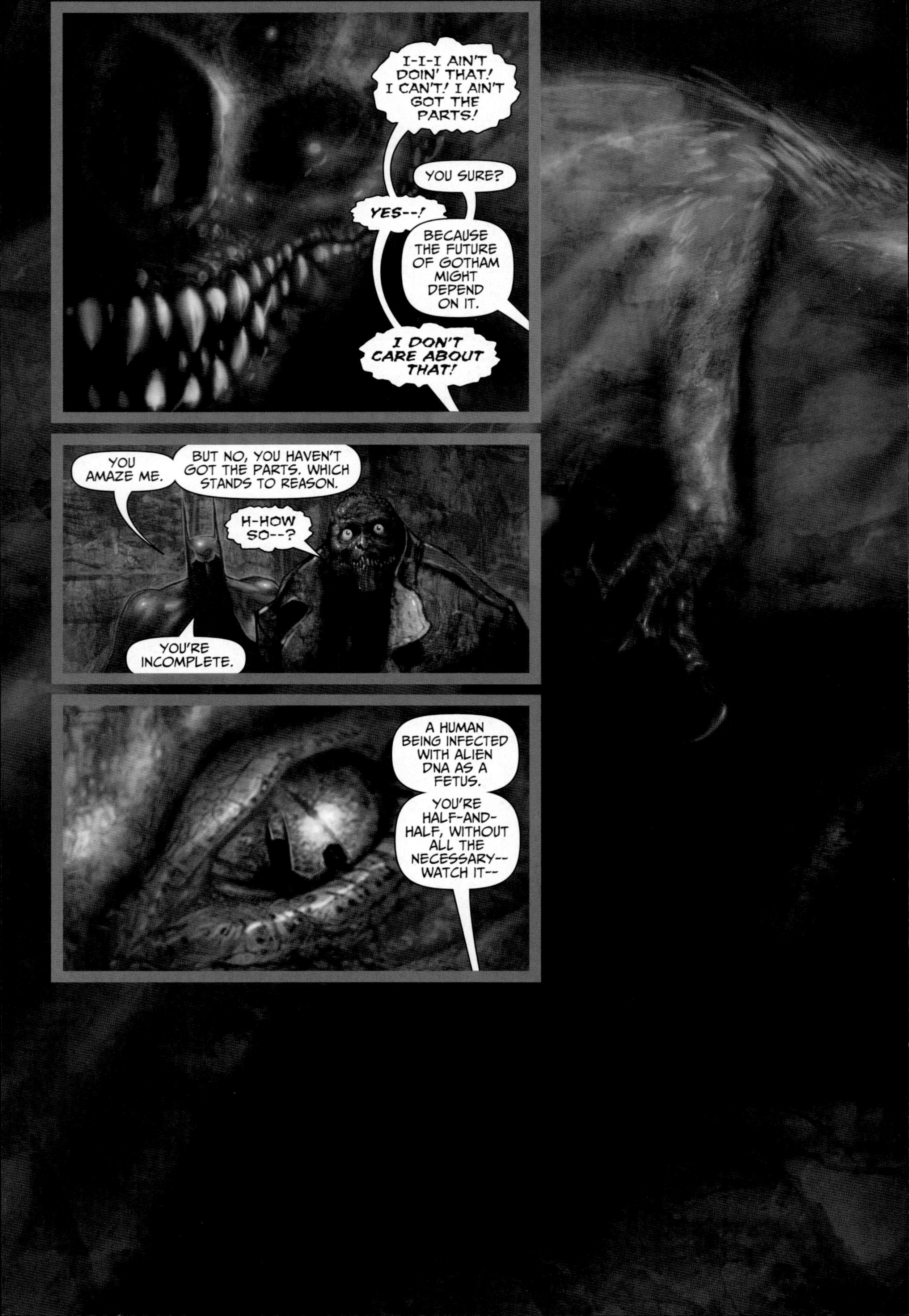
I-I-I AIN'T DOIN' THAT! I CAN'T! I AIN'T GOT THE PARTS!
YOU SURE?
YES--!
BECAUSE THE FUTURE OF GOTHAM MIGHT DEPEND ON IT.
I DON'T CARE ABOUT THAT!
YOU AMAZE ME.
BUT NO, YOU HAVEN'T GOT THE PARTS. WHICH STANDS TO REASON.
H-HOW SO--?
YOU'RE INCOMPLETE.
A HUMAN BEING INFECTED WITH ALIEN DNA AS A FETUS.
YOU'RE HALF-AND-HALF, WITHOUT ALL THE NECESSARY-- WATCH IT--

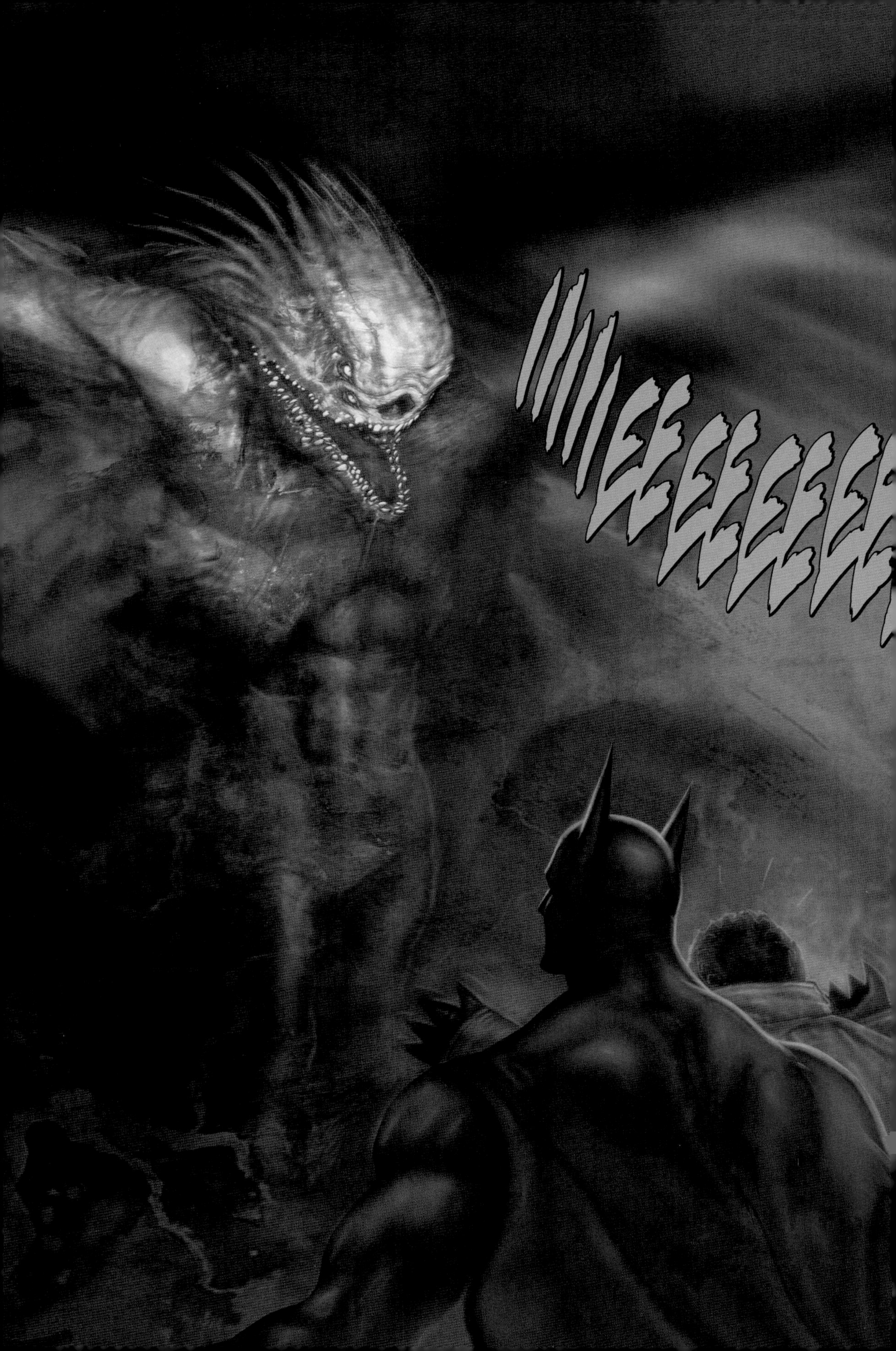
IIIIIEEEEEEE

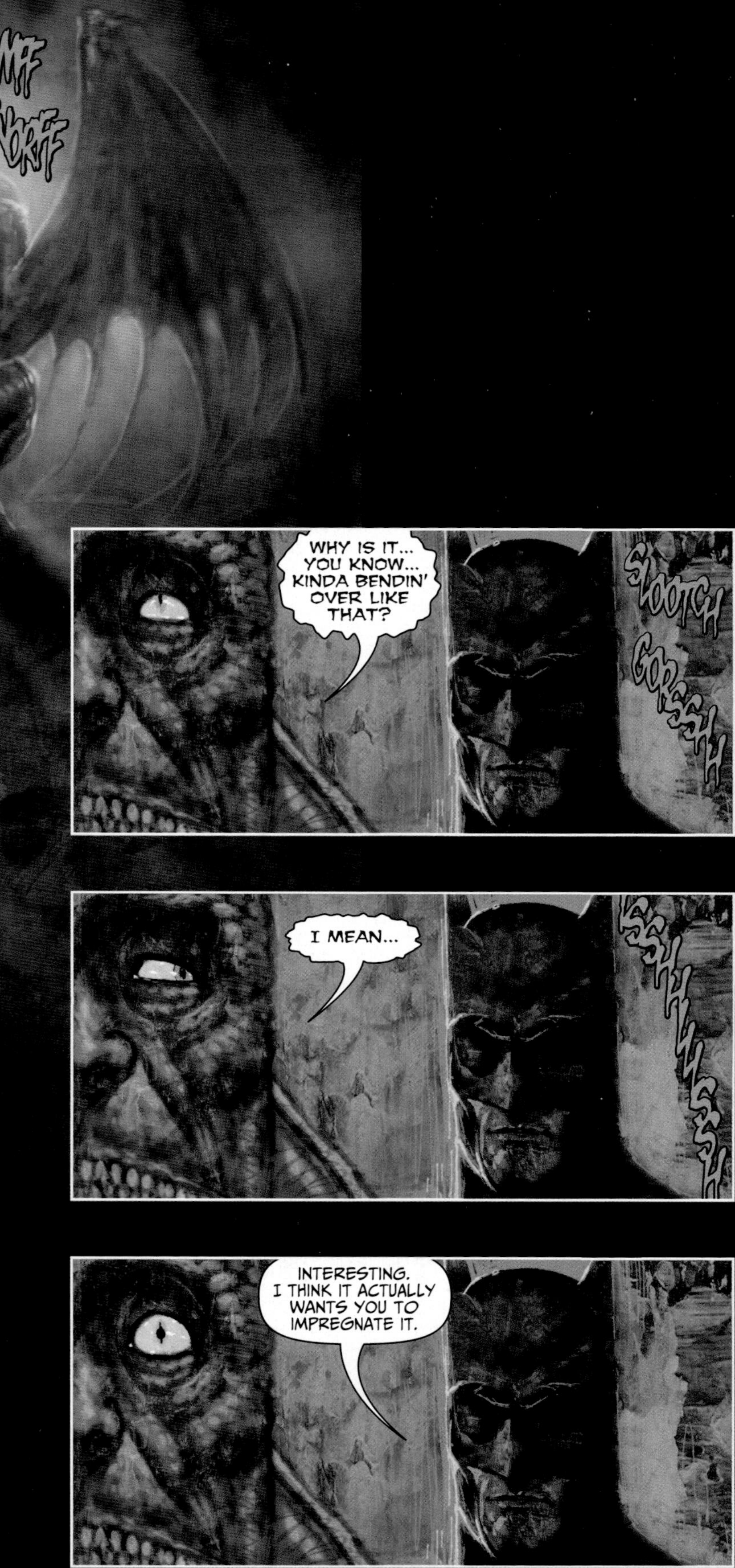
MF
ORFF
WHY IS IT... YOU KNOW... KINDA BENDIN' OVER LIKE THAT?
SLOOTCH
GORSSHH
I MEAN...
SSHHHHSSH
INTERESTING. I THINK IT ACTUALLY WANTS YOU TO IMPREGNATE IT.

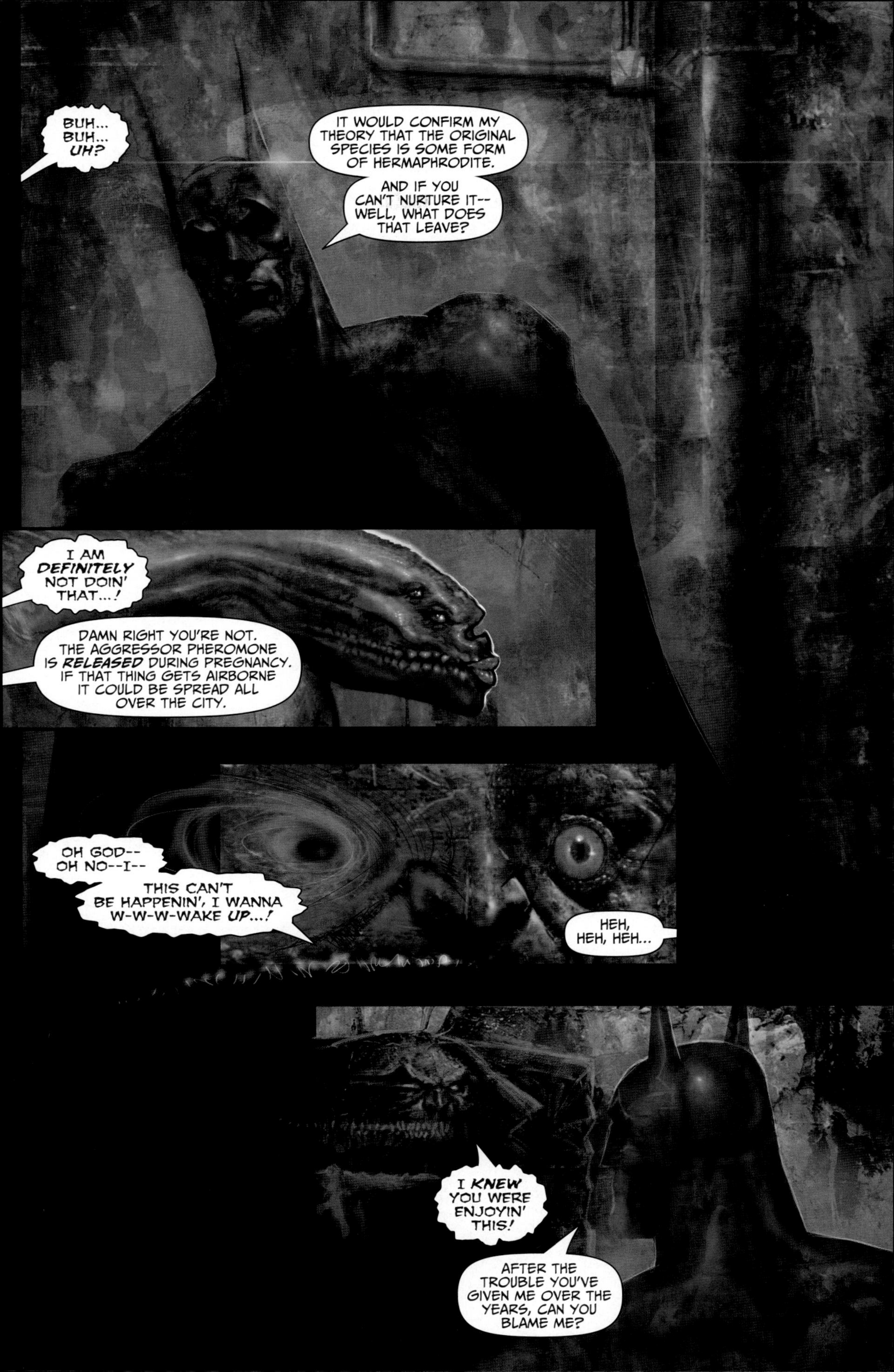
BUH... BUH... UH?
IT WOULD CONFIRM MY THEORY THAT THE ORIGINAL SPECIES IS SOME FORM OF HERMAPHRODITE.
AND IF YOU CAN'T NURTURE IT-- WELL, WHAT DOES THAT LEAVE?
I AM DEFINITELY NOT DOIN' THAT...!
DAMN RIGHT YOU'RE NOT. THE AGGRESSOR PHEROMONE IS RELEASED DURING PREGNANCY. IF THAT THING GETS AIRBORNE IT COULD BE SPREAD ALL OVER THE CITY.
OH GOD-- OH NO--I--
THIS CAN'T BE HAPPENIN', I WANNA W-W-W-WAKE UP...!
HEH, HEH, HEH...
I KNEW YOU WERE ENJOYIN' THIS!
AFTER THE TROUBLE YOU'VE GIVEN ME OVER THE YEARS, CAN YOU BLAME ME?

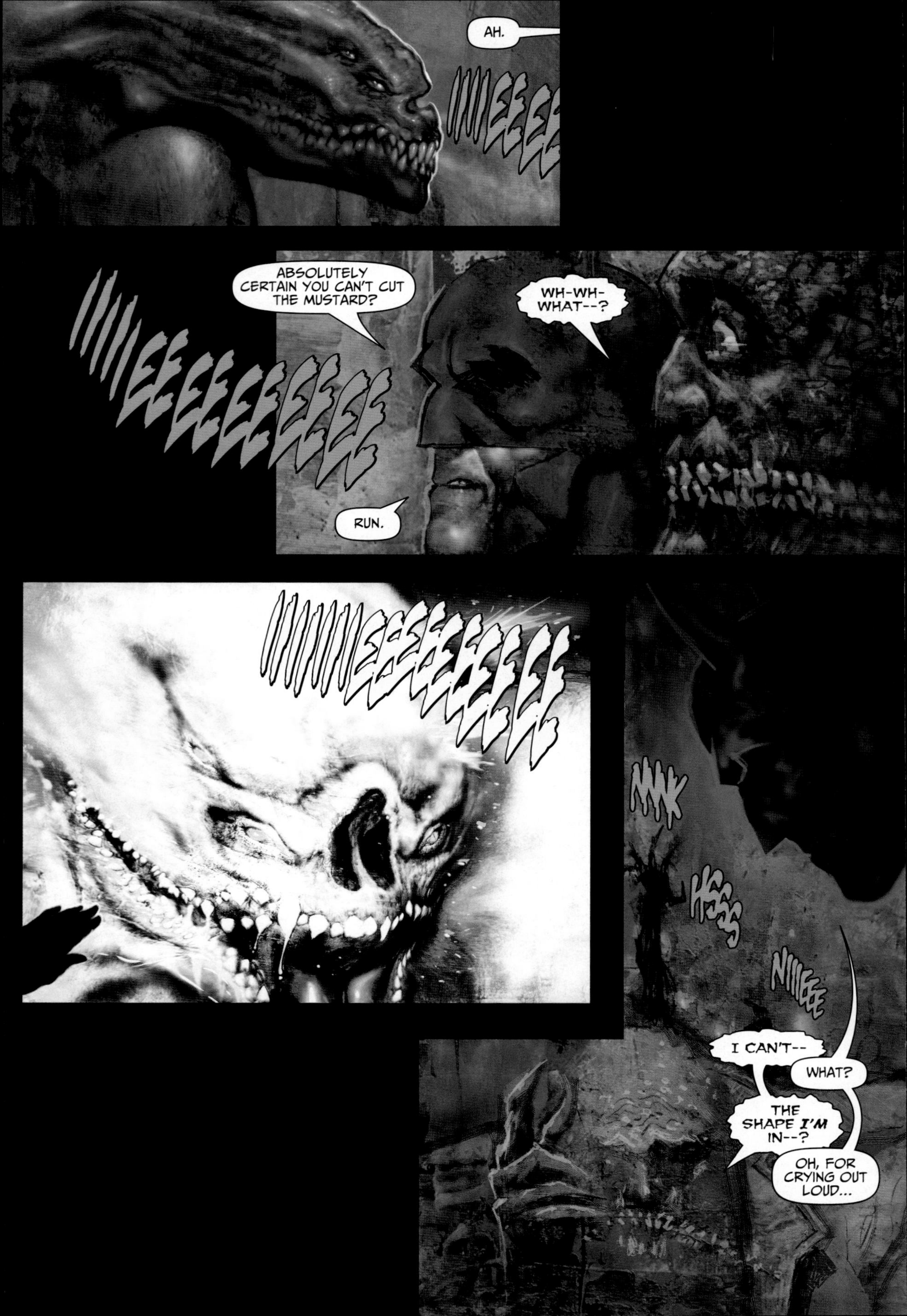
AH.
IIIIIEEEEE
IIIIIIIEEEEEEEEEEEE
ABSOLUTELY CERTAIN YOU CAN'T CUT THE MUSTARD?
WH-WH-WHAT--?
RUN.
IIIIIIIIEEEEEEEEE
NNNK
HSSS
NIIIEEE
I CAN'T--
WHAT?
THE SHAPE *I'M* IN--?
OH, FOR CRYING OUT LOUD...

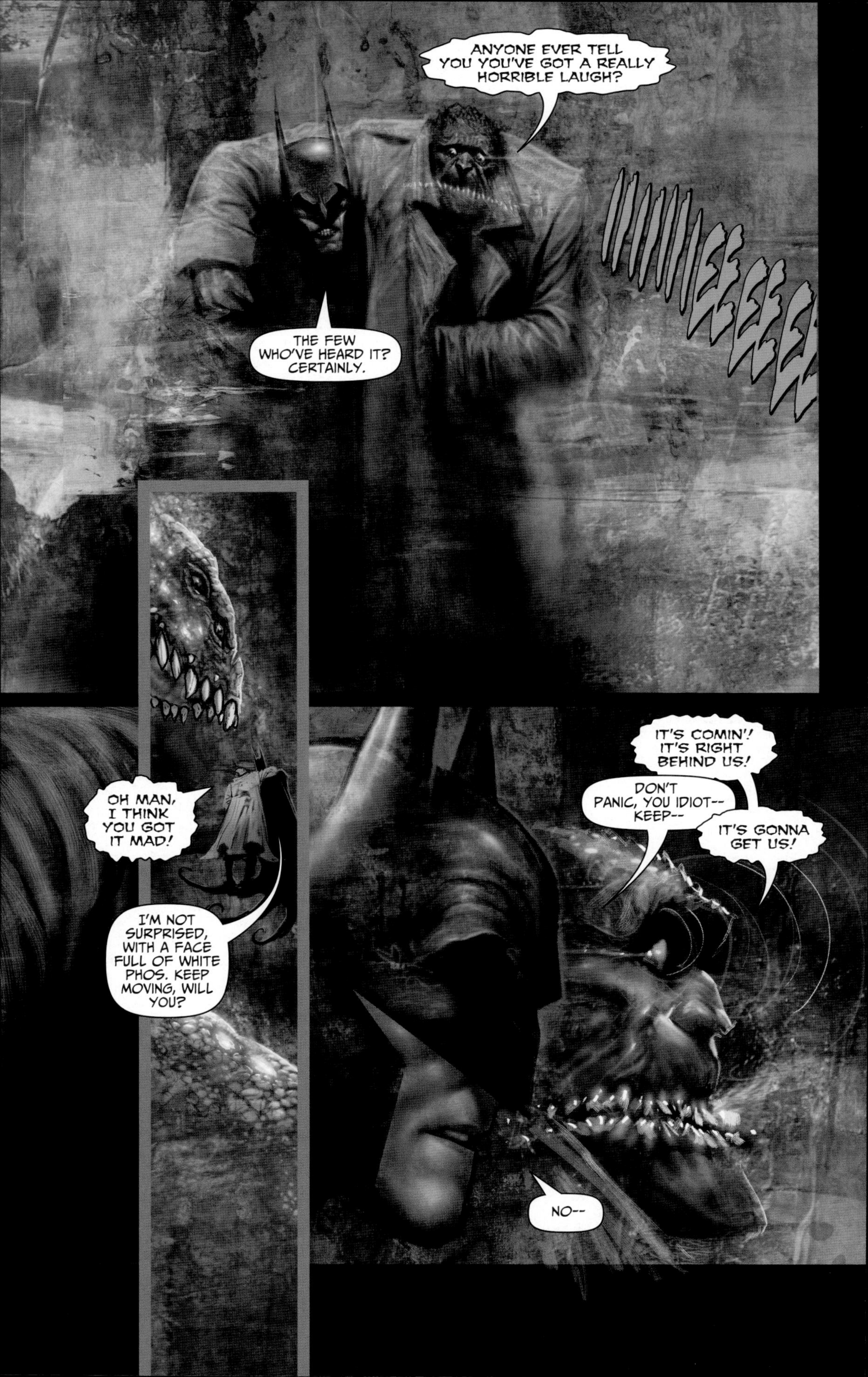
ANYONE EVER TELL YOU YOU'VE GOT A REALLY HORRIBLE LAUGH?
THE FEW WHO'VE HEARD IT? CERTAINLY.
IIIIIIIEEEEE
OH MAN, I THINK YOU GOT IT MAD!
I'M NOT SURPRISED, WITH A FACE FULL OF WHITE PHOS. KEEP MOVING, WILL YOU?
IT'S COMIN'! IT'S RIGHT BEHIND US!
DON'T PANIC, YOU IDIOT-- KEEP--
IT'S GONNA GET US!
NO--

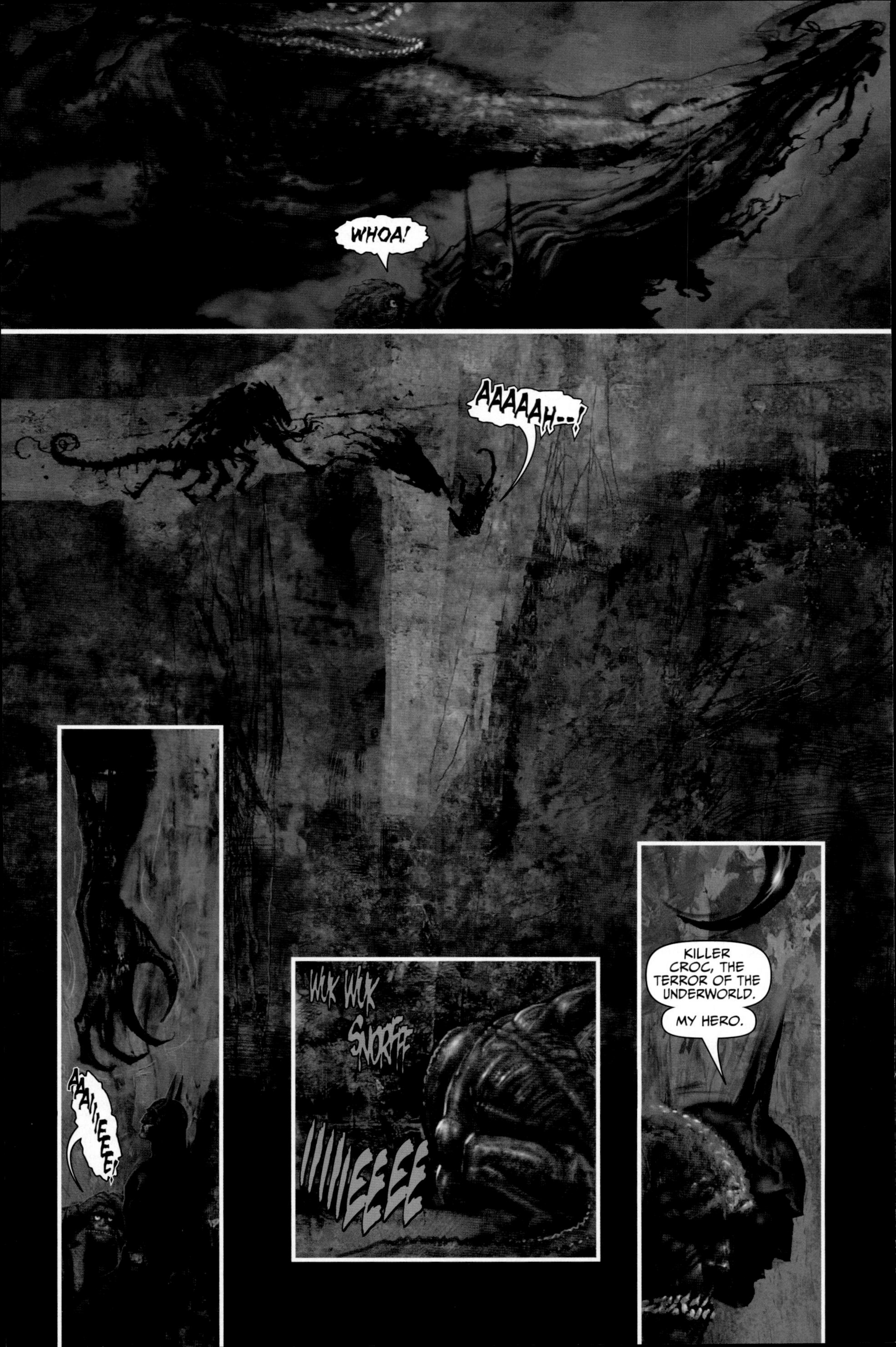
WHOA!
AAAAAH--!
AAAIIIEEEE!
WUK WUK
SNORFF
IIIIIEEEE
KILLER CROC, THE TERROR OF THE UNDERWORLD.
MY HERO.

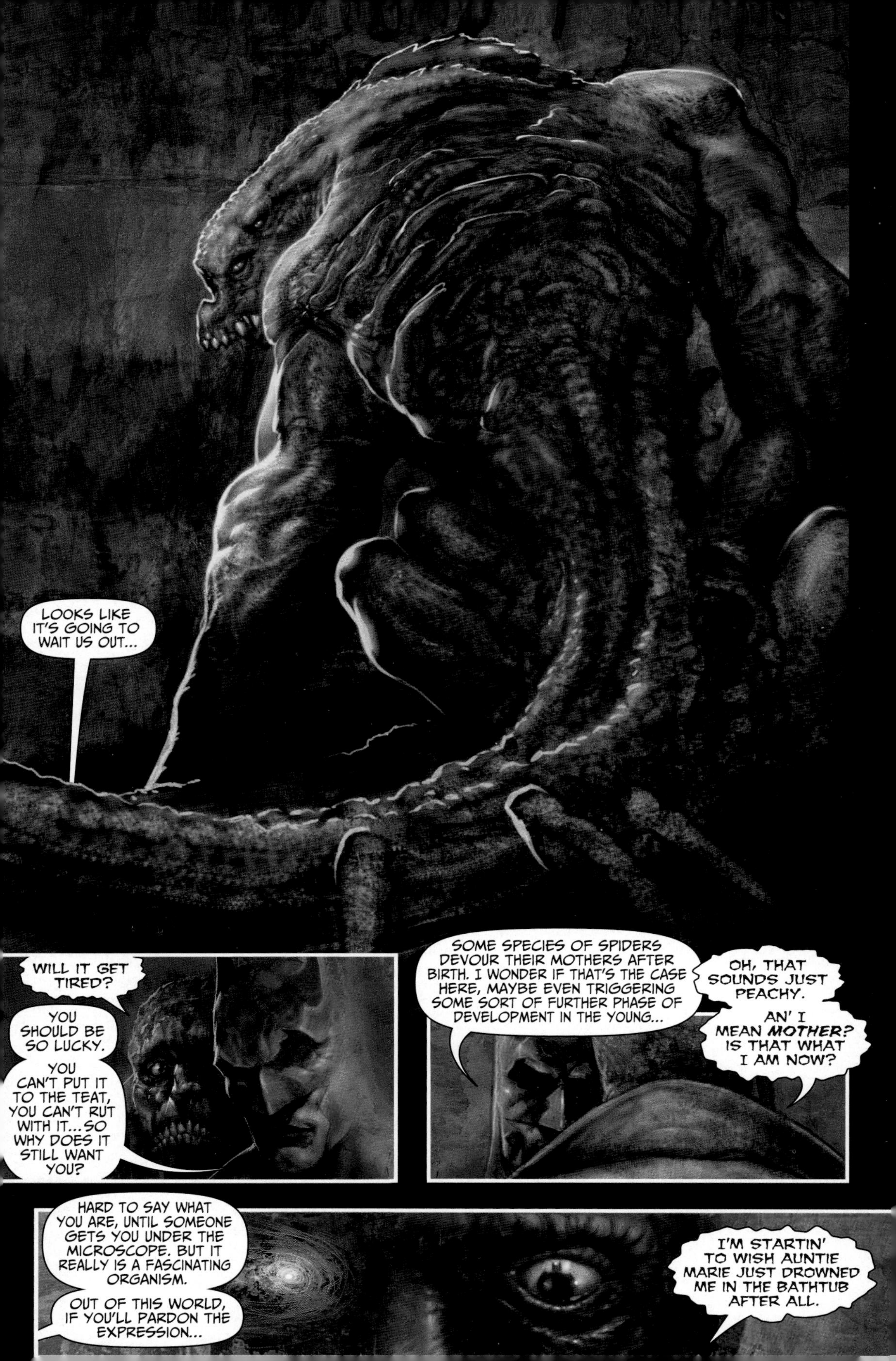

LOOKS LIKE IT'S GOING TO WAIT US OUT...
WILL IT GET TIRED?
YOU SHOULD BE SO LUCKY.
YOU CAN'T PUT IT TO THE TEAT, YOU CAN'T RUT WITH IT...SO WHY DOES IT STILL WANT YOU?
SOME SPECIES OF SPIDERS DEVOUR THEIR MOTHERS AFTER BIRTH. I WONDER IF THAT'S THE CASE HERE, MAYBE EVEN TRIGGERING SOME SORT OF FURTHER PHASE OF DEVELOPMENT IN THE YOUNG...
OH, THAT SOUNDS JUST PEACHY.
AN' I MEAN *MOTHER*? IS THAT WHAT I AM NOW?
HARD TO SAY WHAT YOU ARE, UNTIL SOMEONE GETS YOU UNDER THE MICROSCOPE. BUT IT REALLY IS A FASCINATING ORGANISM.
OUT OF THIS WORLD, IF YOU'LL PARDON THE EXPRESSION...
I'M STARTIN' TO WISH AUNTIE MARIE JUST DROWNED ME IN THE BATHTUB AFTER ALL.

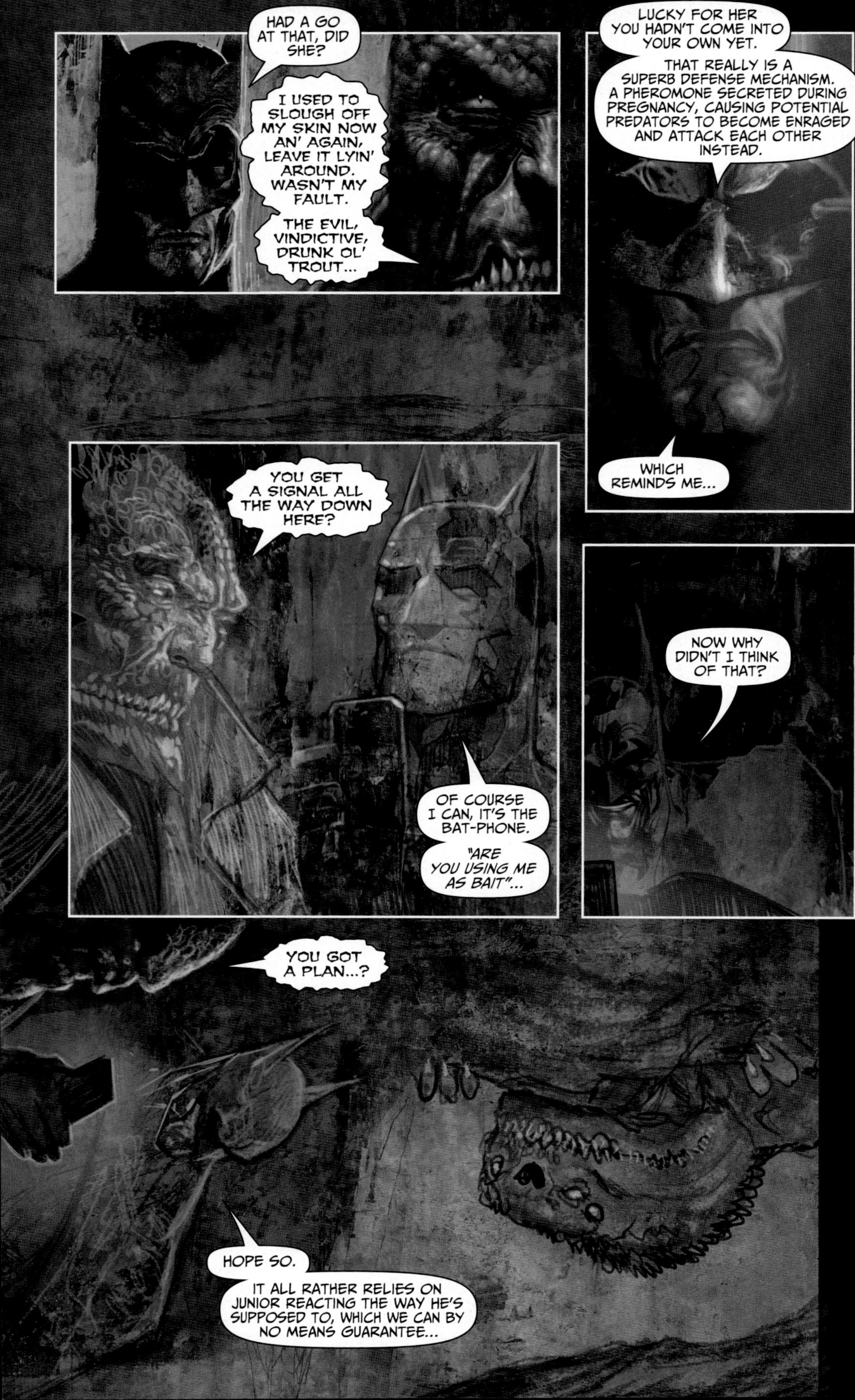

HAD A GO AT THAT, DID SHE?
I USED TO SLOUGH OFF MY SKIN NOW AN' AGAIN, LEAVE IT LYIN' AROUND. WASN'T MY FAULT.
THE EVIL, VINDICTIVE, DRUNK OL' TROUT...
LUCKY FOR HER YOU HADN'T COME INTO YOUR OWN YET.
THAT REALLY IS A SUPERB DEFENSE MECHANISM. A PHEROMONE SECRETED DURING PREGNANCY, CAUSING POTENTIAL PREDATORS TO BECOME ENRAGED AND ATTACK EACH OTHER INSTEAD.
WHICH REMINDS ME...
YOU GET A SIGNAL ALL THE WAY DOWN HERE?
OF COURSE I CAN, IT'S THE BAT-PHONE.
"ARE YOU USING ME AS BAIT"...
NOW WHY DIDN'T I THINK OF THAT?
YOU GOT A PLAN...?
HOPE SO.
IT ALL RATHER RELIES ON JUNIOR REACTING THE WAY HE'S SUPPOSED TO, WHICH WE CAN BY NO MEANS GUARANTEE...

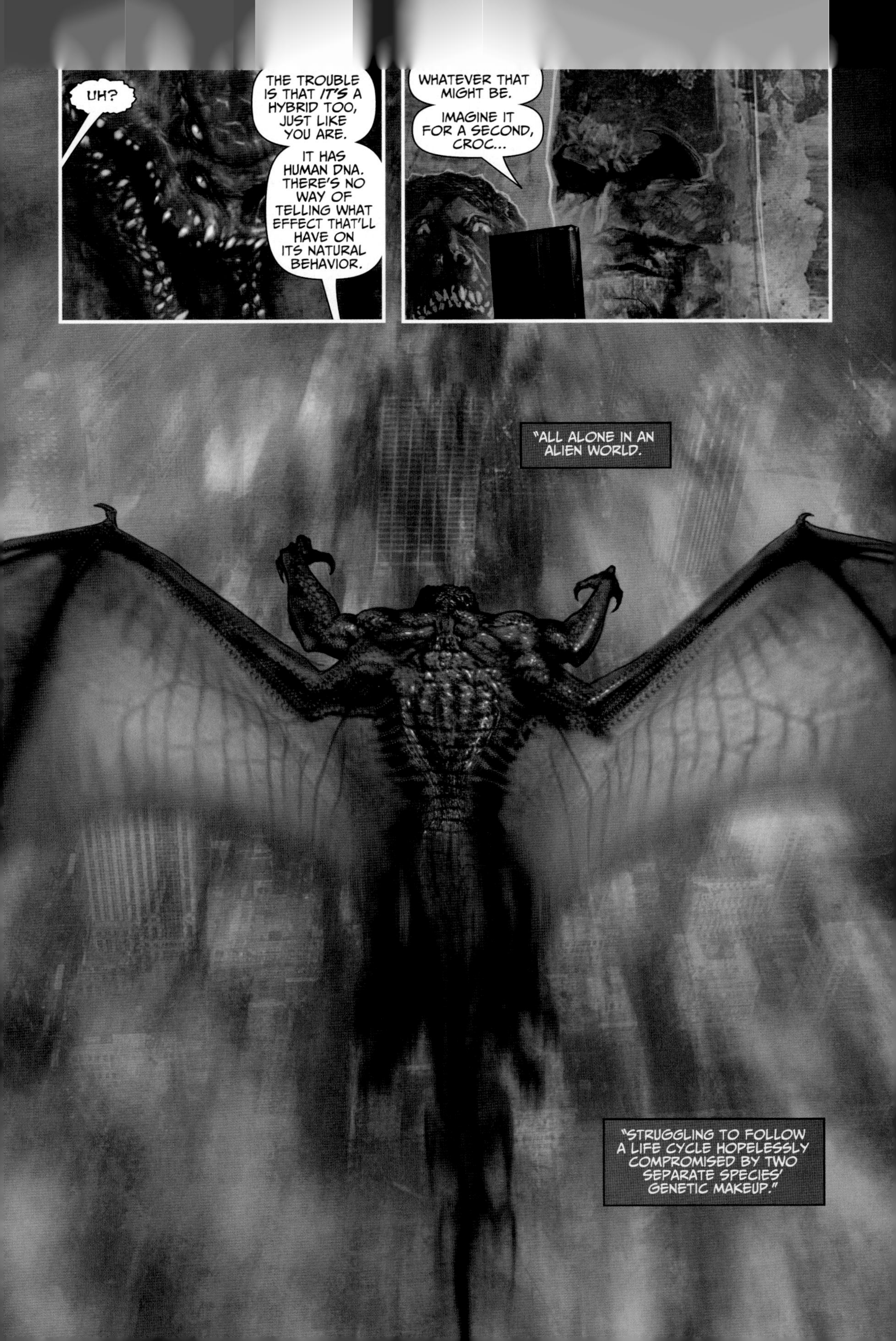
UH?
THE TROUBLE IS THAT IT'S A HYBRID TOO, JUST LIKE YOU ARE.
IT HAS HUMAN DNA. THERE'S NO WAY OF TELLING WHAT EFFECT THAT'LL HAVE ON ITS NATURAL BEHAVIOR.
WHATEVER THAT MIGHT BE.
IMAGINE IT FOR A SECOND, CROC...
"ALL ALONE IN AN ALIEN WORLD.
"STRUGGLING TO FOLLOW A LIFE CYCLE HOPELESSLY COMPROMISED BY TWO SEPARATE SPECIES' GENETIC MAKEUP."

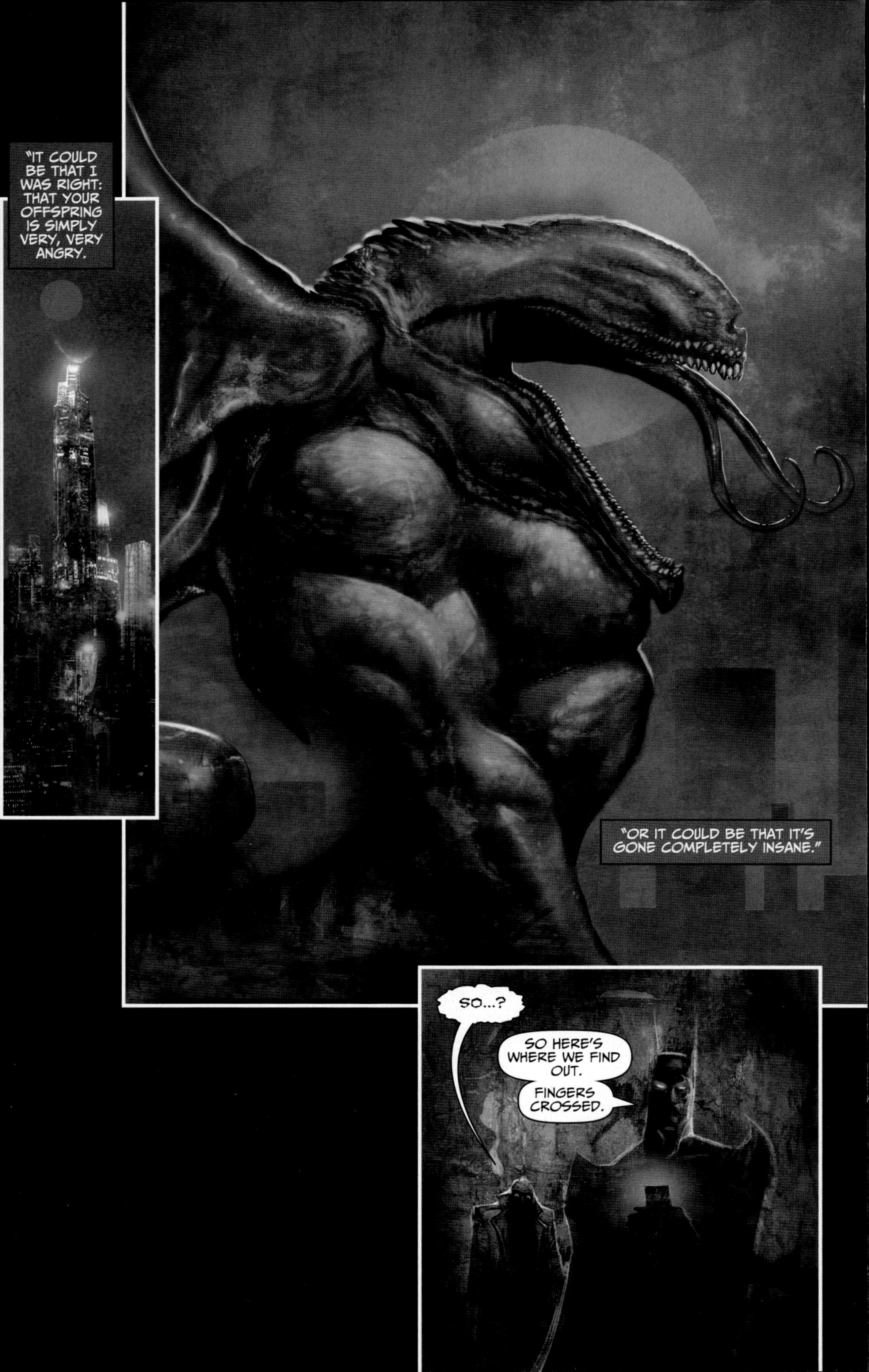
"IT COULD BE THAT I WAS RIGHT: THAT YOUR OFFSPRING IS SIMPLY VERY, VERY ANGRY.
"OR IT COULD BE THAT IT'S GONE COMPLETELY INSANE."
SO...?
SO HERE'S WHERE WE FIND OUT.
FINGERS CROSSED.

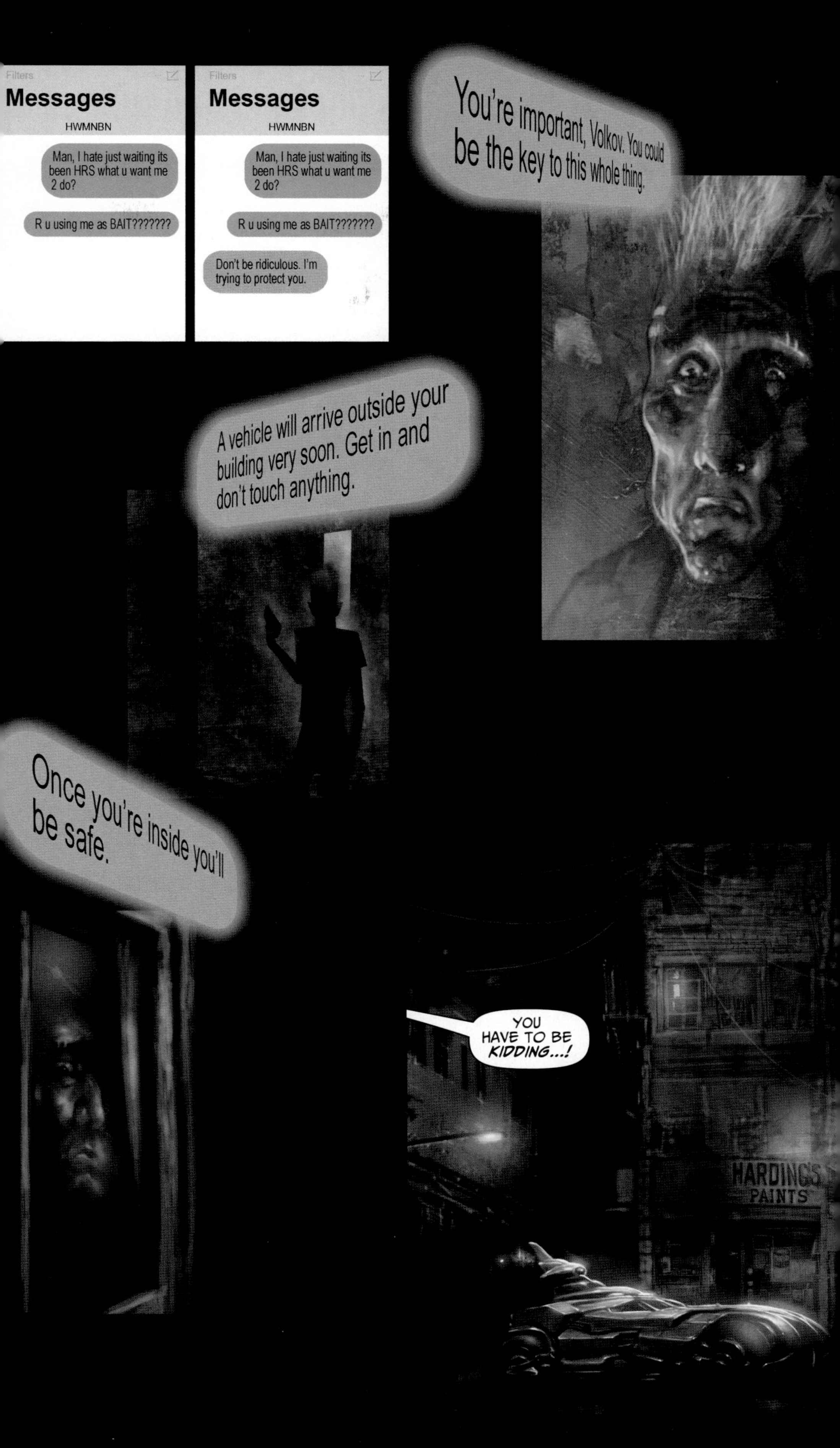
Filters
Messages
HWMNBN
Man, I hate just waiting its been HRS what u want me 2 do?
R u using me as BAIT???????
Filters
Messages
HWMNBN
Man, I hate just waiting its been HRS what u want me 2 do?
R u using me as BAIT???????
Don't be ridiculous. I'm trying to protect you.
You're important, Volkov. You could be the key to this whole thing.
A vehicle will arrive outside your building very soon. Get in and don't touch anything.
Once you're inside you'll be safe.
YOU HAVE TO BE *KIDDING...!*
HARDING'S PAINTS

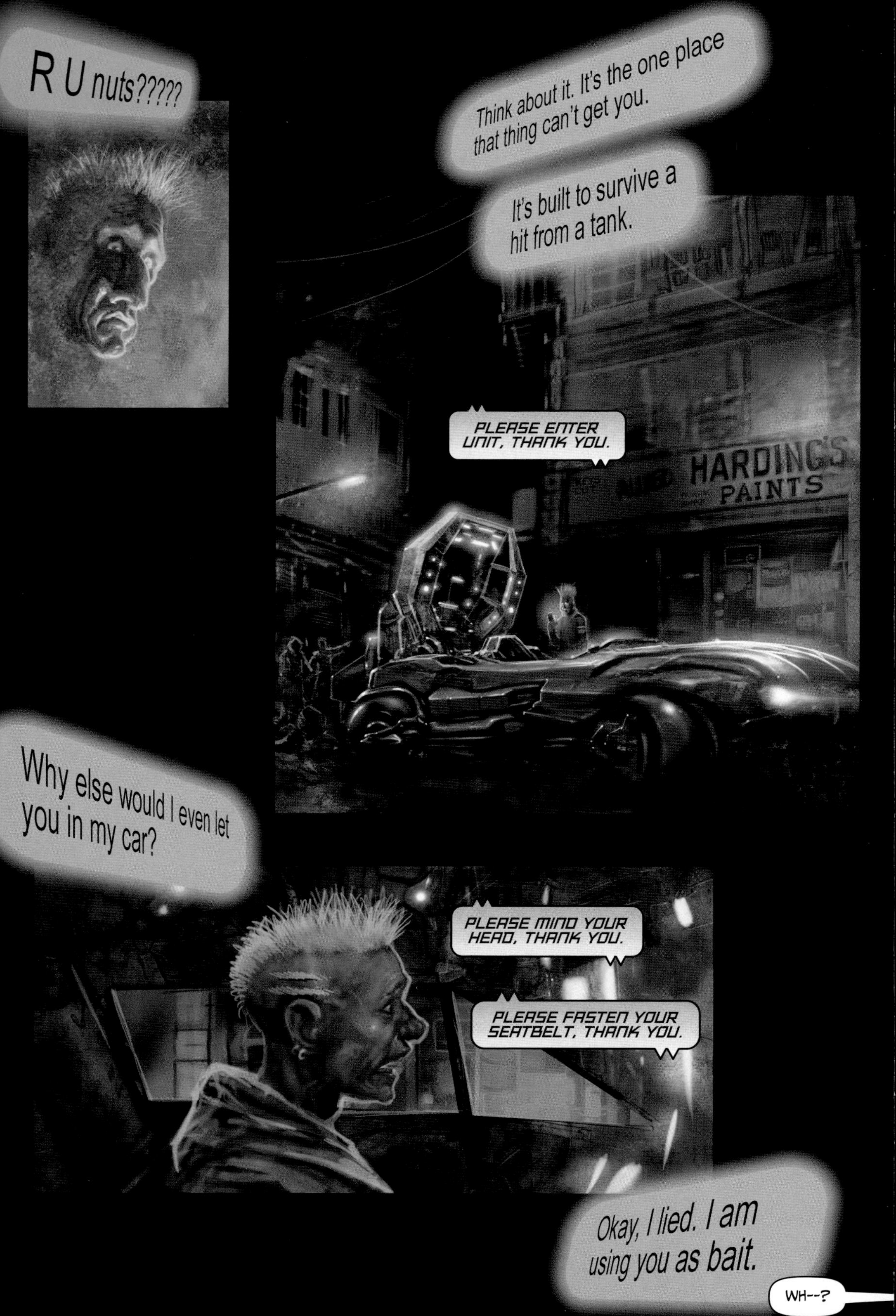
R U nuts?????
Think about it. It's the one place that thing can't get you.
It's built to survive a hit from a tank.
PLEASE ENTER UNIT, THANK YOU.
HARDING'S PAINTS
Why else would I even let you in my car?
PLEASE MIND YOUR HEAD, THANK YOU.
PLEASE FASTEN YOUR SEATBELT, THANK YOU.
Okay, I lied. I am using you as bait.
WH--?

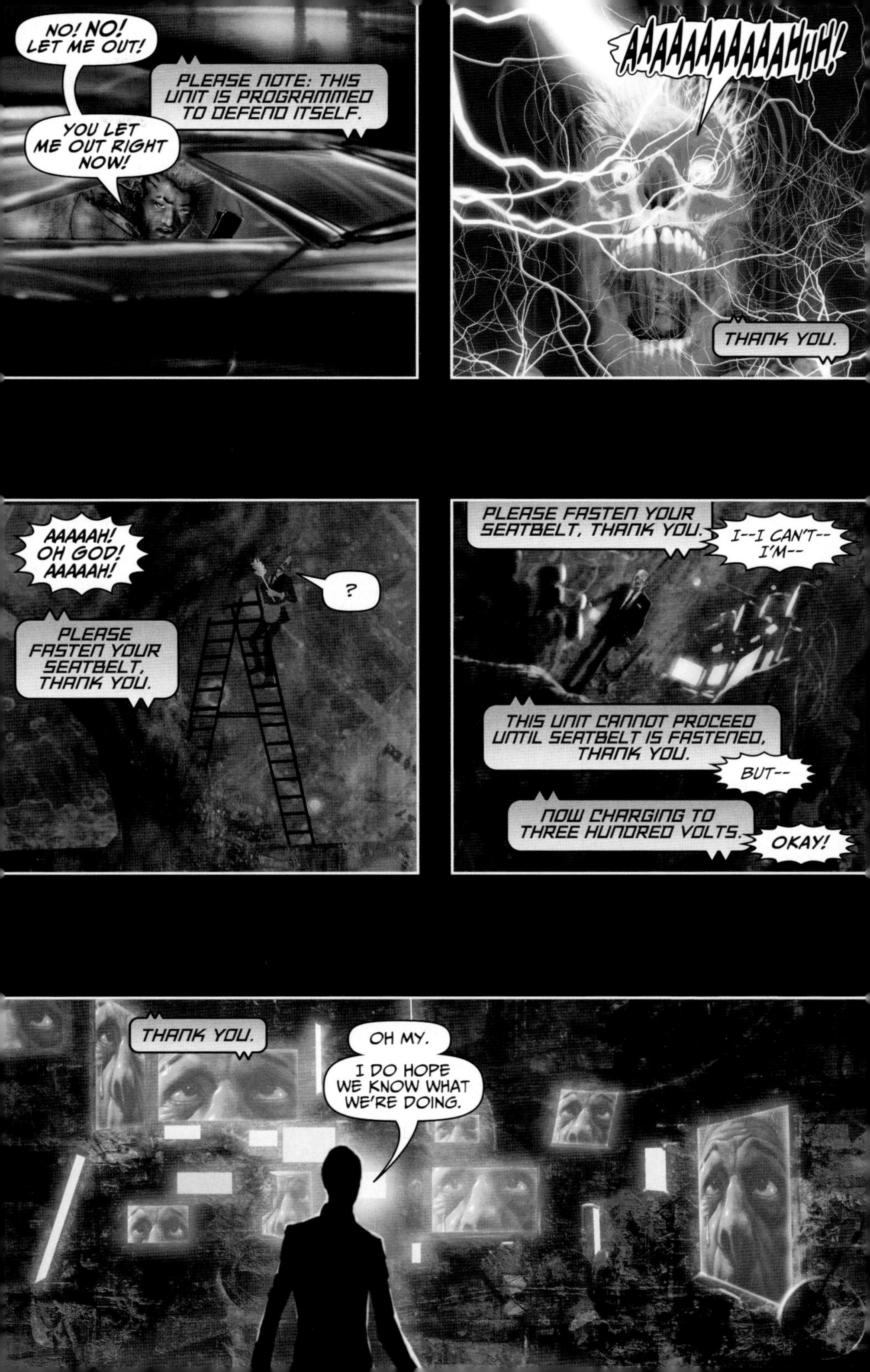

NO! NO! LET ME OUT!
PLEASE NOTE: THIS UNIT IS PROGRAMMED TO DEFEND ITSELF.
YOU LET ME OUT RIGHT NOW!
AAAAAAAAAAAHHH!
THANK YOU.
AAAAAH! OH GOD! AAAAAH!
?
PLEASE FASTEN YOUR SEATBELT, THANK YOU.
PLEASE FASTEN YOUR SEATBELT, THANK YOU.
I--I CAN'T-- I'M--
THIS UNIT CANNOT PROCEED UNTIL SEATBELT IS FASTENED, THANK YOU.
BUT--
NOW CHARGING TO THREE HUNDRED VOLTS.
OKAY!
THANK YOU.
OH MY.
I DO HOPE WE KNOW WHAT WE'RE DOING.

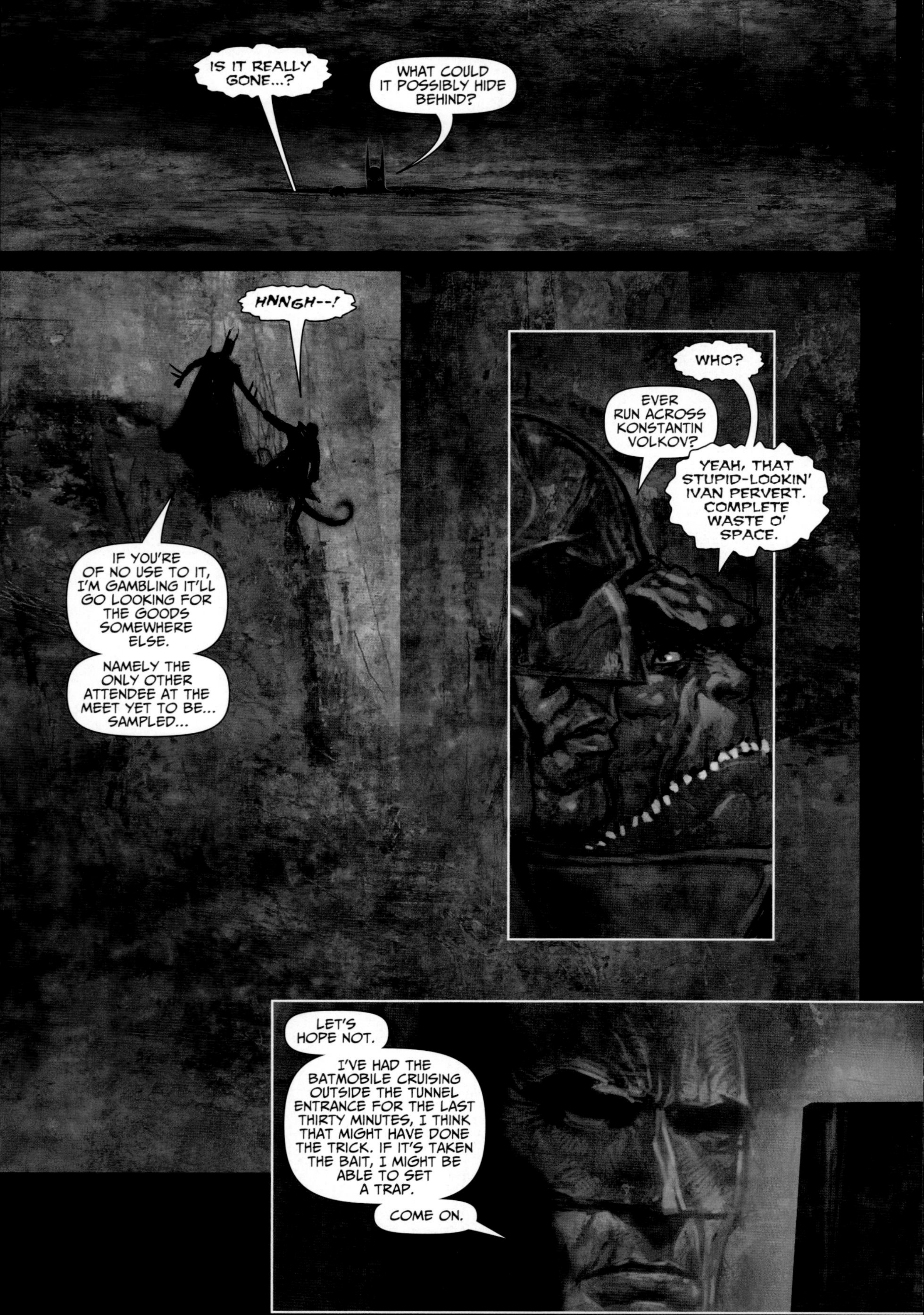
IS IT REALLY GONE...?
WHAT COULD IT POSSIBLY HIDE BEHIND?
HNNGH--!
IF YOU'RE OF NO USE TO IT, I'M GAMBLING IT'LL GO LOOKING FOR THE GOODS SOMEWHERE ELSE.
NAMELY THE ONLY OTHER ATTENDEE AT THE MEET YET TO BE... SAMPLED...
WHO?
EVER RUN ACROSS KONSTANTIN VOLKOV?
YEAH, THAT STUPID-LOOKIN' IVAN PERVERT. COMPLETE WASTE O' SPACE.
LET'S HOPE NOT.
I'VE HAD THE BATMOBILE CRUISING OUTSIDE THE TUNNEL ENTRANCE FOR THE LAST THIRTY MINUTES, I THINK THAT MIGHT HAVE DONE THE TRICK. IF IT'S TAKEN THE BAIT, I MIGHT BE ABLE TO SET A TRAP.
COME ON.

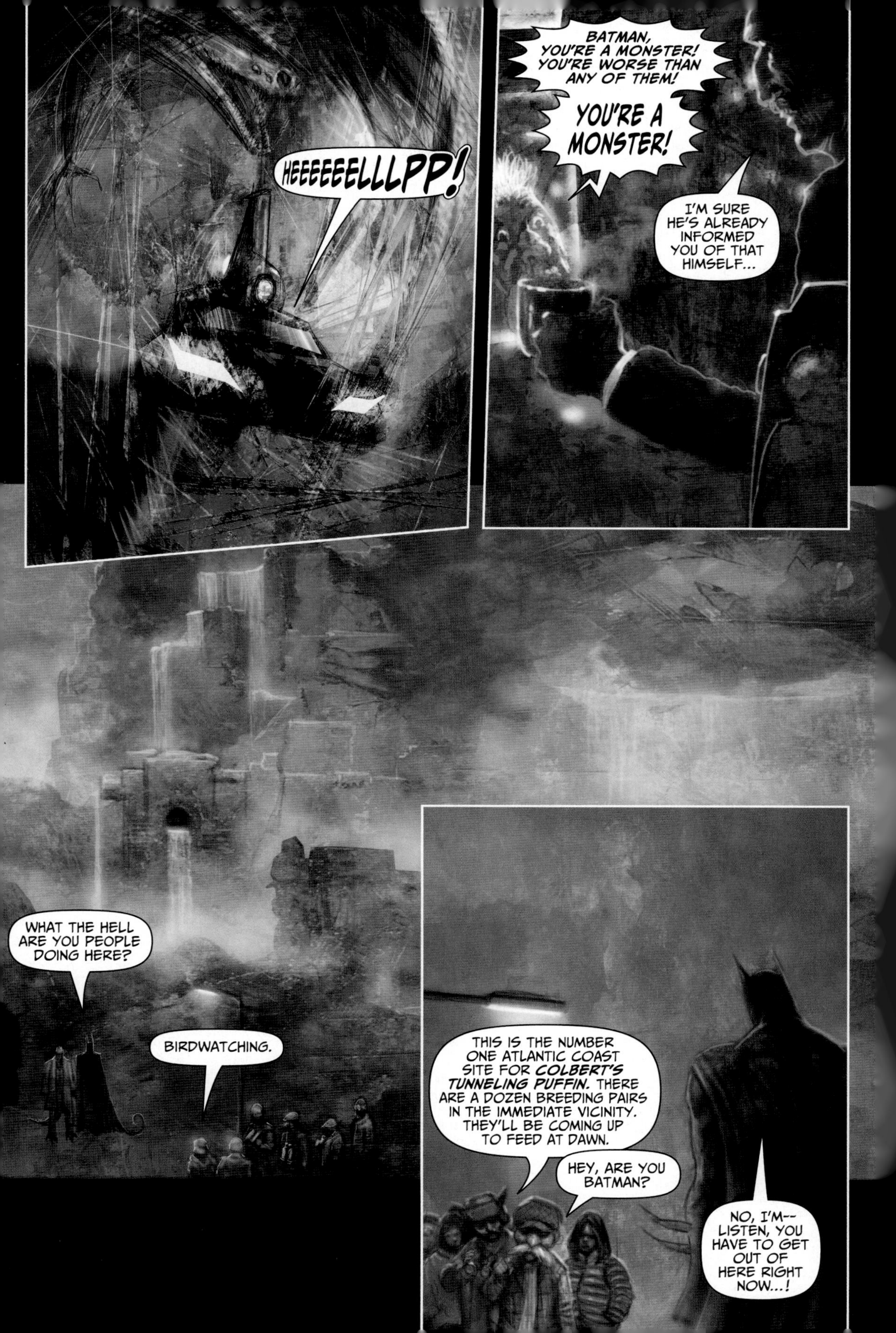
HEEEEEELLLPP!
BATMAN, YOU'RE A MONSTER! YOU'RE WORSE THAN ANY OF THEM!
YOU'RE A MONSTER!
I'M SURE HE'S ALREADY INFORMED YOU OF THAT HIMSELF...
WHAT THE HELL ARE YOU PEOPLE DOING HERE?
BIRDWATCHING.
THIS IS THE NUMBER ONE ATLANTIC COAST SITE FOR COLBERT'S TUNNELING PUFFIN. THERE ARE A DOZEN BREEDING PAIRS IN THE IMMEDIATE VICINITY. THEY'LL BE COMING UP TO FEED AT DAWN.
HEY, ARE YOU BATMAN?
NO, I'M-- LISTEN, YOU HAVE TO GET OUT OF HERE RIGHT NOW...!

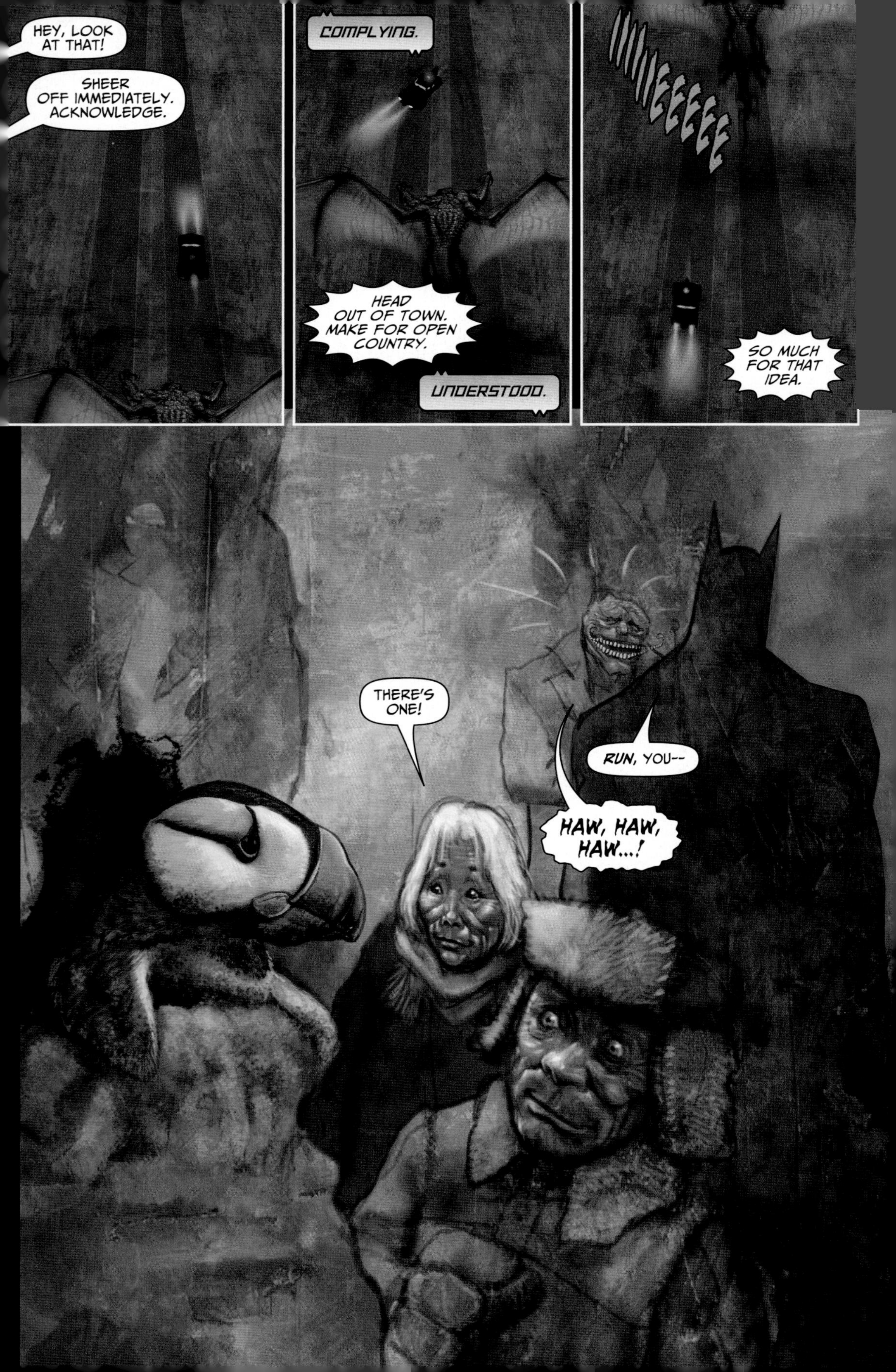
HEY, LOOK AT THAT!
SHEER OFF IMMEDIATELY. ACKNOWLEDGE.
COMPLYING.
HEAD OUT OF TOWN. MAKE FOR OPEN COUNTRY.
UNDERSTOOD.
IIIIIIEEEEEE
SO MUCH FOR THAT IDEA.
THERE'S ONE!
RUN, YOU--
HAW, HAW, HAW...!

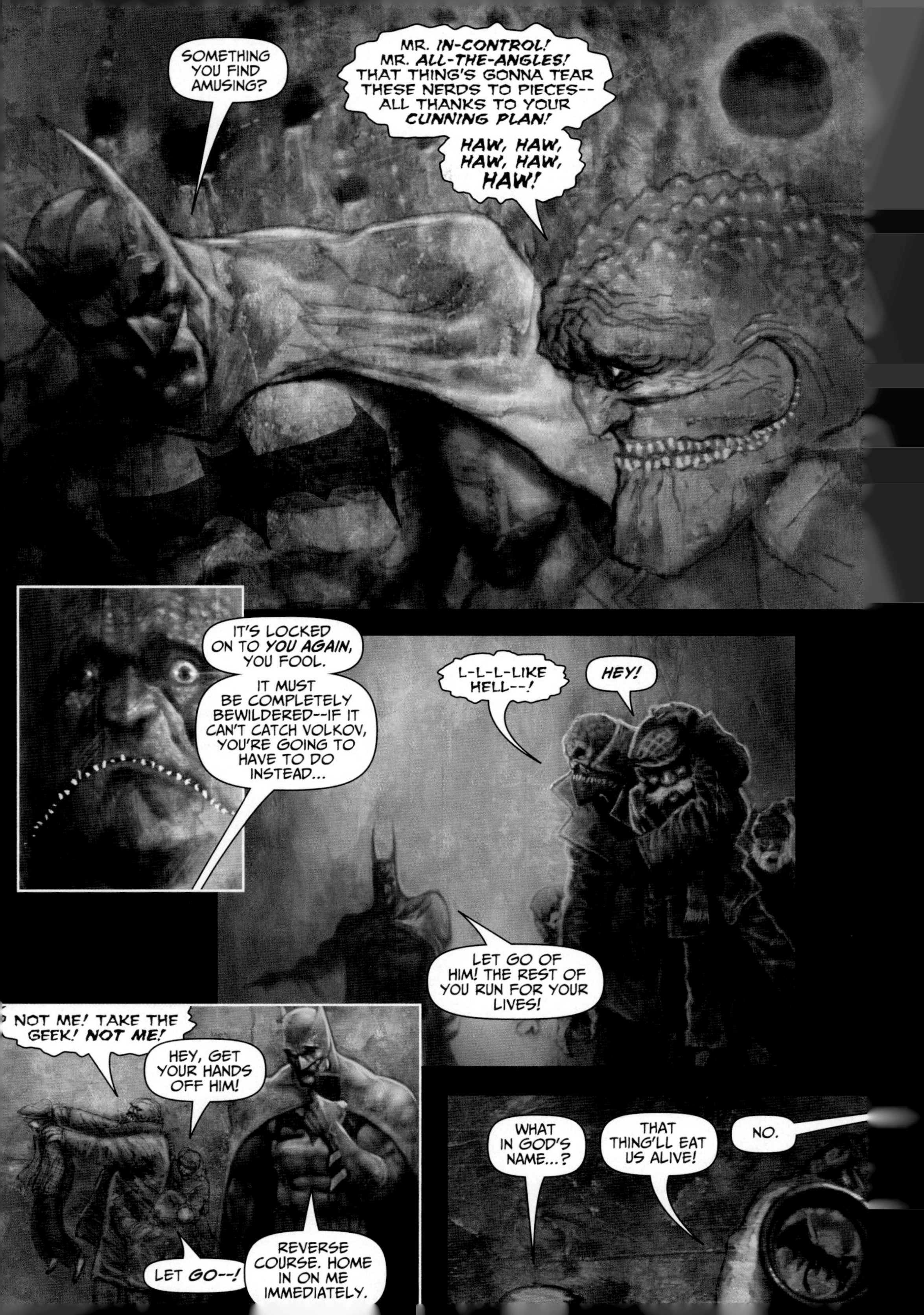
SOMETHING YOU FIND AMUSING?
MR. IN-CONTROL! MR. ALL-THE-ANGLES! THAT THING'S GONNA TEAR THESE NERDS TO PIECES-- ALL THANKS TO YOUR CUNNING PLAN!
HAW, HAW, HAW, HAW, HAW!
IT'S LOCKED ON TO YOU AGAIN, YOU FOOL.
IT MUST BE COMPLETELY BEWILDERED--IF IT CAN'T CATCH VOLKOV, YOU'RE GOING TO HAVE TO DO INSTEAD...
L-L-L-LIKE HELL--!
HEY!
LET GO OF HIM! THE REST OF YOU RUN FOR YOUR LIVES!
NOT ME! TAKE THE GEEK! NOT ME!
HEY, GET YOUR HANDS OFF HIM!
LET GO--!
REVERSE COURSE. HOME IN ON ME IMMEDIATELY.
WHAT IN GOD'S NAME...?
THAT THING'LL EAT US ALIVE!
NO.

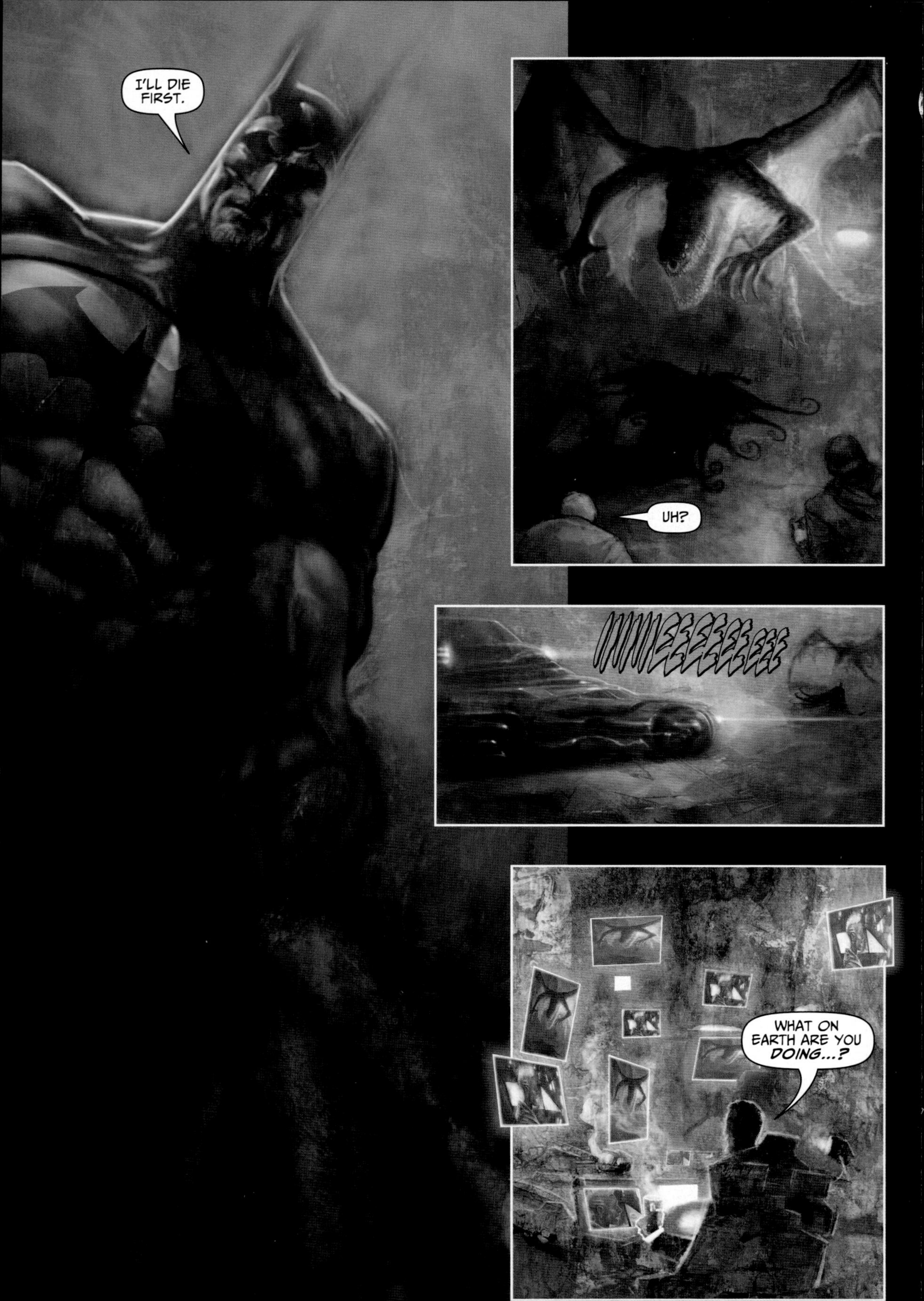
I'LL DIE FIRST.
UH?
IIIIIIEEEEEEEEEEEE
WHAT ON EARTH ARE YOU DOING...?

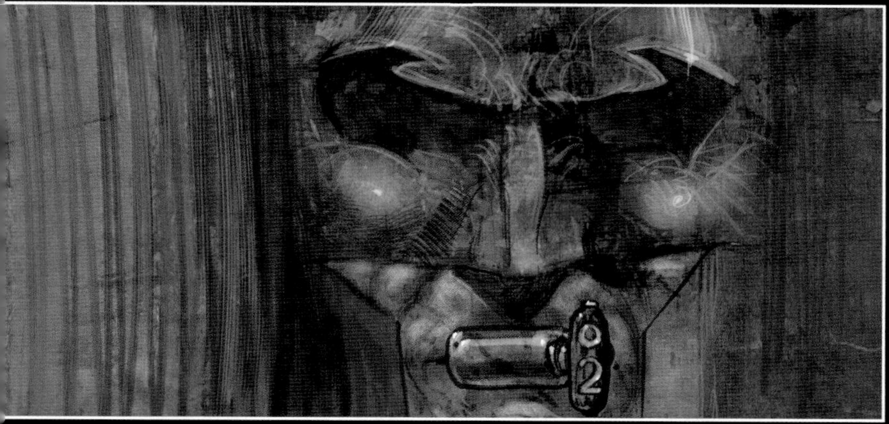
O2

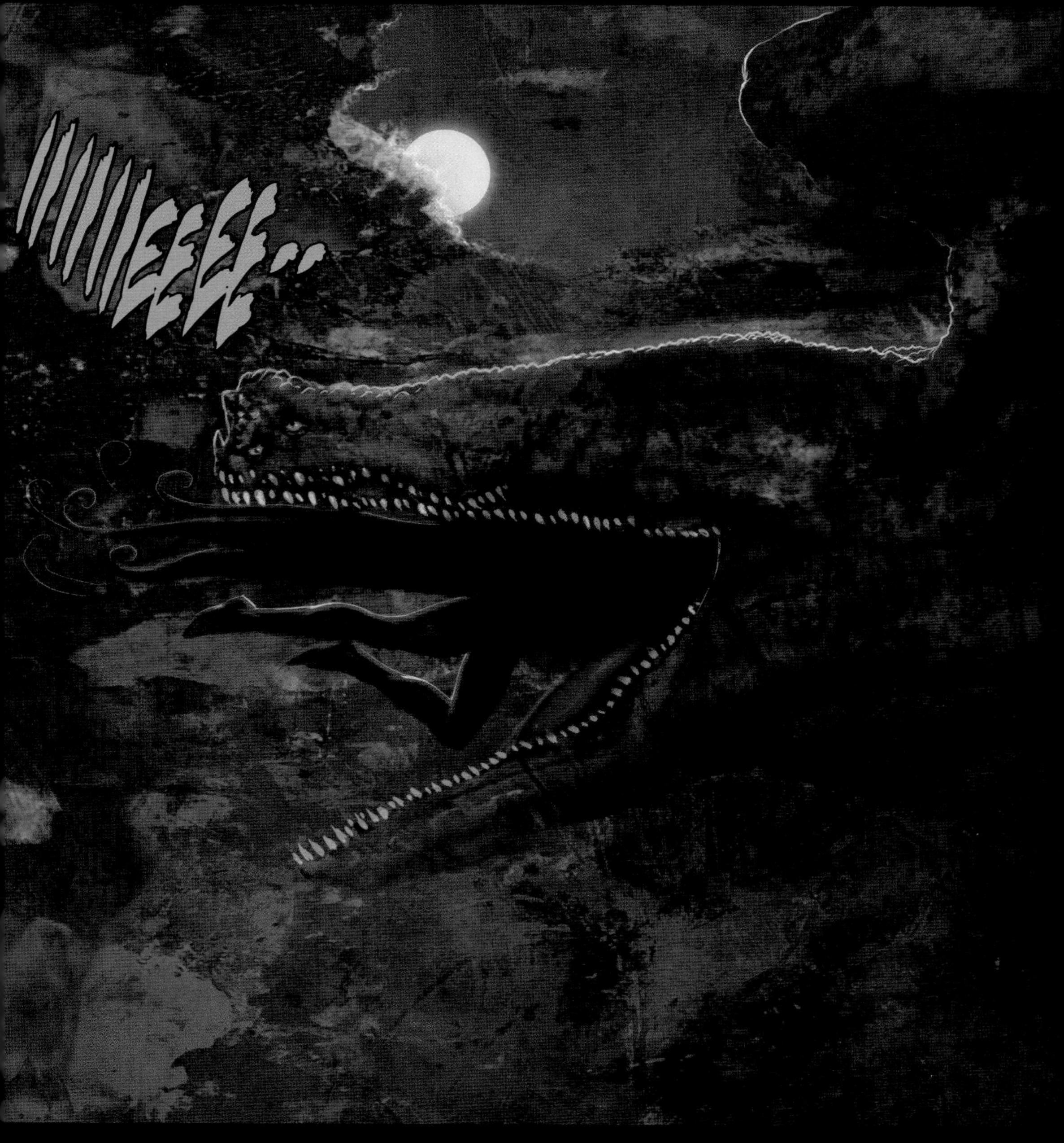
IIIIIIEEEE..

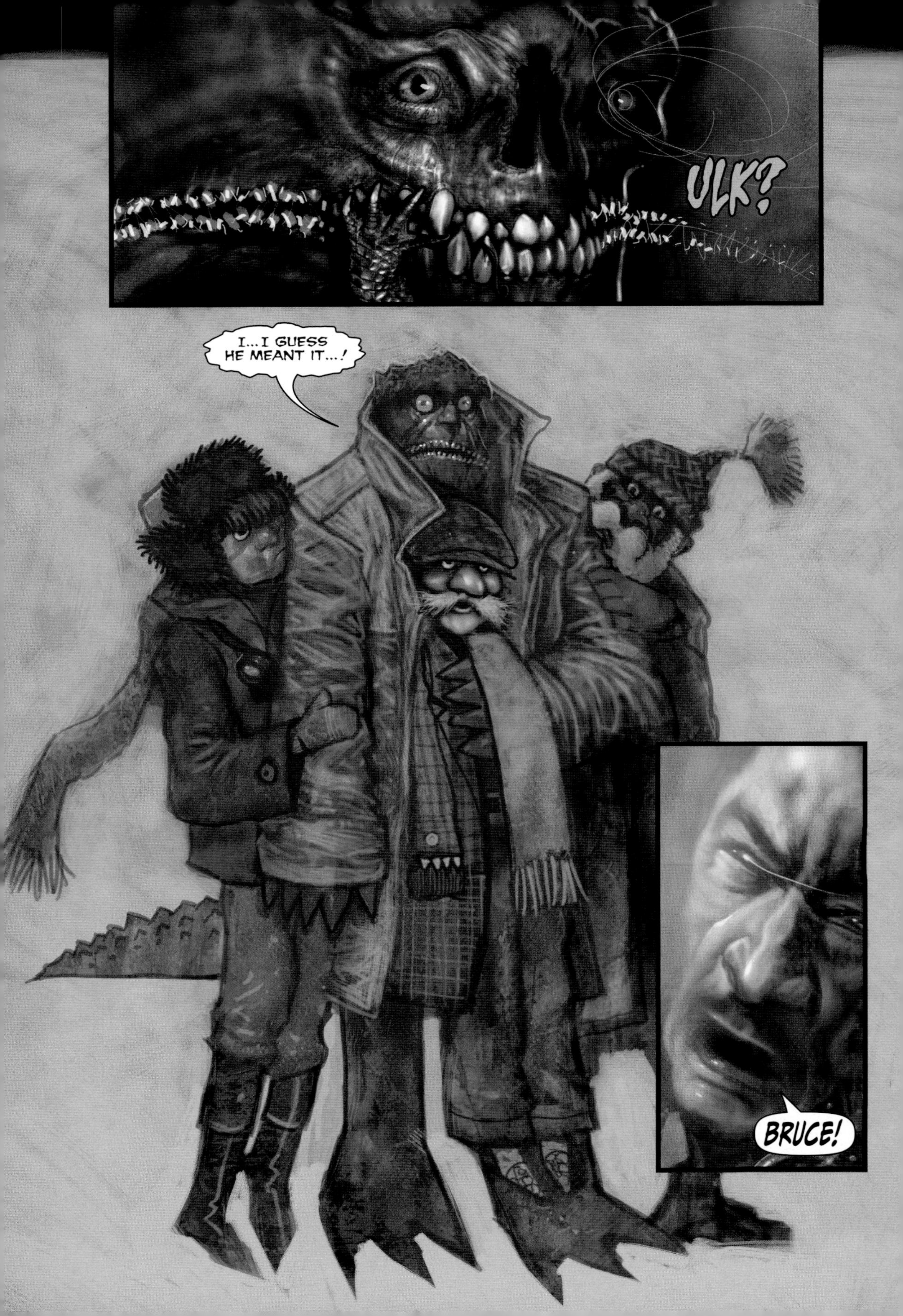
ULK?
I... I GUESS HE MEANT IT...!
BRUCE!

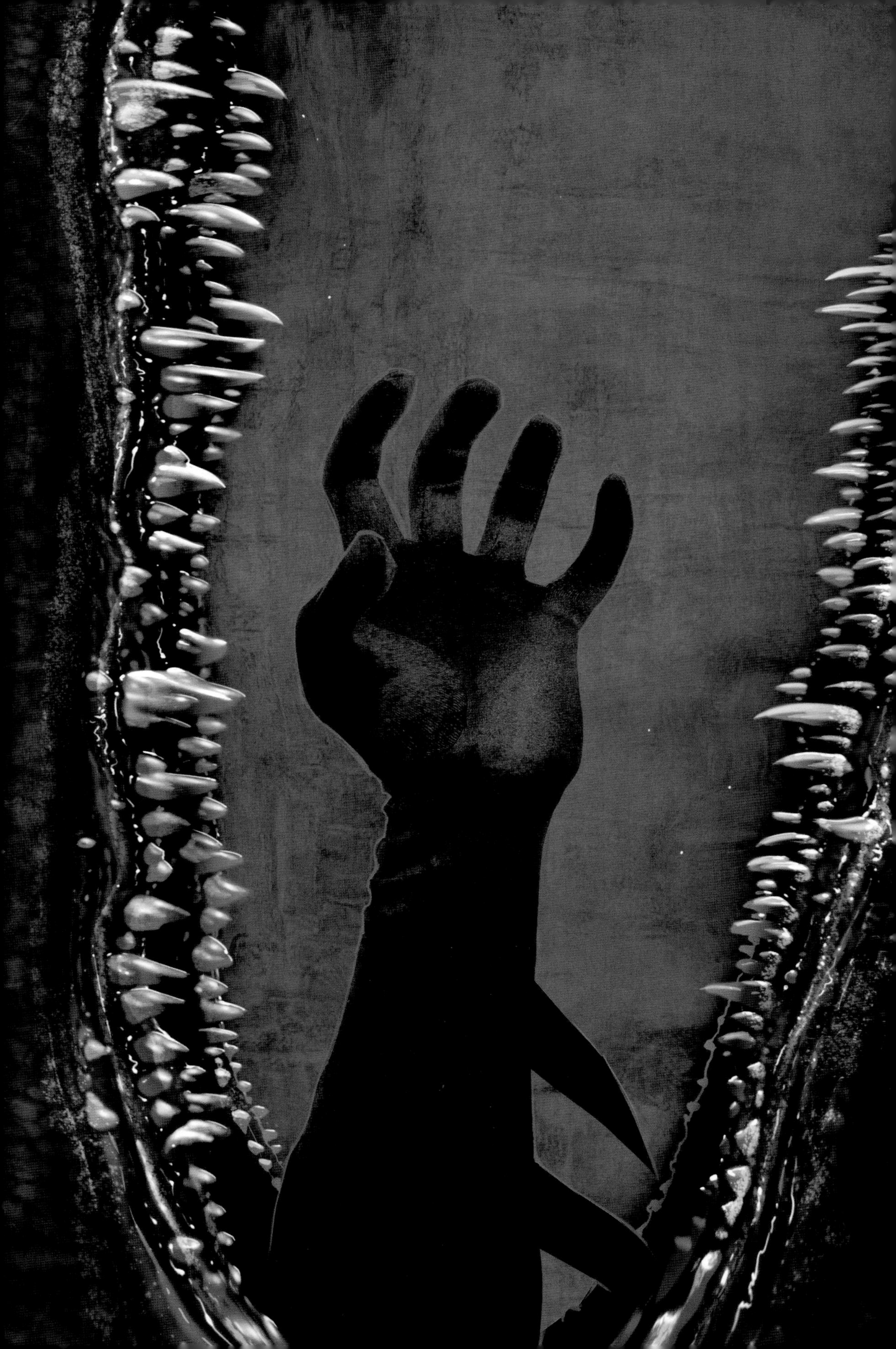

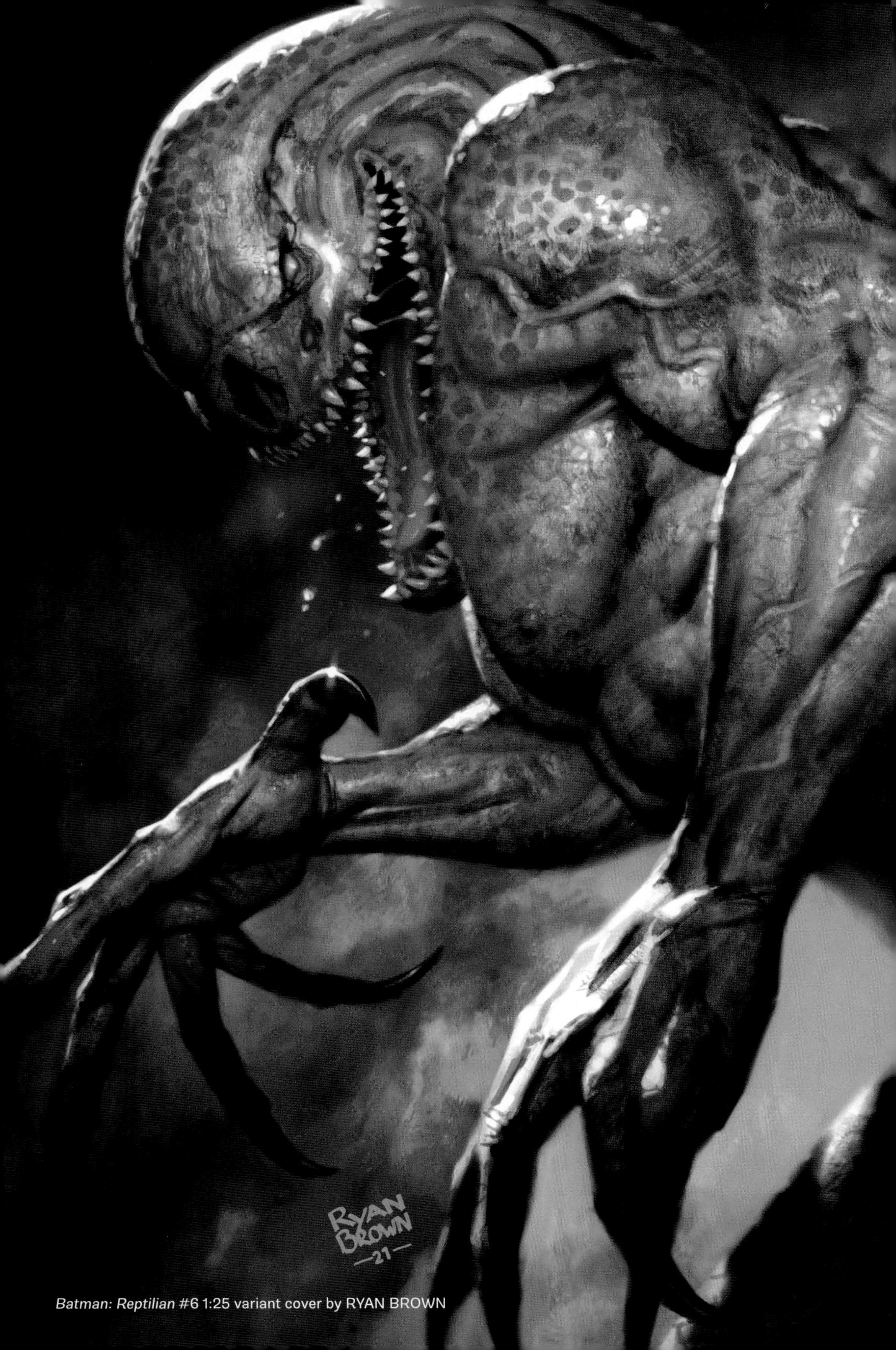
RYAN BROWN
21

Batman: Reptilian #6 1:25 variant cover by RYAN BROWN

6: DEATH & TAXES

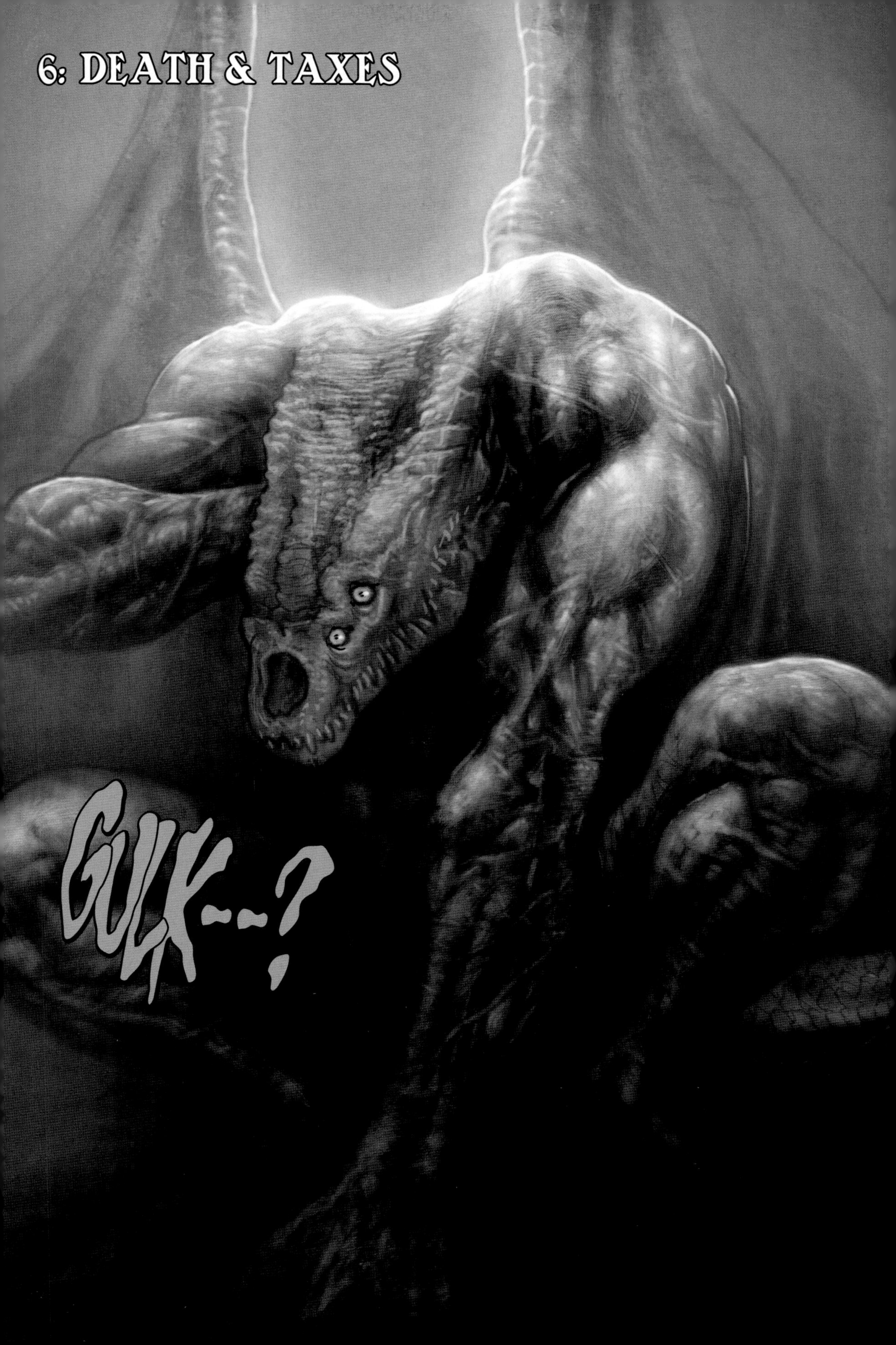
GULK--?

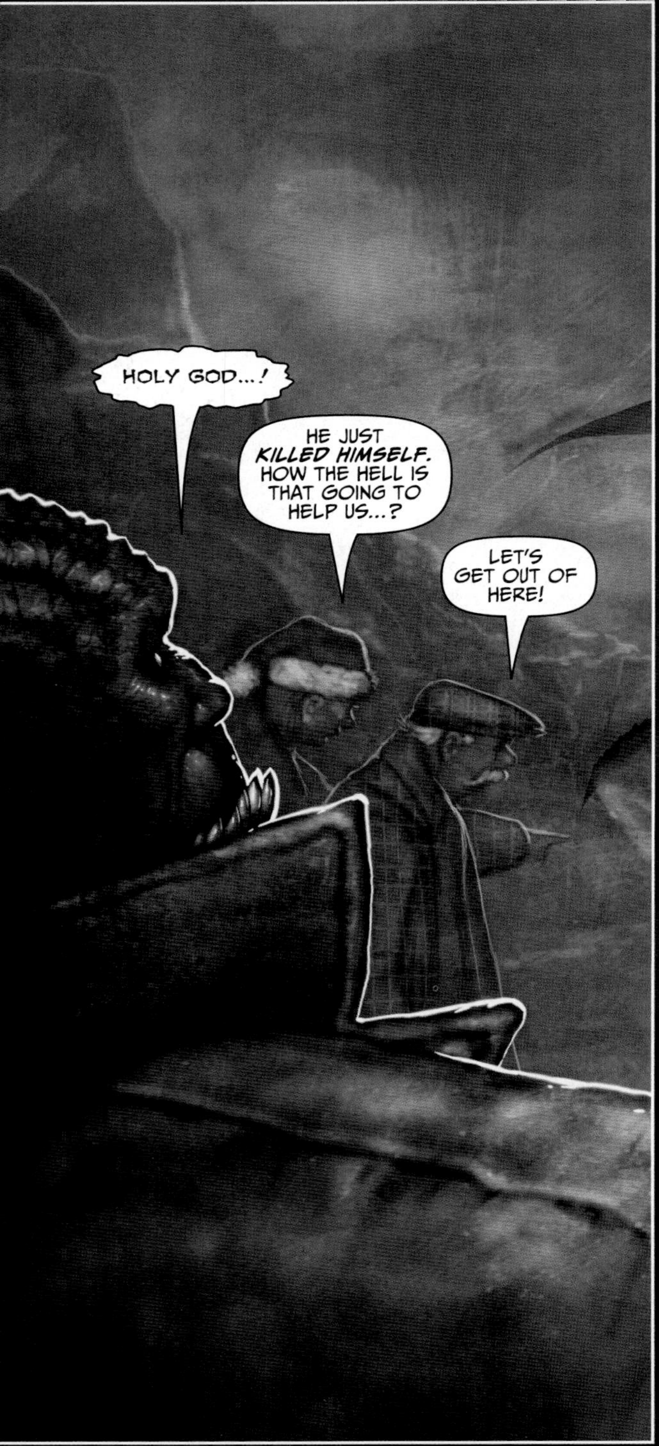
HOLY GOD...!
HE JUST KILLED HIMSELF. HOW THE HELL IS THAT GOING TO HELP US...?
LET'S GET OUT OF HERE!
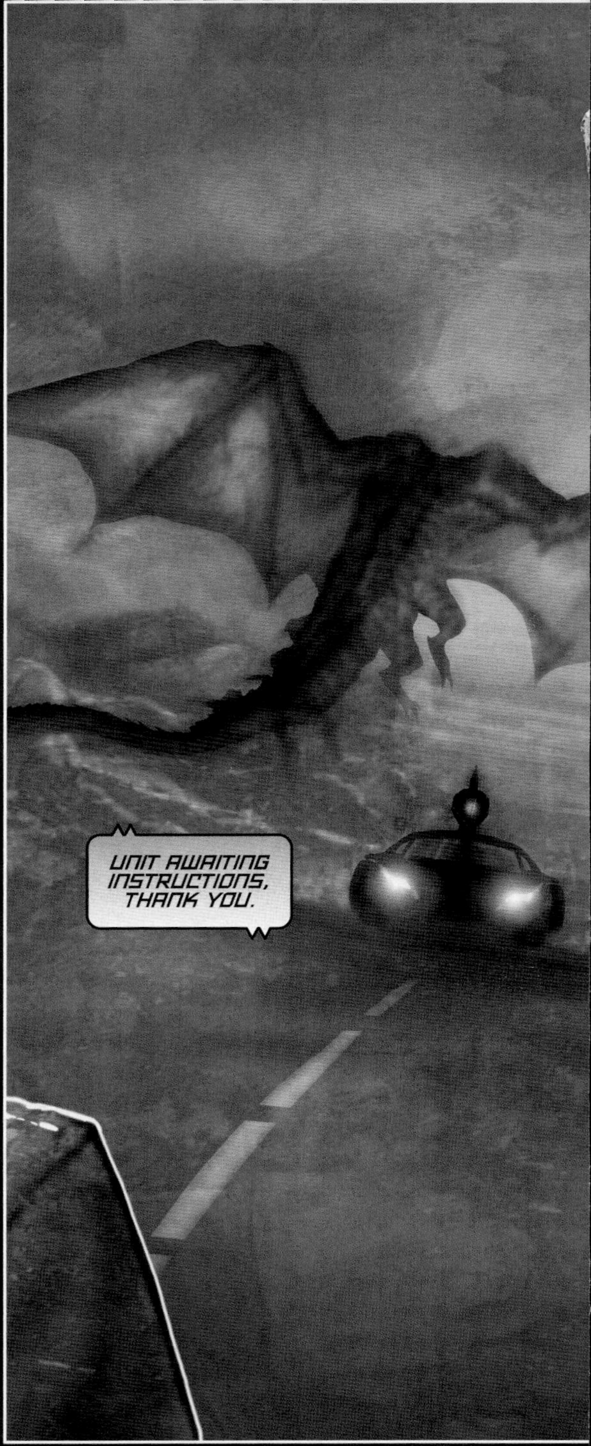
UNIT AWAITING INSTRUCTIONS, THANK YOU.

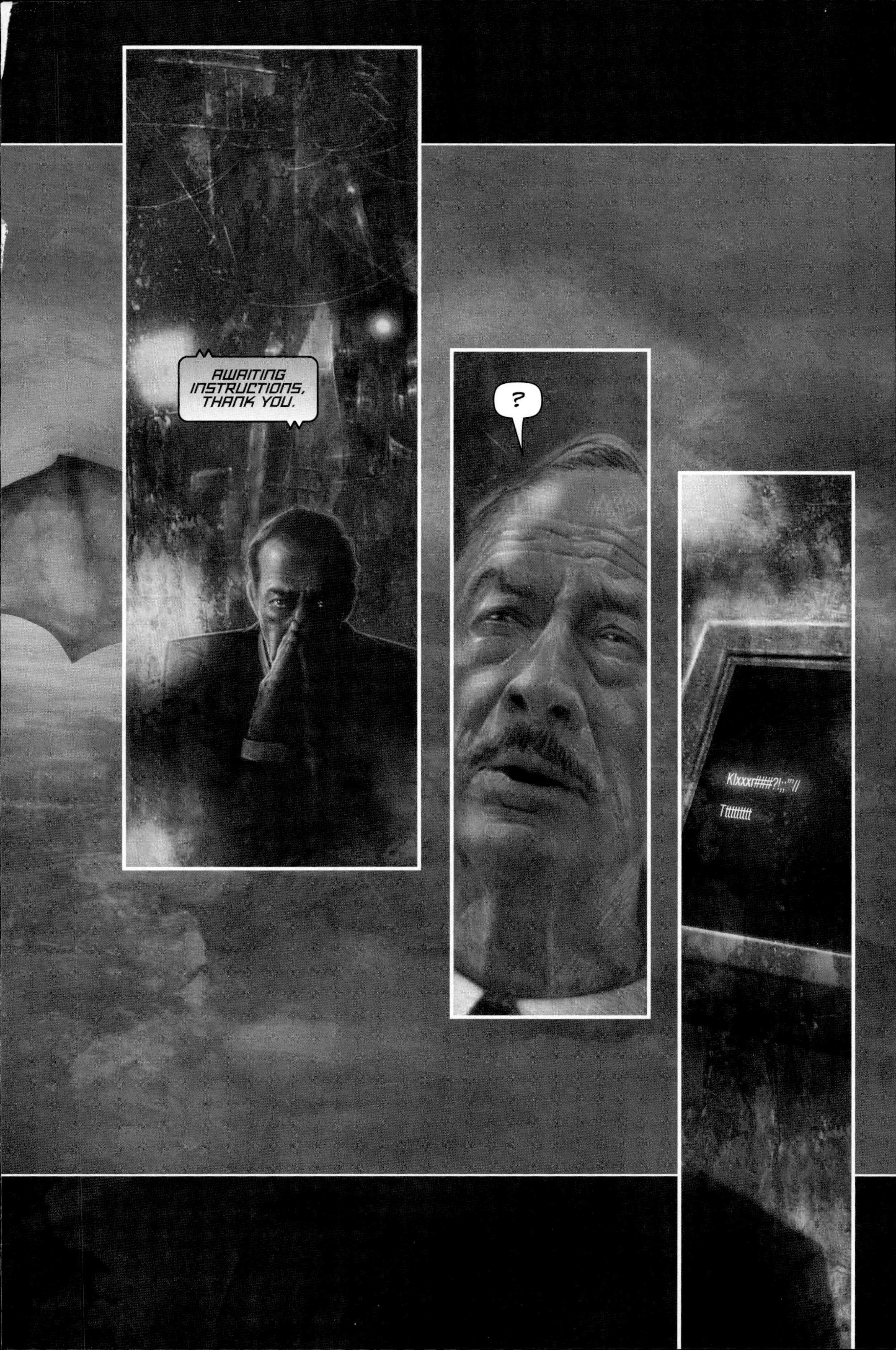
AWAITING INSTRUCTIONS, THANK YOU.
?
Klxxxr###?!;;'''//
Tttttttttt

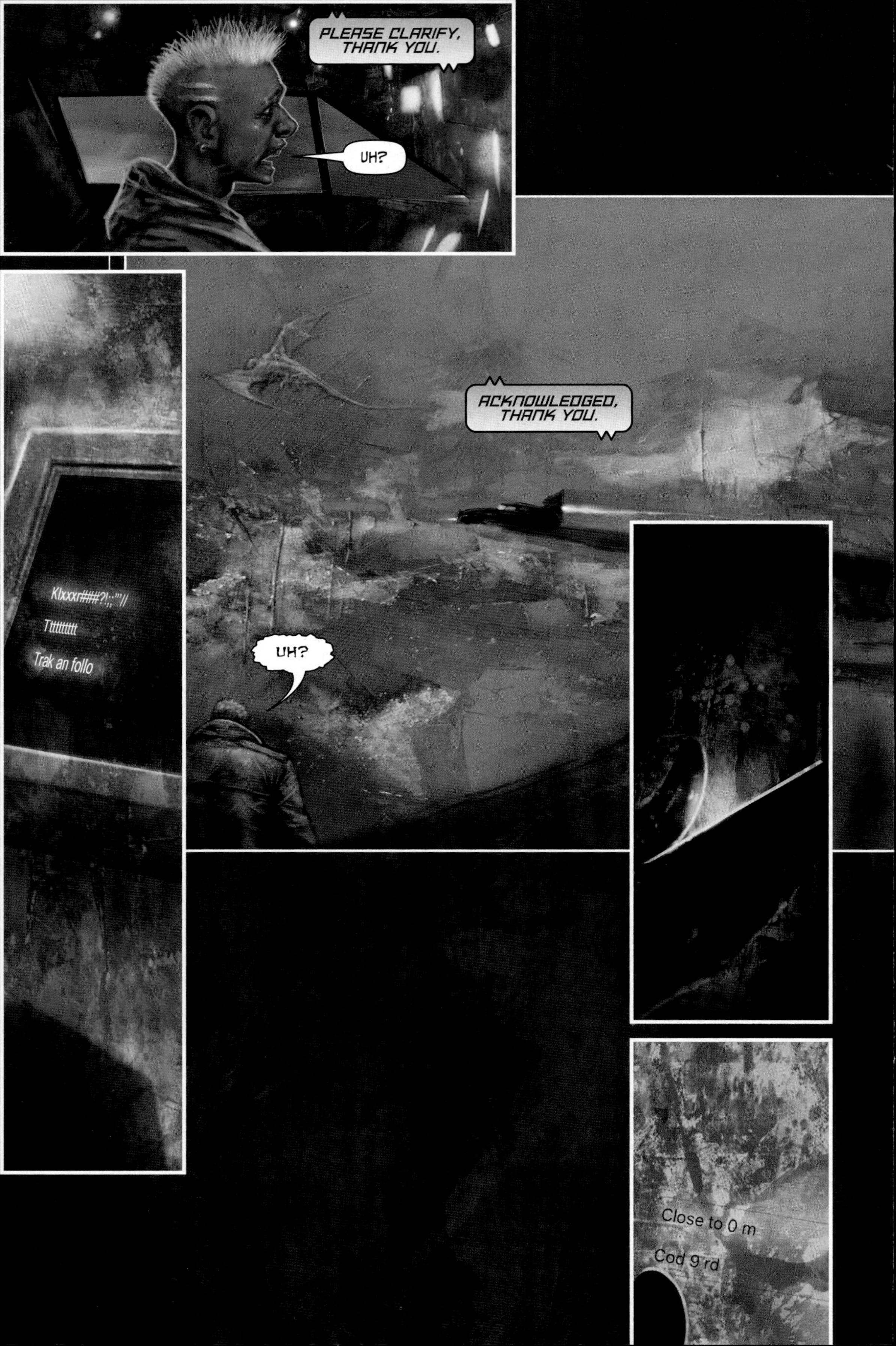
PLEASE CLARIFY, THANK YOU.
UH?
Klxxxr###?!;;"'//
Tttttttttt
Trak an follo
ACKNOWLEDGED, THANK YOU.
UH?
Close to 0 m
Cod 9 rd

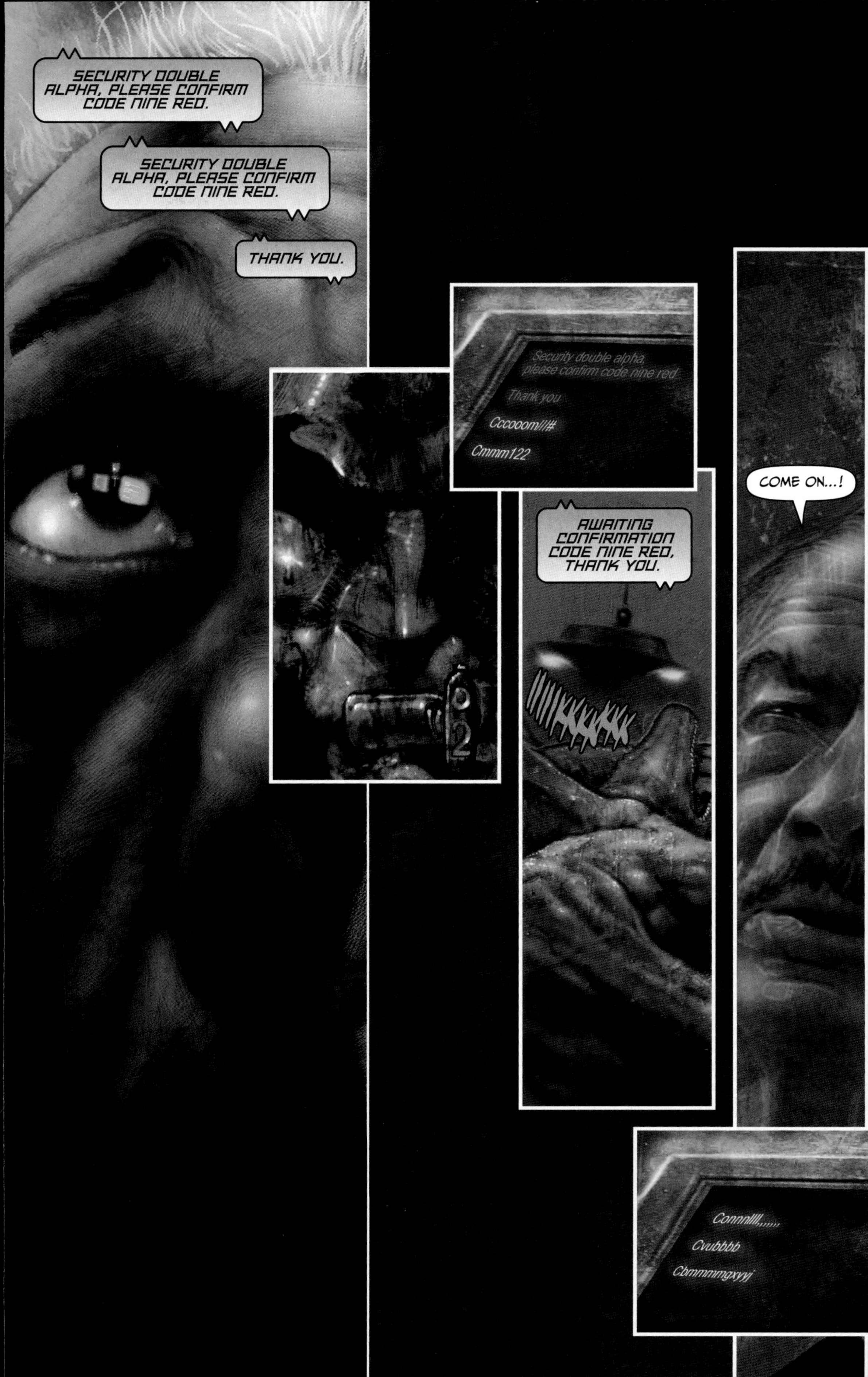
SECURITY DOUBLE ALPHA, PLEASE CONFIRM CODE NINE RED.
SECURITY DOUBLE ALPHA, PLEASE CONFIRM CODE NINE RED.
THANK YOU.
Security double alpha, please confirm code nine red
Thank you
Cccooom///#
Cmmm122
AWAITING CONFIRMATION CODE NINE RED, THANK YOU.
COME ON...!
Connnllll,,,,,,
Cvubbbb
Cbnmmmgxyyj

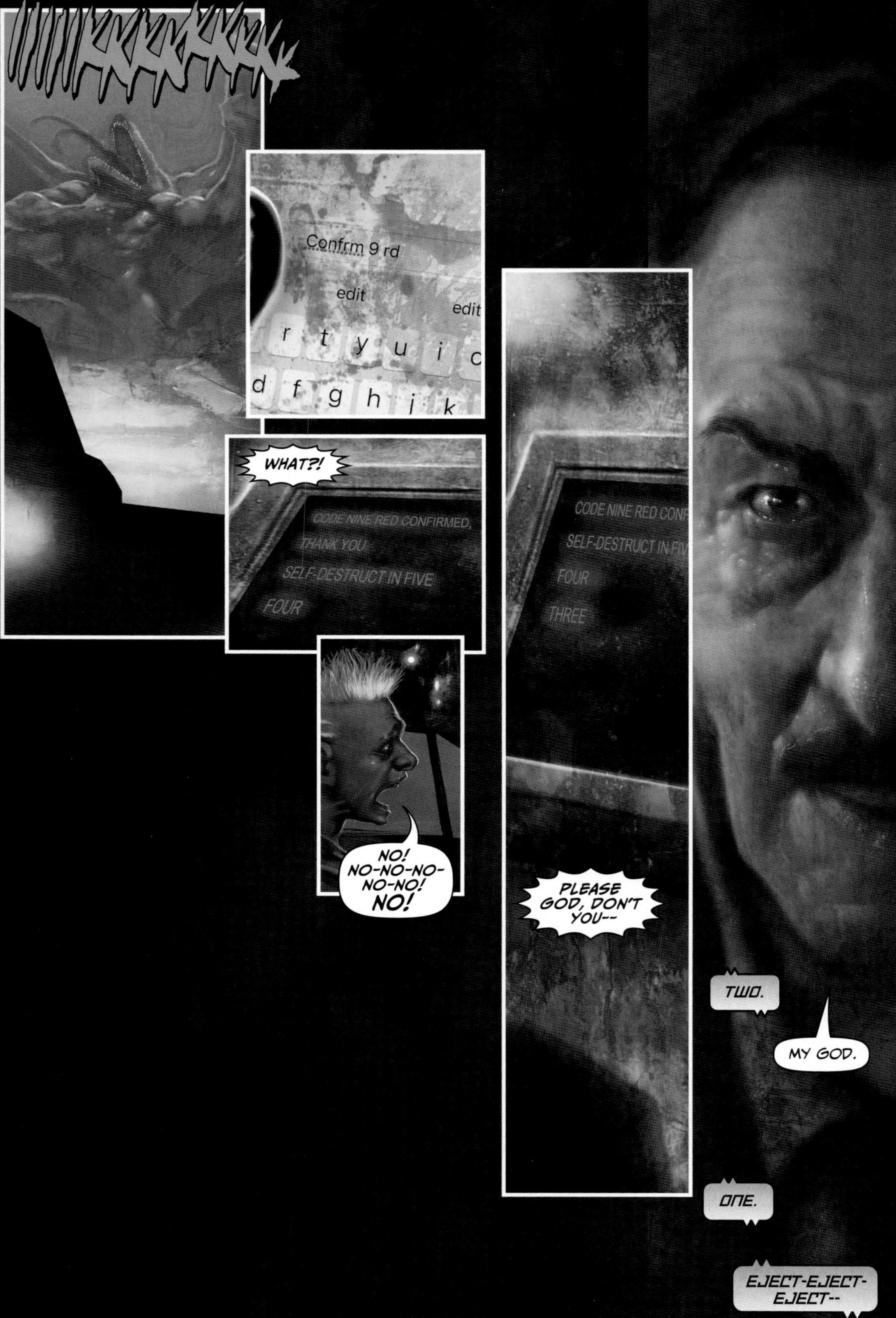
KKKKKKK
Confrm 9 rd
edit
edit
WHAT?!
CODE NINE RED CONFIRMED.
THANK YOU.
SELF-DESTRUCT IN FIVE
FOUR
NO! NO-NO-NO-NO-NO! NO!
CODE NINE RED CONF
SELF-DESTRUCT IN FIVE
FOUR
THREE
PLEASE GOD, DON'T YOU--
TWO.
MY GOD.
ONE.
EJECT-EJECT-EJECT--

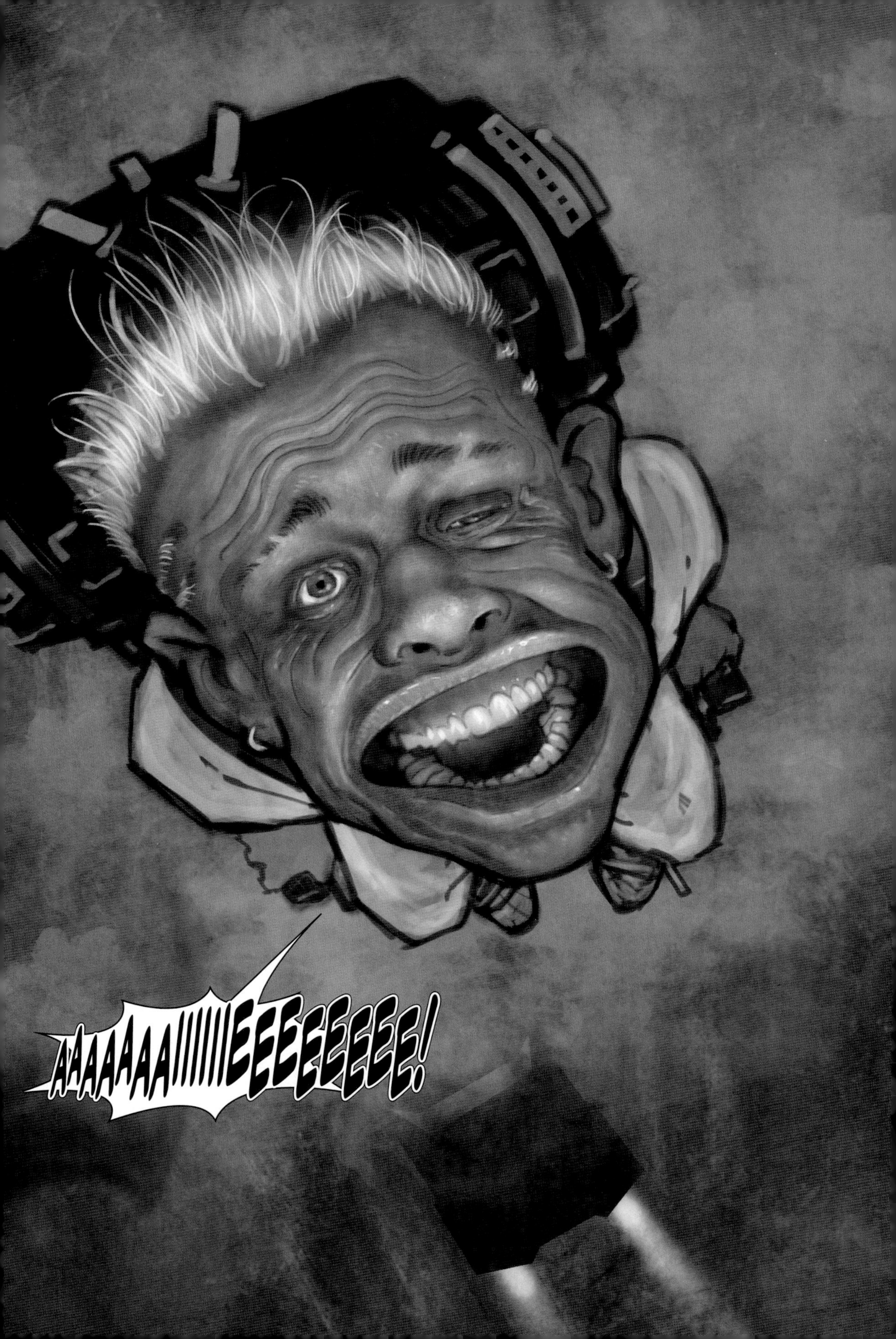
AAAAAAIIIIIIIEEEEEEEE!

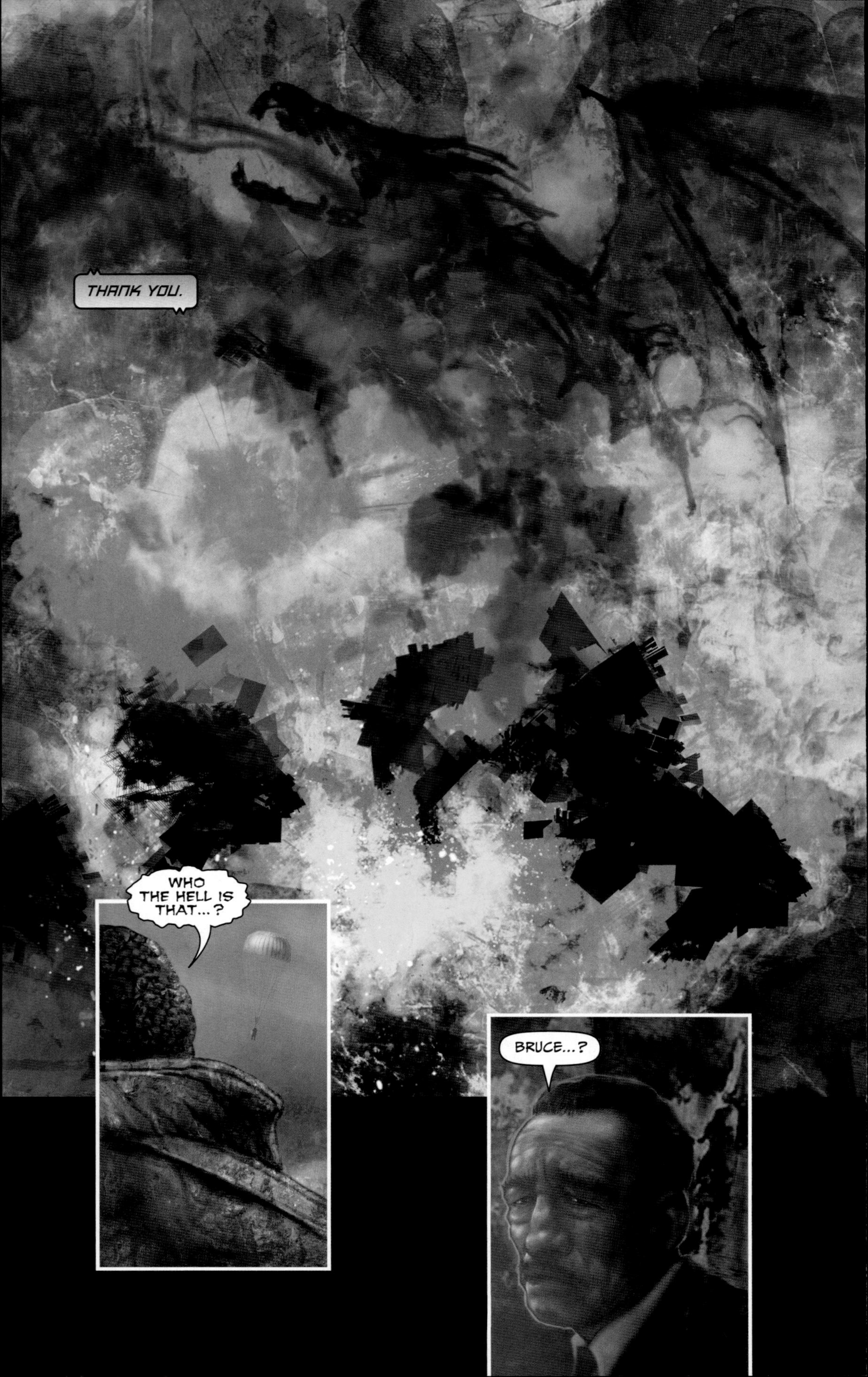
THANK YOU.
WHO THE HELL IS THAT...?
BRUCE...?

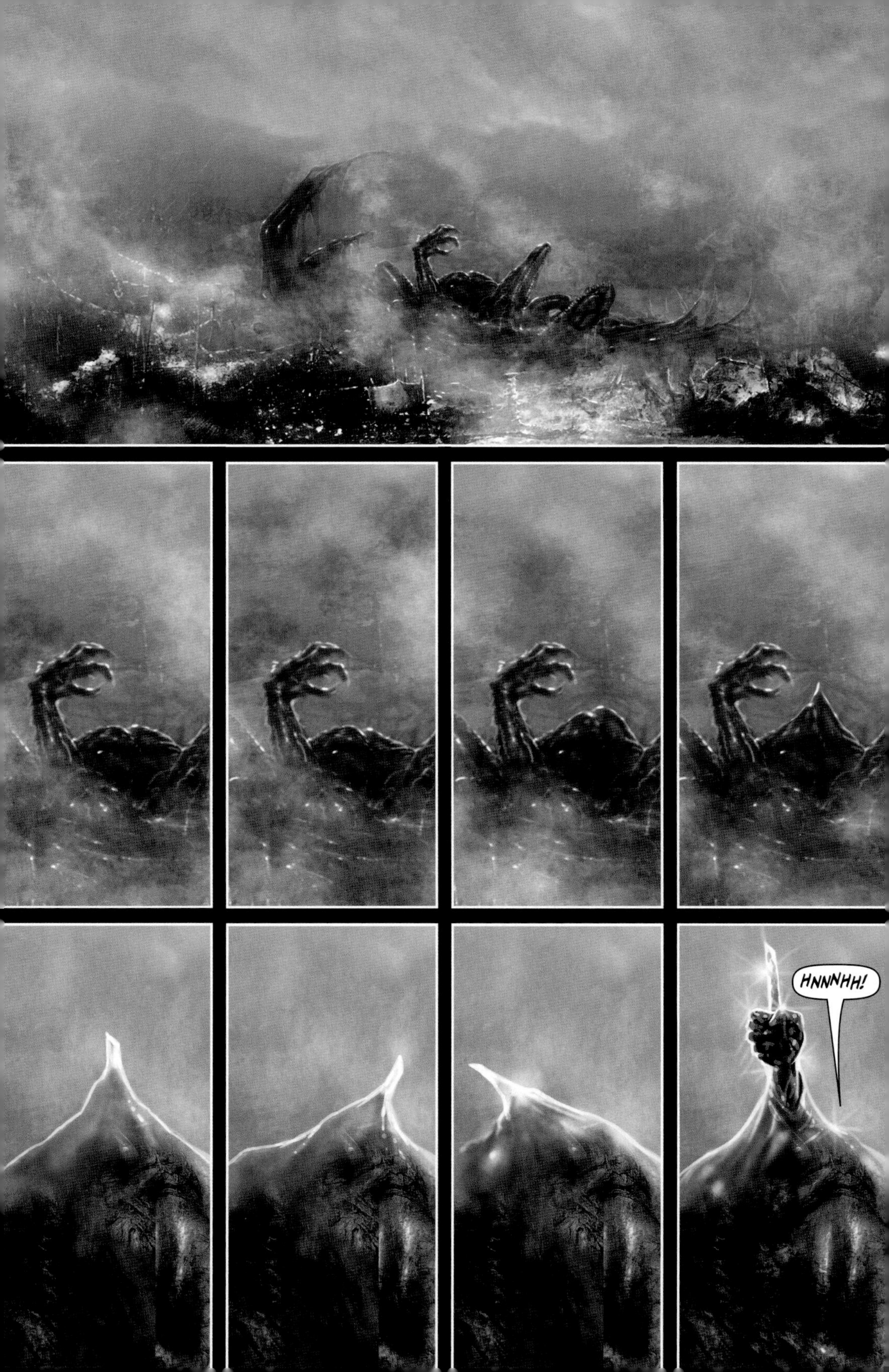
HNNNHH!

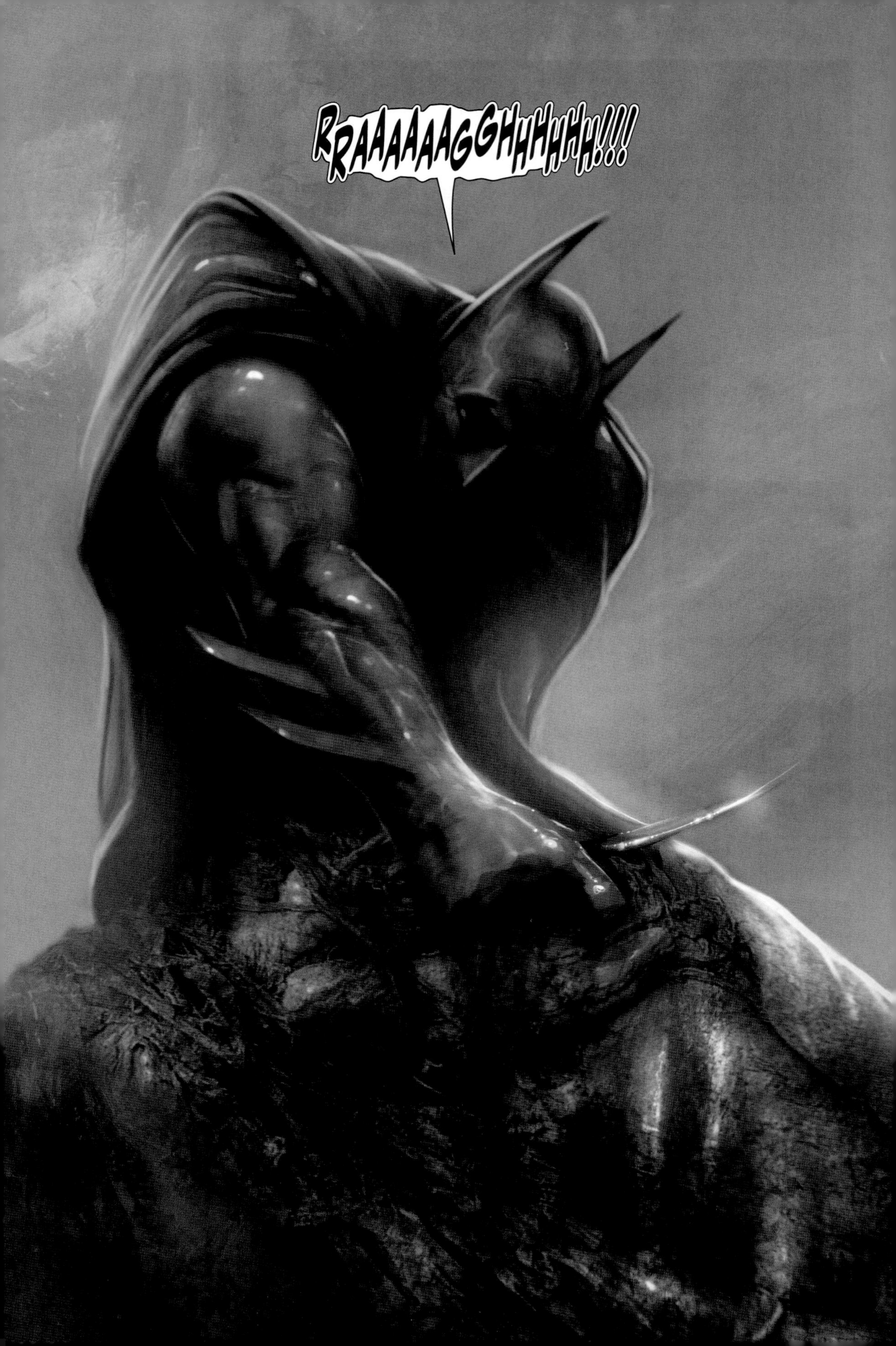
RRAAAAAAGGHHHHHH!!!

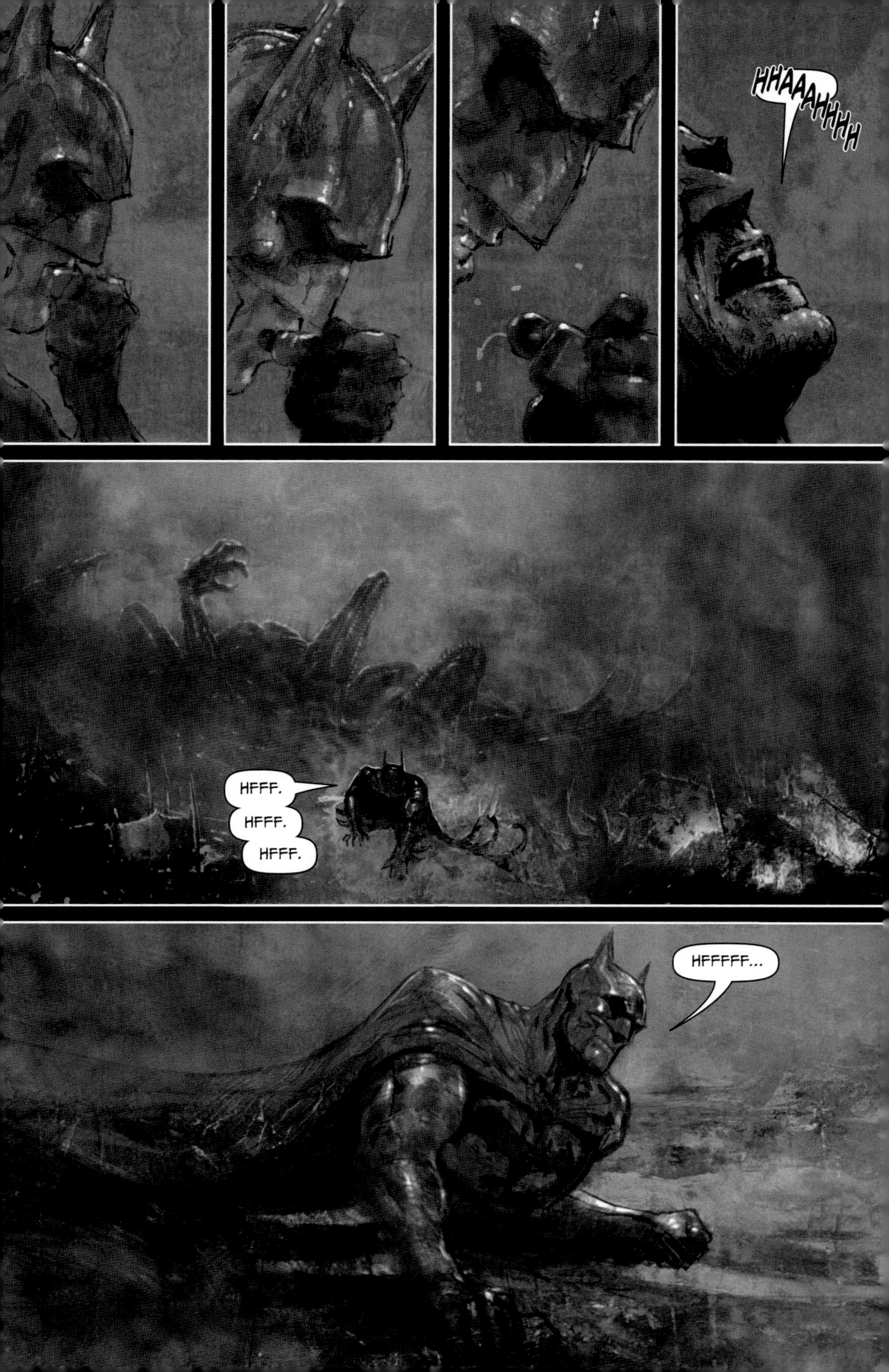
HHAAAAHHHH
HFFF.
HFFF.
HFFF.
HFFFFF...

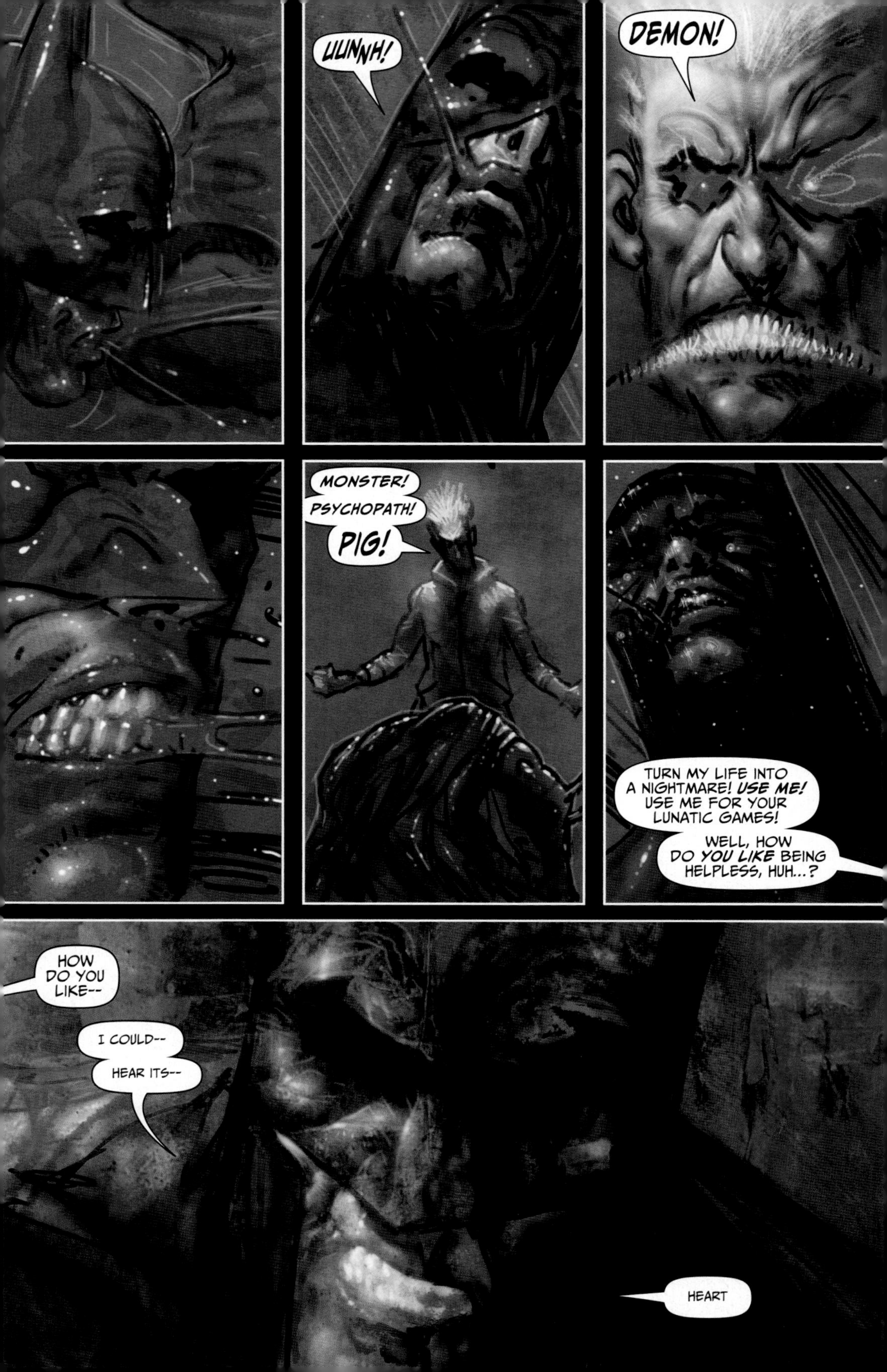
UUNNH!
DEMON!
MONSTER!
PSYCHOPATH!
PIG!
TURN MY LIFE INTO A NIGHTMARE! USE ME! USE ME FOR YOUR LUNATIC GAMES!
WELL, HOW DO YOU LIKE BEING HELPLESS, HUH...?
HOW DO YOU LIKE--
I COULD--
HEAR ITS--
HEART

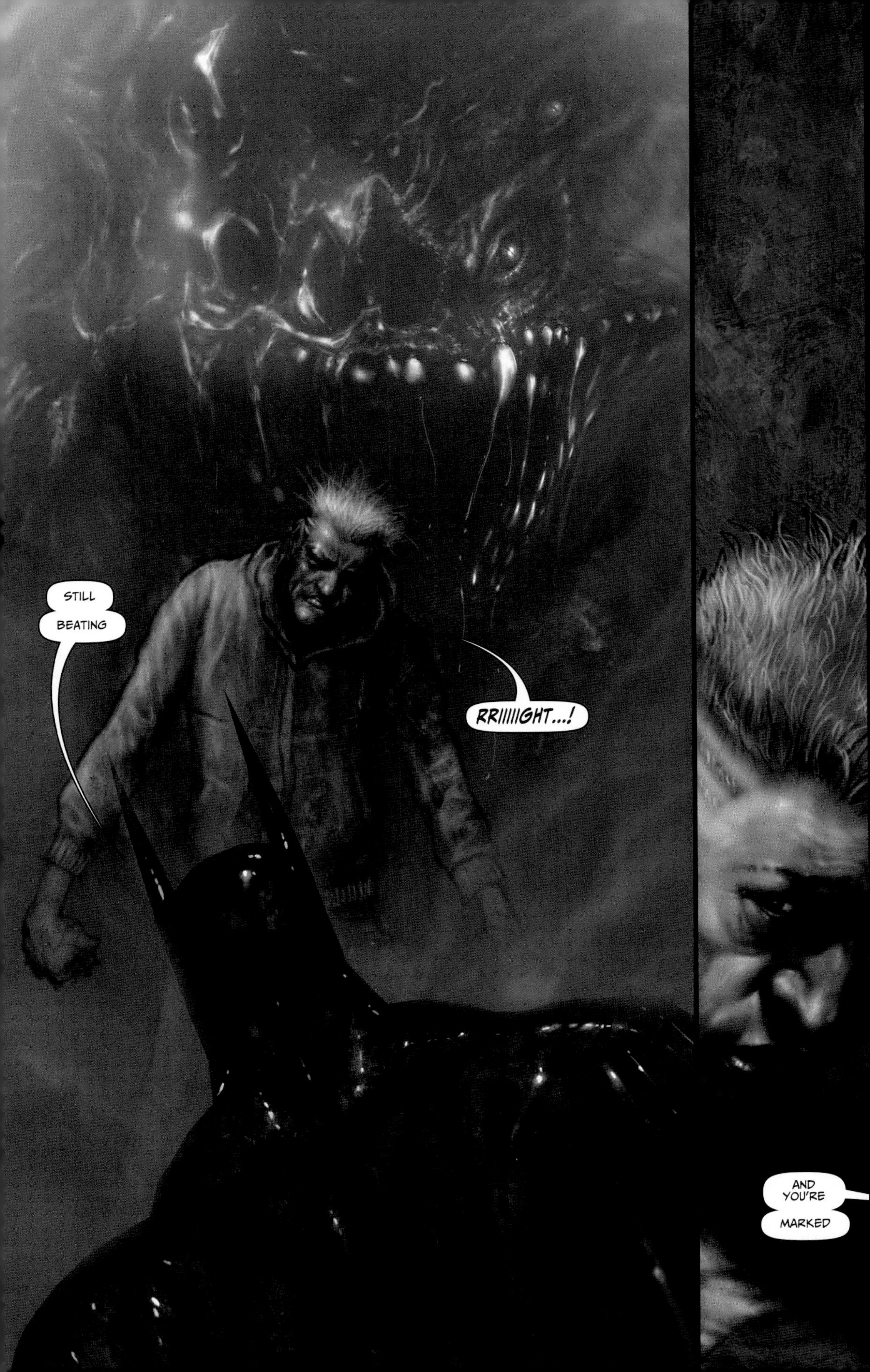
STILL
BEATING
RRIIIIIIGHT...!
AND YOU'RE
MARKED

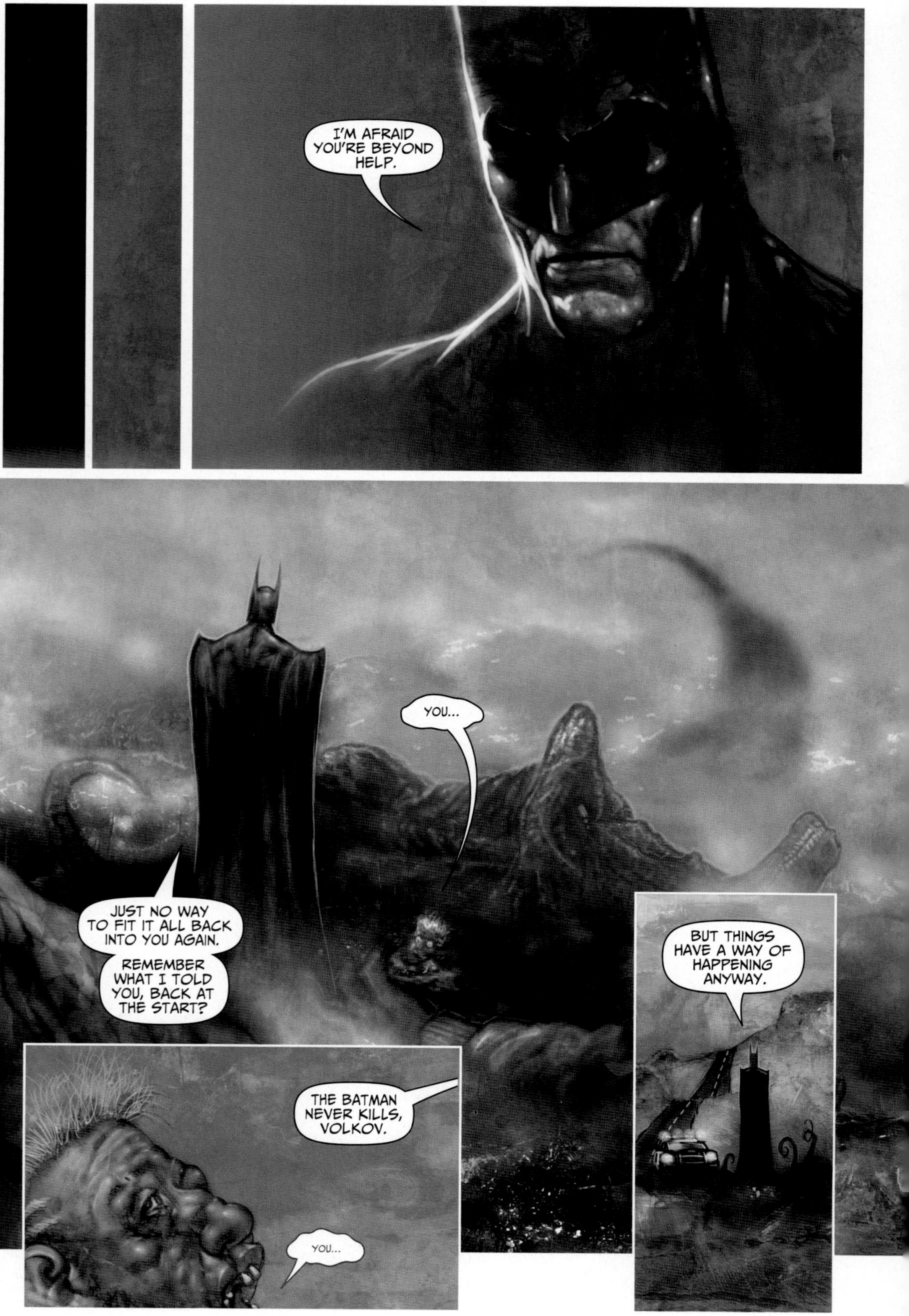
I'M AFRAID YOU'RE BEYOND HELP.
YOU...
JUST NO WAY TO FIT IT ALL BACK INTO YOU AGAIN.
REMEMBER WHAT I TOLD YOU, BACK AT THE START?
THE BATMAN NEVER KILLS, VOLKOV.
YOU...
BUT THINGS HAVE A WAY OF HAPPENING ANYWAY.

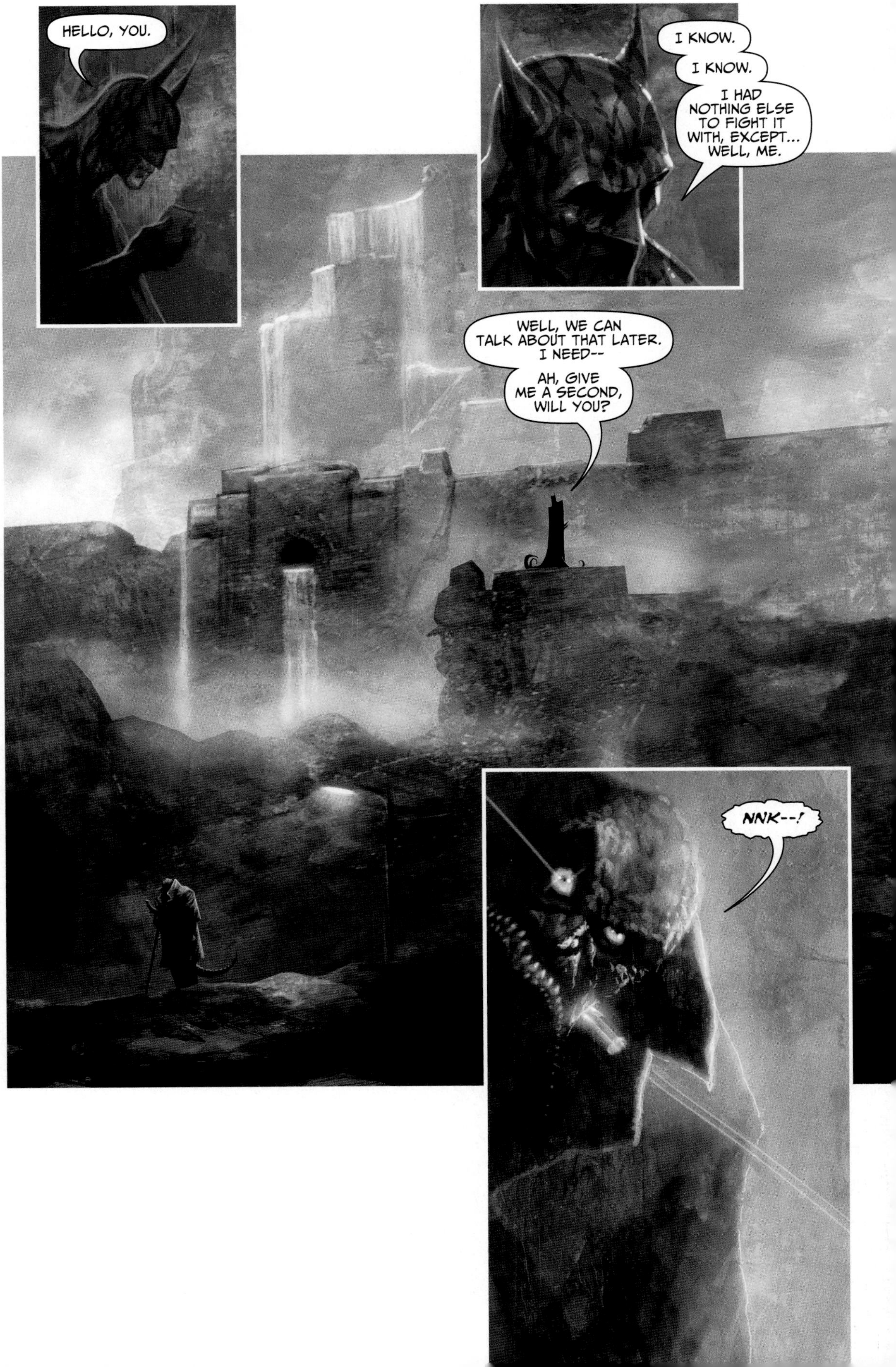
HELLO, YOU.
I KNOW.
I KNOW.
I HAD NOTHING ELSE TO FIGHT IT WITH, EXCEPT... WELL, ME.
WELL, WE CAN TALK ABOUT THAT LATER. I NEED--
AH, GIVE ME A SECOND, WILL YOU?
NNK--!

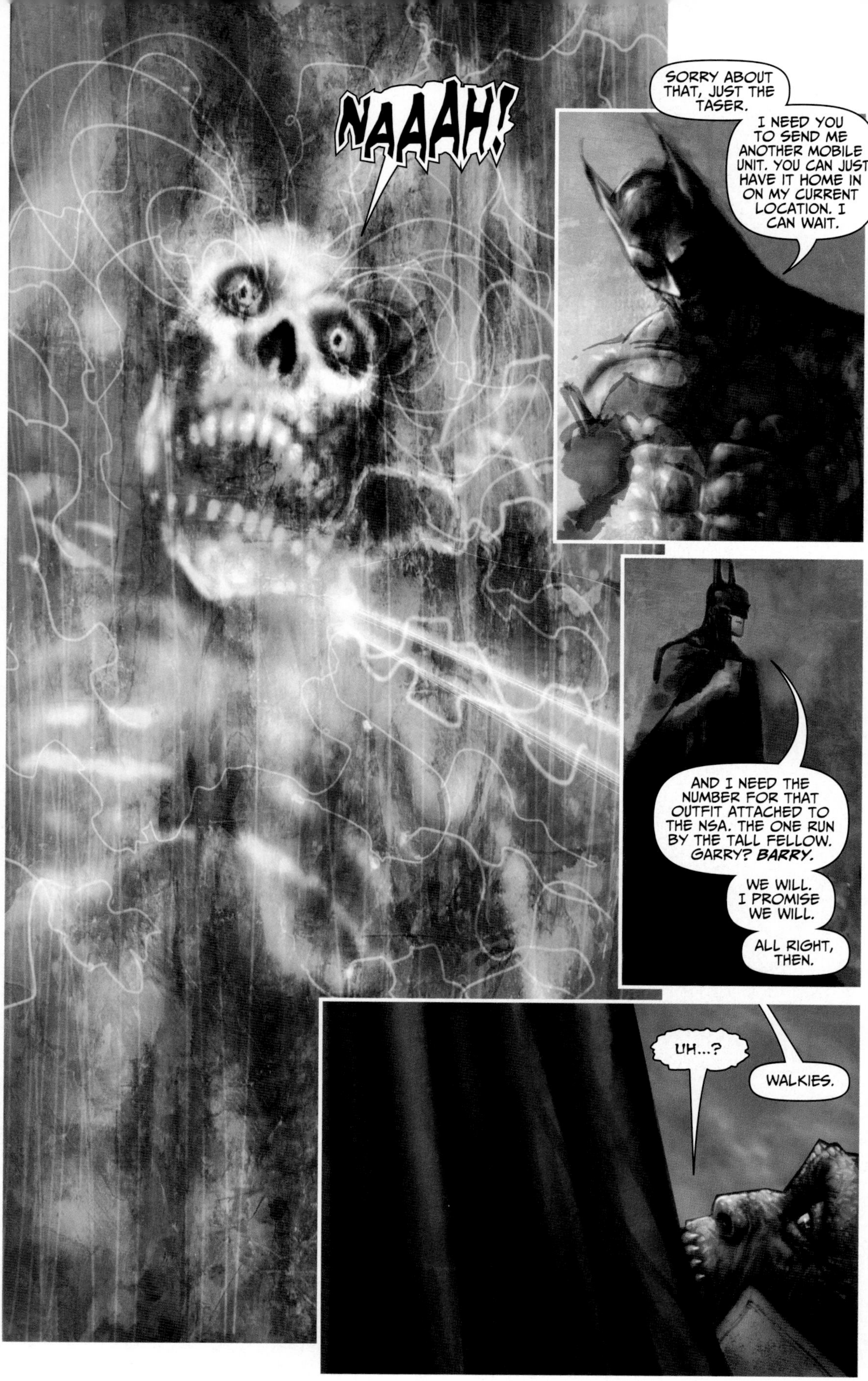
NAAAH!
SORRY ABOUT THAT, JUST THE TASER.
I NEED YOU TO SEND ME ANOTHER MOBILE UNIT. YOU CAN JUST HAVE IT HOME IN ON MY CURRENT LOCATION. I CAN WAIT.
AND I NEED THE NUMBER FOR THAT OUTFIT ATTACHED TO THE NSA. THE ONE RUN BY THE TALL FELLOW. GARRY? ***BARRY.***
WE WILL. I PROMISE WE WILL.
ALL RIGHT, THEN.
UH...?
WALKIES.

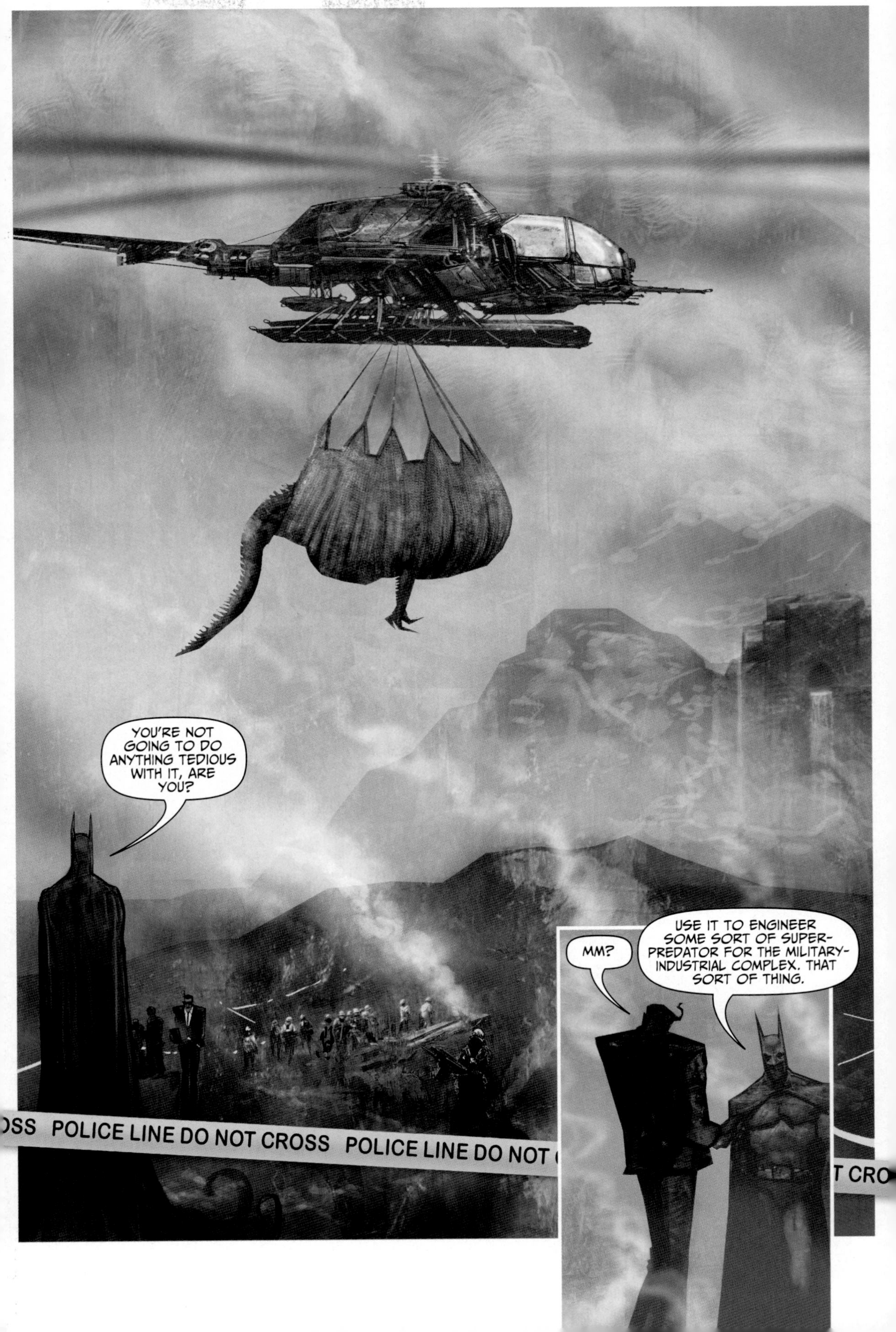
YOU'RE NOT GOING TO DO ANYTHING TEDIOUS WITH IT, ARE YOU?
OSS POLICE LINE DO NOT CROSS POLICE LINE DO NOT C
MM?
USE IT TO ENGINEER SOME SORT OF SUPER-PREDATOR FOR THE MILITARY-INDUSTRIAL COMPLEX. THAT SORT OF THING.
T CRO

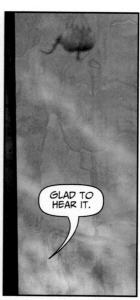

HONESTLY, WHAT DO YOU TAKE US FOR?

WE'RE THE UNITED STATES GOVERNMENT, NOT SOME DREADFUL ROGUE CORPORATION...!

GLAD TO HEAR IT.

BECAUSE LET'S FACE IT, YOU'RE NOT THE ONE WHO'D HAVE TO CLEAN UP THE MESS.

OH, YOUR LIFE'S SUCH A TRIAL.

IT IS *INCREDIBLY TOUGH*, ISN'T IT? I MEAN, TO STILL BE BREATHING AFTER THE DAMAGE IT'S TAKEN, I'VE NEVER HEARD OF ANYTHING QUITE LIKE IT...

YES, WELL, YOU HAVEN'T MET ITS MOTHER.

WELL NOW.

AW, HEY, MAN, YOU GOTTA GET ME OUTTA HERE...!

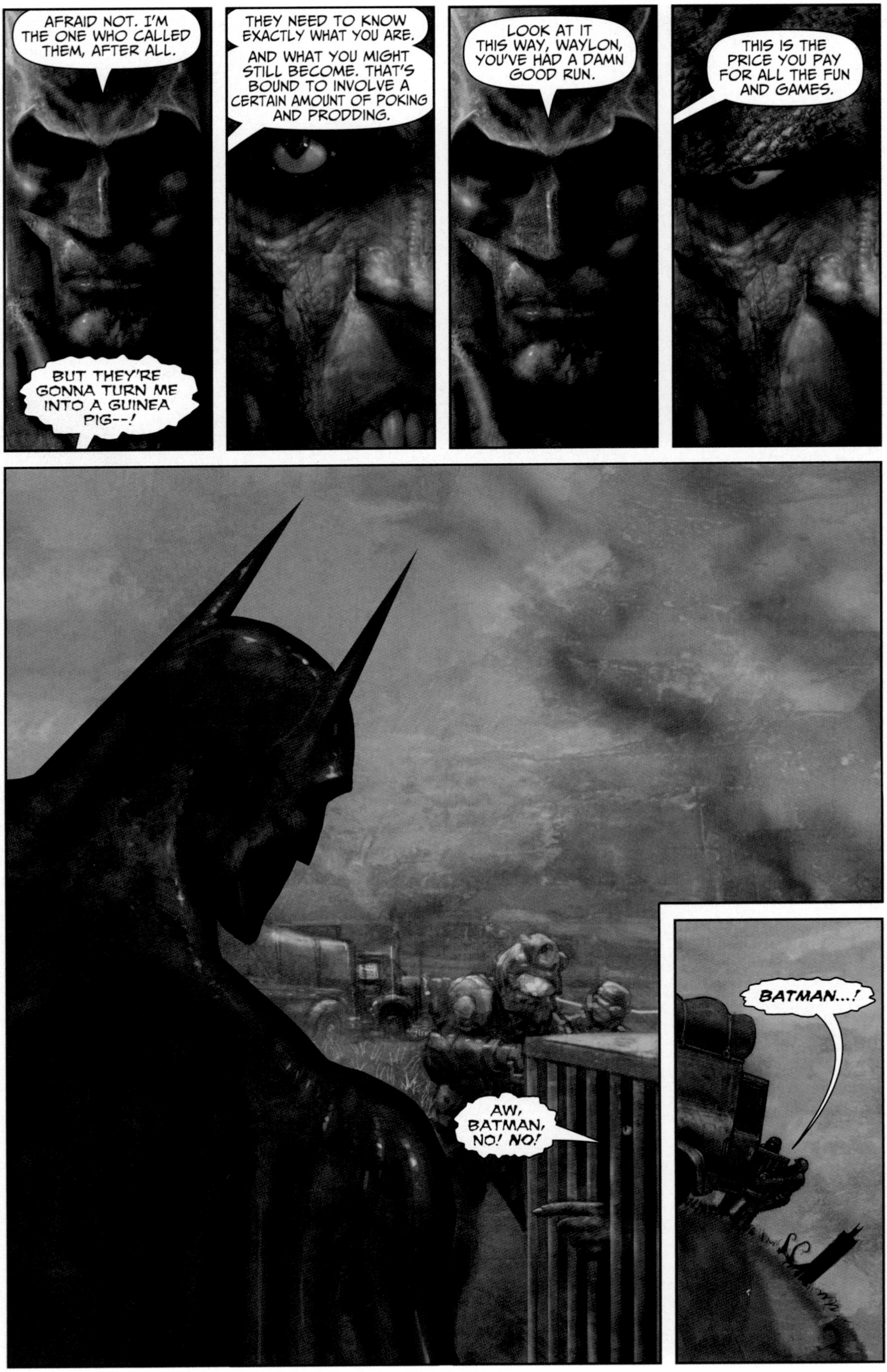
AFRAID NOT. I'M THE ONE WHO CALLED THEM, AFTER ALL.
BUT THEY'RE GONNA TURN ME INTO A GUINEA PIG--!
THEY NEED TO KNOW EXACTLY WHAT YOU ARE.
AND WHAT YOU MIGHT STILL BECOME. THAT'S BOUND TO INVOLVE A CERTAIN AMOUNT OF POKING AND PRODDING.
LOOK AT IT THIS WAY, WAYLON, YOU'VE HAD A DAMN GOOD RUN.
THIS IS THE PRICE YOU PAY FOR ALL THE FUN AND GAMES.
AW, BATMAN, NO! NO!
BATMAN...!

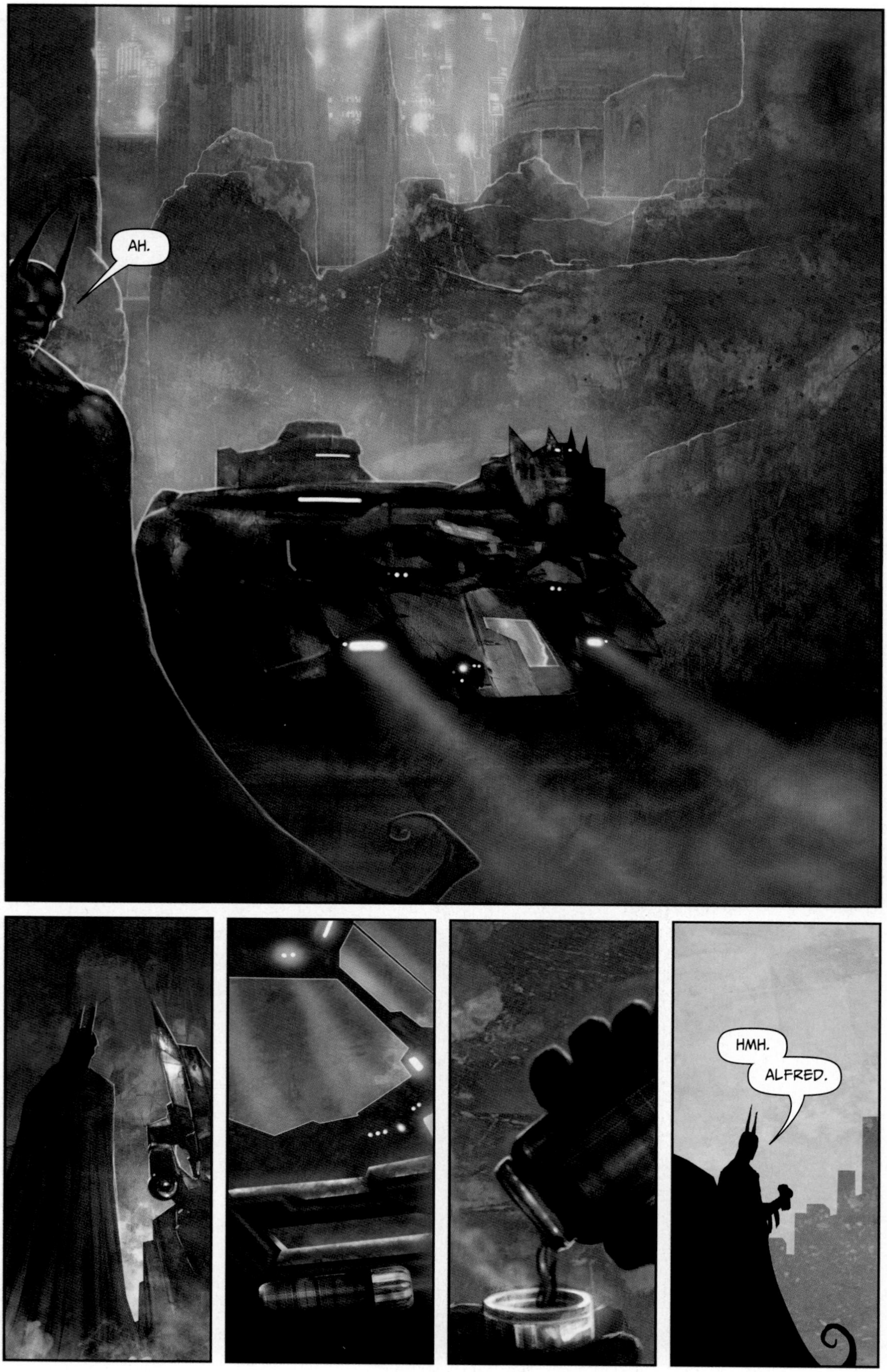
AH.
HMH.
ALFRED.

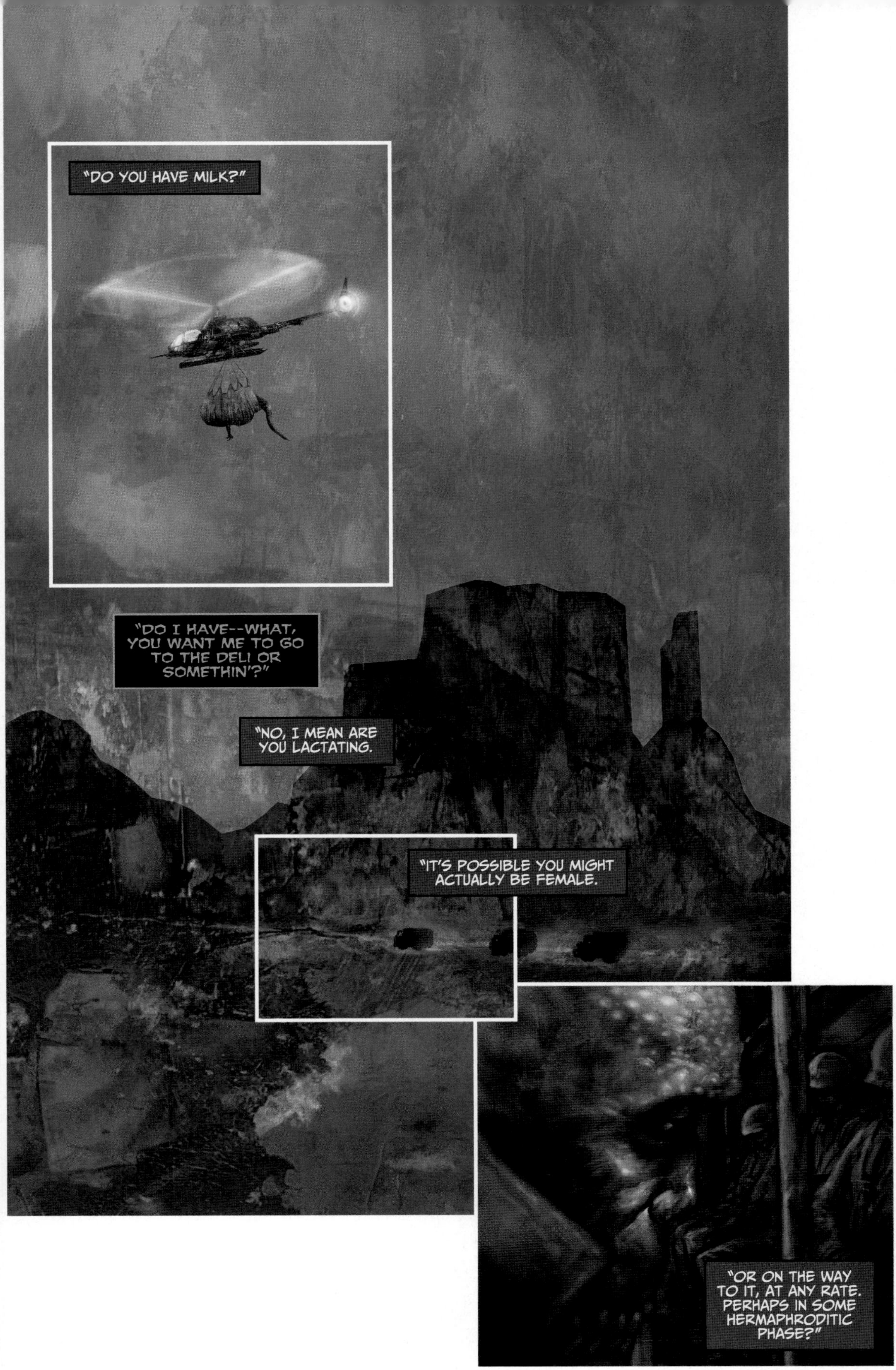
"DO YOU HAVE MILK?"
"DO I HAVE--WHAT, YOU WANT ME TO GO TO THE DELI OR SOMETHIN'?"
"NO, I MEAN ARE YOU LACTATING.
"IT'S POSSIBLE YOU MIGHT ACTUALLY BE FEMALE.
"OR ON THE WAY TO IT, AT ANY RATE. PERHAPS IN SOME HERMAPHRODITIC PHASE?"

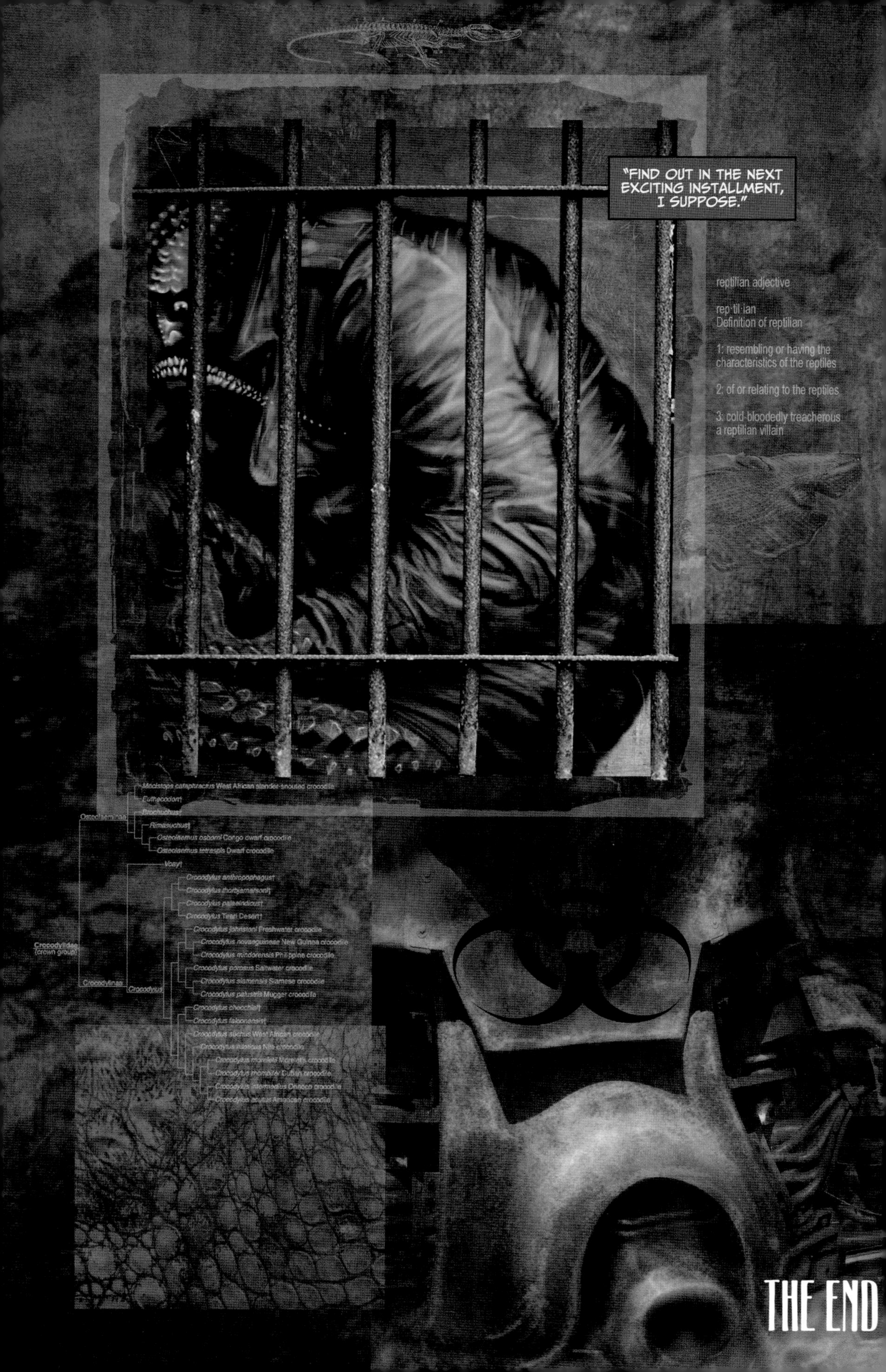
"FIND OUT IN THE NEXT EXCITING INSTALLMENT, I SUPPOSE."
reptilian adjective
rep·til·ian
Definition of reptilian
1: resembling or having the characteristics of the reptiles
2: of or relating to the reptiles
3: cold-bloodedly treacherous
a reptilian villain
Mecistops cataphractus West African slender-snouted crocodile
Euthecodon†
Brochuchus†
Osteolaeminae
Rimasuchus†
Osteolaemus osborni Congo dwarf crocodile
Osteolaemus tetraspis Dwarf crocodile
Voay†
Crocodylus anthropophagus†
Crocodylus thorbjarnarsoni†
Crocodylus palaeindicus†
Crocodylus Tirari Desert†
Crocodylus johnstoni Freshwater crocodile
Crocodylidae (crown group)
Crocodylus novaeguineae New Guinea crocodile
Crocodylus mindorensis Philippine crocodile
Crocodylus porosus Saltwater crocodile
Crocodylus siamensis Siamese crocodile
Crocodylinae
Crocodylus
Crocodylus palustris Mugger crocodile
Crocodylus checchiai†
Crocodylus falconensis†
Crocodylus suchus West African crocodile
Crocodylus niloticus Nile crocodile
Crocodylus moreletii Morelet's crocodile
Crocodylus rhombifer Cuban crocodile
Crocodylus intermedius Orinoco crocodile
Crocodylus acutus American crocodile
THE END

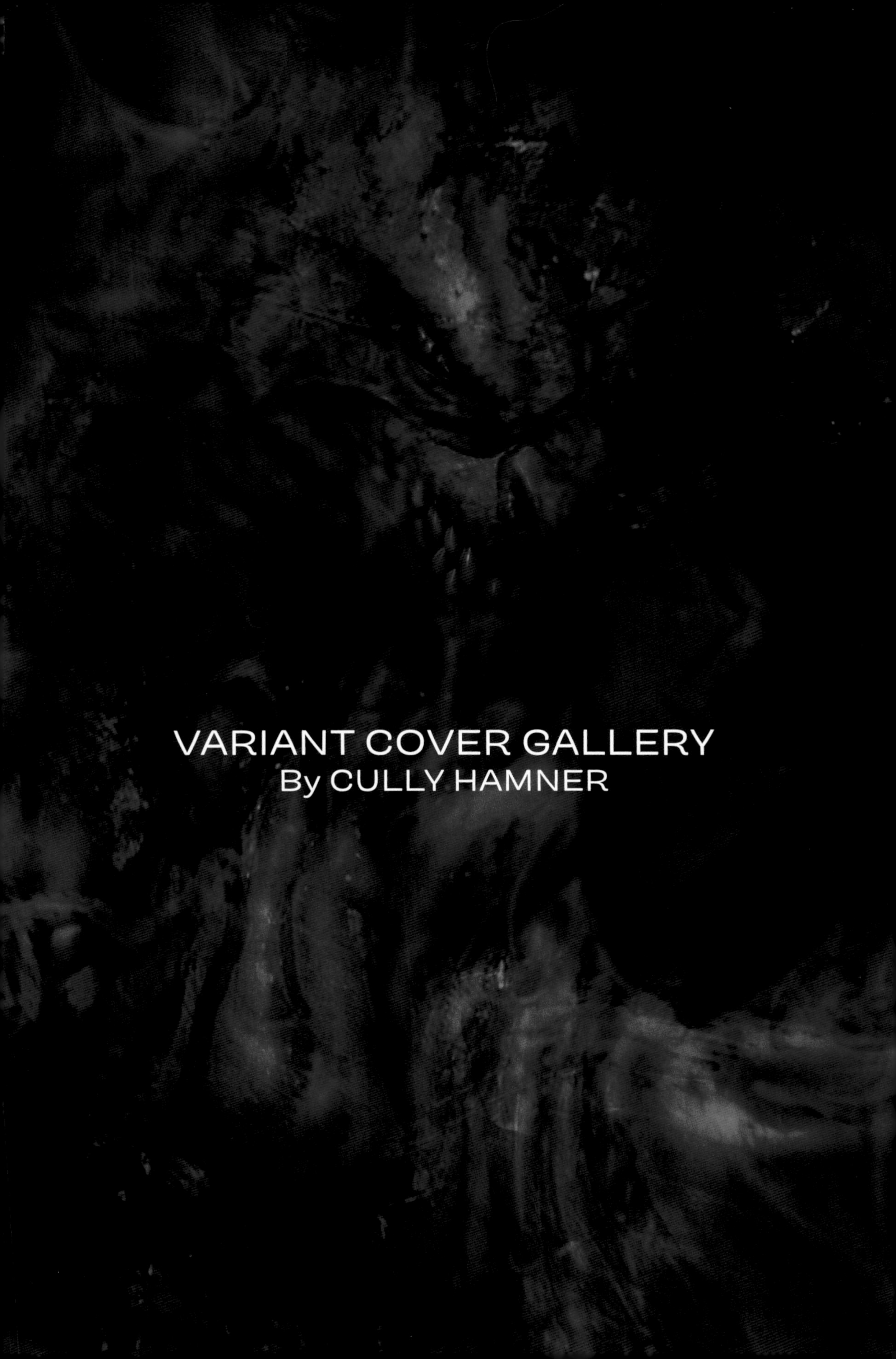

VARIANT COVER GALLERY
By CULLY HAMNER

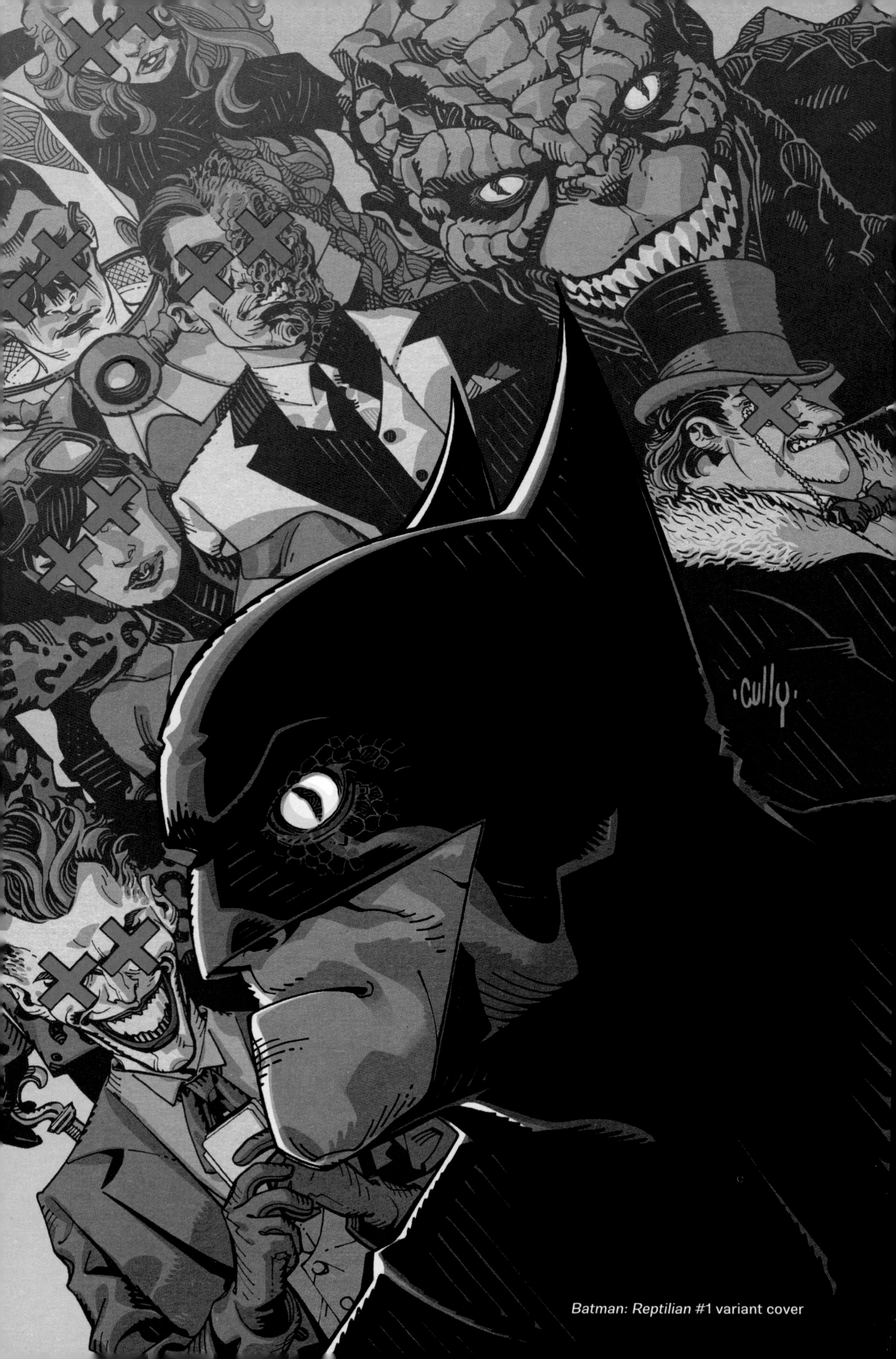

CULLY

Batman: Reptilian #1 variant cover

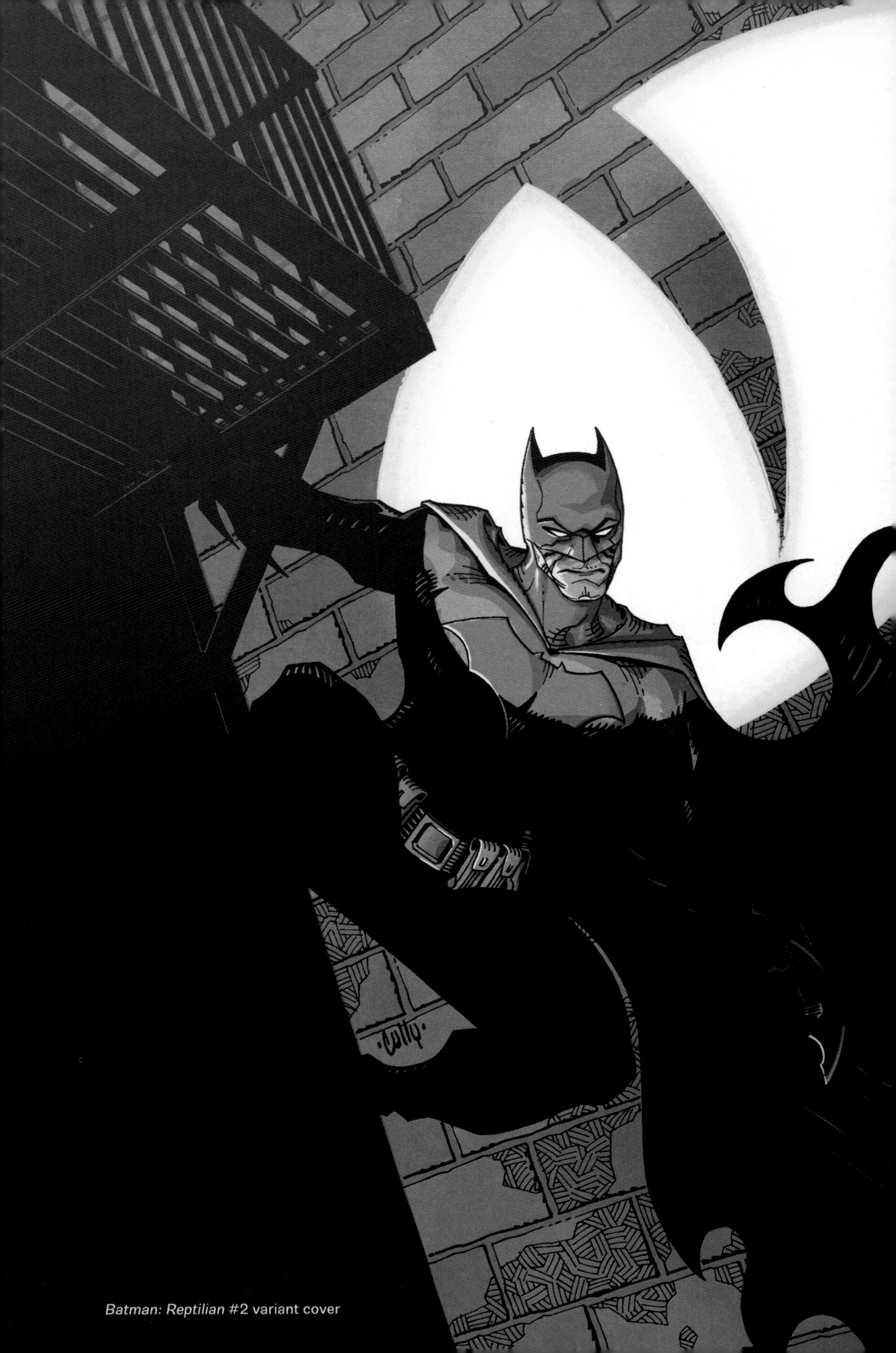

Batman: Reptilian #2 variant cover

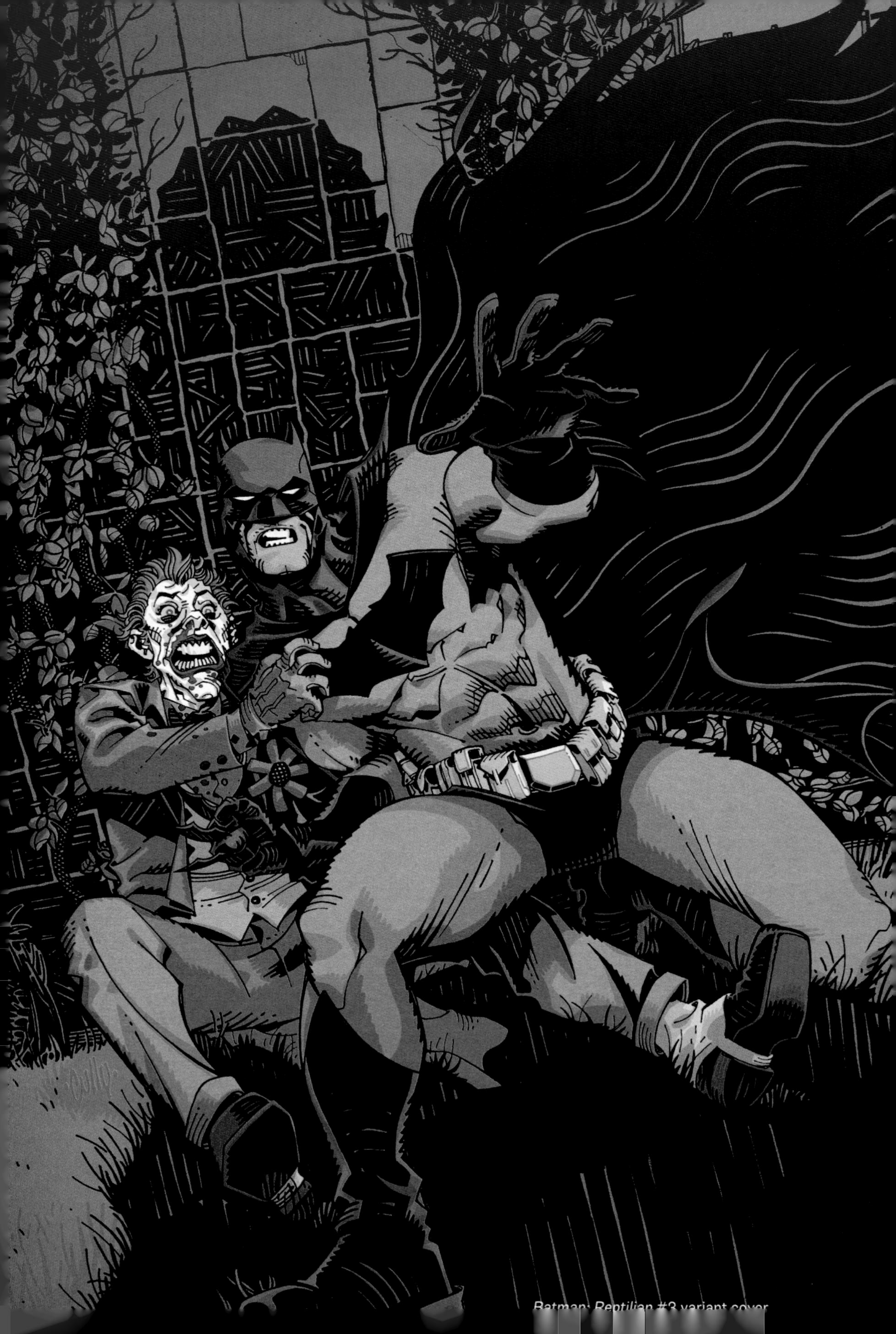

Batman: Reptilian #3 variant cover

Batman: Reptilian #4 variant cover

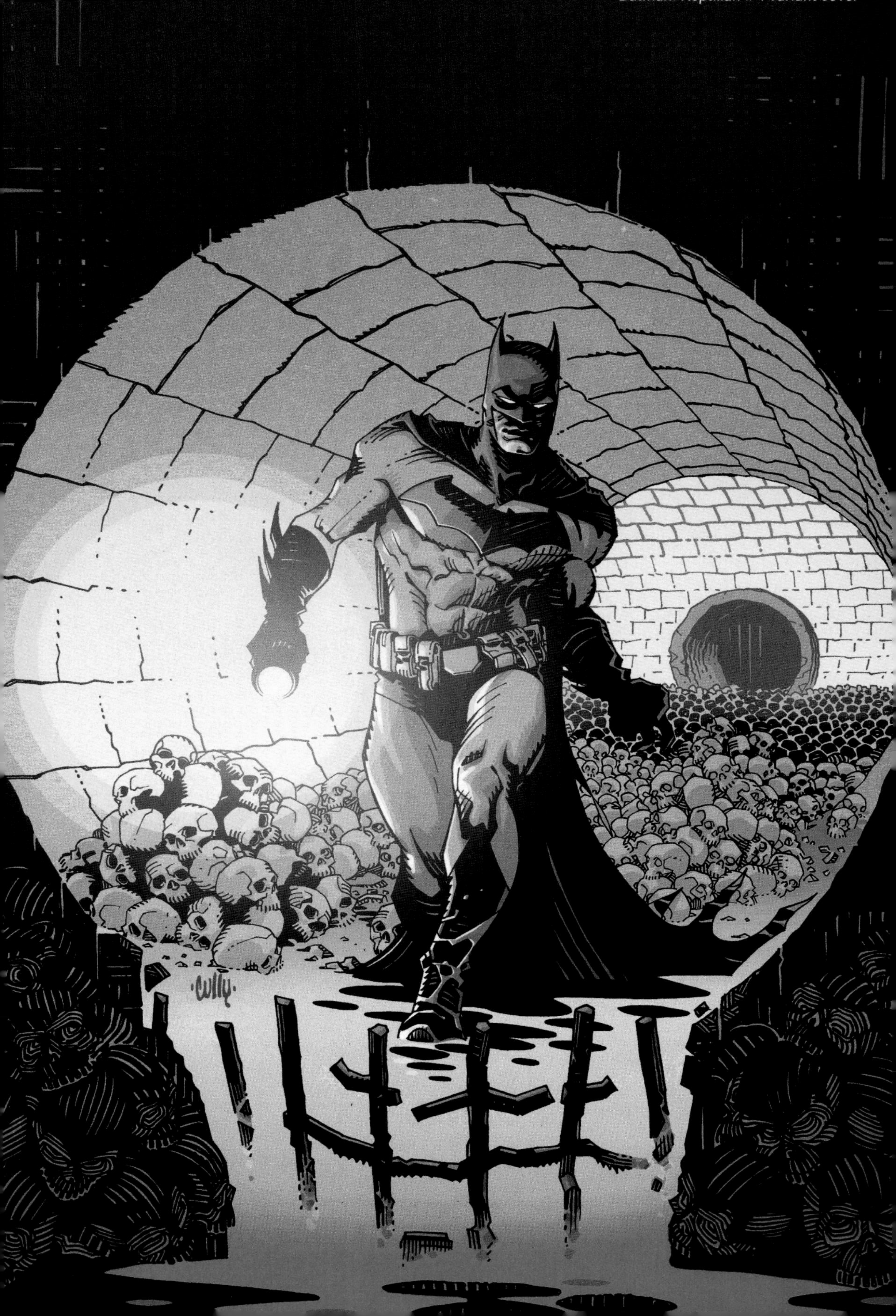

Batman: Reptilian #5 variant cover

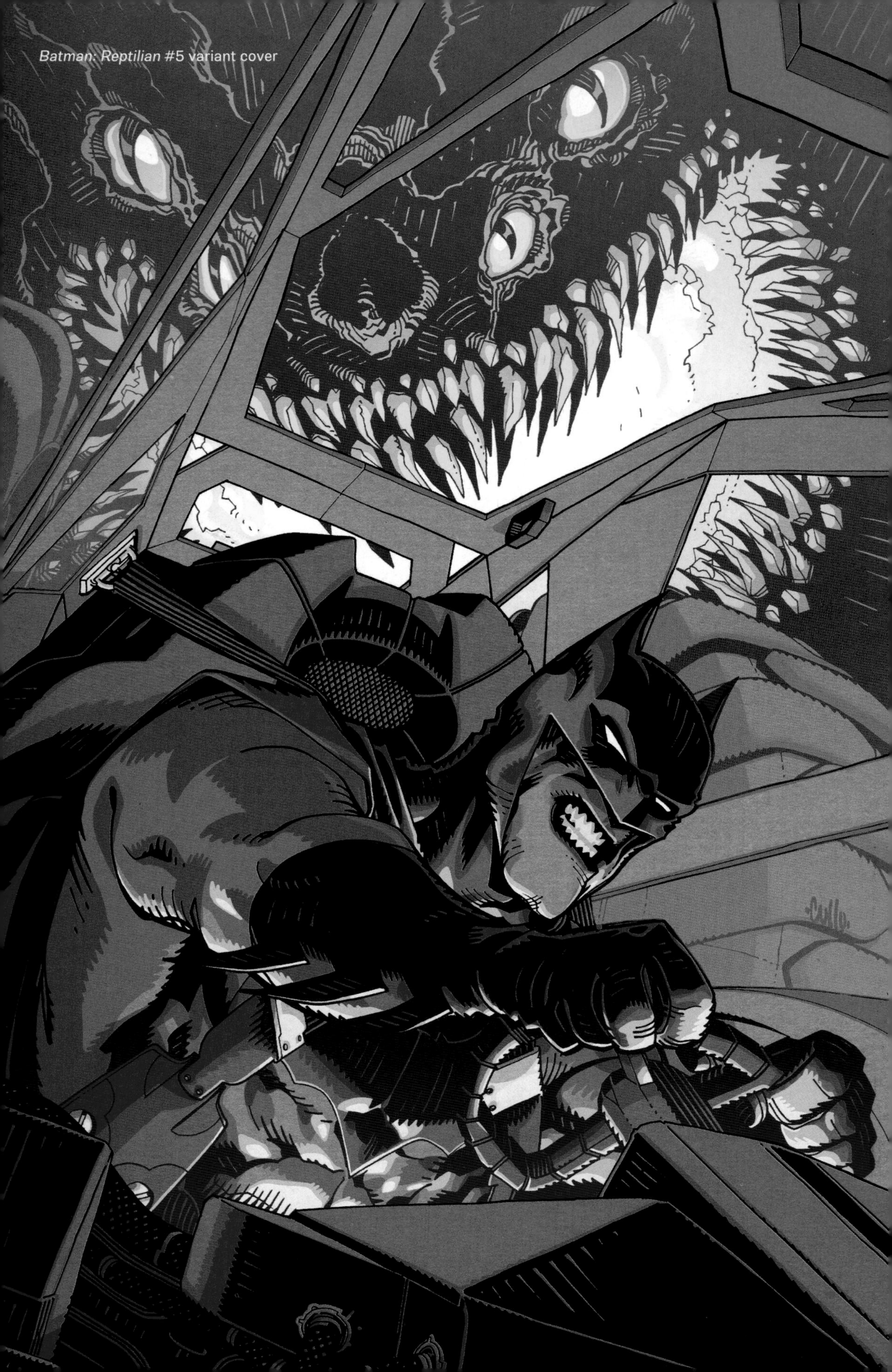

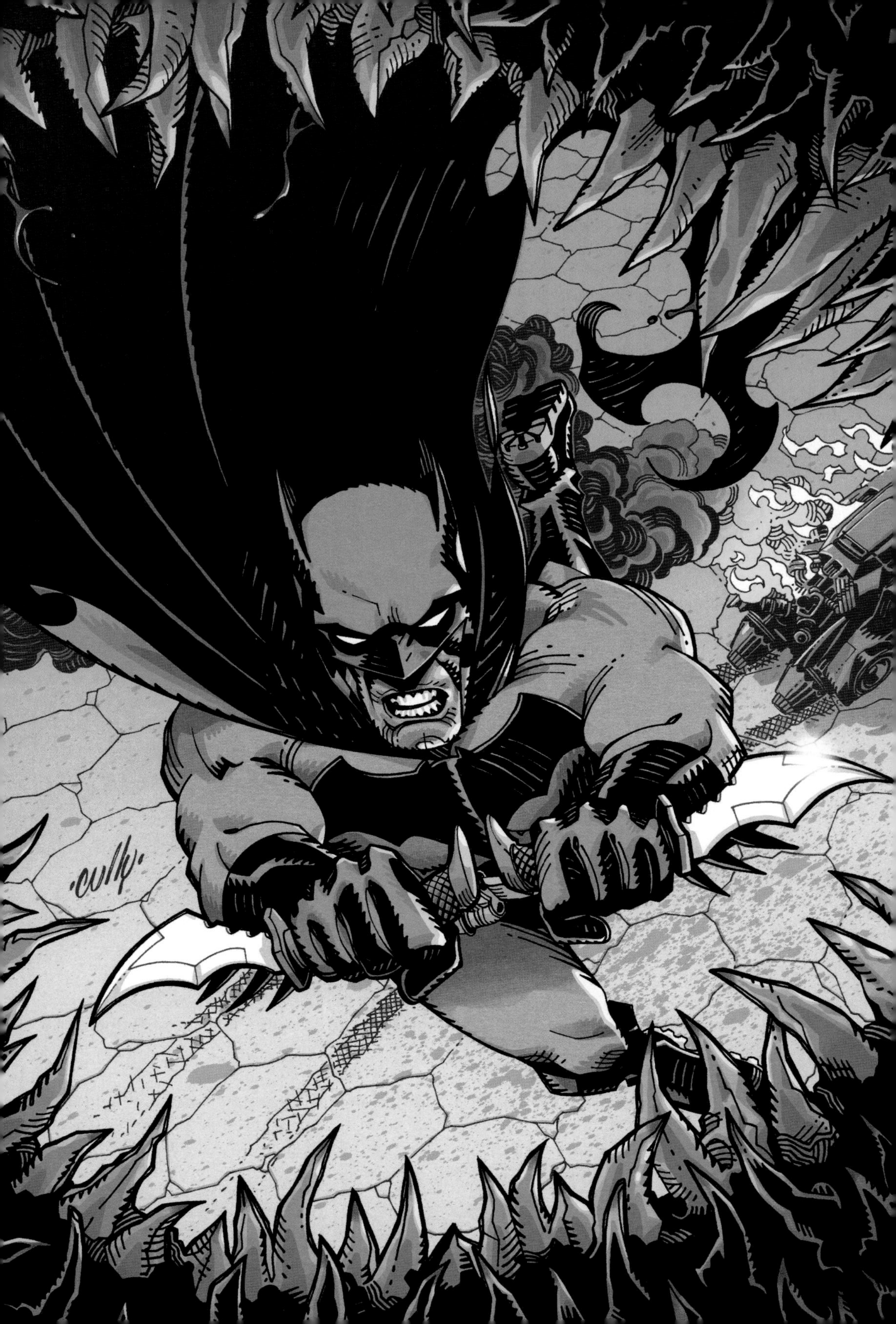

Batman: Reptilian original series pitch by GARTH ENNIS to MARIE JAVINS

This original outline was pitched to Marie Javins and the book was intended for the late great Steve Dillon to draw. Garth notes that he usually dislikes writing outlines, as they frequently bear only a passing resemblance to the finished product, as you'll see here.

BATMAN: LEGENDS OF THE DARK KNIGHT
An ongoing series in arcs produced by high-profile teams

SIX ISSUE ARC WRITTEN BY GARTH ENNIS, DRAWN BY STEVE DILLON

Batman

Not just completely capable but a figure of extraordinary authority, Batman goes through Gotham's underworld like a buzzsaw. He's trained, motivated and in top physical condition, and his opponents are either unskilled, under-fed or mentally ill. Most people don't dare mess with him; the majority of those that do will usually back down if he snaps or even just glares at them. His planning leaves nothing to chance; if he doesn't get you, the booby-trap he left around the corner will.

He is utterly certain of himself and his actions. The mystery that surrounds Batman works to his advantage, with no one ever quite sure of his limits or abilities. When he does appear, he projects an air of cold, hard command that blends with a constant sense of repressed violence- an extremely effective combination. He won't kill, but he has no problem with barely stopping short of doing so. And his mastery of psychological warfare is total, as we'll see in the sequence that opens the story.

An impromptu press conference is underway on the steps of the Gotham City courthouse. A heavyweight champion boxer (and millionaire) has just been released on charges of beating and raping a young woman, the judge having been forced to throw out evidence provided by the Batman. The guy's lawyer is doing a bit of grandstanding, sounding off about the city's reliance on vigilantism. Then, to the amazement of all present, who should arrive to face the press but Batman himself.

Batman confronts the huge boxer and calmly accuses him of cowardice, assaulting someone half his size and a tenth of his strength. The lawyer says that's slander. The boxer just smirks, well-aware Batman's attempting to provoke him. So Batman ups the ante, says he's supposed to be the heavyweight champion of the world but he's letting someone call him a coward in front of millions of people. He'll have to live with that forever. He'll have to remember it when he's kissing his kids goodnight, when he's making love to his wife... the boxer's starting to get angry now, his defenses are crumbling, his lawyer's desperately trying to end the press conference... but Batman keeps going.

The guy loses it and throws an uppercut that Batman dodges with ease, and then we cut to a shot of the reporters gaping in horror as a terrible scream rends the air. Batman is last seen coolly walking away from what's left of the boxer- a sight we're largely spared- in front of the appalled reporters. *Self-defense*, he says.

That gets us as far as page six.

Plot

Someone is killing their way through Gotham's underworld—and it's not the Batman. In fact, something's tearing these guys apart. Several mob figures have been found eviscerated or horribly maimed, and the few survivors have little idea what happened to them—in fact, they seem to be in deep shock (it'd be nice if I could kill a couple of the rogue's gallery here, or at least mutilate them- the way I see it, if I render the Scarecrow quadriplegic you can always have him cured for his next appearance). Batman is curious: if this is some sort of mob takeover, who's doing it and why haven't they made their move yet? But the days go by and nothing happens, except that a couple more victims end up in the morgue.

Batman starts asking questions in the underworld. All the signs point to a Russian hardcase, a Moscow Mafia figure who's apparently getting big ideas. The reality turns out to be very different. The guy's a joke, a would-be loan shark who Batman backs across a rooftop until his heels are off the edge of the building. The guy tries to front it out, babbling about how he knows the Batman never kills and that this is all a bluff, so Batman says that in that case why not just walk away? Because he can't, of course, he can't get past the enormous dude dressed as the bat- and his balance is getting shaky, and it's a long way down, and the wind is getting up…

Okay, he says, he's not involved but he has been hearing things. He'll find out what he can. He'd better. Batman will carry out a blackly comedic campaign of mental torture against this loser throughout the story, forcing him to dig deeper into his criminal contacts (part one will end with him tucked up in bed, a nervous wreck, flipping off his light- only to hear a voice hiss *The Batman never kills.* Jerking upright and flipping his light off, he finds himself in an apparently empty room).

Batman will spend the next few issues having near misses with whoever or whatever it is that's doing all the damage, as more and more villains fall victim to the murderous rampage. Even the Joker is not immune, up to his usual shenanigans at the city botanical gardens, where he's taken a number of hostages and is demanding Batman's appearance. Batman manages to outwit him and free the hostages, and it's then that the real trouble becomes apparent: when the Joker cackles over the radio to Batman that he can hear him coming, the grim response wipes the smile off the villain's face: "Whatever's in there with you, Joker: it isn't me." What's left of the Clown Prince of Crime is soon being scraped into an ambulance.

Eventually all becomes clear. Not so long ago Gotham's rogues and villains met for one of their occasional scheming/plotting/planning get-togethers. As usual, first on the agenda was getting rid of the Batman. As usual, the whole thing fell apart because these lunatics and scumbags all despise each other. But this time, something odd began to happen- in the days following the meeting, the attendees began dying, or suffering ghastly assaults that left them maimed and hospitalized. Batman slowly uncovers the reasons behind this trail of carnage, and name that keeps coming up is… Killer Croc.

Which somehow doesn't make complete sense, because although Croc has motive enough to wipe out his fellow vermin, he seems to be leaving much of the work unfinished- and even the survivors bear injuries that Croc would be hard put to inflict.

Croc in fact it proves to be, but not in the way one might think. Batman finds him deep in the Gotham sewers, so sick he can barely move. He seems to have suffered some kind of hideous biological trauma, there's a lot of loose skin hanging off him, much of it shredded. He has no memory of what's happened, he's weak as a newborn baby. Which is ironic, because as Batman soon discovers, that's exactly what happened to him: he gave birth. The original mutation that caused his condition progressed so that a huge, egg-like spore formed on his back, and soon Croc's hideous progeny came sliding out to wage its campaign of terror on the Gotham underworld. Completely unaware of the results due to his delirious and debilitated condition, Croc has been in a coma-like state ever since.

But why has the creature turned on its parent's criminal associates? Well, emerging from the sewers with no understanding of its surroundings, the thing tried searching for "Mommy" by employing its uncanny sense of smell. And unbeknownst to Croc, he's been exuding a powerful pheromone for some time now, a byproduct of his curious "pregnancy". Everyone who was at that meeting got marked by the pheromone, everyone was eventually tracked down by the ghastly Croc-child, and everyone suffered its wrath when it realized it had an impostor on its hands (or claws. This thing's hideous, a huge mutated bastard like a Velociraptor crossed with a dozen chainsaws). Worse still, when Batman drags the battered Croc out of the sewers to get him medical help, there's no overpowering smell of shit to mask the scent of the pheromone…

Pretty soon Junior comes calling, but Croc is in no rush to be reunited with his misshapen offspring. Too bad, says Batman, it looks like it wants to be held- and you'd better do it, because I need time to figure out how to subdue the damn thing. Croc reluctantly cuddles the mewling monstrosity, but when he realizes it wants to be fed- well, that's a step too far. Croc's rejection of the beast causes an instant meltdown, with the creature going on a rampage that even Batman can't stop. He tries and almost loses his life in the process, but even a 100mph collision with the Batmobile doesn't stop Junior. It turns out that only Croc can do that, soothing his child with whispers and caresses until Batman can turn the flamethrowers on it.

All Croc wants now is a nice, safe, cosy prison cell to curl up in- but Batman, being Batman, can't resist leaving him with one last thought. If giving birth was a result of an ongoing mutation caused by whatever gave him his misshapen form in the first place… what's next? What else has he got to look forward to?

It takes Croc a while to get to sleep that night.

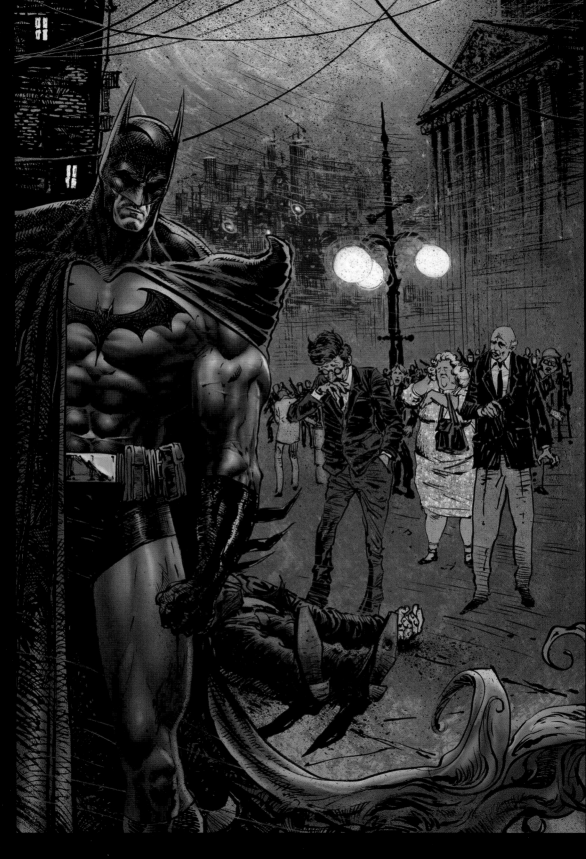

Batman: Reptilian initial concepts by LIAM SHARP

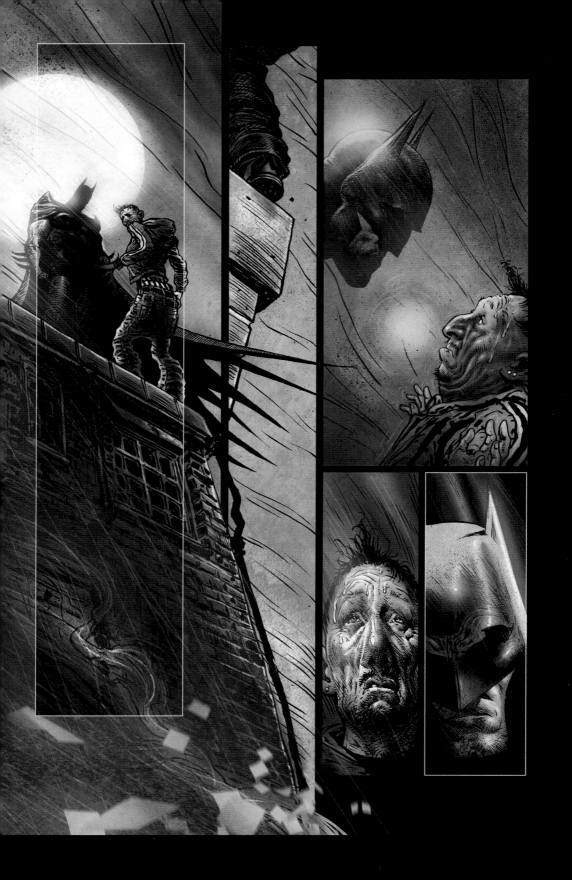